Excel 97 Annoyances

Excel 97 Annoyances

Woody Leonhard, Lee Hudspeth,
and T.J. Lee

Cambridge • Köln • Paris • Sebastopol • Tokyo

Excel 97 Annoyances
by Woody Leonhard, Lee Hudspeth, and T.J. Lee

Printed in the United States of America.

Published by O'Reilly & Associates, Inc., 101 Morris Street, Sebastopol, CA 95472.

Editor: Ron Petrusha

Production Editor: Clairemarie Fisher O'Leary

Printing History:

September 1997: First Edition

This book is printed on acid-free paper with 85% recycled content, 15% post-consumer waste. O'Reilly & Associates is committed to using paper with the highest recycled content available consistent with high quality.

ISBN: 1-56592-309-X

Four years ago, Linda and I started a non-profit organization called the Tibetan Children's Fund. As of this writing TCF sponsors more than 150 refugee children in northern India and Nepal. These children are chosen on the basis of financial need and scholastic performance—particularly in English, math, and science. Most of them come from families that can only be described as destitute; many have been orphaned. Few of the refugee families have more than one room to call their own, many live in shanties, and none can afford medical care on even the most basic level.

TCF exists because of people like you. A significant portion of the proceeds from the sale of this book go to the TCF. Donations from people like you make TCF possible. Yes, computer geeks *do* care. And the donations are deductible.

The Tibetan Children's Fund is a unique organization. Nobody draws a salary. There's no "overhead." Volunteers who travel to India pay their own way. They don't solicit donations by phone, or hire companies to mount advertising campaigns. When they need to put something together—say, a new brochure, or a newsletter, or a web page—volunteers do the work, and companies donate the supplies. The net result: every single penny donated by individuals goes directly to the children. I know. I keep a close eye on it. My money's in there, too.

TCF isn't a religious organization. It isn't a political organization. It isn't a welfare organization, either. Sponsored kids must maintain good grades or they're put on probation. If they still can't keep their grades up, we remove them, to make way for kids who can. TCF has no particular axe to grind or point of view to impose: they just want to give the kids a chance to succeed in the world at large. Heaven knows the Tibetans have had a terrible time just surviving.

I could write about TCF's successes, and its failures, but the tales would fill a book. Suffice it to say that TCF has been very fortunate to find and support a handful of really brilliant refugee kids—and it's been unfortunate enough to see more than a few children die, when good medical care at the right time would've made all the difference.

If you would like to know more about TCF, please write to:

Tibetan's Children Fund
Post Office Box 473
Pinecliffe, Colorado USA 80471
Phone: (303) 642-0492
Email: *woody@wopr.com*

Thanks for your help.

— Woody Leonhard
Coal Creek Canyon, Colorado

Table of Contents

Preface

There you are, clicking along in Excel, crunching numbers left and right, when you get that . . . feeling . . . again. A sudden goosebump premonition that something's not right. With all the computer horsepower you've got, plus 30 megabytes of Redmond's flagship spreadsheet program, just why the heck doesn't it work better than it does?

Why is the toolbar covered with buttons you never use? Why do you have to drill down through labyrinthine dialog boxes to find the command you want? Who decided which tabs appear in Excel's File ➤ New dialog? Why does each new workbook look like it came out of the factory, not like you want it to? And what's all this add-in stuff that Excel discharges onto your hard disk, and does it do anything useful?

Starting to get annoyed? Welcome to the club.

The good news is that you are not alone, nor are you imagining things. *Excel can be quite annoying.* A lot of times it just doesn't work like it should. Many features within its powerful but complex and enigmatic structure could be a darn sight easier to use than they are. Beginners, advanced users, and even the full-blown spreadsheet gurus get annoyed with Excel.

The better news is that you don't have to live with it. In this book we help you pound your annoyance level down as close to zero as humanly possible. We cover everything from simple workarounds to ripping out the default demoware interface and replacing it with toolbars and commands that *make sense for you!* Create smart spreadsheets that help monitor themselves. Get the software doing more of the grunt work.

The Book's Audience

Buying yet another version of the User's Manual (remember when you used to get a real User's Manual when you bought a piece of software?) won't help you. Why should you shell out good currency for a rehash of Redmond's marketing drivel? You shouldn't. You don't need to be told you're a dummy, an ignoramus, or an idiot, and that that annoying feeling is all your fault. What you need is for someone to help you out and tell you something useful.

This book is geared toward Excel users who have doggedly marched along spending days trying to get Excel to do what they need to get done, getting more and more annoyed at what they perceive to be their own stupidity and inadequacy in trying to get this very powerful software to do something useful.

There's another group of Excel users, those who have been working with Excel long enough to be steamed at the software for *its* stupidity and inadequacy. Those users who grit their teeth at the problems and convoluted features and grind their way through their spreadsheets, knowing there must be a better way but not having the time or patience to ferret it out. This book is for them as well.

If you've ever gotten really annoyed at Excel and wondered how anyone ever achieves full guruhood with this powerful, wonderful, exasperating piece of software—this is the book for you.

Organization of This Book

The book contains eight chapters.

Chapter 1, *Required Reading*, discusses the causes and nature of annoyances in Excel. An annoyance can arise because Excel doesn't work like it's supposed to or because it doesn't work like you want it to. The most common cause of annoyances in Excel: things should just work a darn sight easier than they do. This chapter covers all the settings you can tweak in Excel and Windows to make Excel less annoying. We dive right in and get you maneuvering through your worksheets like a pro.

Chapter 2, *Excel as Workhorse*, covers all the new specifications of Excel 97 and how you can capitalize on them. Understanding the new command bar paradigm is the first step in being able to completely customize Excel. Find out how the pan-Office utility Office Art works, and get the latest on the virus threat in Excel.

Chapter 3, *Tale of the Toolbar and Other Aides-de-Camp*, walks you through a complete reworking of Excel's Standard and Formatting toolbars. Don't be saddled with the demoware versions of the toolbars that Microsoft's Marketing Department designed. Turn the toolbars into customized collections of the buttons you need to get real work done. Also, spend a few minutes getting to know Bob, the semi-intelligent new help system in Excel.

Chapter 4, *How Excel Works*, is a from-the-ground-up, feature-pounding review of the tools in Excel you need to be using to increase your productivity and lower your annoyance level. Make absolute and relative references work for you. Book-level and sheet-level names, tips, tricks, and useful workarounds abound in this chapter.

Chapter 5, *Using VBA to Customize Excel*, is a no-bull introduction to Visual Basic for Applications (VBA) as it is used from within Excel. This chapter gets you oriented in the VBA Editor and shows you how to approach writing VBA programs, with step-by-step examples on how VBA can control Excel and on making VBA programs run from inside Excel.

Chapter 6, *Excel Strategies*, shifts into high gear and tackles some of Excel's most egregious annoyances: dealing with the macro virus threat that is starting to plague Excel; creating error traps and self-monitoring formulas; using Excel's extensive set of auditing tools; creating simple VBA macros to solve some major spreadsheet annoyances; finding hidden gems buried deep inside Excel—all this and more! We'll delve into the new Internet features in Excel and how to better present your spreadsheets, both on screen and in print.

Chapter 7, *Excel in the Office*, covers Excel from where you stand in the trenches of everyday office use. How you can control what Excel does when it is first launched. How to utilize templates, get started creating your own custom templates, and how to replace the default book and sheet templates in Excel. How to protect your workbooks and sheets and why. Use Excel's annotation and comments features to document your models. Manage lists and analyze data using the amazing pivot table feature. Rock solid stuff for use every day in the real world.

Chapter 8, *Where and How to Get Help*, is a discussion of your best sources for additional help and information on Excel. Magazines, listservers, and web sites—we point you in the right direction for the latest and greatest sources of news and knowledge on all things Excel.

Conventions in This Book

Throughout this book we've used the following typographic conventions:

`Constant width`
: indicates a language construct such as in VBA for Excel. Code fragments and code examples appear exclusively in constant width text. In syntax statements, text in constant width indicates such language elements as the function's or procedure's name and any invariable elements required by the syntax. Key combinations are also shown in constant width, as are VBA language statements (like `FOR...NEXT`) and constants.

Italic
: in command syntax indicates parameter names. Italicized words in the text also represent the names of procedures and functions, as well as variable and parameter names. System elements like filenames and path names also are italicized.

Obtaining Updated Information

Many of the VBA code listings in *Excel Annoyances* can be found on our web site at *ftp://ftp.ora.com/published/oreilly/windows/excel.annoy.* Updates to the material contained in this book, along with information on the other books in the Annoyance series, are also available on our web site at *http://www.ora.com/publishing/windows*, as well as at *http://www.wopr.com* and *http://www.primeconsulting.com.*

Acknowledgments

Our thanks to Ron Petrusha, without whose help and guidance this series would not exist. Troy Mott also played an important part in getting this book in print. And to Claudette Moore, who was the linchpin that held everything together. Special thanks to Bill Manville for his superb technical editing on Chapter 5. Don Buchanan, the emir of Excel comedy, also provided many technical insights. Both Bill and Don are two of the world's leading Excel developers. Our thanks also to Dan Butler, genius and all-around good fellow.

Thanks to everyone who worked on production of this book. Clairemarie Fisher O'Leary was the project manager and production editor; Seth Maislin created the index; Madeleine Newell provided production assistance; Steve Kleinedler was the proofreader; and John Files and Sheryl Avruch provided quality control.

Woody would like to thank his loving wife Linda, who's been putting up with him for 20 years, and his nine-year-old son Justin, who already describes himself as a computer nerd. Their considerable accomplishments have made him very proud. Woody would also like to mention Jud and Linda Schroeder, and all the folks at Lancer Corporation in Texas, for their help with Tibetan refugee children. You've made a big difference for those kids—given them chances they never would have had—and saved more than a few lives in the process. I appreciate your help from the bottom of my heart. And Jim Vanderford, who taught me how to say, uh, things in one syllable.

From Lee Hudspeth, heartfelt thanks all around to my endearing wife Liz, our son Aaron, my parents Eloise and George, my second mom Gloria, and Scott Fraser for friendship of the highest caliber.

Jim thanks his wife and kids for being as understanding as they are when he's working on a book.

And from all of us, of course, to every spreadsheet jockey who has ever had to build a model. You fight the good fight every day, and we wrote this book for you.

In this chapter:

- *Annoying, Isn't It?*
- *Custom Settings for Everyman*
- *Now That We're Here, Where Are We?*
- *A Selection of Cool Stuff*

1 Required Reading

You popped in that Office 97 CD-ROM and fired up the *Setup.exe* file. It churned away and asked you questions that may have had you scratching your head—just what the heck is a Typical installation, anyway?—but you clicked here and clicked there, and Excel is now on your system along with all the other flotsam and jetsam that makes up the 200-plus megabyte Office 97 suite.

You're primed and set, locked and loaded, and you know exactly where you want to go today. You want to get some work done, crank out some spreadsheets, build a few models, pivot a few tables. But you've got that vague feeling that something is not quite right. This should be easier than it appears to be. You start wondering . . . is it you? Or is it the software?

It's the software.

Annoying, Isn't It?

Ever get annoyed at computer software? Okay, okay, that's a trick question. Take a rich, complex piece of software like Excel. It's got more features than you can shake a stick at, but some of the things it does (or doesn't do) can drive you crazy. Then there's that little feature that you know is in there somewhere, but you can't find, or can't figure out how to use even if you do find it! Arrrgh! Ever get the feeling the designers delight in making it more difficult to use than it has to be? Actually, the Excel development team is one of the sharpest groups on the planet, but they don't always get the last word on things. The Marketing Department has way too much say, and for them, a product has to demo well, not necessarily be useful. That leads to all kinds of little demoware annoyances, because instead of demo-ing Excel, you're trying to use it to do actual work.

That's where this book comes in. In this tome we're gonna try to squash as many annoyances as we can. Flat. Get you up to speed and running; show you how to undo the demoware damage, and help you get your money's worth out of this incredibly powerful spreadsheet program. Deep-six the marketing configuration and zero in on setting up Excel to do what you want it to do.

We'll start off from the standpoint that you're a current user of a relatively recent version of Excel, a tad annoyed at some of the things Excel does and doesn't do, and perhaps more than a bit overwhelmed by the immensity of this amazing program.

Annoyances come in all shapes and sizes, and what may annoy the heck out of one user may be a joy to another. Basically, we've found that the annoyances that drive users to want to reprogram Excel with an ax break down into one of three annoyance categories:

- Excel doesn't work like it's supposed to. These annoyances are thankfully fewer than in some of Excel's Office counterparts (like Word), but they're around, and can really be annoying when you run into them. We'll try to give you a fix or workaround when we come a'cropper with these.
- Excel doesn't work the way you want it to. Excel is just not very good at helping you get the most out of it. It dumps a ton of stuff on your computer's hard disk, leaves some handy things behind on the CD-ROM, and then it's strictly up to you to ferret out the best way to get things done. The demoware features that you'll run into on the Standard toolbar fall into this category. Forget about ignoring the man behind the curtain, we'll help you wrestle the controls from the Marketing wizards and make Excel dance to your tune.
- Some Excel procedures should be a darn sight easier than they are. This includes the hidden jewels that seem to have been buried in this incredibly powerful spreadsheet program or that could certainly be more intuitive or obvious. This is the most common type of Excel annoyance. We'll point out the hidden gems as we come across them and try to show you all the various shortcuts and less than obvious tricks for getting the maximum use out of Excel while keeping the annoyance level to a minimum.

With this in mind we'll strike out across the Excel tundra and start squishing these annoying, ah, annoyances. Fill your canteen and put on your pith helmet, we're off into the very heart of the beast!

Key Files—What They Are, Where to Find Them

When you install Excel, it dumps lots of stuff onto your disk. Excel alone consumes a fair size chunk of your disk real estate, and if you are installing all of Office 97, you can wave bye-bye to over 200MB. All that's apparently left to commemorate the installation event are some entries on your Start button's Program menu. Sure, in Windows 95, Microsoft decided to make things easier on the poor user, but in this case we don't think ignorance equals bliss! Talk about annoying!

Whether you're about to install Excel 97 on your system for the first time or if you've already done the deed, in this section we'll show you where your disk space went and how you can see for yourself where on your system Excel has scattered its many files.

When installing Excel, you can drill down through the installation options (see Figure 1-1) and decide what you want and don't want installed. (If you've already installed Excel, you can do the same thing and install any components you did not originally install or just review the locations that the install defaults to so you can see where Excel has put things.) But the real question is just where is the road map that tells you what each component does (and maybe gives you a hint about whether you might actually need it or not)? Or what gets installed where? Odds are that sooner or later you're going to want to know.

As you can see, a full-blown Excel install is going to chomp up a tad over 31 megabytes of your disk space. A big chunk of that is the Help files for Excel. If you click on the Help and Sample Files line and then on the Change Option button, you'll see that the Help for Visual Basic file is taking up the lion's share of space at 6724K (see Figure 1-2).

Don't expect two nice neat .HLP files, one for Excel and one for Visual Basic. Everything is modular these days. Excel breaks up its help across a number of files (most of which you'll find in the *C:\Program Files\Microsoft Office\Office* folder, assuming you accepted the defaults for file locations when you installed Office 97). The *Xlmain8.hlp* file has the bulk of the Excel Help (2,599K), but different topics and how-tos are stored in separate files.

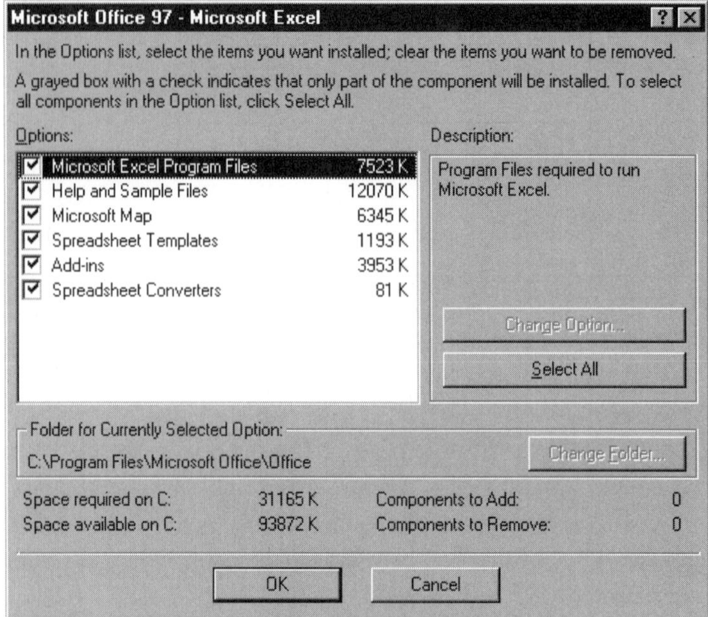

Figure 1-1: The Excel components installed by Office 97

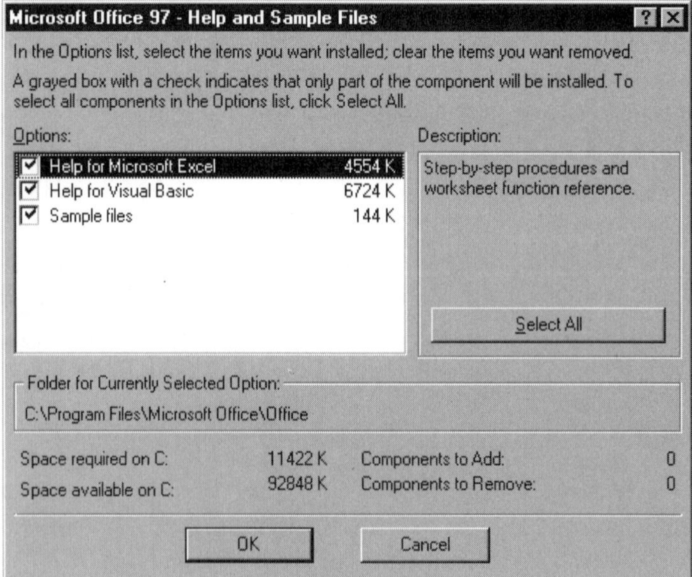

Figure 1-2: Excel's Help and Sample Files

NOTE Remember when you could just drag a folder (or `xcopy` a directory structure, if you're long in the tooth enough to grok DOS) from *here* to *there* to reorganize your drives and still have your applications run? Okay, maybe you'd have to do some editing of an INI file under Windows, replace one directory location with another, but certainly nothing too daunting for most users. It's an annoying fact of life that with new goodies like the Windows Registry and shared common files, you can't casually move your programs around manually. Fooling around with the Registry is *rocket science* compared to editing good old INI files. You'll have to get used to uninstalling and reinstalling your programs to move them around on your disk. And if you run both Win95 and NT on the same machine, you have to install your applications under both operating systems; you can't assume that a program installed under one will necessarily run under the other.

Just what is the story with those "Sample files"? What files might they be, do you want them, and where are they going to wind up if you install them? One good thing that the install Wizard does is to show you the destination folder it plans on installing the selected option to, just above the "Space required/available" information. On our test machine this file ended up as *C:\Program Files\Microsoft Office\Office\Examples\Samples. xls.* That's right, file, as in singular.

The *Samples.xls* is a great little primer on handy worksheet functions like index matching and conditional summing (awesome tools . . . if you haven't used them, you should take a look). It has some very nice VBA coding examples for working with arrays, standard looping techniques like `For...Next`, `For...Each`, `Do...Loop`, etc. For the database-inclined, it has examples for working with Data Access Objects and ODBC. It also contains some OLE Automation code suitable for cutting and pasting into your own macros and a general discussion of event programming to make your models interactive in a big way.

Not bad for 144K, eh?

As long as we're talking about samples, Excel 97 comes with three sample templates: Expense Report, Invoice, and Purchase Order, in the form of *Expense.xlt, Invoice.xlt, Purorder.xlt,* respectively (see Figure 1-3). These wind up in *C:\Program Files\Microsoft Office\Templates\Spreadsheet Solutions.*

You also get a bonus that does not appear in the installation list—*Village.xlt,* which is from Village Software, the company that developed

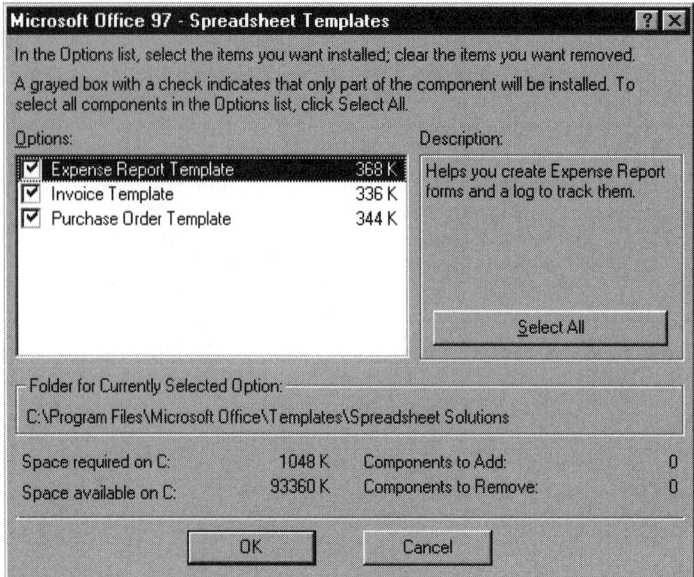

Figure 1-3: The sample spreadsheet templates . . . or most of them, anyway

the other three templates. This template offers to connect you to the Village Software web site where you can get more information on their products, and it includes their 800 number. Funny, this advertisement does not appear in the installation list, and it's kind of annoying that you have to manually delete it if you don't want it on your system.

All of the templates show up if you go to File ➤ New and select the Spreadsheet Solutions tab. You get a nifty set of automated business forms, and you can customize some aspects of them to suit your own company. They're worth a look, but don't expect to see any of the VBA code that drives them. The templates are locked, which means you can run the code but can't view or edit it.

The last major piece of the installation is the add-ins that come with Excel 97. (See Figure 1-4.)

There are a number of add-ins; some you'll find indispensable, some perhaps not relevant to your use of Excel. When you install Excel, you can decide whether or not to include the add-ins that are listed in Figure 1-4. Others are automatically included whether you like it or not. A complete list of Excel 97 add-ins appears in Table 1-1.

Consult Excel's Help file and do an index search on "add-in programs"—check them out to see what might be of use or interest. The Conditional Sum Wizard is one we bet you'll come to love. All the add-ins appear in

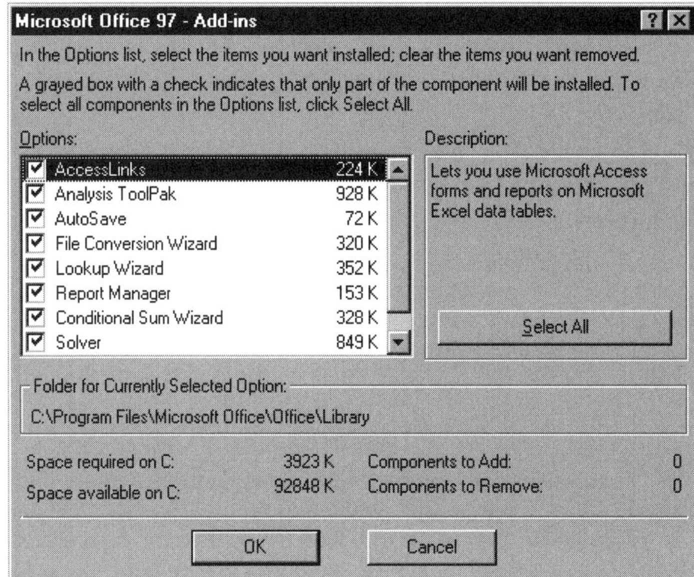

Figure 1-4: Excel's many add-ins

the Help file under add-in programs, except AutoSave. Search the help index separately for this add-in by name, "AutoSave."

Table 1-1: Add-ins Included with Excel 97

Add-in Program	Description
AccessLinks (optional)	For use with Microsoft Access, creates Access forms and reports linked to data in Excel. Requires Microsoft Access 97.
Analysis ToolPak (optional)	A collection of functions for calculating financial, engineering, and statistical results. Not as esoteric as it sounds, as it includes some very handy everyday functions like QUOTIENT and MROUND.
AutoSave (optional)	Lets you specify how often your workbooks are automatically saved to disk.
File Conversion Wizard (optional)	Walks you through converting files to the Microsoft Excel format in batch mode (i.e., converting a bunch of files all at once).
Lookup Wizard (optional)	Takes you step by step through creating a Lookup formula to look up specific data from a list.
Report Manager (optional)	Lets you define a number of reports that can contain various print ranges from within the workbook, different custom Views, and scenarios.
Conditional Sum Wizard (optional)	You can use this Wizard to create a formula that sums only the items in a list that meet specific criteria.

Table 1-1: Add-ins Included with Excel 97 (continued)

Add-in Program	Description
Solver (optional)	Lets you run various "what if" scenarios using variable amounts and constraints entered into specific cells.
Template Wizard Data Tracking (optional)	Helps you create Excel forms that can enter data directly into an Excel database.
Microsoft Bookshelf Integration	You get this if you install Office Professional or if you install Microsoft Bookshelf. It supports look-up and copy to Excel from Bookshelf.
MS Query Add-in for Excel 5 Compatibility	Lets you use MS Query with files created with older versions of Excel.
ODBC Add-In	Lets you onnect directly to external data sources.
Update Add-In Links	Workbooks created with earlier versions of Excel may reference add-ins that have been replaced by built-in Excel functions. This add-in finds these references and changes them to use the built-in functions.
Web Form Wizard	Takes you through creating an HTML table from a range in an Excel worksheet.

Excel creates some additional key files that you should know about, like the *Username8.xlb* file that stores custom toolbar settings. We'll point these files out as we come across them throughout the book.

What's This "Enable Macros" Thing All About?

If you've been following along, you probably opened *Samples.xls* or maybe one of the templates we've discussed. If you did, you had to deal with this dialog box that pops up, shown in Figure 1-5, that can only be described as annoying.

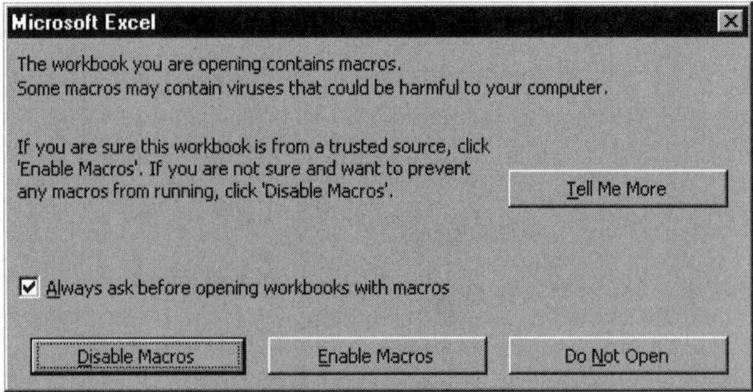

Figure 1-5: Excel's last line of defense to avoid a document virus infection

Unfortunately, this is an annoyance that you'll have to learn to live with. When macro languages added the functionality to trigger a piece of code by initiating a routine action—like opening, closing, or printing a file—the macro gurus smiled and started cranking out massively useful applications. But some of us were a bit uneasy. Auto macros made some very destructive things theoretically possible.

Don't let the term *macro* throw you! It was coined to describe the ability to record a series of keyboard actions that could be played back by pressing a single key or key combination—a macro key as it were. But VBA isn't a macro language under this original definition. It's a full-blown, Katie-bar-the-door, high-powered programming language. And therein lies the rub.

Back in 1995 somebody with too much time on his or her hands wrote the Word Concept virus in WordBasic to demonstrate this theoretical possibility in practice. It was designed to simply demonstrate the potential risk that existed with document-borne viruses. But two things went wrong.

First, it was released—or got loose accidentally—and spread like wildfire. By 1996, it was the most widely reported virus infection. Other viruses got more press, but Concept got more computers. Second, while Concept itself was really annoying, it was relatively harmless. However, it was a dandy build-your-own-macro-virus kit. It showed just how to build a real nightmare-inducing, self-replicating, document virus.

And now these same principles have been applied to Excel macro modules. We'll discuss this topic in some detail a bit later, but for now, whenever you open a workbook that contains macros, you'll have to deal with this warning message.

Basically, you have to make a split-second decision to either open the file with macros enabled (and hope for the best), open the file with the macros disabled (they won't run but aren't deleted or damaged in any way), or forget the whole thing and don't open the file at all. Some set of choices, huh? Pretty annoying. We'll talk more about the macro virus threat to Excel in Chapter 6, *Excel Strategies*, and how you can give yourself a few more options in dealing with workbooks that include macros.

Custom Settings for Everyman

First things first. Let's take a look at the things you should deal with before you grab the controls and take off in the cockpit of this spreadsheet building monster program. You can bypass a number of annoying little gotchas with this pre-flight run-through.

Record Your CD-ROM Key

Unless you are a glutton for punishment, you hopefully have a CD-ROM as your original media for Excel or, more likely, your copy of Office 97. This is good because flipping floppies can get old, real fast!

But the CD requires you to enter a "key" number when you install the software. This key is a 10-digit number that you'll find on a sticker on the back of the CD-ROM plastic case. If you're like us, you probably get the cases and the CDs mixed up on a regular basis, so we recommend you write the number on the front of the CD itself. Yep, right across the printed side of the disk, using a permanent marker. This won't hurt the CD—unless you write it on the wrong, non-printed side—and now you always have the disk and the number in the same place.

You can also pop open the Help ➤ About dialog in Excel to see the Product ID number (see Figure 1-6). The middle two groups of numbers (making 10 digits) are the same as your key number. So if you've already misplaced your key number, you can read it in the Help ➤ About box and record it on your CD. Consider doing this right now, as in right this very minute. You may not have a chance to read the ID number from Help ➤ About when you need it most because a frequent reason for reinstalling Excel (and thus the need for the number) is that Excel has gotten trashed and you ain't gonna be opening the Help ➤ About dialog.

Disable Find Fast

This annoyance is not Excel-specific but is more an irksome feature of Office. Although Microsoft touts Find Fast as the greatest idea since a pocket on a shirt, we've had nothing but troubles with it. The concept is pretty simple: Windows waits until you aren't doing anything, and then scans and indexes the contents of all the files on your hard drives. Then, when you're searching for a particular word or phrase in a document, Windows' Start ➤ Find ➤ File (and Office) can simply look at the index, instead of having to scan the innards of all the files. Great theory.

In practice, though, Find Fast hasn't worked out as well as the Marketing Department would like us to believe. Every couple of hours it takes over the machine—the PC starts acting as if it's gone berserk, with disk lights flashing and the keyboard freezing. In Excel, typing suddenly becomes an exercise in herky-jerky futility. We've also hit General Protection Faults

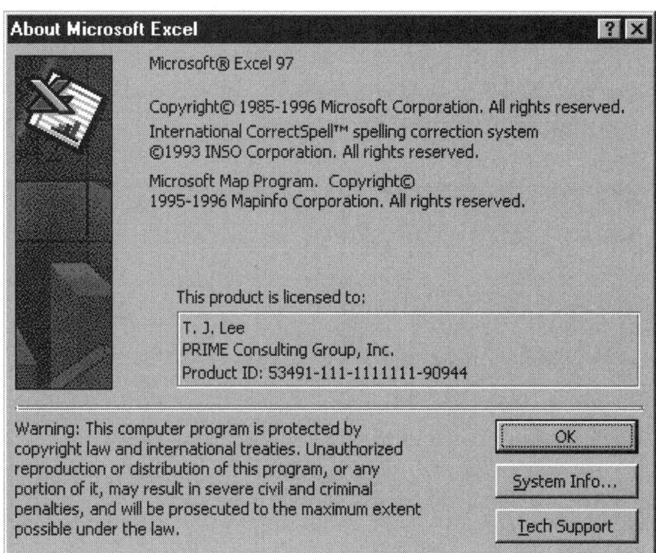

Figure 1-6: The About Microsoft Excel dialog box

caused by Find Fast. Some of the "cascading" GPFs get very humorous: leave your machine on overnight, and at least ten GPF boxes, delicately interleaved, may appear on your screen. We have no idea what caused the GPFs, and we couldn't replicate them, but they were very real.

Besides, we don't look for data inside spreadsheets all that often. We'd rather take the performance "hit" when we're searching for that data, rather than withstand a hit every couple of hours during a busy model building day. So the simple answer is: shut it off. Your situation may be different; if so, you have our sympathies.

To turn off Find Fast on all your drives, click Start ➤ Settings ➤ Control Panel. Double-click on the Find Fast icon. Click each drive in turn, then click Index ➤ Delete Index, OK. (See Figure 1-7.) If you ever want to start Find Fast again on a specific drive, reverse the procedure, clicking Index, Create Index.

If you want to get rid of Find Fast entirely—and never expect to use it again—you should also remove it from the Startup program group. To do so, just delete the Microsoft Find Fast shortcut icon from your PC's *C:\Windows\Start Menu\Programs\Startup* folder.

Maybe Microsoft will get it right some day.

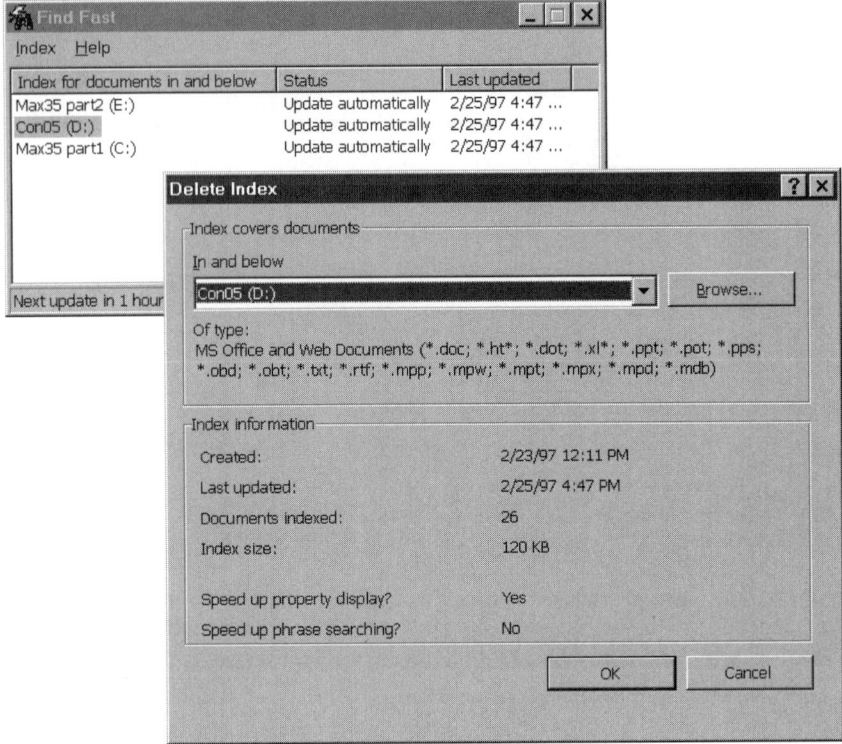

Figure 1-7: Turn off Find Fast by deleting the indexes

Getting Explorer to Reveal All

To make your life easier, you should undo some of the "I'll protect you from yourself" nonsense that Windows 95 thrusts upon you (if you have not already done so). This is true whether you are working in Excel or any other Office application. We're talking about the way the Windows Explorer hides filename extensions. Sure, Microsoft may like everyone to think that DOS is dead and that filename extensions don't matter any more, but whom do they think they're kidding?

Until the basic file format is redesigned to let applications determine a file type in a more sophisticated manner, applications are still partially dependent on the extension to give them a clue as to what file belongs to which application. Oh, if you rename an extant Excel file, Windows will continue to fire off Excel when you double-click it (assuming the new extension is not associated with another application), but by and large the extension is still important. As long as the applications are keeping track, you should too.

Fire up Windows Explorer (Start ➤ Programs ➤ Windows Explorer), click on View ➤ Options, and then click on the View tab (see Figure 1-8). Check the button labeled "Show all files," and uncheck the "Hide MS-DOS file extensions for file types that are registered" (the middle check box at the bottom). These settings affect almost all of your Office (and Windows) applications. The top and bottom check boxes affect only your view within the Windows Explorer application, so you can check them or not at your discretion.

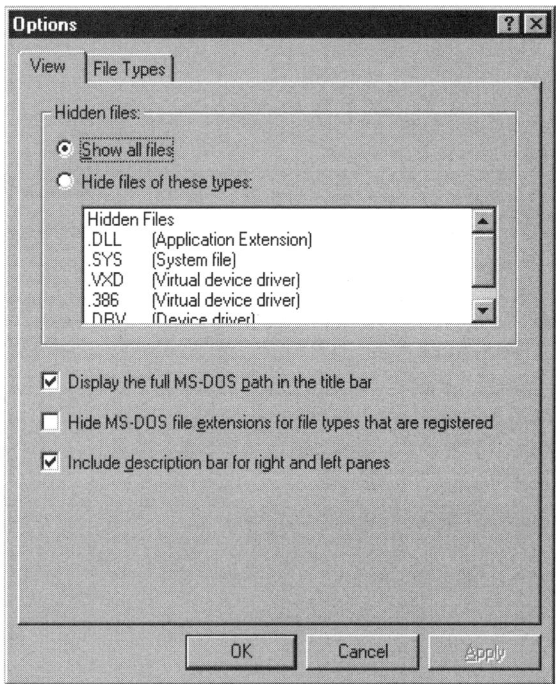

Figure 1-8: Windows Explorer View options

Relocating Your "My Documents" Folder

Excel has a nifty setting you can use to determine the folder it looks in whenever you do a File ➤ Open. Down in Tools ➤ Options ➤ General ➤ Default file location, you can type in a qualified path, and Excel uses this new folder as the default when it first fires up. But unless you change this setting, it defaults to the *My Documents* folder. More to the point, most of the other Office applications do the same, as does the Open Office Document item on the Start menu as well as the button of the same name on the Office Shortcut Bar.

Therefore you might want to consider just going with the flow and having the My Documents folder be your default folder (with sub-folders for organizing your files). Of course, if you find the folder name a bit too cutesy to stand, you certainly have our sympathy. Rename it by all means: select the folder, right-click it, and choose Rename (or just hit the `F2` function key) and change the name. You can relocate it by dragging it around your Explorer window as well. Just don't try to rename or move it outside of Explorer.

You'll have to restart Windows for the changes to be recognized by your applications.

Before You Start

Do you have the current version? Patches, bug fixes, interim releases—Excel has had them all in the past. So you should keep tabs on what the most recent release is. (It's a sure bet that Microsoft won't be notifying you!) The fact that Excel 7 had a 7.0a release went widely unnoticed. Microsoft does not like to send out fixes and interim releases unless you are having a problem that is corrected in the latest version.

Open Help ➤ About and you can get the current version number. The example in Figure 1-9 is Excel 7.0a, so you can see how they list an interim version.

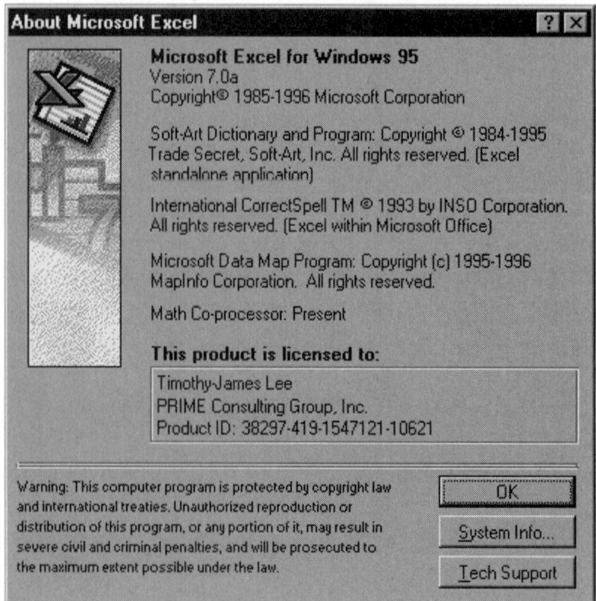

Figure 1-9: Excel 7.0a interim release version number

When in doubt, call up Microsoft (800-360-7561 in the U.S.A.; outside the U.S.A. call your local Microsoft office) and tell them you want to verify that you've properly registered your copy of Excel. The clerk will want your Product ID, which is also in the Help ➤ About box. Verify that Microsoft has your correct name and address on file. Then ask whether you have the latest version. If you don't have the latest version, squawk and tell them you've been having problems and your company computer guru said the latest version fixes the problem. Squawk loudly enough and they'll probably waive the shipping and handling charges on sending you the update.

And as long as we're talking about getting free stuff from Microsoft, be sure to visit their FreeStuff page on the World Wide Web. Point your browser at *http://www.microsoft.com/OfficeFreeStuff/excel/* and check out the latest Excel add-ins and freebies that Microsoft has made available.

Tools ➤ Options and You

As part of our pre-flight, let's take a look at some of Excel's default settings and discuss what things you might want to change before you go much further. Excel has a myriad of options, and the optimal settings for many will depend on how you are going to use Excel, but some are good candidates for changing right out of the box.

A change of view

Pull down the Tools menu and click on Options. You'll get the tabbed dialog box that lets you tweak Excel's settings to your heart's content. (See Figure 1-10.)

The View tab should be selected, and this is a good place to start. If you find you don't need the status bar, you can uncheck the "Status bar" check box in the Show group. This gives you the advantage of displaying another row of your sheet on the screen. The downside is you lose the very handy AutoCalculate box. That's the spiffy little box that sums (by default) any cells you highlight that contain values. You can right-click on it to change the default behavior (see Figure 1-11).

Comments (which were called Notes in earlier versions of Excel) are not annoying at all. Quite the contrary, they are a big help, and you have three choices on how comments are displayed on your worksheet. "None" is just that. You'd never know that a note, excuse us, a comment, exists on your sheet. Second, you can select the "Comment indicator only" setting. This gives you a small red triangular spot in the upper left

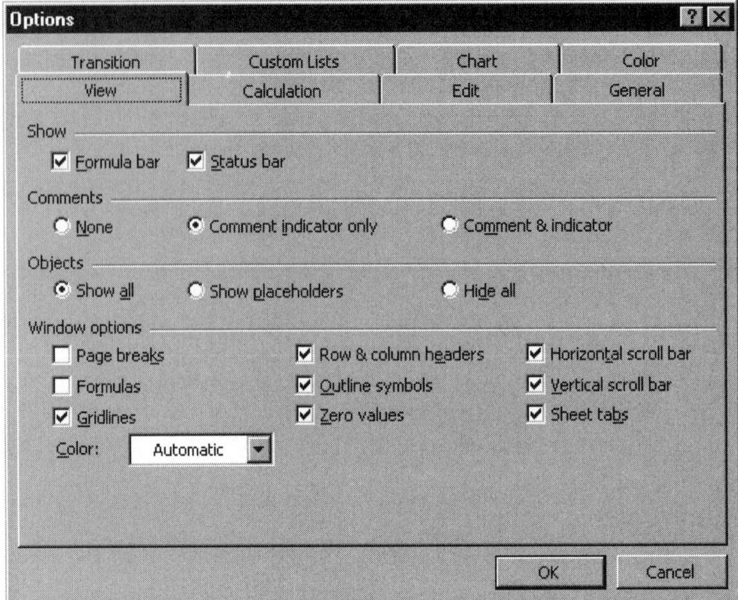

Figure 1-10: Excel's Tools ➤ Options dialog box

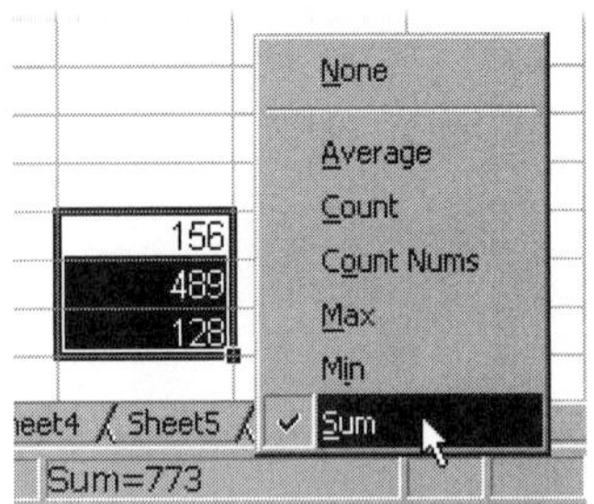

Figure 1-11: The AutoCalculate box on the status bar

corner of each cell that has a comment attached to it. Third, you can make Excel display the comments themselves as well as the indicators (see Figure 1-12).

We like to check the "Page breaks" box under the Windows options. This forces the display of page breaks throughout the sheet, every 9 columns and every 51 rows (assuming you have not changed the default font). This lets you see the space you have to work with on a page as you build your model. Printing is not affected by displaying the page breaks—if you have data only in cell A1, that's the only cell that will print. Your printer will not start spewing every empty cell out to column I and row 51. For that, you'd have to explicitly set the print range.

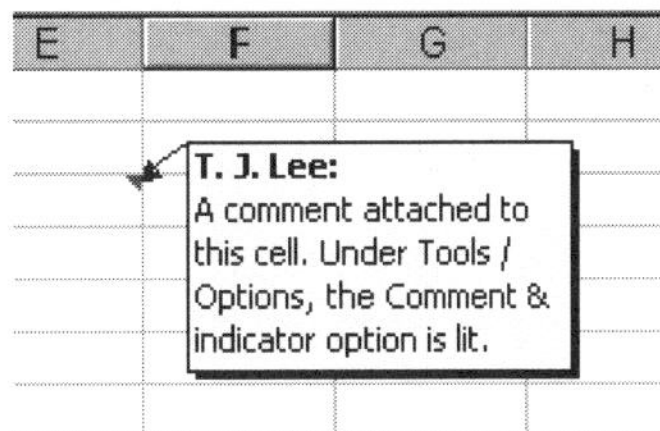

Figure 1-12: The ultra-useful cell comment

This print area display can be affected by explicitly setting the print range (via File ➤ Print Area ➤ Set Print Area, or via File ➤ Page Setup ➤ Sheet ➤ Print Area). Doing so causes the page breaks to conform to the range you've set.

You get a very different effect if you have multiple noncontiguous areas defined as the print range. It used to be that when you did this no page breaks appeared at all, but new in Excel 97 you get the page break delimiters showing up around each noncontiguous group of cells in your print range. (See Figure 1-13.)

	A	B	C	D	E	F
1						
2		Print this range B1:D4				Print
3						this
4						range
5						F2:F6
6		And print B6:D6				
7						

Figure 1-13: Page breaks on noncontiguous print range

Make a note of the location of the check box marked Formulas, just under the "Page breaks" box in the Windows options section. We'll be using this to do a little trick we call "flipping the sheet" whereby you make Excel show you the actual formula in a cell instead of the result of the formula, which is what Excel usually does. We'll come back to this in greater detail in Chapter 6, so leave it unchecked for now.

You can turn off the gridlines if you prefer that look. We like to flip the gridlines on and off depending on the type of model we're building, so later we'll add a button to a toolbar to toggle this setting.

If you find having zeros appearing in your sheets to be annoying, you can turn them off globally by unchecking the "Zero values" box. Formulas that resolve to zero, and cells with the value zero entered into them, all show up empty with this box unchecked.

Speaking in general

Now click on the General tab to display the general settings. (See Figure 1-14.)

The Excel developers at Microsoft did a nice job of reorganizing this dialog from the previous Excel 5/95 versions. The "Ignore other applications" option should not be checked unless you want to prevent your workbooks from responding to other applications that may be trying to get their attention using Dynamic Data Exchange. For example, if you check this option, and double-click on several workbook files in Windows Explorer, you'll get a new instance of Excel running for each workbook. Uncheck it and each workbook is opened in a single instance of Excel.

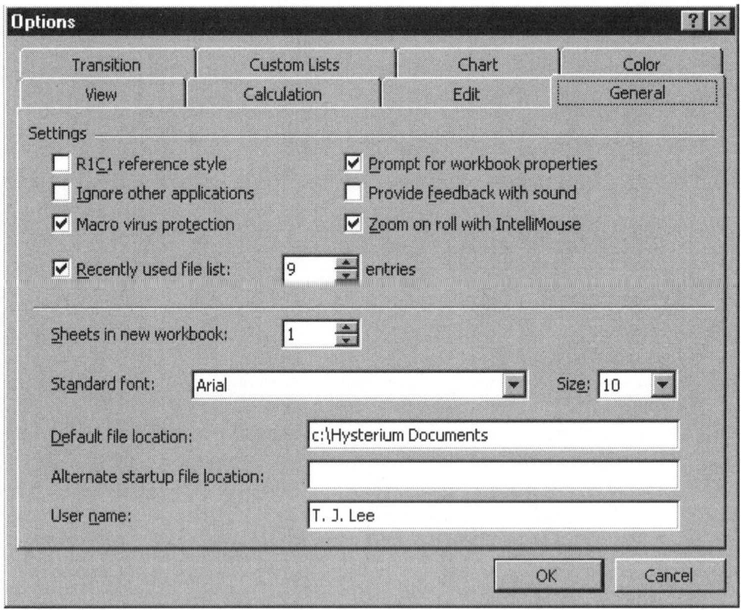

Figure 1-14: The General tab settings

The "Macro virus protection" check box controls the "this workbook has macros" warning message you saw earlier. You should turn it off only at your own risk.

Some people really like the recently used file list and others find it annoying. This is the list of last opened files that appears at the end of the File menu. Commonly known as the MRU (most recently used) list, you can set it to display from zero (unchecked) to a maximum of nine filenames. Set it for as many or few as you want or have the screen real estate for. We'll talk about some tricks for managing files you work with regularly in just a bit.

You can adjust the number of sheets that appear in new workbooks as well as change the standard font and point size for new workbooks you create. You have to shut down Excel and restart it for any font and/or point size changes to take effect.

If you have a particular folder where you like to keep all your Excel files (and it's not the *My Documents* folder), you can specify a default file location in the text box of the same name. This entry will cause Excel to default to the specified path whenever you first do a File ➤ Open. Subsequent File ➤ Open operations place you in the same folder that stores the last file you opened. Excel still has no Browse button beside this text box, which is extremely annoying, especially since we've been asking Microsoft to provide one since Excel 5! You have to type in a correct path, or you get a message box telling you Excel cannot access the directory (see Figure 1-15). Sheesh!

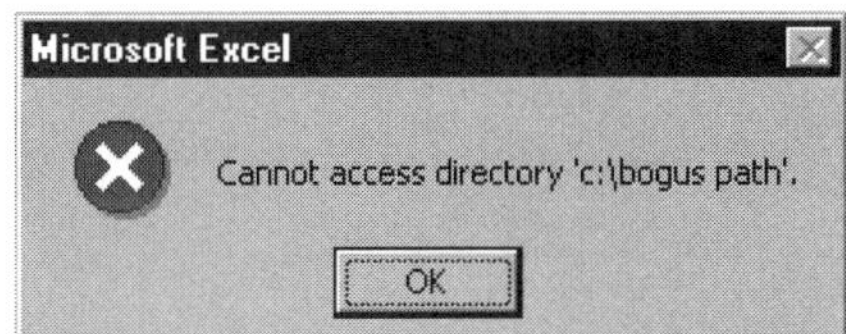

Figure 1-15: It can't access the folder either

Below the default file location, you can specify an alternate startup file location. You see, Excel's installation routine creates a folder called *Xlstart* (usually just below the location of the folder that houses the *Excel.exe* file). Excel will attempt to load any files it finds in the *Xlstart* folder when you first fire it up. Well, the alternate start file location lets you specify a folder of your choice to be the equivalent to *Xlstart.* Any files in this alternate folder get loaded automatically *in addition to* those in *Xlstart.* This is very handy if you're on a network and want to autoload some files from the net and some from your local disk. Still no Browse button, though. What's worse, if you type in a non-existent folder path, Excel won't offer to create it for you.

Saving the best for last, there's the "Prompt for workbook properties" check box. Check it.

Sure, it'll be annoying at first. But this is an annoyance you should learn to love, or at least put up with. Every time you save a workbook, up pops the Properties dialog box with the Summary tab selected (see Figure 1-16). You just need to get into the habit of filling out this information for any workbook you create. The keyword and category fields are especially useful when you create a lot of workbooks and need to be able to search quickly through them later.

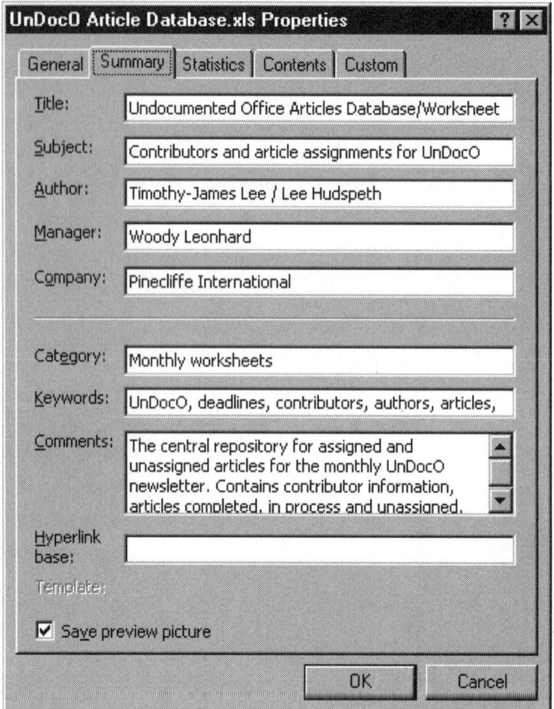

Figure 1-16: Summary tab in the Properties dialog box

When you do a File ➤ Open, you can click on the Advanced button and search the property information stored in each file. This is very slick when you're dealing with a large number of files. Pop in a keyword—perhaps a client name or project number—and up come all the files with that information stored in the Property Summary. Really neat, but you must have entered the summary information in the first place.

You can carry this to the next level by creating your own custom fields and setting data types and values for them. See Figure 1-17.

You can even dynamically link information in the worksheet to fields in the property list. No kidding! You could then search for all worksheets that have a common value that is over a specified amount.

When in Excel, do as Excel does

If you are a new convert to Excel from Lotus 1-2-3, you may have twiddled on the Lotus transitional settings. Click on the Transition tab to display the settings (see Figure 1-18).

The setting that we're most concerned about is the "Transition navigation keys" check box about halfway down the dialog box. If you're a recent

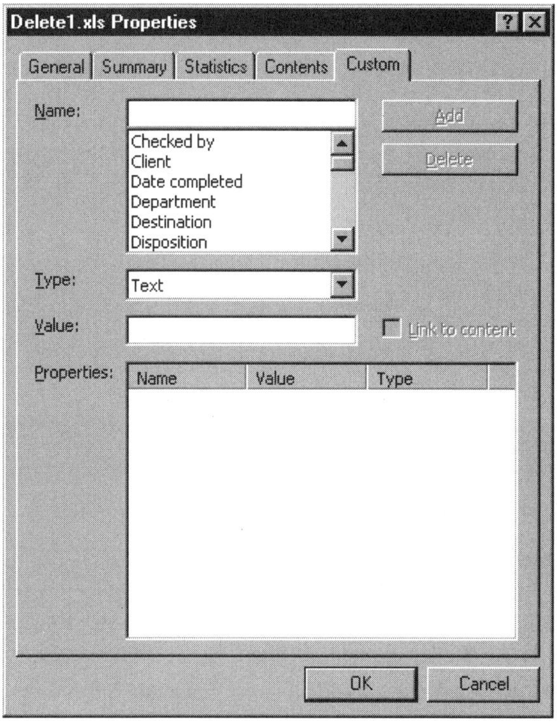

Figure 1-17: Roll your own custom property fields

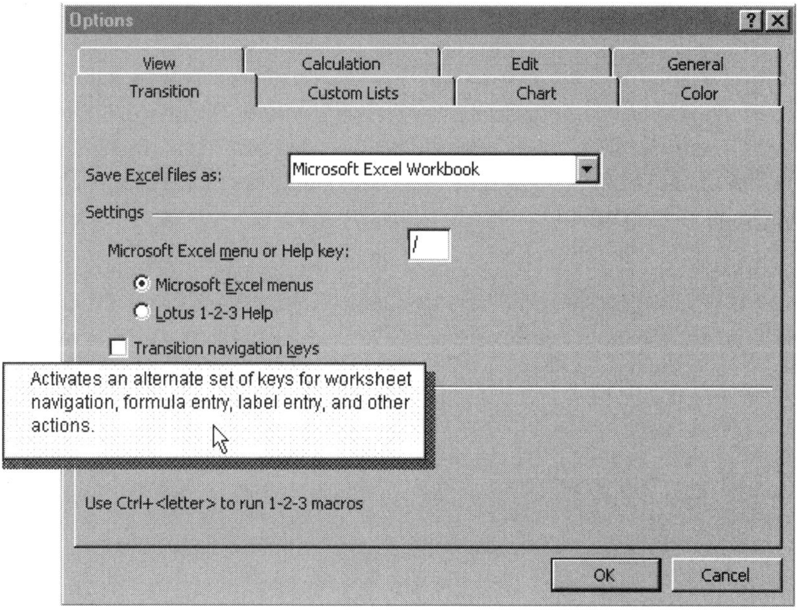

Figure 1-18: The Transition options

Lotus convert, it is tempting to check this box and use the keystrokes you are familiar with in Lotus 1-2-3. But Excel is not Lotus, and you would be well rewarded to forgo this crutch, make a clean break, and learn the Excel way of doing things.

Checking this box changes all sorts of navigation keys and how formulas and labels are entered. It will also make a lot of the examples in this book misbehave, so please uncheck it.

As long as we're here, there is a nifty feature that lets you change the default file type that Excel will use whenever you do a File ➤ Save. The drop-down list at the top of the dialog lets you select from among a number of file types, including all the earlier Excel version formats as well as Lotus 1-2-3 formats, CSV, DBF, and such. This is worth making a note of in case you need to create a number of workbooks that have to be saved in another format.

Now That We're Here, Where Are We?

Excel is a number crunching machine. Chomp! Sure, you can do lots of other nifty stuff with Excel, but the bottom line is numbers. Spreadsheets started out as the electronic equivalent of an accountant's 14-column work paper. It's an environment suited to manipulate numbers in remarkable and meaningful ways.

To this end, you get a workbook that contains a number of individual sheets. Each sheet has 256 columns and 65,536 rows (up from 16,384 in previous versions). That's a heap of rows any way you slice it! A four-fold increase in individual sheet size from Excel 95, over 16 million individual cells. If you printed out an entire sheet—using the default settings—it would be about 15 feet wide and 852 feet from top to bottom, or about 12,780 square feet. Whew!

What do you do with this giant matrix? You enter stuff into the individual cells, and you define relationships between them. A cell can only contain one of three things—a number, text, or a formula. That's it. You use formulas to define relationships between the contents of the cells containing numbers and text (called constants).

Let's run though some of the basics and learn how to navigate the typical sheet.

Working with the Same Files

We've discussed the MRU list, which tracks up to the last nine files you've opened, and how to search a bunch of files for property information. But some of you work with a small set of files, day in and day out: departmental budgets that must be regularly updated, expense report spreadsheets, cost models, and the like. Invariably, though, the one workbook you want never seems to be on that MRU list.

Here's a tip that works well for us. First, create a custom Office Shortcut Bar (OSB) as follows:

1. Right click on the OSB and select Customize... from the pop-up menu.
2. Select the Toolbars panel and click on Add Toolbar.
3. The first button, "Create a new, blank Toolbar" is selected, which is what you want. Type in a name for this custom toolbar, like **`Excel Docs`**, and click OK.
4. Click OK in the Customize dialog box.

Now you've got an empty custom toolbar. Next, open Windows Explorer and you'll see that you have a folder of the same name as your new toolbar under the `Shortcut Bar` folder (most likely *C:\Program Files\Microsoft Office\Office\Shortcut Bar*). Create shortcuts for the Excel files you work with on a daily, weekly, or monthly basis, and put them into this folder. They'll appear as buttons on your custom toolbar.

Another way to get the shortcuts on the toolbar is to just drag the filenames directly from Explorer to the displayed toolbar. Windows will automatically create the appropriate shortcut file in the correct folder. See Figure 1-19.

Figure 1-19: A custom OSB toolbar

That Annoying Little Mouse Pointer

First, let's come to grips with the mouse as regards Excel. Ever try to use the mouse to do one thing, only to have something else altogether happen? Or try to click or drag something and have the mouse balk and refuse to obey your commands?

Love it or hate it, the mouse is an integral part of the graphical user interface (also known as Plan 9 for World Domination or "Windows" for short). In Excel the mouse pointer changes when you least expect it, depending on what it's touching. Cross hair, pointy thing, arrow doohickey—nobody knows what to call these sundry shapes. Very annoying (to say nothing of needing the hands of a surgeon to make the pointer perform correctly for certain tasks). Since we'll be showing you some nifty stuff that depends on knowing what pointer the mouse is manifesting, we'd better define some terms for the common pointer shapes. We made these names up eons ago for our own peace of mind, and they've stood us in good stead. These names, and their corresponding mouse pointers, are shown in Table 1-2.

Table 1-2: Mouse Pointers Used by Excel

What It Looks Like	What We Call It
	Traditional Northwest Mouse Pointer—this is the standard selector used for clicking on menus, buttons, scroll bars, file names, and what have you.
	Selection Cross hair—this is the pointer you see when your mouse is over a sheet. You can select a cell, a range of cells, rows, columns, and if you right click with it in a cell, you'll get a pop-up menu of options.
	I-Beam—the I-Beam manifests itself whenever you touch a control that accepts text directly (like the zoom, font, or font size controls on Excel's default toolbars).
	Fill Handle Grabber—the fill handle is the aptly named gizmo that lets you perform "AutoFill" in a range of cells. You need to touch the teensy little square block in the lower right-hand corner of the active cell (or active range).
	Horizontal Sizing Grabber—the sizing grabbers are used to change column width and row height using the mouse. Touch the black line between any two column headings. Click and drag to resize it.
	Vertical Sizing Grabber—this works the same as the horizontal grabber, only for rows. Very handy.
	Horizontal Split Bar Grabber—this grabber is used to split the sheet into independently scrolling windows.
	Vertical Split Bar Grabber—works the same as the horizontal flavor.

Table 1-2: Mouse Pointers Used by Excel (continued)

What It Looks Like	What We Call It
	Bidirectional Split Bar Grabber—if you split a sheet both horizontally and vertically and touch the pointer to the intersection of both split bars, the grabber will change again into a four-headed arrow that points north, south, east, and west, letting you resize in two directions at once.
	Pointing Index Finger—pass the mouse over a graphical object that has been assigned a macro, a hypertext link or URL, or a jump topic in a help window, and you'll get the pointing finger. This tells you that if you click, something will happen. Hopefully, something wonderful.
	Help Button Pointer—pull down the Help menu and click on What's This. You'll get the Help pointer (a traditional Northwest pointer with a big question mark tacked on). You can use this to click on anything in Excel to get help on that particular thing.
	Zoom Pointer—in Preview mode you get the little magnifying glass pointer when you touch the active sheet. Left-click once to enlarge (pointer changes to a Northwest arrow configuration); click again to restore the preview to its original size.
	Drag-Copy Pointer—indicates that you are dragging something that will be copied when you release it.
	No-Drop Zone Pointer—if you drag something where it is illegal to drop it, you get this "no-can-do" pointer.

Shhhh! Programming . . .

Does Excel sometimes seem annoying to you on general principle? Something you can't quite put your finger on but that annoys you nevertheless? We know that feeling. It can debilitate new Excel users and cause even regular users to feel uneasy with the program. We think this odd syndrome is caused by a misconception about spreadsheets in general (one that Microsoft helps maintain, by the way). Fire up Excel and what do you get? Nothing. A workbook with three empty sheets in it (assuming you didn't change the default setting earlier). Take a close gander at Sheet1. Emptiness. Now, you could make the same argument about Word: open it up and all you get is an empty document. But a document in Word is a relatively simple container for text. A word-processed document is something that most everyone understands, at least conceptually.

A spreadsheet, however, is void of form and meaning until you build something with it. From complex models for hydraulic force and motion analysis on deep-hole petroleum exploration to a simple list of expenses you ran up over the weekend, Excel is first and foremost a development environment. D-E-V-E-L-O-P-M-E-N-T. And this is a scary (or at least unsettling) thought.

Fortunately, spreadsheets drove the personal computer revolution in its early days, and people found themselves fooling around with Lotus 1-2-3 and MultiPlan long before they knew they were actually doing programming. We say "fortunately" because if they knew that programming was involved, users might have written off spreadsheets as "too hard" to use. Microsoft would certainly rather you think that a spreadsheet is just like an accounting program, word processor, or your email program, just an easy-to-use everyday appliance that will take you wherever you want to go today. But it isn't, and that's what gives you that uneasy annoying feeling.

Take a very simple example of a formula in Excel: You have some numbers in a range of cells `B2:B5`, and you get their average with the formula entry shown in Figure 1-20. So how is this programming, you ask?

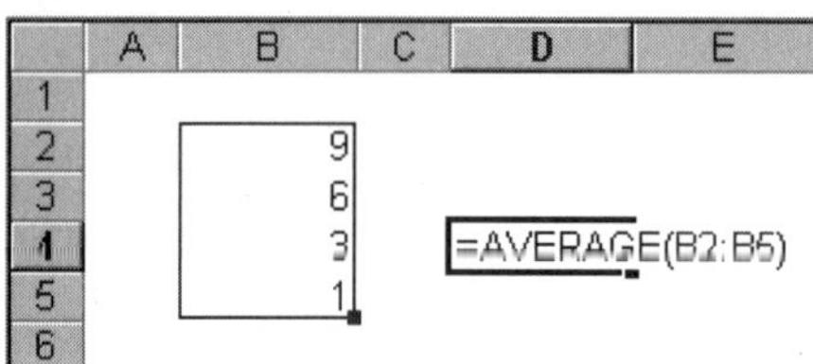

Figure 1-20: Averaging a range of values

This is a function, that is, a routine that returns a result. You give the function, in this case **AVERAGE**, an argument—the range of cells containing the values you want averaged—and you get back the result. Programming.

You program your Excel sheets at the cellular level. Each cell can hold a program in the form of a formula, and that program code gets executed whenever Excel updates the sheet. Excel updates or calculates the entire workbook when it is opened or closed. The individual sheets are calculated when you enter something into a cell or change an existing entry. Actually, it's a bit more involved. Excel is smart (well, the programmers who built it are), and to keep performance snappy, it tries to calculate only the cells that depend on other cells whose values have changed. And you can force a recalculation of the entire sheet at any time by pressing the F9 function key.

To lower your annoyance threshold, you have to come to grips with the fact that Excel is a programming environment in which you develop your own applications.

Tips on Tabs

A single workbook can contain a plethora of sheets, as the only limitation is available memory. But as the number of sheets in a workbook grows, the complexity of working with them can become a bit annoying.

Each sheet has a tab located at the bottom of the workbook. (See Figure 1-21.) You can make a particular sheet active by clicking on the tab for that sheet. You can turn off the tab display in Tools ➤ Options ➤ View by unchecking the "Sheet tabs" check box. We don't know why you'd ever want to do this, but you can.

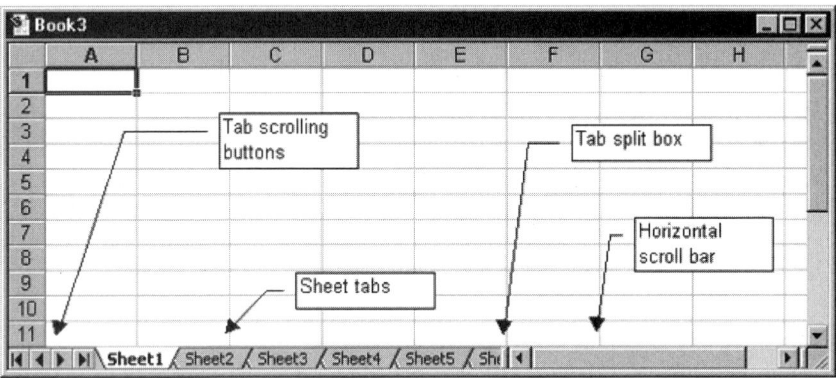

Figure 1-21: Sheet tabs and various related controls

That's fine and dandy, but what do you do when you have more sheets in a workbook than you have screen space for displaying the tabs? First, you can reduce the space allotted to your horizontal scroll bar by placing your mouse over the tab split box (you'll get the vertical split bar grabber mouse pointer) and dragging it left or right. Left for less room for displayed tabs, right for more tab screen space. Double click on the tab split box to restore the default setting.

You can also click on the tab scrolling buttons. The outer left and right VCR-like controls move the tabs all the way to the beginning/left or end/right. The inner two buttons scroll you one sheet left or right. You can also hold down the `Shift` key and click the inner buttons to move one display's worth of tabs in either direction.

When you have a bunch of sheets the quickest way to get to a particular one—or to just see all the sheet names at once—is to right click on any of the tab scrolling buttons. (See Figure 1-22.)

Excel also has an annoying habit of inserting new sheets before the selected sheet, and not after, as you might expect. And there is not even

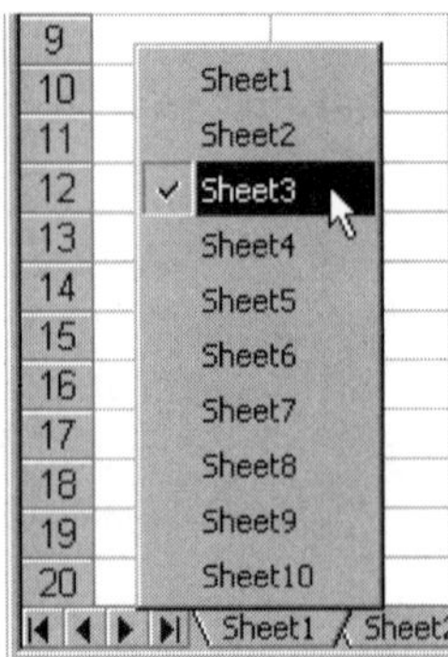

Figure 1-22: Excel's sheet menu—just right-click on the tab scrolling buttons

a preference setting that might allow you to choose whether you'd like to insert before or after the selected sheet. Once your sheets are inserted, you have to move them around to reorder them. You do this by left-clicking and dragging the sheet's tab to a new location. Hold down the `Ctrl` key while you click-and-drag, and you'll copy the sheet to a new location instead of moving it. This handy trick with the `Ctrl` key comes up again when we discuss copying and moving cells.

Working with multiple sheets

Here is a major time saving trick: Say you want to enter some data in several sheets. Same data in the same place, in several sheets. Or you want to format several sheets in an identical manner. Just select all the sheets you want to work with *before* you start entering or formatting. Click on the first sheet's tab and then `Shift`-click on the last sheet's tab (assuming the sheets you want are contiguous), or hold down the `Ctrl` key while you select each tab (if they are noncontiguous). Now whatever you do to the active sheet happens on every sheet selected.

Hmmm, it's annoying that getting out of this multi-sheet selection mode is not more intuitive than it is. You have to select a sheet that is not part of your current selected set, unless, of course, you've selected every sheet in the workbook, in which case you just click on the tab of any sheet to deselect the set and have only one sheet active again.

What's in a name?

By default, each sheet starts life with a dull and uninteresting name of Sheet*x*, where *x* is the sequential number of the sheet. The number of the sheet is sequential, but as we mentioned earlier, the sheet is inserted to the left of the current sheet no matter where the sequential number might fit in the overall sheet order. When we discuss templates, you'll see how you can change the default sheet name, but for now, let's talk about renaming sheets.

Just right-click on a sheet tab and you'll get a pop-up menu like the one shown in Figure 1-23. Click on Rename, and you can rename your sheet to anything you want, as long as it's 31 characters or less, and as long as none of the characters includes * ? / \ : ' or [, all of which are reserved, meaning hands off. The Help file says you can't use the right bracket ( ]) either, but we haven't had a problem using it. Of course the Help file doesn't say anything about the apostrophe being forbidden, so go figure.

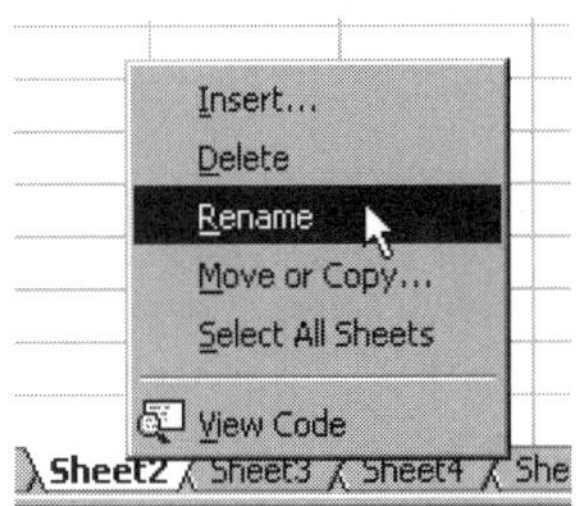

Figure 1-23: Renaming sheets via the pop-up menu

Make your life easier and get out of the habit of using spaces in your sheet names. Use *Income_Statement* or *IncomeStatement* instead of *Income Statement.* Why? When you use sheet names in formulas, database stuff, and some VBA programming, you'll find that the space in the sheet name gives you some major headaches.

Navigating the Worksheet

You'd be surprised at how much time gets wasted by inefficiently scrolling around a worksheet. The seconds spent waiting—while rows and columns scroll by on the screen—can really add up. If these pauses are bothering you, then let's go over the basic navigation methods and tricks that can save you a ton of time.

Zooming

This is an underutilized feature that's been in Excel a long time. Of course, its lack of use may be explained by its really poor implementation. But a massively useful thing it is, to zoom out, reducing the screen image of your spreadsheet, letting you see a thumbnail of your sheet like the one shown in Figure 1-24.

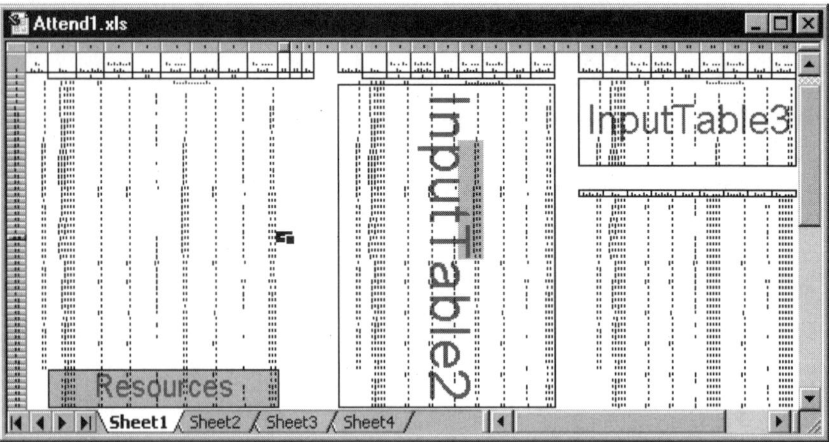

Figure 1-24: The birds-eye view

There are two primary ways to zoom a sheet (not counting the IntelliMouse, which is discussed at great length in Chapter 2, *Excel as Workhorse*): the menu method (View ➤ Zoom, select your setting, and click OK), which is not recommended because it's way too slow; or the Zoom button on the Standard toolbar. (See Figure 1-25.)

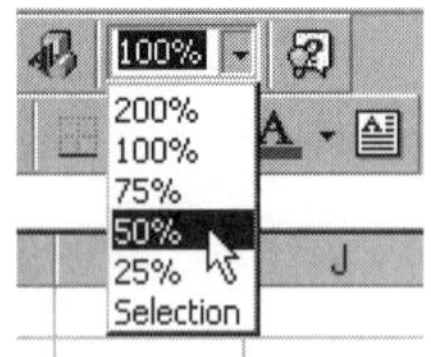

Figure 1-25: Handy-dandy Zoom control

The problem with this implementation is the limited number of preset settings and your inability to add any new custom settings. But you really kick up your efficiency in navigating about a worksheet by just zooming out to 25%, clicking on the area of the sheet you want to be in, and zooming back to 100%. Four clicks and you're there, no scrolling required. Another advantage in Excel 97 is how your range names are displayed on the actual sheet when you zoom out (assuming your ranges consist of more than a single cell and that the name is of a length that can be displayed in the range area). This feature kicks in at around 39%, but your mileage may vary depending on your screen resolution. (Look back to Figure 1-24.)

If you need a bit more finesse, you can just click on the Zoom control, type in your desired percentage, and hit the `Enter` key.

Go To'ing

The Go To command works very nicely for maneuvering your way around a sheet or a group of workbooks. The fastest way to access Go To is to hit the `F5` function key. Up pops the Go To dialog box (see Figure 1-26).

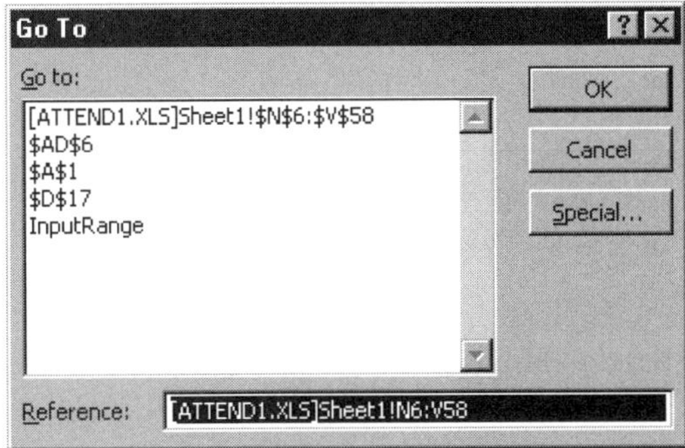

Figure 1-26: Go To—Instant transportation anywhere

You can type in a cell address and you are instantly transported. The Go To dialog keeps track of the last five addresses you've visited using Go To. This lets you jump to a sheet or workbook, work in that section, and then very quickly return to your previous location.

You can enter range coordinates as well, like B10:E15, and that range is selected. You can do multiple selections just as easily. Just separate your ranges with a comma: B10:E15,H1:J7.

The Go To dialog box also displays all the range names in the current active sheet.

The Name box

You can use the Name box to move around a sheet. (See Figure 1-27.) Click in the box, type your destination cell address, and hit `Enter`. Bang! There you are.

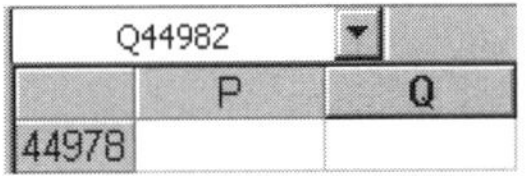

Figure 1-27: Excel's Name box

The jumps you make via the Name box are remembered by the Go To dialog box and show up in its history. You can also pull down the Name box and select from any named ranges that you have in your sheets, and you'll be instantly transported to that range.

Zapping

This is a keyboard technique that every spreadsheet jockey should know inside and out. For this, a little hands-on would be useful. Open a new workbook. Cell A1 of Sheet1 is active. Hold down the `Control` key and press the right arrow key. Zap! You just flew 256 columns to the right, out to the end of the sheet.

Now do a `CTRL+DOWN ARROW`. Instantly, you are 65,536 rows down in your sheet, down at the very bottom row.

When you zap in any direction, the active cell moves in the chosen direction until it hits a cell with contents (text, number, or formula) and stops with that cell selected, or until it reaches the end of the sheet.

There's a mouse-only variation of the zap, but it behaves a bit differently. Start with an empty sheet. If you have very precise mouse control, you can double-click on the top or left edge of the active cell and you'll zap up or left. But double-click on the right or bottom edge of the active cell and nothing happens.

	A	B	C	D	E	F	G
1							
2							
3				Col 1	Col 2	Col 3	Col 4
4			Row 1	100	110	120	130
5			Row 2	120	130	140	150
6			Row 3	130	140	150	160
7							

Figure 1-28: A sample worksheet

Now, consider the example shown in Figure 1-28. If you have cell contents to the right or below the active cell, the double-click right or down does work. But the mouse trick generally moves one cell less, i.e., instead of stopping when it hits a cell with contents, it stops one cell short, in the cell just before the cell with contents. With the active cell A3, you double-click on the right edge, and you zap to cell C3, one cell short of the first cell in that row that has contents.

A practical application of this technique would be when you need to find the very last entry in a given column. If the contents in the cells are all contiguous, you just `CTRL+DOWN ARROW` and there you are. If the cell contents are not contiguous (a few entries, some empty cells, some more entries), you use the Go To dialog or Name box to jump to the last cell in the column (say D65536), then `CRTL+UP ARROW` and there you are.

You can build on the zap technique for selecting large areas of your sheets. For small selections, you just click-and-drag across the target cells with the mouse. Make noncontiguous selections by selecting the first cell or range, then hold down the `Ctrl` key and make your additional selections. This works great until you have to scroll off the displayed area of the sheet.

By adding the `Shift` key to the `CTRL+` key zap method, you can quickly select a large area of your worksheet. This works best for large tables where you have some contiguous ranges of cells—column headings across a number of columns, and a number of row descriptions running down the left edge of the table, for example. Select the upper left-most cell, `CTRL+SHIFT+RIGHT ARROW`, then `CTRL+SHIFT+DOWN ARROW`. Your table is selected.

Favorite keys

The `Page Up` key takes you one screen of rows up, `Page Down` the same in the other direction. `ALT+Page Up` takes you one screen of columns left; `ALT+Page Down`, one screen of columns right. `CTRL+Page Up` activates the next sheet to the left of the active sheet; `CTRL+Page Down`, the next sheet right.

The `Home` key takes you to column A—the row you were on remains unchanged—while `CTRL+Home` takes you to cell A1.

`CTRL+End` takes you to the lower right-most cell that defines the last row and the last column with contents. But this "end" setting is not dynamic. If you delete rows and columns, thereby changing the last row and column with contents, Excel stays stuck on the previous setting until you close and reopen the workbook. It sure would be nice if Excel could dynamically reset this, but since this behavior has remained unchanged since Excel was a sapling, don't look for it to get fixed anytime soon.

A Selection of Cool Stuff

Don't get the wrong impression and think that Excel is just a pit of annoyances. Not only is it the most amazing spreadsheet program on the planet, it is continually being expanded, polished, and generally improved upon. The Redmond Rangers do not idly rest upon their laurels, not by a long shot.

There are a number of very cool improvements and new features in Excel 97. New stuff like data validation with custom error messages, a sprinkling of new worksheet functions, the Page Break Preview feature that should save a forest or two in printing jobs, and the ability to actually merge cells. You can now rotate text within cells, do conditional formatting (how often we've wished for this one!), use several new chart types and the improved Chart Wizard, and slice and dice your data with a plethora of pivot table goodies.

In keeping with the new focus on the World Wide Web, there are now hyperlinks, an HTML Wizard, the ability to save workbooks directly to an FTP site, and you can use Excel forms on the Web. This is all very happening stuff.

We'll touch on some of these blockbusters in more detail in later chapters, but just consider a few of the following smaller improvements that you'll find in Excel 97, and see if you don't start feeling less annoyed already.

Yes to All

When you quit Excel with several open workbooks (that have unsaved changes), you used to get a message box prompting you to save it. This message box would pop-up once for each worksheet. Very annoying. Well, they've added a "Yes to All" button to this dialog box so you can tell Excel to save every blessed sheet and shut down. (See Figure 1-29.) Yea!

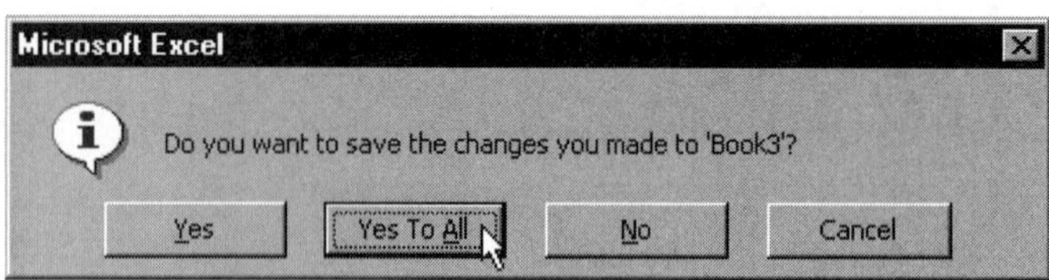

Figure 1-29: Save 'em all!

Multi-Level Undo

Wow! Bet you were counting the days until they added a multiple-level undo to Excel (Word has enjoyed this one for a while now). As Figure 1-30 shows, it's finally arrived. Sure, they limited it to 16 actions, which is pretty annoying in itself, and there are some other gotchas as well, but by golly, it's a start!

Magically Shrinking Dialog Boxes

This used to be a major annoyance. You are trying to do something that involves highlighting a range, only the bloody dialog box that wants the

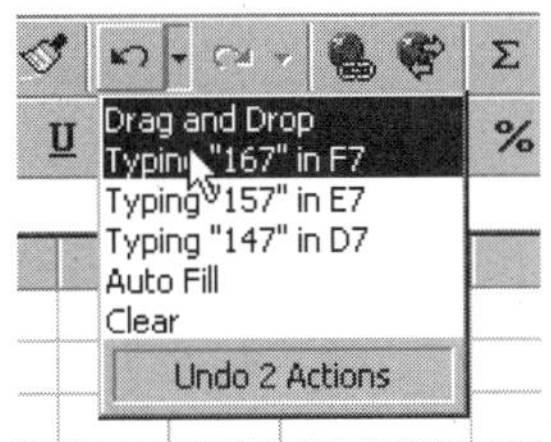

Figure 1-30: Multiple Undo at last

range is covering 60% of the screen. This used to drive users crazy when they were setting repeating rows and columns in the Page Setup dialog. Now, when you start to select your range, the dialog box shrinks and gets out of your way, as illustrated by the dialog box in Figure 1-31.

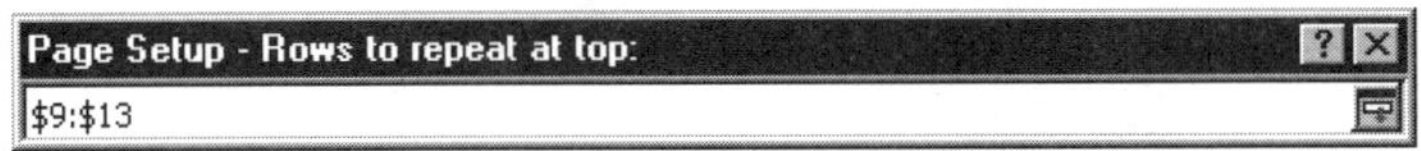

Figure 1-31: The handy shrinking dialog box

Drawing in Excel

Drawing gizmos, doohickeys, thingys, and more! An improved drawing layer and numerous tools to make flowcharting or line-drawing enhancements to your spreadsheets a snap. (See Figure 1-32.) You can even pop-up WordArt right in Excel and avail yourself of all the special text editing features that this handy utility has. Very nice indeed.

Expanded Entries

Ever run into the 255 characters in a cell limitation? Okay, okay, calm down, yes, that was a trick question, too, but you'll be thrilled when you discover that Excel 97 lets you run that number up to 32,000 characters.

Range Finder

Now, whenever you edit a formula, all the referenced ranges are displayed in color, and the corresponding cells are bordered in that same color. So, for instance, if a cell contains the formula `=B3*B4`, the letters B3 will appear in one color (blue, for instance), and the cell B3 will be highlighted in the same color, while the letters B4 will appear in a different color (like green), while the cell B4 will be highlighted in the second color. By color-coding your form for easy reference, Excel gives you instant visual confirmation of which cells each part of your formula is dealing with.

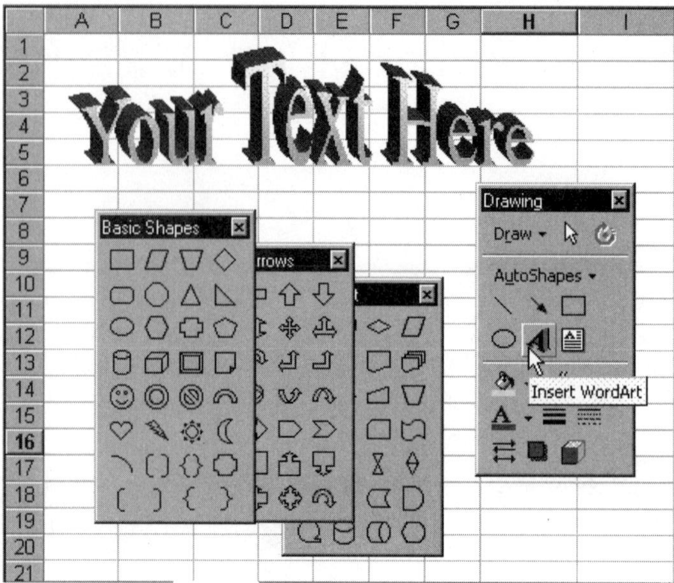

Figure 1-32: Drawing tools galore

Indented Text

This is a cosmetic improvement, but one that should have spreadsheet builders jumping with glee! Finally, just highlight a series of labels, and with one click, indent all of them. (See Figure 1-33.) Splendid!

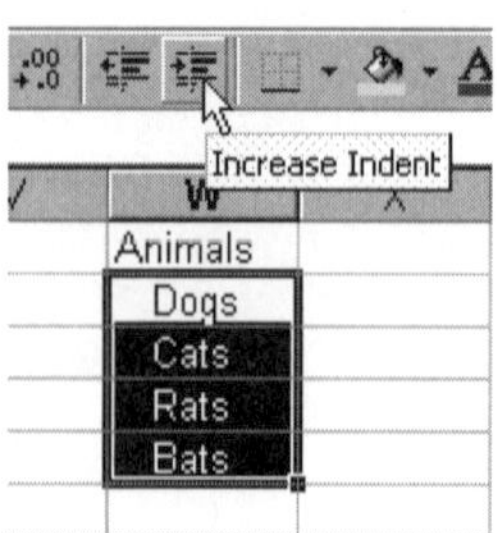

Figure 1-33: The long-awaited ability to quickly indent text in cells

In this chapter:

- *New Specs*
- *Mouse Wheelies*
- *Dancing Row and Column Indicators*
- *Undo, Undo, Finally, a Multiple Undo!*
- *Command Bars*
- *Office Art*

2

Excel as Workhorse

In Chapter 1, *Required Reading,* you saw a brief synopsis of some of Excel's new features. In this chapter we give you a close look at Excel's newest "user" features; those that directly impact how you interact with Excel day in and day out, keystroke by keystroke. We'll be getting into Excel's "data" features in subsequent chapters.

By drawing your attention to these critical user features, we guarantee you'll begin to viscerally appreciate and better understand Excel's mind set—how it thinks, moves, glides, and gesticulates during the intricate dance we all do with it that some stuffed shirts call, er, work. These new features empower you not only by being new or improved (thereby eliminating prior annoyances), but they also provide you with more and easier ways to customize Excel to suit your needs, not those of the Microsoft marketeers. We'll take a look at the very fundamental enhancements to Excel's dimensions, a new pointing device, row/column orienteering à la a fighter jet's HUD, a long-overdue undo facelift, command bars (menu and toolbars renamed and gussied up), a completely new drawing layer, and last but certainly not least, the unfortunate meteoric rise of macro viruses and what you can do to defend yourself.

New Specs

The upper limit on the amount of text you can type into a cell has undoubtedly frustrated more Excel users than any other limitation. Up until Excel 97, the upper limit was a paltry 255 characters. We can't think of a single Excel user we encountered in either a personal or a professional setting who didn't rail against this head-banger. The Excel designers made sure they exceeded this constraint—by two orders of magnitude! Now you can loquaciously type up to 16 pages of material in a cell—well, 32,000 characters to be exact. (See Figure 2-1.)

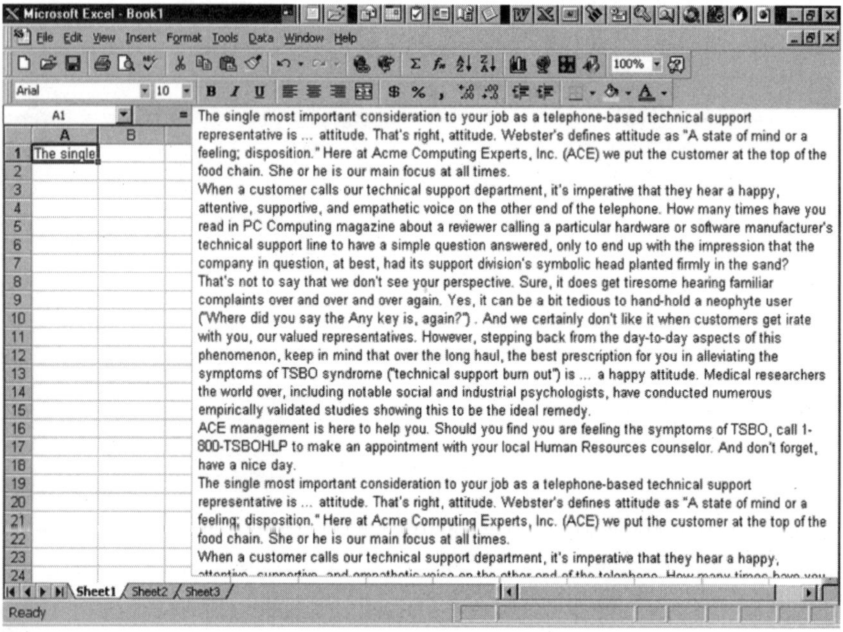

Figure 2-1: A single Excel cell loaded with 32,000 characters

Excel 95 supported a maximum of 16,384 rows. Excel 97 ups the ante fourfold to 65,536 rows per worksheet. The maximum column count remains unchanged at 256. That's 16,777,216 cells, thank you, so everyone run out and upgrade your RAM to 64 MB so you can use all that real estate.

Figure 2-2 shows the view from the dark recesses.

Speaking of improvements, Excel 95 annoyingly produced new workbooks with 16 sheets by default, unless you went in and sniffed around the Tools ➤ Options tabbed dialog long and hard enough to find the setting to make it a more reasonable number, say, 3 (Tools ➤ Options ➤ General, "Sheets in new workbook"). We all complained loudly about this one, and the Redmond Rangers listened up. Excel now creates a sensible 3 worksheets in a new workbook unless you ratchet it up yourself (the maximum in a default workbook is 255).

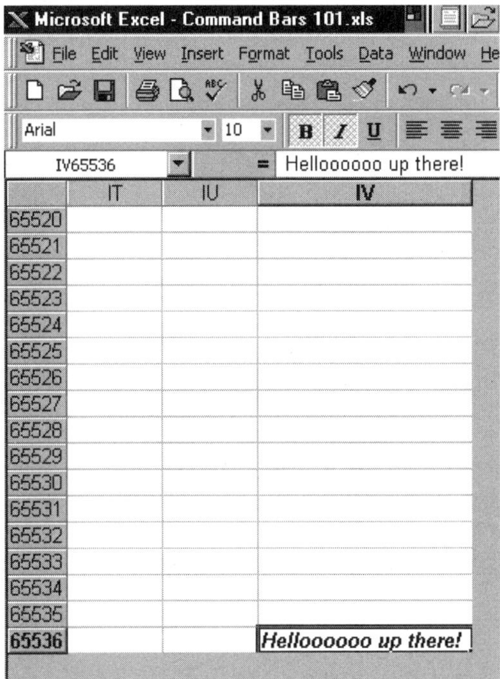

Figure 2-2: Cell IV65536 sure knows what lonely's like

If you're curious about additional Excel specifications, fire up Robert, er, Office Assistant (Robert was OA's code name) and type in **`specifications`**—exactly please—and drill down from there to your heart's content. We say exactly because if you give Robert the actual Help topic title instead—which is "Microsoft Excel 97 specifications"—in a fit of myopia it won't see that topic and instead just points to one topic—"What's new in Microsoft Excel 97." This is a classic example of a "doesn't work like it's supposed to" annoyance. If you use Help instead of Office Assistant, then you get a correct list of all the related topics. (Click Help ➤ Contents and Index ➤ Find ➤ "Microsoft Excel 97 specifications.") In fact, of the remaining four Office applications, PowerPoint and Word produce no relevant items in a Robert-based query! It seems to us that there should be pan-Office consistency on these key informational Help topics and the way both Robert and the Help engine locate them for you. You can read more about this gaffe in O'Reilly & Associates' *Office 97 Annoyances*.

Anyway, you'll certainly find lots of good reading by asking Robert "what's new," as shown in Figure 2-3.

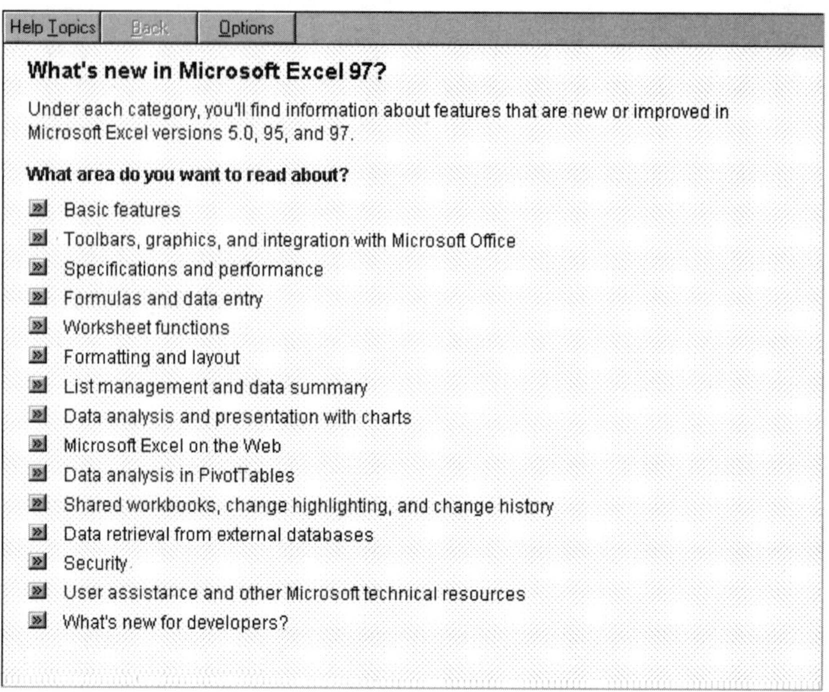
Help Topics Back Options

What's new in Microsoft Excel 97?

Under each category, you'll find information about features that are new or improved in Microsoft Excel versions 5.0, 95, and 97.

What area do you want to read about?

- Basic features
- Toolbars, graphics, and integration with Microsoft Office
- Specifications and performance
- Formulas and data entry
- Worksheet functions
- Formatting and layout
- List management and data summary
- Data analysis and presentation with charts
- Microsoft Excel on the Web
- Data analysis in PivotTables
- Shared workbooks, change highlighting, and change history
- Data retrieval from external databases
- Security
- User assistance and other Microsoft technical resources
- What's new for developers?

Figure 2-3: Just ask Office Assistant, "what's new" and take its first suggested topic

Mouse Wheelies

When it comes to hardware—especially hardware we come in close personal contact with for 12, 16, or more hours a day—we're awfully opinionated. As far as we're concerned, with one exception, Microsoft's forays into hardware have been uniformly disastrous, stretching back almost a decade. We hate the "natural" keyboard. But we've always loved Microsoft's old dove bar mouse. It just feels "right"—and none of the hundred-plus competitors we've tried have weaned us away from the plain little beast. Until Magellan, er, IntelliMouse, uh, IntelliPoint. (All right, the official terminology is IntelliMouse for the device itself and IntelliPoint for the software controlling the mouse. Official or not, we'll use IntelliMouse to refer to the whole enchilada throughout.)

The IntelliMouse looks just like the old dove bar mouse, except it has a wheel between the left and right buttons. When you roll the wheel "up" (generally with your middle finger), the document scrolls up. Roll it down and the document scrolls down. But you can also click the wheel itself—and once it's been clicked, simply moving the mouse up and down controls the scrolling. The sensitivity has been finely calibrated (and can be adjusted): move the wheel or the mouse slowly, and you scroll slowly;

move it quickly and you jump across documents at lightning speed. It takes a while to train your fingers to use the wheel, but once you've realigned your synapses, you'll wonder how you ever lived without it.

Windows applications have to be written specifically to use the mouse, but Win95's Explorer, Help, Internet Explorer 3, and Office 97 all use it. (The fact that not all applications use it will make training your fingers all the more difficult.) There are lots of bells and whistles that you'll definitely want to explore while calibrating the IntelliMouse to your liking. See Figure 2-4.

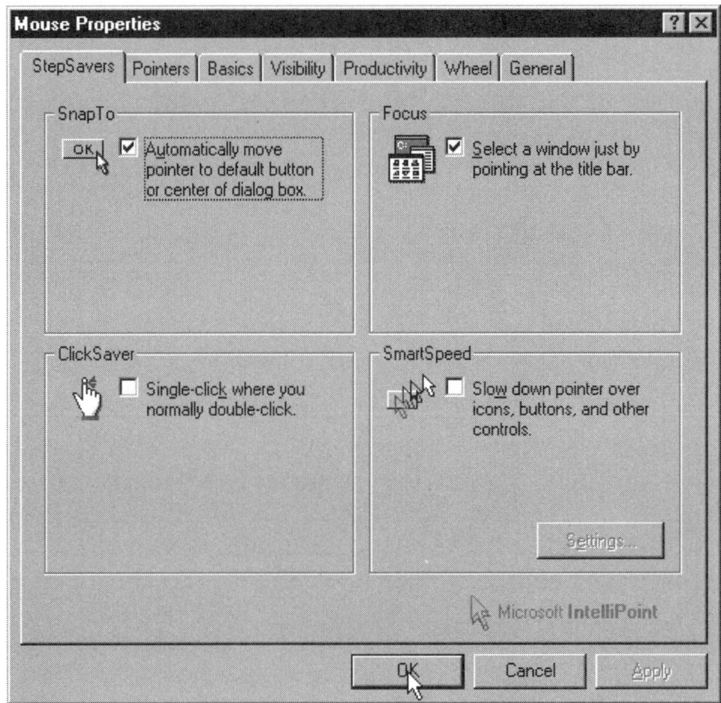

Figure 2-4: The top-most tab in the IntelliPoint Mouse Properties dialog box (notice the mouse pointer centered perfectly on the OK button)

We also like the Focus feature that provides a clickless way to change the focus between title bars, icons, folders, menus, and dialog boxes. Just move your mouse pointer over the object, and it pops into focus automatically.

Aside from the IntelliMouse wheel-scroll-zoom feature set (clearly its main draw), we like the SnapTo feature. The IntelliPoint software looks at dialog and message boxes and tries to figure out which button is the default (meaning, the button that has the focus when the dialog is initially opened). For example, with SnapTo active, if you right-click a file in Explorer and choose Delete, the mouse pointer will land dead-center on the Yes button before you can say "Truth by the gleaming merciless truck-load." It takes some getting used to, and occasionally the pointer ends up somewhere you don't expect it, particularly if you switch back and forth between a primary PC that has IntelliMouse on it and others that don't. There's a trick to reducing the unexpectedness of the pointer's SnapTo behavior. If IntelliPoint can't figure out what button is the default, it jumps to the physical center of the dialog box; however, you can set the pointer to instead simply stay put. Here's how (you'll be editing your Registry so proceed very carefully*):

1. To edit the Registry, select Start ➤ Run ➤ regedit ➤ OK.
2. Locate the key `HKEY_CURRENT_USER\Control Panel\Microsoft Input Devices\Mouse`.
3. Change the setting of the `SnapToCenterOfWindow` value from `ON` to `OFF`.
4. Exit the Registry Editor.
5. Restart your PC and the change will be enforced.

Our favorite Excel features that coordinate with IntelliMouse are:

- Pan through a sheet. Click the wheel button once anywhere inside the sheet display space. This displays what the IntelliPoint literature calls the "origin mark" cursor. Now, move the mouse pointer (it's a unidirectional pointer shaped like a triangular arrow with a round dot at its base) down to pan down, right to pan right, and so on. The panning speed changes in direct proportion to how far away from the origin mark you move the mouse. Click any mouse button or the wheel to turn panning off.
- Zoom. Simply press and hold `Ctrl`, and move the wheel down to zoom out and up to zoom in (each wheel click is 15%); annoyingly, the IntelliMouse only zooms up to 100%, whereas Excel itself zooms up to 400%, so for over 100% you'll have to use the Zoom control on the Standard toolbar (Excel's zoom range is 10% to 400%).

There are other IntelliMouse/Excel features you can explore on your own; just ask the Office Assistant, "intellimouse." The IntelliMouse solves problems that perhaps none of us knew we had, and in this respect, is a great annoyance eliminator.

---

* For a detailed discussion of editing the registry using RegEdit, see *Inside the Windows 95 Registry*, published by O'Reilly & Associates.

Dancing Row and Column Indicators

This is another example of curing an annoyance that folks weren't keenly aware of before Excel 97, but once you see the new feature, there's no going back. As you move the cell cursor around in a worksheet, Excel now provides two subtle but tremendously useful cues as to which row and column the cursor is currently planted in. The current row and column header cells pop up slightly with a 3-D effect (looking raised relative to its neighbors). The current row and column headings themselves (the "A" in column A, or the "1" in column 1, if you're displaying R1C1 notation) become bold. When the current selection extends beyond a single cell to encompass multiple—even discontiguous—cells or ranges of cells, Excel applies the raised-and-bolded effect to all rows and columns containing any selected cells. (See Figure 2-5.)

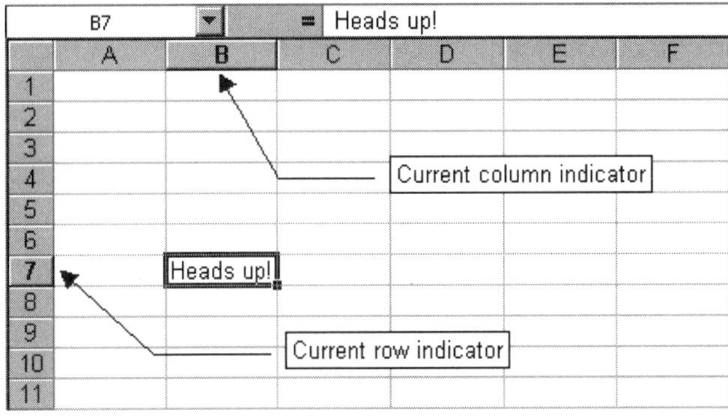

Figure 2-5: Excel's row/column HUD focusing on cell B7

Undo, Undo, Finally, a Multiple Undo!

Until Excel 97 came along, Excel was hamstrung by a single-item undo stack. Harking waaaaaay back to the good old Office 4 days, this is one area in which Word definitely had—and still has—its big brother beat. While Word 6 introduced a 100-action undo capability, Excel 5 shamefully stopped short at one. There were no changes from Office 4 to Office 95—Excel 95 held its ground stubbornly (still just one item), with Word 95 at 100 items. Excel 97 still lags mightily on this dimension, providing a 16-item undo stack, whereas Word 97 weighs in with a whopping 2,417 item undo capability. We'll take 16 undos over a scanty one undo any day, but there's plenty of room for improvement here.

You'll like the user interface of the undo button (located on Excel's Standard toolbar) as shown in Figure 2-6. It provides an amazing amount of detail in a relatively small, compact space. Cool.

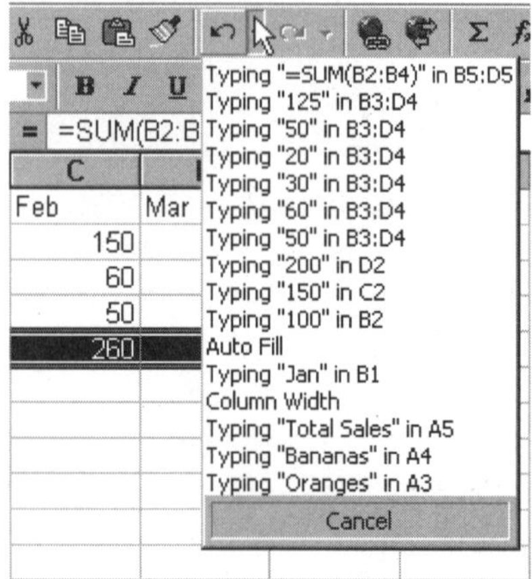

Figure 2-6: Excel's undo stack after creating a small sales table

Command Bars

Command bars represent one of your best weapons in the fight against Excel annoyances. (The other first-choice weapon in this regard is Visual Basic for Applications.) This is because command bars are so easily customized to do your bidding. Yes, Excel ships from the factory in an annoying configuration that reeks more of dog-and-pony show demoware than real-world productivity enhancement. No problem. Just take the knowledge you gain from these sections on command bars and start rooting out annoyances like weeds in a garden.

The following definitions will pay off handsomely as you journey through this section. Read them now, carefully, then earmark this page. You'll be coming back to it often. We do. (Admittedly, some of this is pure semantics, but we prefer to err on the side of an up-front, concise statement of what all the components are when dealing with such an enigmatic topic as command bars.) By the way, you won't find any mention of the term "command bars" in the *Office 97 Resource Kit*'s index; instead look under "toolbars." Another classic example of how much further Office has to go on the much-ballyhooed consistency dimension.

- **Menu**—"Menus list commands available to the user . . . There are several types of menus, including drop-down menus, pop-up menus, and cascading menus."[*] (Note: synonyms for the term *cascading menu* are hierarchical menu, child menu, and submenu.) Example: the File menu on Excel's primary menu bar.

- **Menu bar**—"A menu bar . . . is a special area displayed across the top of a window directly below the title bar. . . . A menu bar includes a set of entries called menu titles. Each menu title provides access to a drop-down menu composed of a collection of menu items, or choices." Example: Excel's primary menu bar.
- **Drop-down menu**—A drop-down menu is "a collection of menu items, or choices" revealed when you click on a menu. Example: click on File in the primary menu bar to see the File drop-down menu.
- **Menu item**—"Menu items are the individual choices that appear in a menu. Menu items can be text, graphics—such as icons—or graphics and text combinations that represent the actions presented in the menu." Example: the New menu item in the File drop-down menu.

NOTE A *menu* and a *menu item* are two entirely different things. It's easy to confuse or misuse these two terms. When unsure, return here and reread their respective definitions.

- **Pop-up menu**—A pop-up menu looks similar to a drop-down menu, is displayed at the pointer's current location, and is usually invoked by a right-click. The benefit of pop-up menus is that they display "commands specific to the object or its immediate context," thereby reducing screen clutter and mouse movement. Example: right-click any cell, as shown in Figure 2-7.
- **Cascading menu**—"A cascading menu (also referred to as a hierarchical menu or child menu) is a submenu of a menu item. The visual cue for a cascading menu is the inclusion of a triangular arrow display adjacent to the label of its parent menu item." Submenu is yet another annoying synonym for cascading menu. Example: select File ➤ Send To to see the submenu that's subordinate to the Send To menu item (see Figure 2-8).
- **Shortcut menu**—See pop-up menu.

---

[*] Unless otherwise noted, all definitions cited in this bulleted list are from *The Windows Interface Guidelines for Software Design* (Microsoft Press), ISBN 1-55615-679-0. We'll use the abbreviation *TWIGSD* hereafter.

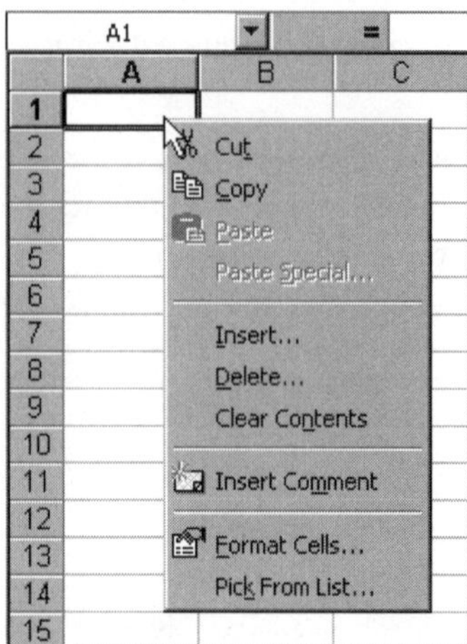

Figure 2-7: Excel's "cell" pop-up menu, seen when you right-click on a cell

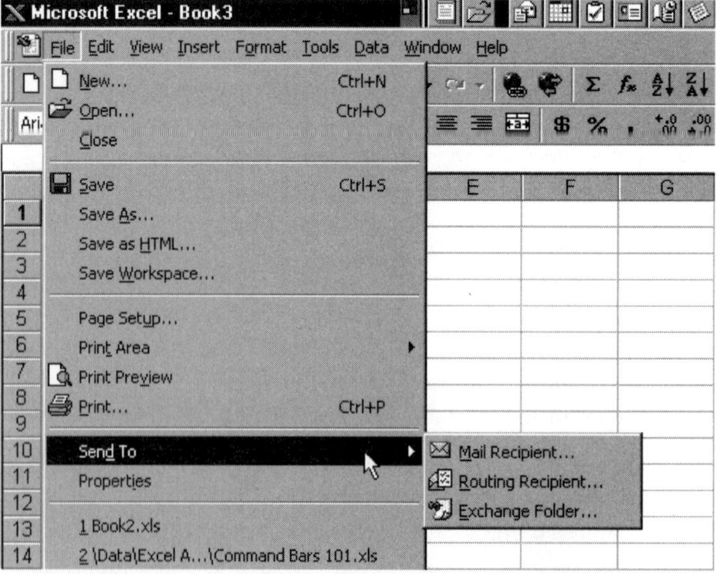

Figure 2-8: Send To is the parent menu item, while Mailing Recipient, Routing Recipient, and Exchange Folder comprise the cascading menu (submenu)

- **Toolbar**—"A toolbar is a panel that contains a set of controls . . . designed to provide quick access to specific commands or options." Example: Excel's Standard toolbar.
- **Command bar**—You won't find any definitions related to command bars in *TWIGSD*; rather, this is—for now at least—strictly an Office vocabulary item. A command bar is a menu bar, toolbar, or shortcut menu.

- **Command bar control**—Objects that can exist on a command bar include a wide variety of controls; as stated in the Microsoft Office Visual Basic Help, these are "buttons, edit boxes, drop-down list boxes, combo boxes, and pop-up controls (controls that display a menu or submenu)." However, in this chapter we're talking strictly about the aspects of command bars exposed by Excel to you, the user, via its user interface. Some of these controls cannot be added manually and instead must be added with VBA code. Controls you can add manually are buttons, combo boxes, and pop-up controls, although we prefer to say "menu control" instead of "pop-up control" in keeping with the official lexicon of user interface (or UI) design. Simply put, in Excel you can manually add buttons, combo boxes, and menus to command bars. Later in this chapter we point you to a listing of all the types of controls supported by command bars.
- **Button control**—A button is only one type of control that can be placed on a toolbar, although in the vernacular (and often in Microsoft's own Help text and user guides) you'll hear folks referring to any kind of control on a toolbar as a button. Ordinarily, this would be okay. But if you're working your way through Excel's Help material on toolbars and how to customize them, you'll be quickly confused by undefined terms, thinly defined terms, and lack of an overview. It's annoying that the documentation for such an important and often used feature is so mediocre. In the next few paragraphs we take you through the intricacies of command bar control terminology:

NOTE As you work through these next few paragraphs, keep in mind that the real power of command bars is their customizability. You can shake and bake 'em to look the way you want and to invoke the commands and custom macros of your choosing. You don't have to accept the demoware mix served up by Redmond. Understanding the terminology should help you exercise that freedom.

  — Excel's Standard toolbar has a Zoom control on it (second control from the right); it's officially a combo box control (of the type `msoControlComboBox`, which you can determine from inside the VBA development environment, which we'll cover later in this book). If it were a button control in the absolute strictest sense of the object model vocabulary, it would be of the type `msoControlButton`, an example of which is the New control on the Standard toolbar (first control from the left). Zoom is not a button control, it's a combo box control. New is a button control. So . . .

— When talking about command bars, if we say "button control" we mean exactly this—a control that (1) can display an image, text, or both (all of which are manually editable via the user interface); (2) is of the type `msoControlButton`;* and (3) is not a menu (pop-up) control, meaning you do not see a menu when you click a button control. What about placement? Well . . .

— A button control can be sitting directly on a command bar, in which case it's perfectly safe to call it a button control. Or, it can be a menu item on a menu that is in turn on a command bar, in which case the semantic waters turn a bit murky. In this case it's still a button control (VBA can prove this to you by revealing the type `msoControlButton`). But you won't be able to manually change this control to be image-only. Presumably because it's a menu item and good UI design dictates that you *always* display text for a menu item and display an image as a secondary support feature, the Office designers wanted your custom UI to conform to this rule. You can't change this control to be image-only via VBA either (we tried it—if you set its Style to `msoButtonIcon` it appears as text only). Nonetheless, we'll still call this thing a button control even when it's a menu item on a menu, and even when the image isn't displayed.

— There is a smidgen of documentation on this topic. Too bad it's partly wrong, and it doesn't bother to explain the logic behind the rules. The last note in Excel's "Display an icon and text or text only on a menu command" Help topic states, "A menu command cannot be displayed as an icon only. However, if you click the Icon Only format for a menu command and then copy or move the menu command to a toolbar, the command displays as an icon on the toolbar." As we'll soon discover, there's no Icon Only format.

— There's a visual clue that almost always differentiates a menu control from a non-menu control: a menu control typically has a triangular arrow on it somewhere. And there's a behavioral clue

* The designers of the Office object model gave names to various types of command bar controls. The name "msoControlButton" is one of these many names. There's very little (if any) documentation from Microsoft on how any of these names came to be, but they do appear from time to time in the Help documentation, and if you use VBA to programmatically manipulate command-bar controls, then you'll use some of them. We provide a complete list of these names—taken from the Help file—later in this chapter.

that almost always differentiates a button control: when you click on it, you do not see a menu, a pop-up list, a drop-down list, a well (a UI design term for a table or grid display of options), or any other kind of "expanding" list of options. You just click a button control and an action takes place. QED.

- **Menu control**—A control that represents a menu.
- **Child menu**—See cascading menu.
- **Hierarchical menu**—See cascading menu.
- **Submenu**—See cascading menu.

Options Over Easy

Before we delve any further into the command bar miasma and see what annoyances and benefits await you, here's a productivity tip guaranteed to save you untold time deciphering button controls on command bars. First, make sure that you've got ScreenTips turned on—select Tools ➤ Customize ➤ Options, select the "Show ScreenTips on toolbars" check box, click Close. A ScreenTip (née ToolTip—why, oh why, can't those 'Softies leave their terminology unchanged for more than six months at a stretch?*) appears like a pop-up yellow PostIt note whenever you touch a button control (and some menu controls, for example, Font Color) with the mouse pointer. It provides a brief, well, screen tip. You can further embellish ScreenTips to show their keyboard shortcut equivalent (if any)—select Tools ➤ Customize ➤ Options, select the "Show shortcut keys in ScreenTips" check box, click Close. "Wait, you guys!", you cry beseechingly. "I don't see the 'Show shortcut keys in ScreenTips' check box anywhere. What gives?" We were rubbing our eyes on this one ourselves. Turns out that as we keyed the above steps into Word, we were accidentally testing the steps in Word, not Excel. So? Well, the much-touted Office 97 "core consistency" among applications still has some annoying rough edges. A case in point: Word's Customize dialog box has a "Show shortcut keys in ScreenTips" check box, and Excel's doesn't. No kidding. Score for the entire Office family on this dimension: Access, yes; Excel, no; PowerPoint, yes; Word, yes; and Outlook is not applicable. (Outlook, sadly, lacks customizable command bars.) Excel's the wayward sibling, as you can see in Figure 2-9. It's annoying that Excel doesn't offer this setting, and even more annoying that Excel doesn't display shortcut keys in ScreenTips at all.

---

* *The Windows Interface Guidelines for Software Design* defines the correct term as tooltip and makes no reference to screentip. "Tooltips are small pop-up windows that display the name of a control . . . "

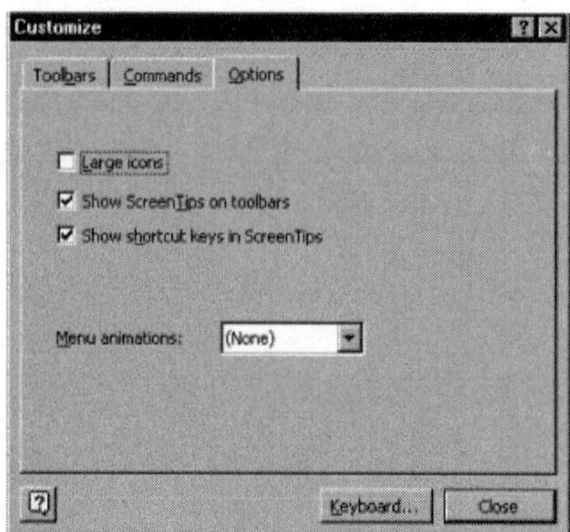

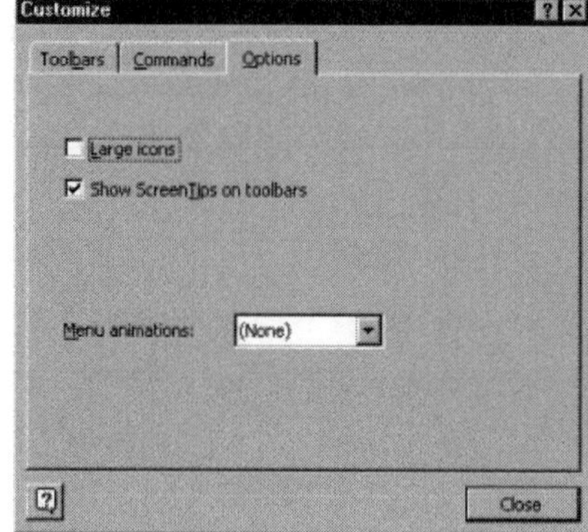

Figure 2-9: Word displays ScreenTip shortcuts (left), Excel doesn't (right)

NOTE A *sticky setting* is one that, once set, remains set even after you close the application or even Windows itself. A sticky setting can apply to a single application, or, in some cases, apply across all Office applications.

ScreenTips shortcuts is a sticky and Office-wide preference setting; once set in any Office application—Excel excepted, natch—the preference holds for all the other Office applications.

How far does the lexical confusion extend in the case of screentip vs. tooltip? Take a gander at the Visual Basic for Applications Help file's description of the ToolTipText property: "Returns or sets the text displayed in the specified command bar control's ScreenTip." We kid you not, they use the UI-proper term (ToolTip) for the object model's property name, but it appears that some marketeer stuck in the annoying new term (ScreenTip).

The Options tab in the Customize dialog box also proffers a "Large icons" check box. Let personal preferences dictate whether you turn this option on or off, but be forewarned, if you do turn it on, Office 97 annoyingly applies this option across all Office applications open now or opened later, not just the app you're in currently. Whoa, Nelly! This is exactly the opposite of how things worked in Office 95, and although we aren't rabid reactionaries, we do know that we prefer each application to maintain its own toolbar button size setting independently of its siblings. After all, that's what the ponderous Registry is for. Hey Redmond, we don't care what the usability lab rats said on this one, switch it back!

What about the Options tab's "Menu animations" drop-down list? If you're not prone to fits of vertigo, then you just might like animated menus. You can choose among unfolding, sliding, and random effects. As for us, no thank you on all counts. Why any disk real estate would be wasted on such marginal frills is beyond us; perhaps WordPro had this feature before Word did, and this is a case of marketing catch-up (Microsoft and all the other big software vendors have always tried to outgun each other in the never-ending Application Feature War). Go figure. Visual animation, sound, 3-D effects, et al., certainly play a critical role in pumping ever more realistic and helpful cues direct to the brain of you, The User. But this particular animation feature seems inconsequential and useless.

A Command Bar of the Toolbar Variety

In this section let's get familiar with the basic steps involved when creating a new (or, by extension, modifying an existing) toolbar. Remember, customizing a toolbar is an easy way for you to apply your own personal spin to Excel and to rid yourself of the annoyances we bring to your attention as well as those you discover on your own. To create a new toolbar:

1. Select Tools ➤ Customize, click the Toolbars tab, click New, type in the name of the new toolbar (e.g., **`Command Bars 101`**), click OK. The Customize dialog box is still visible, as is a new toolbar that's a tad wider than one button.
2. To add a built-in command, say, for creating a new default file, click the Commands tab, select File in the Categories list box, select the New command in the Commands list box (this is the second New command in the list, the one without a trailing ellipsis). If you stop right here and want to see a description of the currently selected command before committing to using it, click the Description button. (See Figure 2-10.)
3. Drag the control from the Commands list box and drop it on the new toolbar (it's ready to drop at the position shown by a bold vertical I-beam on the target toolbar). Click the Close button to end the operation.

To see how to modify a command's display on a toolbar, let's first add the built-in Close command to our new toolbar. You know the drill. Tools ➤ Customize ➤ Commands, select File in Categories, select Close in Commands, and drag-and-drop it to the right of the extant New button control. You should see the text label "Close" on the button control, but we're gonna change that, and pronto. Click the Modify Selection button,

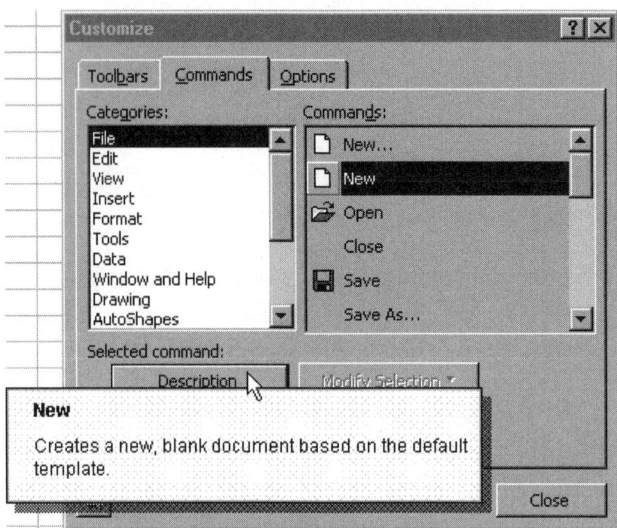

Figure 2-10: Customize dialog's nifty Description button for built-in commands

choose Edit Button Image, and lo and behold an image appears where there was none before—not even in the previous dialog box's Commands listing. Weird, eh, or just plain annoying? Excel knew which image to display in edit mode, so why not display it in the Commands list box to begin with, as it does for many of the other available commands? Anyway, click OK. If you don't like seeing the text label, you can Modify Selection, choose "Text Only (in Menus)", then click the Close button (in the Customize dialog box). Now just the image is displayed.

If you want to save one mouse stroke per customization operation, you can use the right-mouse approach for invoking the Customize dialog box. Right-click anywhere on any toolbar, then choose Customize. (We simply present the menu selection steps in this text for the sake of consistency.) If you want to delete a control from a toolbar, Tools ➤ Customize, then drag the desired item off the toolbar and click the Customize dialog box's Close button.

You can also invoke the Modify Selection's pop-up menu by right-clicking on any toolbar control while the Customize dialog box is visible; this applies not just to the work-in-progress toolbar but to any other visible toolbar. Cool! In a moment we'll use this feature to quickly copy an image from one toolbar button control to another. There are some useful toolbar drag-and-drop tricks, too. You can copy-drag and move-drag button controls from one toolbar to another while the Customize dialog box is visible. For example, to copy the Office Assistant button control from the Standard toolbar to the Command Bars 101 toolbar, start the Customize dialog box and `Ctrl`+drag the Office Assistant button control onto the Command Bars 101 toolbar. To move this button control, simply drag the Office Assistant button control onto the Command Bars 101 toolbar.* As always, click Close when done.

Now for some button control image tips. While in Customize mode, you can copy an image to the clipboard. The trick is to have the desired image available (visible) to be copied. For example, say you want to add the Hide command (which belongs to the Window and Help category) as a button control on the Command Bars 101 toolbar and use the fetching on-off switch image associated with the Forms toolbar's Run Dialog button control. Here's how:

1. First display the Forms toolbar if it's not already visible (View ➤ Toolbars ➤ Forms).
2. Start the Customize dialog box.
3. Add the Hide command to the Command Bars 101 toolbar (in this case, you'll find the Hide command in the Window and Help category).
4. Right-click the Forms toolbar's Run Dialog button control and choose Copy Button Image from the pop-up menu.
5. Right-click the Command Bars 101 toolbar's Hide button and choose Paste Button image from the pop-up menu. We leave it to your personal taste whether you leave the Hide command's default Hide text displayed or not; we're gonna leave it there for clarity's sake.
6. Click Close. To compare yours to ours, see Figure 2-11.

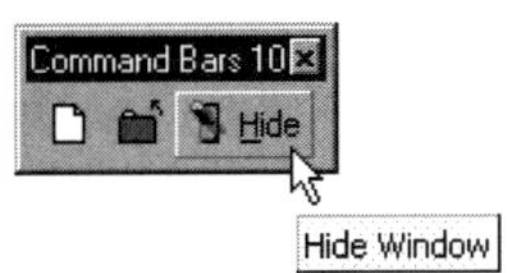

Figure 2-11: Your Command Bars 101 toolbar-type command bar should look like this

You can copy an image from an outside source, too. For more on this neat feature, see the Help topic "Copy an image from a graphics program to a toolbar button or menu command."

* Drag-and-drop hint: typically, plain vanilla drag operations perform a move on the object, and `Ctrl`+drag performs a copy. The mnemonic trick we use is "'c' for copy."

The remainder of the Modify Selection's pop-up menu commands warrants discussion. From top to bottom:

- **Reset** completely resets the selected item to some cryptic hard-wired state, whatever that might be. As best as we can tell, it seems to depend on whether the item thinks it's currently a button control on a command bar or a button control acting as a menu item on a menu control that's in turn on a command bar. More on this in a moment.
- **Delete** does what it says, same as dragging the item off the toolbar.
- The **Name** field allows you to change the text of the item up to a maximum length of 120 characters.
- **Reset Button Image** is a more focused form of Reset; it only returns the item's image (if any) to its built-in state.
- **Edit Button Image** displays the Button Editor dialog box, shown in Figure 2-12. This self-explanatory dialog box allows you to tweak the image at the pixel level to your heart's compulsion, er, content.

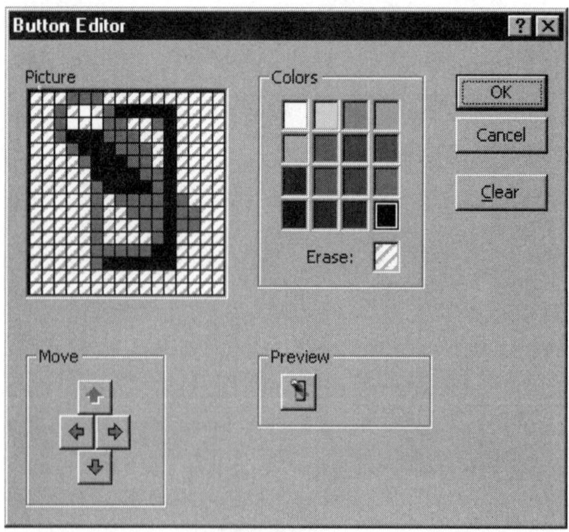

Figure 2-12: The Button Editor dialog box in all its pixelized glory

- **Change Button Image** provides you with a measly 7 row by 6 column table of cheesy images to choose from. This menu item should provide a nice, clean dialog box to access all of the several hundred intrinsic button control images stored inside Excel. No excuses.
- **Default Style**—and its three neighboring commands (see following)—is only available for button controls, not for menus or combo boxes. Its effect varies by the placement context of the control. Default Style for a built-in command that's a button control on a command bar

reverts to being an image only. Default Style for a built-in command that's a menu item reverts to being an image plus text. Try it out on different button controls and see for yourself.

- **Text Only (Always)** does just what it says.
- **Text Only (in Menus)** displays only the text if the item is a button control menu item in a menu and displays only the image (if any) if the item is a button control not in a menu. Again, watch out for odd-ball imageless commands like Hide.
- **Image and Text** does just what it says. See Table 2-1 for examples of what these four style settings look like for the New command in the context of a button control.
- **Begin a Group** inserts a separator bar to the left of (or above) the current item.

Table 2-1: Styles You Can Choose for a Command Item

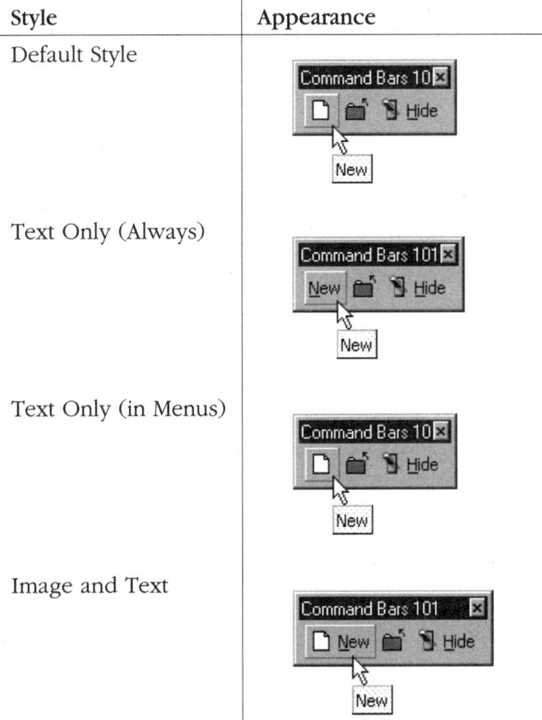

Style	Appearance
Default Style	
Text Only (Always)	
Text Only (in Menus)	
Image and Text	

Stir in Some Menus and Menu Items

Now that we've had our brains thoroughly saturated in the gestalt of adding and manipulating button controls on a toolbar, let's see what head-shrinking permutations the command-bar commandos have in store for us regarding menus and menu items placed on a toolbar. Here are the steps for adding the built-in Name menu to your Command Bars 101 toolbar:

1. Start the Customize dialog box.
2. Click the Commands tab.
3. Select the Built-in Menus item in the Categories list box.
4. Drag the Name menu and drop it onto your Command Bars 101 toolbar.
5. Click Close.

Adding a custom menu and populating it with stuff is, well, interesting. Here goes:

1. Start the Customize dialog box.
2. Click the Commands tab.
3. Select the New Menu item in the Categories list box (it's at the bottom).
4. Drag the New Menu item from the Commands list box and drop it onto your Command Bars 101 toolbar.
5. Let's give this menu a unique name right now: right-click on it on your toolbar, and type **My Special Menu** in the Name field, then press Enter.
6. Steady as she goes, partner . . . here you left-click—do not right-click—on the My Special Menu item on your toolbar to unveil an empty gray square dangling off the lower left corner of the My Special Menu item.
7. Back in the Customize dialog, select the desired category and command. For example, let's add in quick succession the three items already on this toolbar—namely, File ➤ New, File ➤ Close, and Window and Help ➤ Hide: select the File category, select the New (not New...) command, and drag it onto the empty gray square. Repeat these steps for File ➤ Close and Window and Help ➤ Hide.

If you click on the My Special Menu menu right now, you'll see New, Close, and Hide commands in that order; all three commands display a text label, but only New has an image (see Figure 2-13). Bear with us for a minute on this, and keep some Alka Seltzer handy, too. Right-click the New item on My Special Menu—it's set to Default Style. If you add File ➤ New (not New...) again to the toolbar right now just as a test, it will

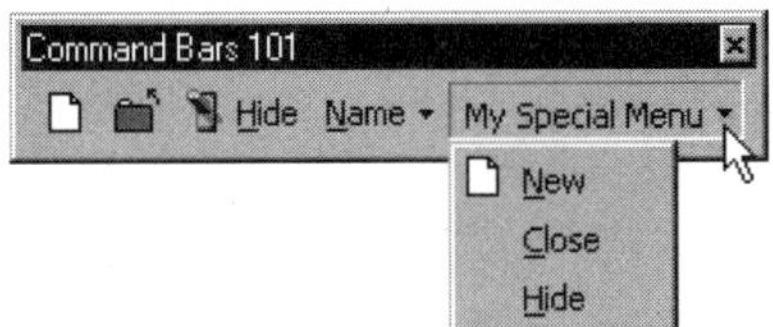

Figure 2-13: My Special Menu's submenu in its initial "just dropped in" state

display as an image with no text. Right-click the freshly added New item on the toolbar—it's set to Default Style. Hmmm. That's right, both items are Default Style and they represent the same built-in command, but they look different depending on their command-bar placement context. The command that's a button control menu item on the menu (said menu being, in turn, on the toolbar) displays an image plus text; the command that's simply a button control on the toolbar displays only an image. It makes sense when you keep in mind Office is keeping you on the straight-and-narrow path and enforcing the good UI design rule of always displaying text for a menu item control.

Here's a brain teaser: In the Commands list box, File ➤ Close reveals no image. Why not? Dunno. Add File ➤ Close to any toolbar as button control, right-click it to see that it's set to Text Only (Always); reset it and it's still just text; set it to Default Style and it's an image only. Add File ➤ Close to any menu on a toolbar, right-click it to see that it's set to Text Only (Always); reset it and it doesn't change; set it to Default style and it's an image plus text. Why would it set itself to Text Only (Always) when directly on a toolbar? We don't know.

Yet another: Why does the Window and Help ➤ Hide command have no image associated with it, but File ➤ Close does? No rule we can discern here. Go figure.

The terminology and behaviors here are so subtle that in our judgment it's best to think in terms of this simple process:

1. Manually add controls to toolbars as needed, where a control can be either a button directly on a toolbar, a menu, or a button (menu item) on a menu on a toolbar.
2. Manually turn on images and/or text at your own discretion.
3. Manually modify images and/or text at your own discretion.

What about menu bars as the target? In Excel it's also possible to manually work through the above process when the target command bar is a menu bar. Excel's user interface does support this. However, you can't create a custom menu bar with Excel's user interface—you have to use VBA to do this—but once created and rendered visible, you can use Excel's user interface to manipulate controls on the custom menu bar.

Submenu Subterfuge

Fifty demerits to the 'Softies for another lexical gaffe, this time surrounding the slippery term "submenu." Office Help uses the term submenu, but doesn't define it. You won't find it in the *Office 97 Resource Kit*'s index either. Here's the skinny.

You see submenus all the time. For example, the File menu's Print Area is the first menu item you'll encounter (moving from left to right across Excel's ship-with menu bar) that leads to a submenu. The Print Area menu item has the telltale triangular arrow on it. When you land the mouse pointer on Print Area, you see a two-item submenu. Another nearby example is Send To.

But wait, there's more. An example of a menu with a submenu that's floatable (also known as "tear off") is Font Color on the default Formatting toolbar, as shown in Figure 2-14.

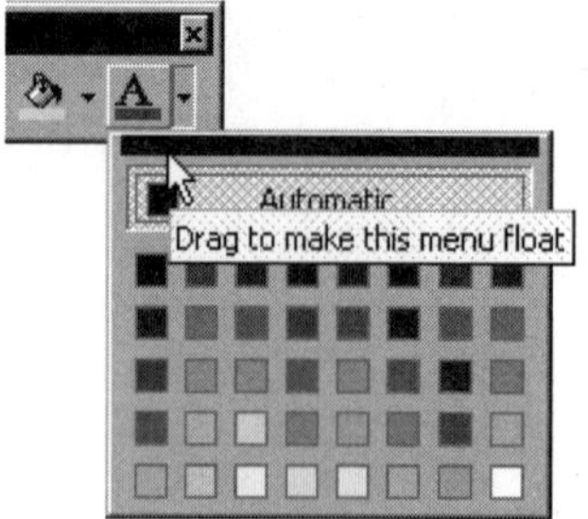

Figure 2-14: The horizontal gray bar across the top of Font Color's submenu is where you grab to "tear it off" and make it float

Violating our own rule never to waste any time on command bar lexicon, let's give it a try. The Font Color control itself is a menu (that looks like a button) on a toolbar, and when you click on its triangular arrow you see its submenu—a five row by eight column matrix of color squares. Along the top of the submenu is a move handle that you can grab; in fact, just touch it with your mouse pointer and a screen tip reads "Drag to make this menu float." Drag the submenu by its move handle and you can actually tear it off its parent menu, thus the slang "tear off." Now it's floating and has its own title bar that reads "Font Color."

A Control Menagerie

The Office object model currently lists a total of 21 distinct types of command bar controls. See the Microsoft Office Visual Basic Help topic "Type Property" (first select the "CommandBarControl Object" topic, click the Properties link, then choose "Type Property (Microsoft Office)"), which has nice pictures of each control type (some of which are reserved for future use). Here they are listed by their built-in constant names.*

The first five are valid for use in your VBA code, and manually, too, in the sense that you can use the Customize user interface to add built-in commands (that already present themselves via these control types) to command bars. If we don't list an example, we couldn't find one to match in the set of Excel's ship-with toolbars.

- `msoControlButton` (example: the New control on the Standard toolbar)
- `msoControlComboBox` (example: the Zoom control on the Standard toolbar)
- `msoControlDropdown` (note: even though Help shows a graphic of the Zoom control as an example of this control constant, Zoom's Type is actually `msoControlComboBox`)
- `msoControlEdit` (example: none in the ship-with set of command bars)
- `msoControlPopup` (example: the Name menu control in the Insert drop-down menu)

If you try to use VBA to add any of the remaining 16 control types, including those *not* reserved for future use, you'll get run-time error 5, "Invalid procedure call or argument." These control types are:

- `msoControlButtonDropdown`
- `msoControlButtonPopup` (example: Line Style on the Drawing toolbar)
- `msoControlCustom`
- `msoControlExpandingGrid`
- `msoControlGauge`
- `msoControlGenericDropdown`
- `msoControlGraphicCombo`

* If you're already familiar with VBA and want to check this out with the Object Browser yourself, these constants are all members of the msoControlType class.

- `msoControlGraphicDropdown`
- `msoControlGraphicPopup`
- `msoControlGrid`
- `msoControlLabel`
- `msoControlOCXDropDown` (example: More Controls on the Control Toolbox toolbar)
- `msoControlSplitButtonMRUPopup`
- `msoControlSplitButtonPopup` (example: Borders on the Formatting toolbar)
- `msoControlSplitDropdown` (example: Undo on the Standard toolbar)
- `msoControlSplitExpandingGrid`

Thus far we've been dealing with adding built-in items to command bars, or, in the case of the My Special Menu menu, creating a custom menu which we then populated with built-in commands. What about causing custom macros (procedures, in VBA-speak) to run in response to selecting a command bar control? Sure thing! We describe how to do this in Chapter 5, *Using VBA to Customize Excel.*

Office Art

Even if you're only an occasional user of Excel's drawing capabilities, you'll find that Office Art levels the graphics playing field. Earlier versions of the Office applications implemented different drawing features, whereas Office Art enables you to take advantage of the "learn it once" approach. Completely new to Office 97, Office Art (code name Escher) is a stunning collection of drawing tools that is—more or less—common to three members of the Office 97 family: Excel, PowerPoint, and Word. Office Art allows you to do the following:

- Choose from a large number of pre-drawn shapes (called AutoShapes,* of course) organized into various categories
- Draw Bezier curves (a curve is an AutoShape)
- Choose from a set of pre-defined smart connectors (a connector is an AutoShape specifically designed to intelligently connect two shapes; for example, an arrow-style connector between two sequential steps A and B in a flow chart)

* We'll often use "drawing object" as a synonym for the term AutoShape.

- Add text and hyperlinks to drawing objects
- Position, align, and distribute drawing objects
- Group and ungroup drawing objects
- Apply shadow effects
- Apply 3-D effects
- Apply sophisticated shading, fill, texture, and transparency effects

We could write a book about the subtleties and permutations of Office Art, but instead we'll cover the highlights, have some fun, then leave it to you to fiddle and play to your heart's content. Don't forget that Excel is all about data analysis; however, if you need images for any purpose whatsoever—whether to adorn a worksheet or as a set of sophisticated shapes to serve as a front-end to custom programming—then Office Art is at your disposal.

NOTE You'll find that many of the Drawing toolbar commands are tear-off submenus and can be quite useful in their floating state. For example, the AutoShapes submenu itself is nice to have floating when you're working with multiple shapes (as in a flowchart or process diagram). Another of our favorites is the Draw ➤ Nudge submenu for precisely aligning individual (or multiple-selected) objects once drawn.

AutoShapes Are the Foundation

First things first. Office Art's communications, command, and control center is the Drawing toolbar. (See Figure 2-17.)

Figure 2-17: The Drawing toolbar, Office Art's central node

Table 2-2 provides a listing of the predefined AutoShape categories supported by Excel.

AutoShapes Step by Step

Let's work our way through the various key capabilities of Office Art by adding a plain vanilla Rectangle object (it may seem boring at first, but this simple shape lends itself to lots of playful 3-D effects, so bear with us).

Table 2-2: The AutoShapes Submenu and Accompanying Sub-Submenus

Category	Submenu
AutoShapes	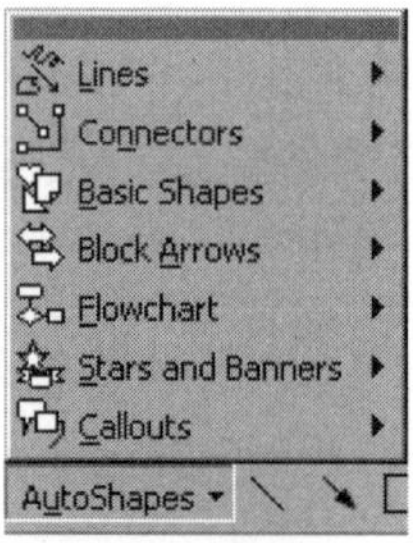 Lines Connectors Basic Shapes Block Arrows Flowchart Stars and Banners Callouts AutoShapes
Lines	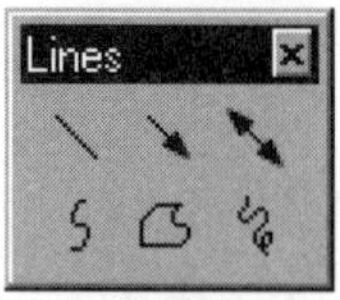 Lines
Connectors	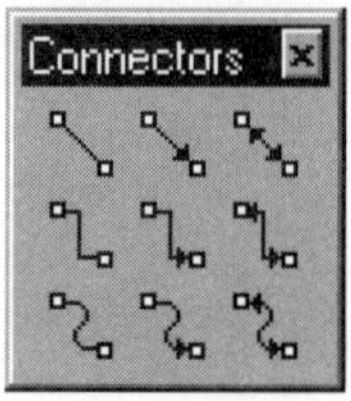 Connectors
Basic Shapes	 Basic Shapes

Table 2-2: The AutoShapes Submenu and Accompanying Sub-Submenus (continued)

Category	Submenu
Block Arrows	
Flowchart	
Stars and Banners	
Callouts	

1. Turn on the Drawing toolbar if you haven't already—View ➤ Toolbars ➤ Drawing.
2. Let's use Excel's underlying cell grid to position this AutoShape: click the Draw button, choose Snap, and make sure the submenu's To Grid command is selected (the button will look depressed).
3. Click the AutoShapes menu button, choose Basic Shapes, choose the Rectangle object (upper-left corner), left-click where you want the AutoShape's upper-left corner to go, and then drag to the appropriate size and release the mouse. (Alternately, since Rectangle is a commonly used shape, it's already on the Drawing toolbar as an independent button.)
4. Your rectangle is now selected (it's framed by eight sizing handles). To see what formatting actions you can apply to it right now, right-click it and choose Format AutoShape to display the Format AutoShape dialog box. We leave it to you to explore the dialog box's four property sheets: Colors and Lines, Size, Protection, and Properties (see Figure 2-18). For the time being, look but don't touch, and let's click Cancel to dismiss the dialog box.

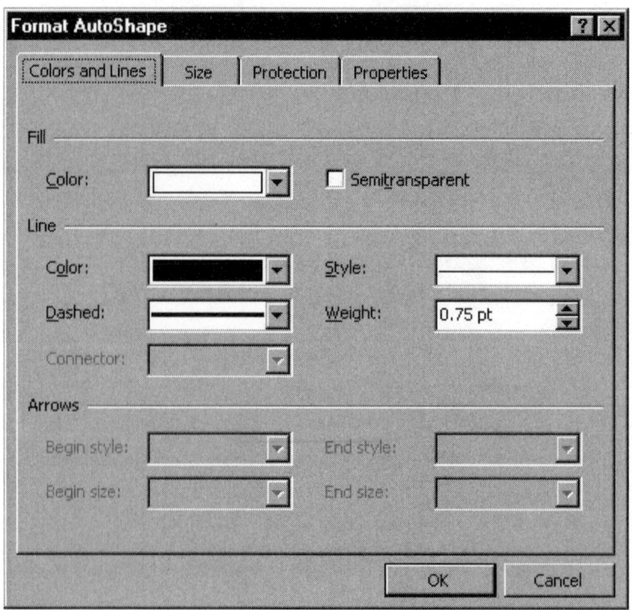

Figure 2-18: The Format AutoShape dialog box for a no-text AutoShape

To move an AutoShape, left-click and drag it to its new destination. To resize it, select it (one left-click anywhere on the shape will do nicely), then drag any of its sizing handles in the appropriate direction. More complex AutoShapes may have one or more special sizing handles—they're yellow and diamond-shaped (we call 'em tilt handles)—that allow you to tilt the shape in a particular dimension. For a quick example, insert a Can shape (AutoShapes ➤ Basic Shapes, select the shape in the first column, fourth row). Drag the tilt handle down to give the can a more down-angled appearance. (The trick here is to precisely touch the tilt handle until you see the mouse pointer change to a tailless traditional pointer, then start tilting.)

Yes, Office Art provides all the rotate and flip operations you'd expect, including free rotation. For precise movements, you can use the Nudge submenu (Draw ➤ Nudge). A couple of tips here.

Nudge operations will not move the object beyond the borders of the sheet's current display area (window); instead you have to manually scroll the display, and Nudge some more. Bug or feature? We're ambivalent, so send us your opinions on this. If Snap To Grid is on, then all movements are in row/column grid (one-cell) increments, your keyboard arrow keys produce matching Nudge operations (one-cell increments), and `Ctrl`+arrow keys produce micro-Nudges (one-pixel increments). If neither Snap to Grid nor Snap to Shapes is on, then all movements are in one-pixel increments. Annoyingly, you can't press and hold any Nudge button and have it auto-repeat, but you can get the auto-repeat effect by using your arrow keys.

Watch out for this annoying pothole: Snap settings are not persistent across Excel sessions. If you have Snap to Grid set on, close Excel, then restart it, all Snap settings (to Grid and to Shapes) will be turned off.

Adding Text and a Hyperlink to an AutoShape

Here's a misleading quotation from the *Office 97 Resource Kit*: "Text can be added to any object without creating an additional text box, and any drawing object can have a hyperlink associated with it." We're here to tell you they just didn't properly qualify that statement. You can add text to any AutoShape *except* lines, connectors, and freeforms. For these three shape types, you'll have to hack it by adding a text box next to the shape in question.

To add text to your rectangle shape:

1. Right-click the shape and choose Add Text. The AutoShape is now hatch-bordered and you've got a flashing text cursor inside it as

shown in Figure 2-19. Type in your text. When done with your text, simply press `Esc`.

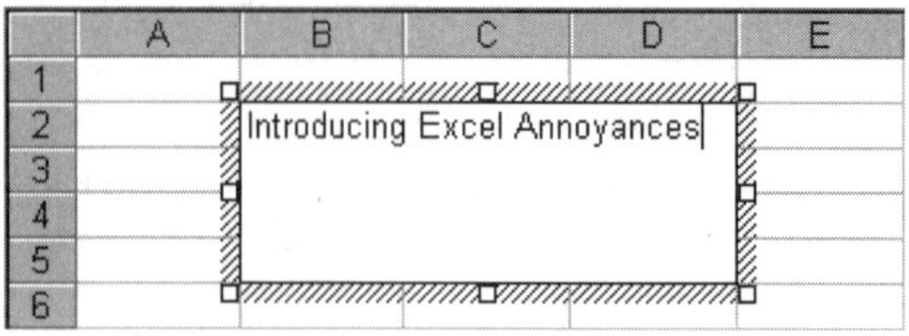

Figure 2-19: Adding text to an AutoShape

2. You can format the text by right-clicking the AutoShape's border, then choosing Format AutoShape. (You'll know you missed clicking the border and that you're still in text-editing mode if the pop-up menu includes the command Exit Edit Text, in which case choose this command, then click carefully on the AutoShape's border.) The Format AutoShape dialog box now includes three new file tabs (relative to its flavor when no text had been added to the shape): Font, Alignment, and Margins. (See Figure 2-20.) You can still selectively format smaller ranges of text within the AutoShape; just select the text, right-click on the selection, choose Format AutoShape and now you'll see only one tab visible—Font.

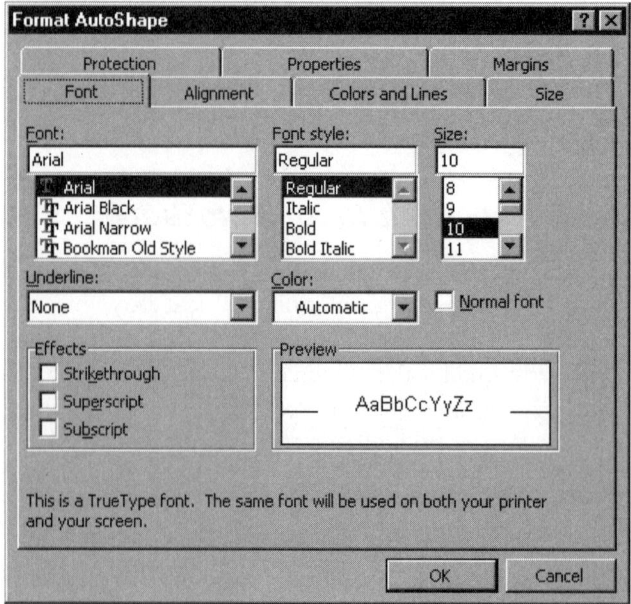

Figure 2-20: Format AutoShape dialog box for an AutoShape with text

Here's how to add a hyperlink to an AutoShape (we'll apply the hyperlink to a new Oval AutoShape):

1. Insert an Oval AutoShape to the right of your rectangle, then add some text to it (we used **`Visit http://www.ora.com`**).
2. Exit text-edit mode and, with only this one shape selected, click the Insert Hyperlink button on Excel's Standard toolbar. Now type in the desired URL into the "Link to file or URL" edit box and click OK (see Figure 2-21). Note that the shape will not appear to have changed, *but it has.* Prove this to yourself by, while it's still selected, right-clicking on it; notice the addition of the Hyperlink command at the bottom of the menu. (See Figure 2-22.)

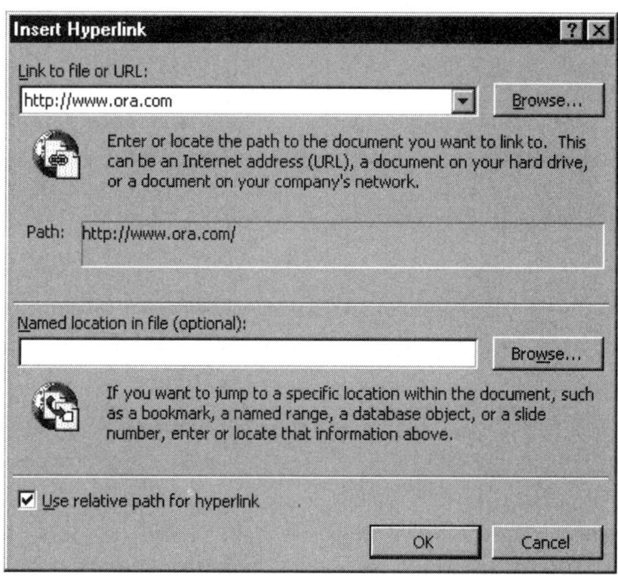

Figure 2-21: Insert Hyperlink dialog box pointing to, you guessed it, www.ora.com

Once an AutoShape with a hyperlink has been unselected, if you later want to edit the AutoShape in any way, you'll be faced with the conundrum of selecting it without triggering the hyperlink. Here's how: *without clicking yet,* touch your mouse pointer to the shape until it turns into a Pointing Index Finger™, press and hold `Ctrl` (the pointer turns into a traditional mouse pointer with a plus sign affixed to it), and left-click to select the shape. Now you can right-click the shape without going off on a wild Web hunt.

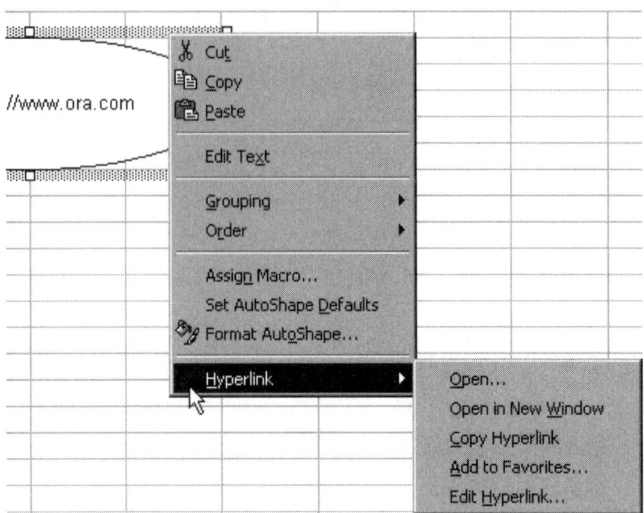

Figure 2-22: The pop-up menu for an AutoShape that includes a hyperlink, showing the Hyperlink submenu

Additional AutoShape Formatting Options

Even more AutoShape formatting options sing their siren song, hoping to lure you from a busy day of data analysis. (Warning: Office Art fiddling is highly addictive; the Surgeon General advises no more than 30 minutes of exposure per day!)

For example, exploring the Fill Effects dialog box has so much to offer (select an AutoShape, click the Fill Color menu button on the Drawing toolbar, then click Fill Effects), you'd better pack some lunch and water for a thorough trek here. See Figure 2-23 for a taste of the plethora of effects you can generate by tweaking gradients, textures, and patterns, and hey, you can even stuff a picture inside an AutoShape (in this example we chose a color—Sky Blue—and opted for the "One color" Colors option and the "From center" Shading styles option).

For shadow effects, click the Drawing toolbar's Shadow button, choose a shadow to your liking, click Shadow again, and this time choose Shadow Settings to display a floating Shadow Settings toolbar.

Finally, for 3-D effects you'll want to click the 3-D button on the Drawing toolbar and choose the 3-D Settings command. This tears off a floating 3-D Settings toolbar, and we guarantee you'll want to check out each of its ten commands. Especially cool are the Depth, Direction, Lighting, and Surface settings. (See Figure 2-24.) Go for it, and don't forget your spelunking helmet and a spare battery pack!

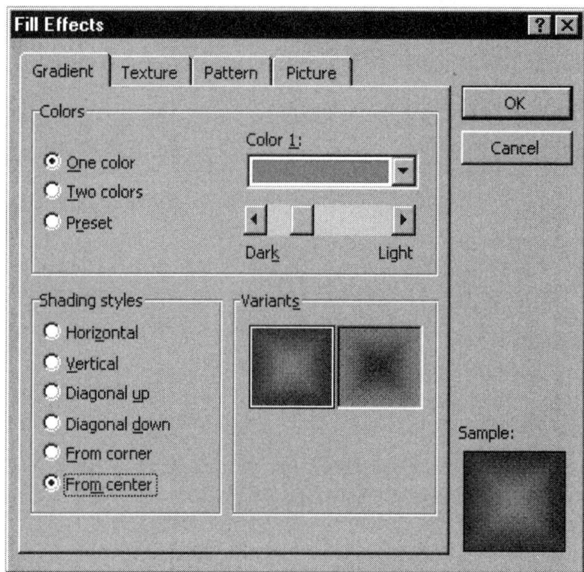

Figure 2-23: Fill Effects dialog box in a classy "From center" shading style

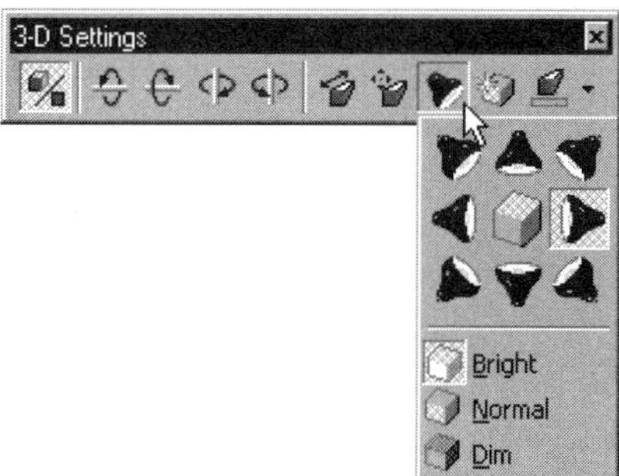

Figure 2-24: 3-D Settings tear off menu with its Lighting submenu displayed

Connector Coolness

Let's say you want to connect the two shapes we've drawn thus far. Here's how:

1. Click AutoShapes, choose Connectors, and then choose from among the nine available connectors. For our purposes, choose Curved Arrow Connector (you'll see why in a moment).
2. Touch the rectangle shape with the connector cross hair (looks more like a HUD gun sight, actually) and each of the shape's edges lights up with a small blue dot in the center. Land on the right edge's connector marker, drag over to the left-most connector marker of the

oval shape, land on it, then release the mouse button. So far so good: you see a right-pointing arrow connecting the two shapes.

3. Now the connecto-fun begins. Select and move the oval shape down six rows (remember, Snap to Grid should be on). Release the shape and the connector is nicely curved, as shown in Figure 2-25. Select it (the connector) and notice it's got a tilt handle. Drag the tilt handle about two column widths to the right and watch the connector bow out. Neat!

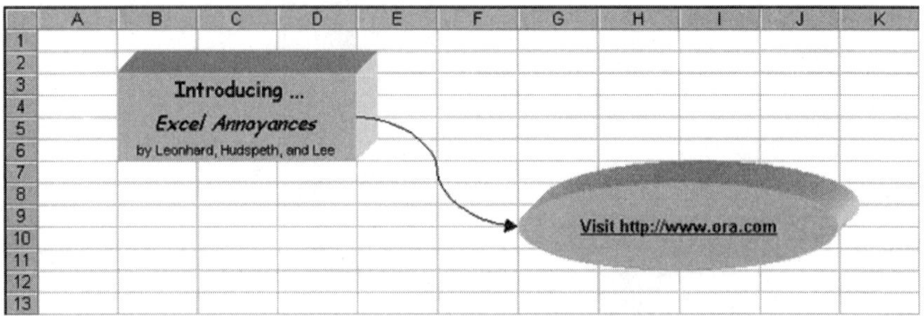

Figure 2-25: Two AutoShapes linked by a smart curved arrow connector

But wait, there's more. If you're moving connected shapes around like a shell game out on the boardwalk, you'll love the Reroute Connectors feature that optimizes the connection points for the connected objects and rethreads the connector's route to take the shortest path without crossing either shape. Try it: drag the oval shape down and around the rectangle shape until it (the oval) is to the left and below the rectangle. The connector has to follow a long, winding route to retain the bond, so right-click the connector and choose Reroute Connectors. The connector instantly finds the closest two points and, well, reroutes itself.

However, if you use both Excel and Word, you're certain to be annoyed with Word when you go looking for the Connectors category. Why? Because it's missing from Word entirely. If you want to connect two AutoShapes in Word, you'll have to fake it with a Line type of AutoShape (an arrow looks best in our opinion, but any line type will do). Unfortunately, this means you'll have to manually line up the pseudo-connector in Word; also, whenever you move an object on either end of the pseudo-connector, the pseudo-connector won't follow along as it does in Excel, and it can't reroute itself as it does in Excel. You'll quickly be pining for Excel's handy smart connector features. Like Excel, PowerPoint also implements smart connector AutoShapes.

AutoShape Adjustment Nuances

To move shapes in unison, first select them all: click the Select Objects button, left-click, and drag the mouse pointer to draw a selection frame that encloses them. To move them, either drag them around with the mouse or use Nudge. To group several objects together logically, select the objects to be grouped, click Draw, then click Group. (A hint about multiple selections: if the objects are positioned such that using the Select Objects selection frame won't work, use `Shift`+left-click to select the objects.) Grouped objects can be flipped, scaled, etc. as a group, and their properties can be set in unison. You'll see the outline of the grouped shapes marked by eight sizing handles (you won't see a border, though).

Once you have the desired group of shapes selected, you can also align and distribute them in several preset ways. Click Draw, then choose Align or Distribute.

3

Tales of the Toolbar and Other Aides-de-Camp

In this chapter:

- *Customizing the Standard Toolbar*
- *Customizing the Formatting Toolbar*
- *Talking to a Paper Clip*
- *Office Goes Brrrrring, Whoosssssh, and Ding Dong*

Excel ships with a total of 86 command bars. Of these, two are menu bars, 39 are toolbars, and 45 are shortcut menus. They are not all, of course, visible at all times. You use some of them more than others. By default, Excel ships with its Standard and Formatting toolbars visible (along with the ever-present Worksheet menu bar). This is where we're going to concentrate our customization energies. We'll let the Worksheet menu bar be.

Imagine if you drove to work every day in your sleek, comfortable, powerful car and that you always station-hopped around on the radio amongst several of your favorite stations. It would be ideal if you used your car radio's station preset feature, thereby saving yourself considerable time toying with the Scan knob, not to mention a heck of a lot safer since you'd have your eyes on the road more often. A seemingly small matter that, taken across enough repeated executions, has enormous consequences in your daily life.

In the same way, a little time spent now setting up your toolbars will go a long, long way to upping your utilization of Excel. Trust us, by the 10,000th time you've issued two mouse clicks to close a file (click the File menu then choose Close)—or worse, dragged the mouse pointer all the way over to the child window's upper-right corner to whack on the ol' X button—you'll be wishing you had created a one-click Close button right next to the Standard toolbar's Save button. See, we just saved you 10,000 needless mouse clicks that amounts to, oh, a mere 167 minutes of your life every year.* And this is only the savings for customizing one control; multiply that by the dozens of other changes you can easily make to Excel toolbars (as detailed later in this chapter) to find yourself saving 10, 15, 20 or more hours per year. At your pay scale, we'll wager that's worth something. So let's start shaving those clicks, shall we?

Excel starts you off with two toolbars visible, the Standard toolbar on top just under the menu bar and the Formatting toolbar beneath that. What if you want to mix and match buttons from the different toolbars into a single modified toolbar set? As you saw in Chapter 2, *Excel as Workhorse*, this is easily done.

Microsoft chose the buttons for the Standard and Formatting bars based on their pet usability lab rats, er, participants, and a predisposition for controls that demo well at Comdex. This love for demoware results in a selection of controls that may not have anything in common with what works for you.

So fix it! We'll get you started with the way we've modified our toolbars. But don't blindly accept our way as gospel anymore than Microsoft's. It's all subjective, and the important thing is to lay out the tools that work for you. Not to worry—if you don't like how it turns out, you can have the default Excel toolbars back. No problem.

Customizing the Standard Toolbar

Before we run pell-mell into the fray of customizing—or perhaps even rebuilding from scratch—your Standard toolbar, let's analyze Excel's Standard toolbar as it comes out of the box. See Table 3-1. (We'll take a closer look at the ID and Type properties in Chapter 5, *Using VBA to Customize Excel.*)

Table 3-1: List of Properties for the Controls on Excel's Default Standard Toolbar

Index	Caption	Id	ToolTipText	Type (Value)	Type (Name)
1	&New	2520	&New	1	msoControl-Button
2	Open	23	Open	1	msoControl-Button

* We're quite serious about all this. Figure you open and close 50 Office documents a day, 5 days a week, 50 weeks a year. That's 12,500 open and close operations every year, so we rounded down to 10,000 close operations to be conservative. Then assume each needless mouse click costs you 1.0 seconds, so one second saved across all 10,000 close operations is 167 minutes.

Table 3-1: List of Properties for the Controls on Excel's Default Standard Toolbar (continued)

Index	Caption	Id	ToolTipText	Type (Value)	Type (Name)
3	&Save	3	&Save	1	msoControl-Button
4	Print (HP LaserJet IIP)	2521	Print (HP LaserJet IIP)	1	msoControl-Button
5	Print Pre&view	109	Print Pre&view	1	msoControl-Button
6	&Spelling...	2	&Spelling...	1	msoControl-Button
7	Cu&t	21	Cu&t	1	msoControl-Button
8	&Copy	19	&Copy	1	msoControl-Button
9	&Paste	22	&Paste	1	msoControl-Button
10	&Format Painter	108	&Format Painter	1	msoControl-Button
11	&Undo	128	&Undo	6	msoControlSplit-Dropdown
12	&Redo	129	&Redo	6	msoControlSplit-Dropdown
13	Hyperl&ink...	1576	Insert Hyper-link	1	msoControl-Button
14	&Web Toolbar	2934	&Web Toolbar	1	msoControl-Button
15	&AutoSum	226	&AutoSum	1	msoControl-Button
16	Paste Function	385	Paste Function	1	msoControl-Button
17	Sort &Ascending	210	Sort &Ascending	1	msoControl-Button
18	Sort Des&cending	211	Sort Des&cending	1	msoControl-Button
19	&Chart Wizard	436	&Chart Wizard	1	msoControl-Button
20	M&ap...	1741	M&ap...	1	msoControl-Button
21	&Drawing	204	&Drawing	1	msoControl-Button

Table 3-1: List of Properties for the Controls on Excel's Default Standard Toolbar (continued)

Index	Caption	Id	ToolTipText	Type (Value)	Type (Name)
22	&Zoom:	1733	&Zoom:	4	msoControl-ComboBox
23	Microsoft Excel &Help	984	Office Assis-tant (F1)	1	msoControl-Button

File It

Now we're ready to customize the Standard toolbar. But instead of customizing it, let's build our own version of it. This way, our version and Microsoft's can coexist, and we don't have to worry about losing our customizations when we click the irrevocable Reset button. To create this new toolbar, click Tools, choose Customize, select the Toolbars tab, click New, type in **`ExcelAnnoy Standard`**, then press `Enter`.

The first three buttons on the Standard toolbar deal with files: creating them with New, opening them with Open, and saving them to your hard disk with Save.

The first thing we have to deal with is the way the New button behaves. This button gives you a new book, instantly! What's wrong with this, you ask? Well, nothing at all. We suggest you leave it be. What's missing here is a single-click control to bring up a list of all the templates currently available to you (more on templates later in the book). Click on this button and choose the template you want to use when creating a new book instead of just being forced to accept the default book template. The Open button and the Save button are both to be kept.

What's missing from this group? Well, if you're like us, you will probably close every file you open at some point, so how about a file close button?

To summarize, the New button is fine as is, but we're going to add a New... button with text (both these commands will be part of a custom menu control we'll call New); the Open button is okay; the Save button is okay; and we're going to add a Close button. Here are the steps:

1. To create a menu control named New: select the Commands tab in the Customize dialog box, select New Menu in the Categories list, drag New Menu from the Commands list over to your new custom toolbar (ExcelAnnoy Standard), then change its Name to `&New` and press `Enter`. Now follow the steps you learned in "Stir in Some Menus and Menu Items" in Chapter 2 when building custom menu

controls to add the New... and New commands (both from the File category) to the menu.

NOTE This approach—using a menu control as a front end to several related controls—is a compelling new feature provided by Office 97 command bars.

---

2. `Ctrl`+drag to copy the Open button from Standard to your new toolbar.
3. `Ctrl`+drag the Save button from Standard to your new toolbar.
4. Drop the Close command on your new toolbar, and change its style to Text Only (in Menus).

When you've finished adding these file-related controls, your toolbar should resemble the one shown in Figure 3-1.

Figure 3-1: ExcelAnnoy Standard under construction—file controls

P. P. S. (Print, Preview, and Spell)

The next three buttons deal with printing and spelling. The first—which we'll call "print default"—prints one copy of the current sheet—no problem there. Next is print preview, which is also a keeper. Next is Spelling, which none of us could live without.

What we'll add here is a command for the flavor of Print that displays the Print dialog, as well as an explicit command for setting the print area. Here we go:

1. Create a menu control named Print just as you did earlier for your New menu control. Use `&Print` for its name.
2. Add the Print, Print..., Print Preview, and Set Print Area commands to your menu control. (If you set and clear the print area often, you might want to add the Clear Print Area command as well.)
3. `Ctrl`+drag to copy the Spelling button from Standard to your new toolbar.

4. To add a separator between this batch and its neighbors to the left, right-click the Print menu control and choose "Begin a Group."

When you've finished with this step, your toolbar should resemble the one shown in Figure 3-2.

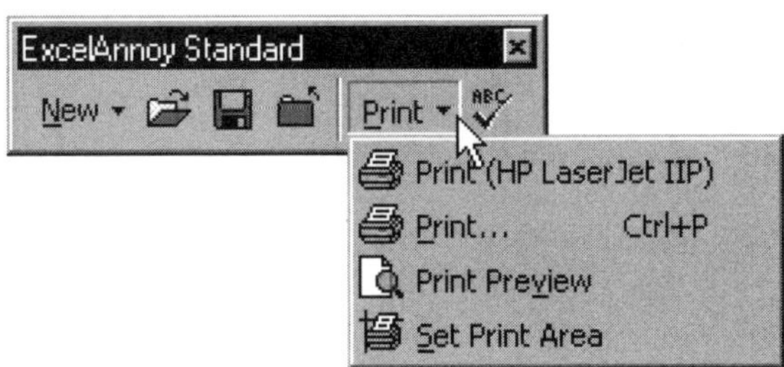

Figure 3-2: ExcelAnnoy Standard under construction—print and spelling controls

Conveyance Controls

The next batch of Standard buttons includes the Cut, Copy, Paste, and Format Painter buttons. We'll leave this batch alone, even though we could make a good case against the Format Painter button. It is difficult to determine just what the Format Painter is going to paint. For instance, say you have this text string in cell A1: "The quick brown fox", and this in cell A3: "jumps over the lazy dog." Format the word "brown" in cell A1 as bold. Select A1, click on the Format Painter button, then click on A3. Hmmm. Cell A3 remains unchanged. Now, in A3 format the entire cell as underlined (select Format ➤ Cells ➤ Font ➤ Underline ➤ Single), click Format Painter, and click on A1. Hmmm again. Only a portion of the text in cell A1—up to the word "brown"—is underlined. So if you ever need some free space on the Standard toolbar, this is a good candidate for the recycle bin.

The steps to reproduce this batch are:

1. Copy all four buttons—Cut, Copy, Paste, and Format Painter—from Standard to your new toolbar.
2. To add a separator between this batch and its neighbors to the left, right-click the Cut button control and choose "Begin a Group."

Your toolbar should now resemble Figure 3-3.

Figure 3-3: ExcelAnnoy Standard under construction—conveyance controls

A Safety Net and a Scrivener

The Undo and Redo controls are absolute must-haves. Here are the steps for creating this control group:

1. Copy the Undo and Redo controls from Standard to your new toolbar.
2. To add a separator between Format Painter and Undo, right-click the Undo control and choose "Begin a Group."

The ExcelAnnoy Standard toolbar should now resemble Figure 3-4.

Figure 3-4: ExcelAnnoy Standard under construction—the life-saving Undo and Redo controls

Hyperlinks, Formulae, and Related Wizardry

If you're excited about the Internet, intranet, and hyperlinking features of Excel (as you should be), then you'll want to hang on to the Insert Hyperlink button. Whether its associate, the Web Toolbar button, is really worth the real estate is open to discussion. After all, you can always access any toolbar by right-clicking a toolbar and choosing the desired toolbar by name. Since the Web Toolbar button is, in our estimation, a classic case of demoware run amok, we remove it; but you may surf the Web—and your local network—often enough to warrant leaving it as is.

The next two buttons—AutoSum and Paste Function—are generally related to creating formulas. The AutoSum button is one of the best ideas Microsoft has ever had. It's another keeper. Paste Function, which fires up the Formula Palette (formerly the Function Wizard), is a nice idea, too, except for one thing. You use the Formula Palette to enter functions into formulas. We always begin formulas by pressing the equal sign key. It's a decade-old habit, it's deeply ingrained muscle memory, and we do it without thinking. So, we're in no mood to unlearn it. Why should we, since it's a perfectly good habit?

What does this have to do with the Paste Function button? When you press the equal sign key, the formula bar is activated, and lo and behold, there is the Formula Palette's drop-down list control on the formula bar. So with the Formula Palette control on the formula bar duplicating the Paste Function button on the toolbar (and the formula bar being where you will most likely need to use it), we don't think you need one on your toolbar. Don't worry though, you'll replace it with something we think is just as useful: the Paste Names command that pastes range names into formulas.

As for the two sorting buttons in this group . . . have you ever screwed up a sort in Excel? We have. You know, you hurriedly select a range, miss the last column, perform a sort, and scramble your data, but you don't notice it until much later when The Boss is venting plasma. These buttons make sorting really easy. Too easy. So, we won't be copying them to our custom toolbar.

Here are the steps for this control group:

1. Copy the Insert Hyperlink button from Standard to your new toolbar.
2. Copy the AutoSum button from Standard to your new toolbar.
3. Add the Paste... command (from the Insert category) to your new toolbar. (If the current worksheet doesn't have any names defined, this control will be grayed out.)
4. To add a separator between Redo and Insert Hyperlink, right-click the Insert Hyperlink control and choose "Begin a Group."

As you can see from Figure 3-5, our new ExcelAnnoy Standard toolbar is now beginning to look a lot different from the Standard Excel toolbar.

Figure 3-5: ExcelAnnoy Standard under construction—hyperlinks, formulas, and related controls

Graphics Galore

The next set of controls are related in that they all allow you to put images in one form or another right on top of your sheet: Chart Wizard, Map, and Drawing.

The Chart Wizard is cool, so it stays. The Map control represents a potentially very useful and powerful feature, but one you're likely to use only rarely. Therefore, we won't be copying it to ExcelAnnoy Standard (of course, if you're into data mapping, you'll want to copy it over). To access this feature absent this button, select the Insert menu, then choose Map. The Drawing button just calls up the Drawing toolbar. As we've stated before, buttons that in turn invoke other toolbars are mostly demoware and easily replaced by simply displaying the toolbar of interest. What we really would like here is a control representing the most often used drawing objects. You'll recall the suave Office Art and AutoShapes from Chapter 2, so let's add the AutoShapes menu control here. Lastly, we find ourselves using text boxes quite a bit, so we suggest adding this as a distinct control as well.

Here are the steps:

1. If the Drawing toolbar is not currently visible, display it.
2. Copy the Chart Wizard button from Standard to your new toolbar.
3. Copy the AutoShapes menu control from Drawing to your new toolbar.
4. Copy the Text Box button from Drawing to your new toolbar.
5. To add a separator between Paste Names and Chart Wizard, right-click the Chart Wizard control and choose "Begin a Group."

Your ExcelAnnoy Standard toolbar should now resemble Figure 3-6.

Figure 3-6: ExcelAnnoy Standard under construction—graphics controls

Zoom and Robert at the Terminus

To finish, let's copy both the Zoom and the Office Assistant (which we affectionately call Robert, its original code name, or Bob) controls:

1. Copy the Zoom control from Standard to your new toolbar.
2. Copy the Office Assistant button from Standard to your new toolbar.
3. To add a separator between Text Box and Zoom, right-click the Zoom control and choose "Begin a Group."

That's it for our new and improved ExcelAnnoy Standard toolbar, which appears in Figure 3-7. It is stripped bare of any vestiges of Microsoft's insidious demoware syndrome. All your most frequently used Standard commands and menus should always be one click away from your digital extremities. On to matters of format . . .

Figure 3-7: ExcelAnnoy Standard is finished

Customizing the Formatting Toolbar

Excel's default Formatting bar, like its sibling Standard, has some flashy controls on it, but some glaring omissions as well. Let's do it right. Table 3-2 lists the default Formatting toolbar's control properties.

Table 3-2: List of Properties for the Controls on Excel's Default Formatting Toolbar

Index	Caption	Id	ToolTipText	Type (Value)	Type (Name)
1	&Font:	1728	&Font:	4	msoControl-ComboBox
2	&Font Size:	1731	&Font Size:	4	msoControl-ComboBox
3	&Bold	113	&Bold	1	msoControl-Button
4	&Italic	114	&Italic	1	msoControl-Button
5	&Underline	115	&Underline	1	msoControl-Button
6	&Align Left	120	&Align Left	1	msoControl-Button
7	&Center	122	&Center	1	msoControl-Button
8	&Align Right	121	&Align Right	1	msoControl-Button
9	&Merge and Center	402	&Merge and Center	1	msoControl-Button
10	&Currency Style	395	&Currency Style	1	msoControl-Button
11	&Percent Style	396	&Percent Style	1	msoControl-Button
12	&Comma Style	397	&Comma Style	1	msoControl-Button
13	&Increase Decimal	398	&Increase Decimal	1	msoControl-Button
14	&Decrease Decimal	399	&Decrease Decimal	1	msoControl-Button
15	&Decrease Indent	3162	&Decrease Indent	1	msoControl-Button
16	&Increase Indent	3161	&Increase Indent	1	msoControl-Button
17	&Borders	203	&Borders	13	msoControlSp-litButtonPopup

Table 3-2: List of Properties for the Controls on Excel's Default Formatting Toolbar (continued)

Index	Caption	Id	ToolTipText	Type (Value)	Type (Name)
18	&Fill Color	1691	Fill Color (Yellow)	13	msoControlSplitButtonPopup
19	&Font Color	401	Font Color (Red)	13	msoControlSplitButtonPopup

The Style Control Should Be Included, Seriously

To create this new toolbar, click Tools, choose Customize, select the Toolbars tab, click New, type in **`ExcelAnnoy Formatting`**, then press `Enter`.

Here's a question we've been asking Microsoft about Excel's Formatting toolbar for the last three versions. (Attention readers: please cover your ears tightly.) <flame on> "*For crying out loud, where's the style drop-down list box?*" <flame off> If users don't grok styles, *educate* them, don't desert them. Since Redmond hasn't yet seen the light on this, let us do it for them: the first thing you have to do is put the Style drop-down control on your customized version of the Formatting toolbar. The Font and Font Size controls are fine as is.

Here are the steps:

1. Add the Style command (in its drop-down version from the Format category) to your new toolbar.
2. Copy the Font drop-down control from Formatting to your new toolbar.
3. Copy the Font Size drop-down control from Formatting to your new toolbar.
4. The Font control is too wide for our taste, so shorten it by grabbing its right edge and dragging just a bit to the left.

You may notice that your ExcelAnnoy Formatting toolbar, which is shown in Figure 3-8, is beginning to resemble the Word Formatting toolbar.

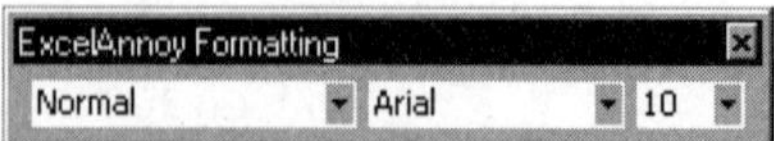

Figure 3-8: ExcelAnnoy Formatting under construction—style and related controls

Frequent Formatting

The next two sets of buttons (seven in all) deal with formatting and aligning cell contents.

Bold, Italic, and Underline are all very useful when creating styles by example. They can stay. (Yes, we keep lauding styles. We'll get into an in-depth discussion of styles in Chapter 6, *Excel Strategies*.)

The next set deals with aligning text in cells: Align Left, Center, and Align Right. These too can stay.

The fourth (and last) control in this set is the Merge and Center button. This button used to just center text entered in one cell across several columns, and thereby probably saved corporate America several person-decades that would otherwise have been frittered away struggling to center text by adding spaces to a label. In Excel 97, it actually merges several cells into a single cell. Shades of functionality! This is amazing, and we'll talk more about it in Chapter 4, *How Excel Works*. This button definitely makes the cut. Here are the steps:

1. From Excel's Formatting toolbar, copy seven buttons in their original sequence over to your new toolbar; they are (in left-to-right order): Bold, Italic, Underline, Align Left, Center, Align Right, and Merge and Center.
2. Add a separator between Font Size and Bold.
3. Add a separator between Underline and Align Left.

Your toolbar should now resemble Figure 3-9.

Figure 3-9: ExcelAnnoy Formatting under construction—more formatting controls

Five for the Recycle Bin

The next five buttons warrant some discussion. Then, to paraphrase Sam Goldwyn, we'll include them out.

The first three—Currency Style, Percent Style, and Comma Style—are Microsoft's attempt to get users to use styles. Not good.* First, these are

* Styles are good. It's Microsoft's adamant refusal to put the Style control on Excel's Formatting toolbar that has us seeing red. This refusal may well stem from a fear that styles don't demo well, hence, another case of the demoware syndrome.

the same default styles already present in the Styles drop-down control that you just added. And the Styles list has *more* default styles, two for currency and two for commas. We won't be copying these buttons.

The increase/decrease decimal demoware buttons definitely came scampering right out of the usability lab. These are two other controls we won't be copying. Instead, we'll replace them with several of our own favorites.

Miscellaneous Formatting Controls

Formatting should be controlled with styles. But there are some types of formatting that you will want to add spontaneously. A good example is the feature of in-cell text indentation that's new to Excel 97. The Decrease Indent and Increase Indent buttons that come on the default Formatting toolbar are keepers.

We have no beef with the Borders button. Bordering regions of the sheet is best done outside of the style paradigm. You can make a similar case for the Fill Color button and its companion Font Color. Use of color is one of those Zen things where less is more. We're not sure that making it easier to color your sheets is a good thing. Nonetheless, in this age of multimedia hyperbole and flaming logos, you may well find occasional use for these controls, so we'll keep them as well.

One of our common ad hoc formatting operations is to border cells or objects with a shadow. So we'll add a button for applying shadow effects to the current selection.

Another type of cell formatting that we frequently use to mark sections of sheets is a light shading, so we'll add a button for it instead of having to hunt around on the Fill Color submenu.

WARNING There's a bug in Excel 97 that may not have a fix available by the time this book gets into print. This bug causes the program to experience a General Protection fault when you run the Chart Wizard with the Light Shading button displayed. If you have either the Light Shading or the Dark Shading buttons visible, you *must* turn off the toolbars on which they reside *before running the Chart Wizard*.

At this point, if you're getting cramped for space (depending on your screen resolution), you can tighten up the Font and Font Size boxes: click on them while the Customize dialog box is displayed and drag the right edge of each one a bit to the left.

The last two buttons we're going to add fall into the general utility category. We like to be able to turn sheet gridlines on and off, so we add a button to do this. Last is the Full Screen button. Full screen view is Spartan but good for concentration, and access via a single-click button is faster than a zooming IntelliMouse. While crunching data in a sheet, you need to see your sheet, not a hodgepodge of toolbars and other eye clutter. Full screen view removes everything from your display except the data entry area (of course), menu bar, column and row headers, and scroll bars.

Here are the steps for including these groups of related formatting controls:

1. Copy the Decrease Indent and Increase Indent controls from Formatting to your new toolbar.
2. Copy the Borders, Fill Color, and Font Color controls from Formatting to your new toolbar.
3. Add the Shadow menu control* (from the Drawing category) to your new toolbar.
4. Add the Light Shading button (from the Format category, third from the bottom) to your new toolbar.
5. Add the Toggle Grid button (from the Forms category) to your new toolbar.
6. Add the Full Screen button (from the View category) to your new toolbar.
7. Right-click the Full Screen button control on your toolbar and select Default Style to display the image only (no text).
8. Add a separator between Merge and Center and Decrease Indent.
9. Add a separator between Increase Indent and Borders.
10. Add a separator between Light Shading and Toggle Grid.

Your finished ExcelAnnoy Formatting toolbar should resemble the one shown in Figure 3-10.

The command arrangements we've recommended for these two industrial-use toolbars work for us, but remember, if these changes don't work for

* The Shadow control is an example of a slightly inconsistent user interface since the image on this built-in control lacks the traditional triangular arrow indicating there's a submenu waiting to reveal itself. There's a submenu, all right, just no hint of one until you've clicked it. Go figure.

Figure 3-10: ExcelAnnoy Formatting is finished

you . . . *change them*! But whatever you do, do not just take the demoware version you're given by the Marketing Department and the lab rats and live with it. Carpe barem.

Activate ExcelAnnoy Toolbars and Don't Look Back

Now that your ExcelAnnoy Standard and ExcelAnnoy Formatting toolbars are complete, it's time to hide Excel's factory default equivalents. Simply select View, Toolbars, select the Toolbars tab, uncheck Standard and Formatting, then click Close. Now, dock ExcelAnnoy Standard and Excel-Annoy Formatting (or not) as you see fit.

Should you ever want the factory default toolbars back, simply hide the ExcelAnnoy versions and display the factory versions.

Talking to a Paper Clip

At first it may sound unusual having a paper clip as an aide-de-camp, but it does work! The most commonly used Office Assistant character is the paper clip, and behind this character and all its siblings is a smart natural language question-and-answer system coupled with Office's Help files.

Although many people find Mr. Clippit endearing, others don't mind the Einstein "Genius" character (which is very nicely rendered). But most advanced users simply leave Office Assistant off until needed, then dismiss it immediately when it has answered the question at hand.

The Help system sitting behind this Office Bob interface works wonders. Don't be put off by the character's annoying appearance and cloying ways. But remember, you can always call up the Office Assistant by clicking on the ? icon on the Standard toolbar, or by pressing F1. So there's really no reason to keep the character around where it simply gets in the way.

To change the character, if you must, just right-click on the Assistant window and pick Options. Bring up the Gallery tab and scroll to the personage you'd prefer. If Excel tells you it's having trouble finding the file associated with the character, you've probably changed the letter of the CD-ROM drive from which Office was originally installed. If that's the

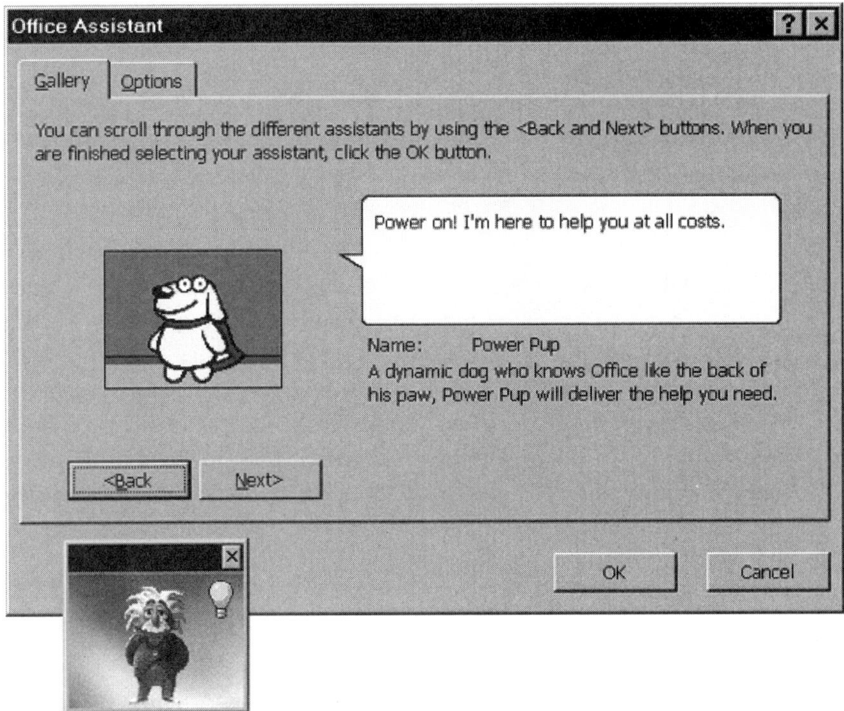

Figure 3-11: Able to leap tall Bobs in a single bound

case, get out your Office CD, look in the *\Office\Actors* folder for the appropriate *.act* file, and drag it to the *C:\Program Files\Microsoft Office\Office\Actors* folder. Excel will find it there.

Office Goes Brrrrring, Whoosssssh, and Ding Dong

This being the age of multimedia and special effects, the Office 97 developers added subtle but important auditory cues to befriend you while working with Office. Unfortunately, if you want to hear Office's remarkably cool sound effects, you're going to have to jump through some hoops. This entire process should be much smoother and seamlessly integrated into Office. One click should do it all. Maybe next time. Let's take this from the top. (This entire discussion assumes you have an installed and functional sound board.)

1. If all the stars are aligned properly, you might just hear Office sounds out of the box. Let's find out. Start Excel (or any Office application), select Tools, choose Options, select the General tab, check the

"Provide feedback with sound" check box, click OK. Do a quick sound check—open any existing file, and, if you're lucky, you should hear a high-end strumming sound (officially, it's *Complete.wav*; more on how to find this out in a moment). If so, you're all done. If instead all you hear is the silent stirring of dust motes in the air, move on to the next step. (You may also be so lucky as to see a message box that reads, "Microsoft Office Sounds are not installed on your system.")

2. Next make sure you've got Windows 95's Audio Compression component installed. We won't go through the detailed steps here, presuming by now you've had some practice at using Control Panel's Add/Remove Programs dialog. Select the Multimedia component on the Windows Setup tab, click Details, then examine the Audio Compression check box. (See Figure 3-12.) If it's already checked, then move on to the next step; otherwise, check it, click OK twice, and now it should be installed. If a sound check that is triggered by opening any existing Office file now plays *Complete.wav*—brrrrring!—then you're all done. Otherwise, move on to the next step.

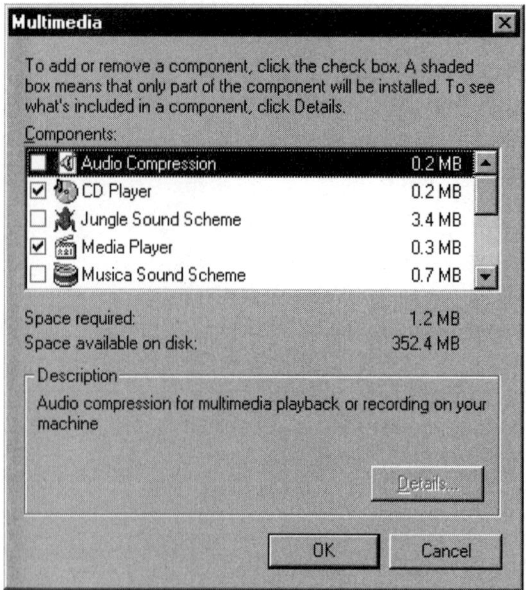

Figure 3-12: Adding Audio Compression via Add/Remove Programs ➤ Windows Setup

3. Unfortunately, Office sounds are not—repeat, not—installed by the Office setup procedure. You have to do this manually. You can obtain *Sounds.exe* from the *\Valupack\Sounds* folder on your Office CD, or on the Web at *http://www.microsoft.com/officefreestuff/*. Install Office

sounds by double-clicking *Sounds.exe* and following the simple instructions. Ahem, time for yet another sound check. If you hear *Complete.wav* now, congratulations. Otherwise, you may have a sound card or multimedia player problem that's beyond the scope of this book. (Quick tip: is your audio volume control applet set to Mute, or perhaps are one or more of the applet's volume potentiometers set to zero? We've had this happen to us, so it's worth a look before you open up your PC's chassis and start fiddling with DIP switches.)

At this point you presumably have Office sounds playing. Did you know that Office sounds can be on (or off) independently of the Office Assistant's sounds feature? To activate the Office Assistant's sounds, right-click on the Office Assistant, choose Options, select the Options tab, select the "Make sounds" check box, then click OK.

If you want to see what files are being played for which actions, fire up Control Panel, start Sounds, scroll down the Events list box until you get to the Microsoft Office node, and select the desired action. For example, Figure 3-13 shows what the Clear action's filename is; click the Play button to hear the sound.

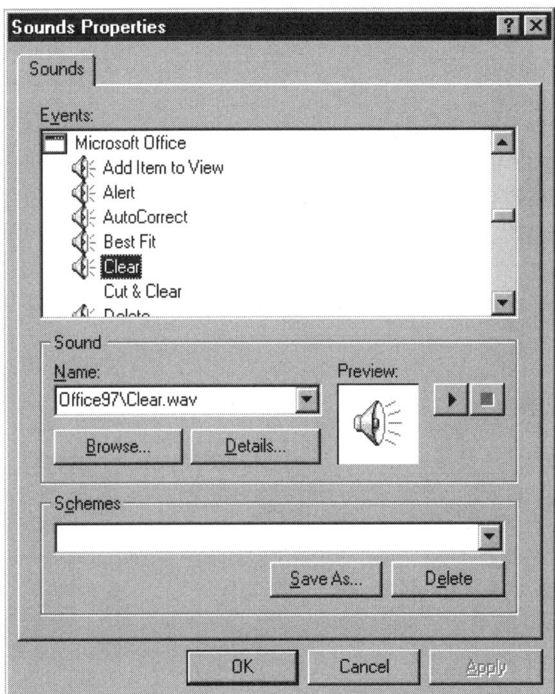

Figure 3-13: Using the Sounds Properties dialog box to reveal an Office action's sound

4

In this chapter:

- *Working with the Workbook*
- *Working with Data*
- *Working with Names, Formulas, and Functions*

How Excel Works

Excel is a feature-rich development environment that is limited primarily by the user's imagination. And the central canvas for this development effort is the workbook. This is the file that Excel produces to hold the various worksheets, charts, macros, etc., that make up your model.

Now, before you toss this book as a boring jargon feast, let's define some terms. *Development environment* simply means that: if you want something in Excel, you're gonna have to build it yourself, or use a template that someone else has built for you. This can be as simple as saying, "If you want to add up a column of numbers in Excel, you're going to have to input the numbers and create a formula to sum them." The term *model* we use to mean this "thing" that you're going to build. We could say *document* to mean the same thing, so don't let the stuffy terms throw you.

In this chapter, we'll start off with the workbook and drill down through the basics of model building.

Working with the Workbook

By default, when you first start Excel you get a new, empty workbook with the name of Book1 (this is one potentially major annoyance all by itself, as you'll see shortly when we talk about saving workbooks). You can change this behavior by utilizing Excel's startup switches and/or creating custom templates. We'll get into templates in Chapter 7, *Excel in the Office.*

The startup switches are pretty straightforward. To add a startup switch, locate the shortcut file you use to run Excel. If you run Excel from the

Start menu, look in *C:\Windows\Start Menu\Programs* for the Excel shortcut, right-click it and select Properties. If you use the Office Shortcut Bar (OSB) look in *C:\Program Files\Microsoft Office\Office\Shortcut Bar* and the appropriate sub-folder for the shortcut (or just right-click on the OSB button and choose Properties).

In the Target text box you'll see the full path to the Excel executable program file (see Figure 4-1). You simply add the startup switch at the end of the text in the Target text box. In this example we've added the **/e** switch, which starts Excel without the default Book1 workbook. To force Excel to open an extant worksheet, you just add the fully qualified path to the end of the Target text. Precede the path to the spreadsheet to be opened with **/r**, and the workbook is opened as read-only. You can specify a particular working folder by including **/p** followed by a fully qualified path to the folder you want to use. Excel's startup switches are summarized in Table 4-1.

Table 4-1: Excel's Startup Switches

Startup Switch	Function
/e or /E	This switch is used to prevent Excel from creating a new default Book1 workbook upon loading (Excel starts *empty*).
/r or /R *c:\path\file-name.ext*	This switch is used in conjunction with a path and filename that specifies a file that you want Excel to open upon loading. The switch causes the file to be opened as *read-only*.
/p or /P *c:\path*	This switch is used in conjunction with a path to specify a folder to be used as the default folder for this session of Excel. It overrides the default file location setting in Tools ➤ Options ➤ General.

The Book You Save

Since you can have more than one workbook under development at any one time, Excel gives each one a name of Book***x*** as you create it, the ***x*** being a numeric value that is incremented each time a new book is created during that particular Excel session. Start Excel, create five workbooks, and the next one that you create will have a default name of *Book6.xls*. Shut down Excel, fire it back up, and you start off with Book1 again.

We don't know about you, but we find this behavior to go beyond annoying all the way up to being downright dangerous. Having both taught Excel classes and manned a Help Desk, we can tell you that people invariably wind up saving a critical workbook under a default name. Create a new workbook, hit Save, and Excel is primed and ready to save it under the Book1 name. (See Figure 4-2.)

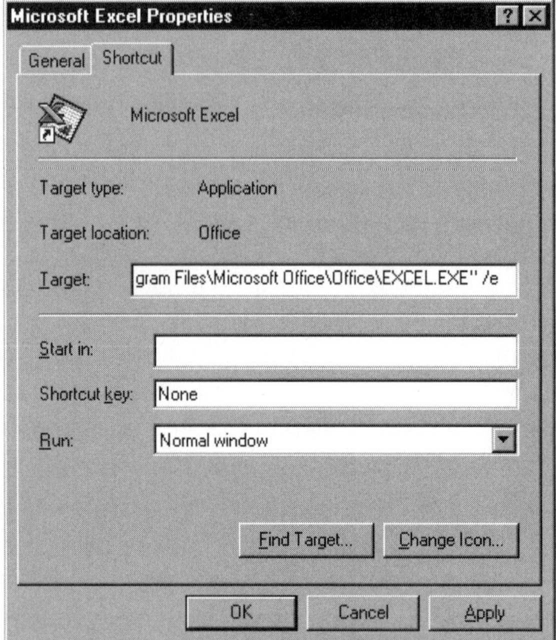

Figure 4-1: Setting startup switches

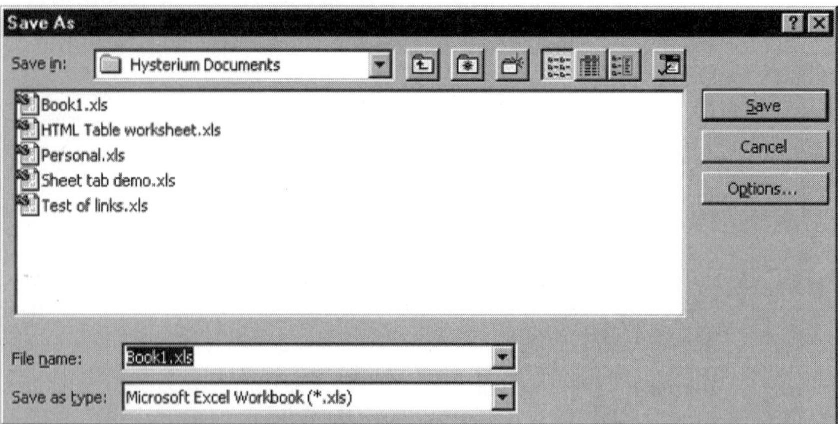

Figure 4-2: An annoying Book name

How annoying is this? We've seen many a user save a book under the default name with every intention of going back later and renaming it. They're in a hurry and click, bang, save, and off they go. But they never quite get around to renaming the book. Then, in a later session, Excel offers to save a different book under the same name used earlier. Is this a service call waiting to happen or what? "Hey Help Desk! Excel keeps giving me the wrong *Book1.xls.* Get someone down here and find the other Book1 file." Ouch!

Excel should never save a file under a default name, and it is a real annoyance that it does. It should force you to give the file a name of your own choosing.

Backward Compatibility Issues

As the upgrade wheel spins faster and faster, you're more and more likely to be working in an environment where different versions of Excel are in use. Maybe even within various departments of the same company.

That makes backward compatibility an issue, and there are several ways to minimize the annoyance level of working with multiple file formats. Excel 5 and Excel 95 share the same file format, so there is no problem there. But Excel 97's native format is incompatible with previous versions.

On the bright side, Excel 97 comes with conversion filters for earlier versions going back as far as 2.1. Even better, there is a filter for creating a dual file format. In addition to the filters you'd expect, there is one called "Microsoft Excel 97 & 5.0/95 Workbook (*.xls)" (see Figure 4-3). When you use this filter, you get the native Excel 97 format *as well as the Excel 5.0/95 format!* Two formats—one file. Open the file with Excel 97 and make changes; the changes are saved in both formats. This adds about one-third to the file's size over a native Excel 97 file.

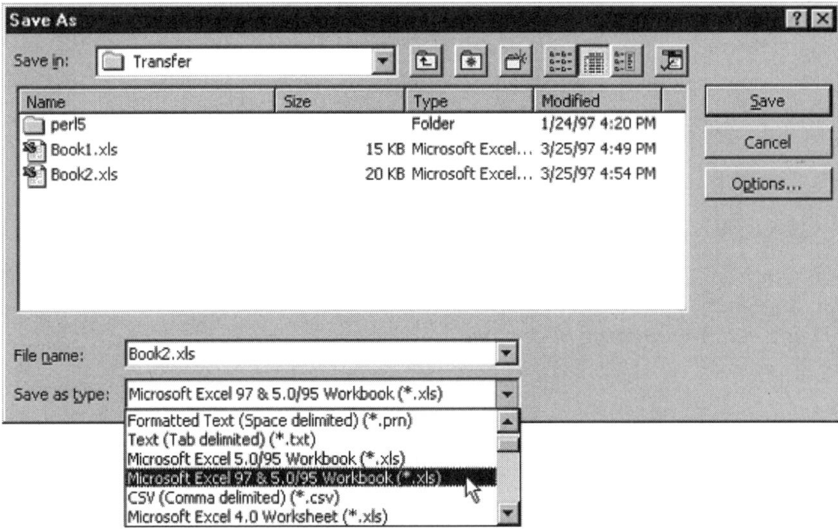

Figure 4-3: Excel's Save As—Save as type list

When the file is opened in Excel 5.0/95, you get the file as though it had been saved in that earlier version (i.e., you don't get any Excel 97 specific features). This is where you have to exercise some caution. If you make any changes to the file and save it, you'll destroy the Excel 97 portion and be left with a straight 5.0/95 workbook. With this in mind, Excel suggests you open the file as read-only (see Figure 4-4) to preserve the Excel 97 format.

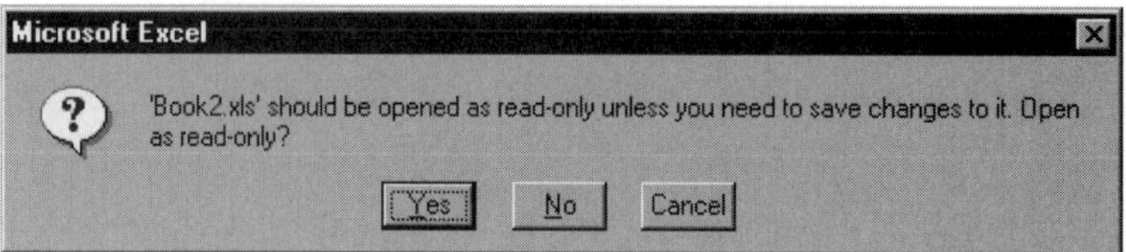

Figure 4-4: Opening dual format file in Excel 95

Fitted Sheets

As we mentioned earlier, the only limit to how many sheets you can have in a workbook is available memory, and you control how many default sheets appear in a new book via the Tools ➤ Options, General tab, "Sheets in new workbook" setting.

You add new sheets via the Worksheet option on the Insert menu or by right-clicking on a sheet tab and choosing Insert from the pop-up menu (see Figure 4-5). New sheets are inserted to the left of the active sheet. You can left-click, drag a new sheet by its tab, and position it wherever you want in the tab order.

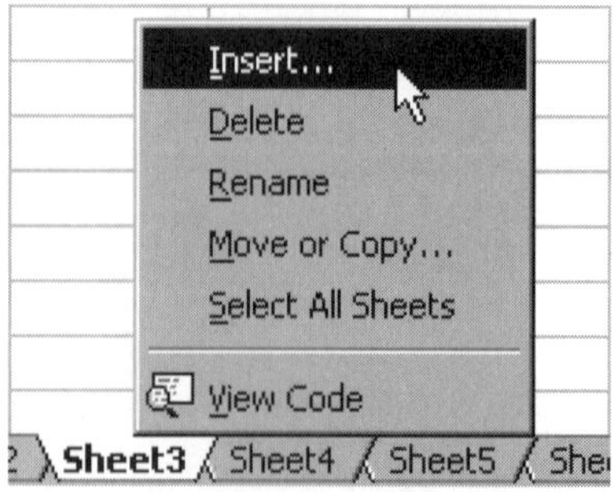

Figure 4-5: Excel's tab pop-up menu

This pop-up menu is pretty slick. You can insert, rename, delete, move or copy sheets, or select all the sheets at once from this menu. You can also start the Visual Basic Editor by clicking on View Code.

To move or copy sheets within a workbook, you're better off using the mouse. Click-and-drag to move, hold down the `Ctrl` key, and drag to copy. Of course, if you have a book with a jillion sheets, the Move or Copy dialog via the pop-up menu is more efficient. (See Figure 4-6.)

To copy instead of move, just check the "Create a copy" check box.

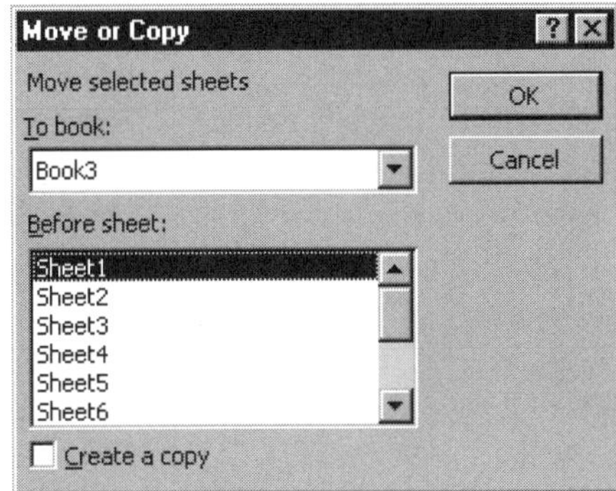

Figure 4-6: Move or Copy

Columns and rows

A worksheet is a really large two-dimensional table that consists of a matrix of 256 columns by 65,536 rows. You can enter constants (text and numbers) and formulas into the cells formed by this matrix. Constants are static data, and the formulas are what you use to define the relationships between the cells and to display calculated results.

The rows and columns are resizable, meaning you can make the columns wider and narrower, and the rows taller or shorter. For most adjustments, you can use the mouse. Just place the mouse near the black line to the right or below the column or row you want to resize. The pointer changes into the sizing grabber shape and you can left-click and drag the right edge of a column or the lower edge of a row. (See Figure 4-7.)

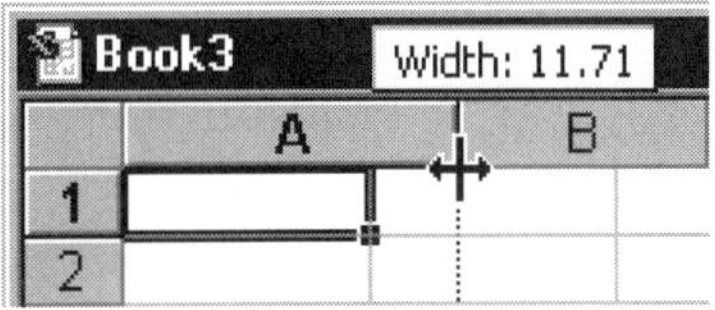

Figure 4-7: Resizing a column in Excel

Notice that when you are resizing this way, you get an on-screen indicator of the numeric height or width as you drag. With a steady hand, you can get pretty precise with the mouse. Of course, if you are just going for a best fit, meaning you want to widen a column to accommodate its widest entry, just double-click when you get the sizing grabber. The column or row immediately snaps to fit the widest (column) or tallest (row) entry. On the Row or Column options on the Format menus, this is called AutoFit. It's a bit annoying that the AutoFit option is not on the cell shortcut menu (right-click on a cell to get the shortcut menu), but as annoyances go, this is a minor one.

If you select multiple columns or rows (but not both), you can resize them all with one mouse operation. For example, select the target columns by clicking on the column letter at the top of the worksheet. Then just resize any one of the selected columns. They'll all change to the new width. You can even work this trick on noncontiguous columns or rows. Hold down the `Ctrl` key while making your selections (this is the same principle we used earlier when selecting sheet tabs).

NOTE Row height is measured in points. There are 72 points to the inch, and a default row is 12.75 points high. The column measurement is a bit trickier. A default column is 8.43 "zeros" in the default font. Excel starts with Arial as its default font, so a standard column is wide enough to fit 8.43 zero digits. How this came about is lost in the folklore of spreadsheet history. If you don't like this default width, you can change it globally via the Format ➤ Column ➤ Standard Width dialog box. Just enter a new value and click OK.

Column width and row height can be set to zero (via either the mouse or the Format menu), thereby effectively hiding the column or row. Setting the width or height to zero is what Format ➤ Row ➤ Hide or Format ➤ Column ➤ Hide does. The content of the cells hidden this way is still there and can be referenced in formulas; you just don't see the cells storing that content. This is an effective way to eliminate intermediate calculations from a printed report because hidden columns and rows do not print.

Once you've hidden a column or row, it can be tricky to redisplay them. Say you've hidden a number of contiguous columns, E, F, and G. To redisplay them, you could select columns D and H (which appear on the display to be contiguous) and resize them (even if you just reset them to their default width). The intervening hidden columns resize to the same width as well. This can play havoc with the structure of your worksheet, since you wind up resizing all the columns.

The mouse can redisplay a hidden column or row as well. Touch the mouse pointer just to the right of the last visible column to the left of the hidden column (see Figure 4-8). When the pointer turns into a vertical sizing grabber (assuming that you want to unhide one or more columns), click-and-drag and you'll resize the hidden column.

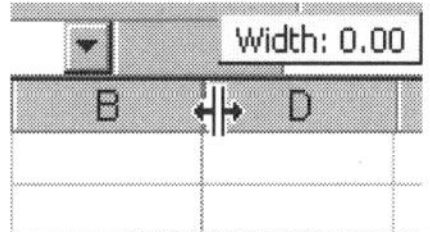

Figure 4-8: Resizing a hidden column

You can also select columns D and H, right-click with the mouse and choose Unhide from the shortcut menu. This avoids having to resize a column and is perhaps the best method.

Using sheets effectively

Since each workbook can contain multiple sheets, you should construct different parts of your model on separate sheets and link the key data that needs to move from one section to another using formulas. Excel makes this easy, perhaps too easy. You can start with a link here and a link there, but, like eating potato chips, once you start, it's sometimes difficult to stop. Pretty soon you've got links going everywhere, and your workbooks become a circular reference waiting to happen. You need to lay out your sheets with some thought and care. Don't link your sheets in a haphazard way, or your model becomes difficult to audit and unreliable (see Figure 4-9).

Keep the number of links to a minimum and move the key data in a one-to-many (dashed arrows) or a many-to-one (solid arrows) relationship. (See Figure 4-10.)

Hyperlinks, objects, and more

As we've discussed, you can input text, numbers, and formulas directly into the cells on the sheet. But each sheet also has what is called a drawing layer on which you can add various objects. You can think of this layer as a clear acetate overlay on which you can draw or embed things that float over the sheet itself. (See Figure 4-11.)

You can add map graphics that are linked to data in your worksheet. Just input the data, select it, and choose Map from the Insert menu. Callouts and numerous AutoShapes and drawing tools are also available from the Drawing toolbar. When you embed a chart on a sheet, it winds up in the drawing layer as a chart object.

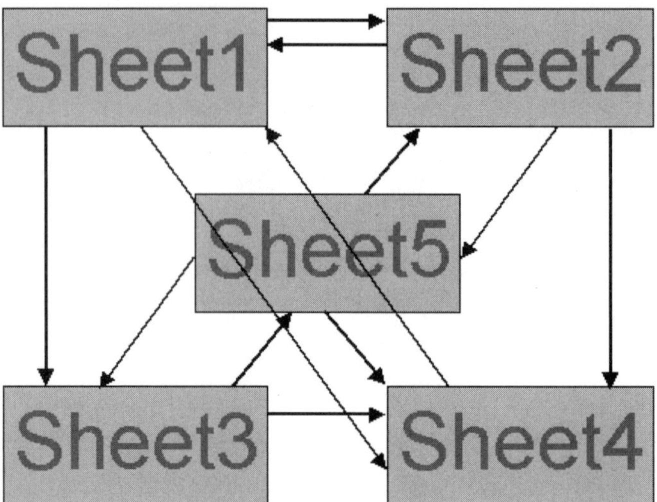

Figure 4-9: Poor layout makes the model difficult to maintain

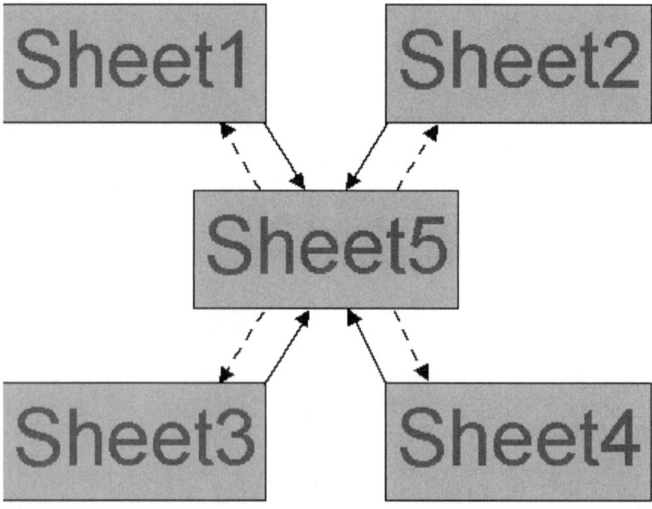

Figure 4-10: A better model for linking sheets

Various and sundry controls can be added to the drawing layer of a sheet from the Form toolbar (for creating interactive forms) or from the Control Toolbox toolbar (for adding ActiveX controls)—things like option buttons, check boxes, drop-down lists, command buttons, and the like. These controls can be hooked to macro code.

In the lower left-hand corner of the worksheet in Figure 4-11, you'll see a hyperlink that has been added to cell A18. Hyperlinks are a new worksheet function in Excel 97 that jump directly to a document that may be

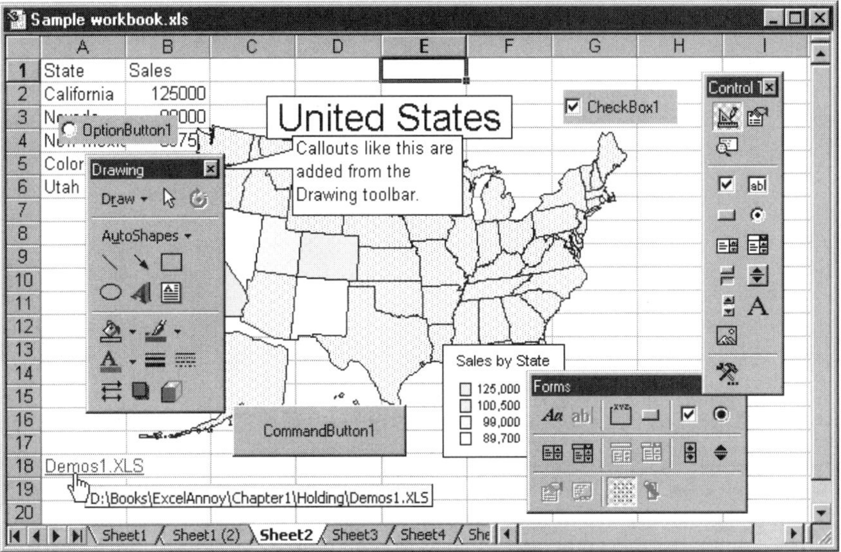

Figure 4-11: Various elements and objects shown on the drawing layer

on your local computer, a network, an intranet, or the Internet. The hyperlink in Figure 4-11 is in the sheet cell, but you can make any object on the drawing layer a hyperlink by selecting the object and choosing the Hyperlink button on the standard toolbar or Hyperlink from the Insert menu. You type in the path (which could be to a file on your disk, or an intranet/Internet URL) and an option locator within the file (a range name or an HTML tag). (See Figure 4-12.)

Constants and Formulas

Text, numeric values (called constants), and formulas are the three basic building blocks of almost every spreadsheet model you are ever likely to build.

By default, Excel tries to give you visual clues as to the nature of a cell's content. As content types go, text is left aligned, numbers are right aligned, and logicals and errors are centered. A formula may return an error or a logical result like TRUE or FALSE in a given context. Or the cell might be blank.

Firing blanks

You can leave a cell blank. This is not the same as a cell being equal to zero as the result of a formula, or entering a zero into a cell (which are both values). A cell can be tested to see if it is blank by using a function,

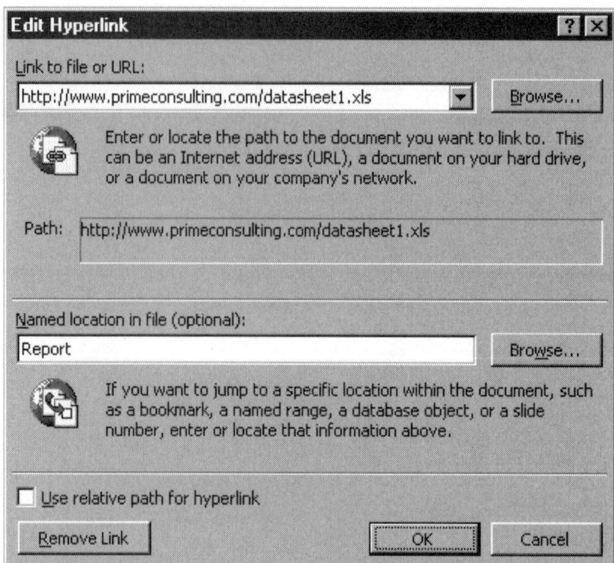

Figure 4-12: Adding a hyperlink

as in the formula `=ISBLANK(B4)`. This returns TRUE if cell B4 is indeed blank. Testing to see what the state of a cell is, at any given moment, is something you'll want to do when building spreadsheets that are responsible for helping to maintain themselves and alerting you to error conditions, so we'll revisit this concept later.

Working with text strings

Text typed into a cell is called a text string or label, and can be up to 32,000 characters in length (up from 255 from earlier versions of Excel). Text can be manipulated using formulas similar to the way numbers are by using the concatenation operator, the ampersand (&).

In the example in Figure 4-13, a string, "Total number of", is concatenated with a text string in cell D1, another string, and a value in cell E5. Note how the value, when concatenated, is treated as text.

There is a gray area between text and values that you need to watch out for. Consider the example in Figure 4-14. In this sheet, we originally entered the values 1, 2, and 3 in columns A, B, and C. Then we formatted cell B1 as text using Excel's Format Cells dialog (Format ➤ Cells ➤ Number ➤ Text). In cell C1, we entered "1" as text using the `=TEXT` worksheet function. These two methods of portraying a number as text are treated differently by Excel, depending on how you manipulate them.

="Total number of " & D1 & " is " &E5

C	D	E	F
	Monster sightings		
	Godzilla	15	
	Rodan	7	
	Mothra	5	
		27	
Total number of Monster sightings is 27			

Figure 4-13: Manipulating text in a formula

C3 =TEXT(1,0)

	A	B	C	D	E
1	1	1	2	4	=SUM(A1:C1)
2	2	2	3	7	=SUM(A2:C2)
3	3	3	1	6	=SUM(A3:C3)
4	6	6	6		
5					
6					
7					
8					

Format / Cells / Number / Text

Figure 4-14: Excel does not always treat text the same way

Next we sorted B1:B3 in ascending order, and then did the same to C1:C3. Note how Excel's sort routine treated the two "text" entries differently. In column B, the value formatted as text is treated as a *number*! When we summed the row across (column E shows you the formulas entered into the adjacent cells in column D), the `=SUM` worksheet function also sees the value formatted as text as a value.

Where things get weird is with the text entry that we originally entered in C1. The sort function treated this entry as real text, i.e., it sorted the text *after* the numeric values. And the `=SUM` function ignored it when it summed the numbers across.

On row 4, we added the cells in rows 1, 2, and 3 using a simple operator formula. The formula in cell C4 is `=C1+C2+C3`, and this method *does* see the text as a value and includes it in the total.

The moral is to be mindful of just how you portray values as text, because sometimes Excel wants to include the value in calculations and sometimes it doesn't.

Text as plain old labels you're probably comfortable with. Type in your text and it aligns to the left of the active cell by default. If the string is too long to display within the active cell and, providing the adjacent cell(s) to the right are blank, the text spills over onto the adjacent cells. The adjacent cell does not actually contain the displayed text; it remains blank, but the text is displayed *over* the cell.

Assume a new, empty worksheet. Type in a long label, and the text spills right. Center the text, and it spills left and right. Right align it, and the text spills left. Pretty standard stuff.

Take a look at Figure 4-15. In column C, rows 2, 3, and 4, the same string, "This is a fairly long label", has been entered. Column A shows you how each cell in column C is formatted for alignment. The cells in columns B and D are blank. C2 is left-aligned and spills to the right as you'd expect. C3 is centered and so spills both left and right. But notice that the left-aligned label in A3 is too wide for that cell, and it spills to the right. Both of the strings (the one in C3 and the one in A3) are spilling over cell B3.

	A	B	C	D	E
1	Alignment				
2	default		This is a fairly long label		
3	centered - x	This is a fairly long label			
4	right	is is a fairly long label			
5					

Figure 4-15: The text runneth over

C4 is right aligned and spills to the left. The string is long enough to spill over into column A, but cell A4 is not blank, so the text is truncated at the edge of column A. The text entry in C4 is still complete, and no characters are deleted; this truncation only affects how the text is displayed.

Text can be wrapped in a cell (Format ➤ Cells, Alignment tab, check the "Wrap text" check box—see Figure 4-16), which increases the row height as more text is entered. If you then reset the row height to standard, the text does not spill over even if the adjacent cells are blank. This is a handy trick if you have blank cells but want to restrict the amount of text that can be displayed.

The Format ➤ Cells, Alignment tab dialog box tab provides some powerful formatting options. You can set a horizontal indent (see Figure 4-17)—a godsend for anyone who has tried to do indented level headings—as well as aligning the text vertically in the cell. New in Excel 97 is the ability to tilt the text, and this dialog provides an angle indicator, under Orientation, that lets you tweak this setting by clicking and dragging the angle control with the mouse.

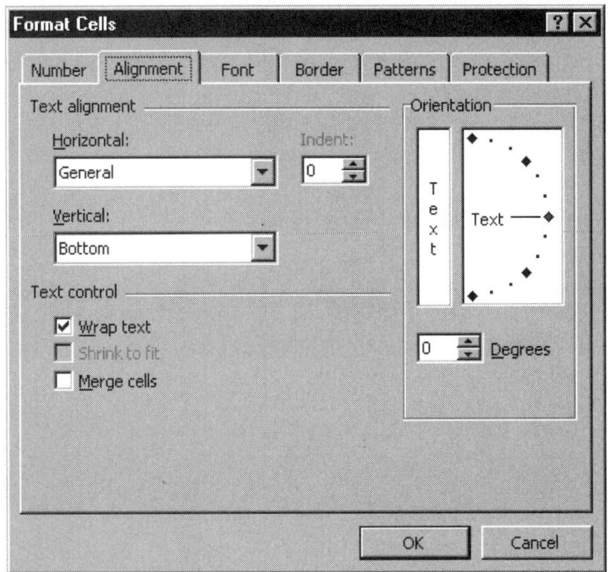

Figure 4-16: Tweaking the alignment of text

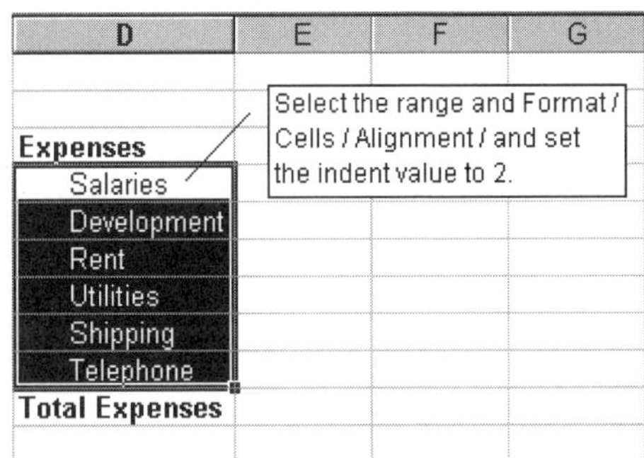

Figure 4-17: Indenting labels

The Merge cells check box is also new in Excel 97 (the old Center Across Columns button on the default formatting toolbar has been hooked to this setting, and its name has been changed to Center and Merge). Word users may be familiar with merging table cells, but this is very new stuff to spreadsheet jockeys.

In Figure 4-18, the one billion value you see has been entered in cell F6. We selected F6:G6 and checked the Merge cells box in Format ➤ Cells, Alignment. If the billion is sitting in F6, where the heck did G6 go? Well, it's still there, but like the post office in Brooklyn, you can't get there from here. Pop up the Go To dialog, type `G6,` hit OK and you wind up in F6. But G6 is alive and well, as the value in G8 indicates. This cell (G8) contains the formula shown to the right (`=ISBLANK(G6)`) and it returns TRUE, so G6 is blank. If you create a formula that references G6 (like the formula in G9), it returns zero. If there had been some content in G6 when we merged the two cells, Excel would have warned us that only the upper left-most data would be retained, and the contents of G6 would have hit the bit bucket. G6 is still there, but you can't put anything in it.

	F	G	H
6	1,000,000,000.00		
7			
8		TRUE	=ISBLANK(G6)
9		0.00	=G6
10		1.E+09	=F6
11			

Figure 4-18: A matter of merging

This ability to merge cells gives you a tremendous amount of control over your worksheet's appearance and layout.

Working with numbers

Values in Excel can be constants (numbers entered into cells) or the result of a formula (those little mini-programs we discussed in Chapter 1). Values are calculated to a precision of 15 decimal places. This means that if you have a value with an indeterminate value (say, pi) or a repeating decimal (like if you divide 98 by 13) Excel is going to lop the number off at 15 places.

Now, this is accurate enough for the majority of spreadsheets most users will ever develop. However, you can get thoroughly annoyed when you start rounding numbers via formatting.

Figure 4-19 shows two sets of numbers being summed in columns G and H. In both cases we're using the `=SUM` function to add 1.04 to 1.04. But in column G the formatting is set to display 2 decimal places and in column H only 1 decimal place. Looks pretty odd, no? You might be tempted to force Excel to use precision as displayed (Tools ➤ Options ➤ Calculation, and check the "Precision as displayed" box). Do not do this unless you really know what you are about. When you check this box, you tell Excel to lop off any decimal place not provided for in the formatting display, and once it does this you cannot get the original value back.

In the example we should have taken care of the rounding necessary to give us the value we desired with something like this formula `=ROUND(H2,1)+ROUND(H3,1)`.

G	H
2 places	1 place
1.04	1.0
1.04	1.0
2.08	2.1

Figure 4-19: Watch the rounding

Dates are just numbers with special formatting applied. January 1, 1900, is equal to 1, and each day thereafter is incremented by one. This allows you to do math with dates. Speaking of which, if you do a lot of date calculations (especially if you work in payroll or Human Resources), check out the `=NETWORKDAYS` function that is available in the Analysis ToolPack that comes with Excel. It lets you enter a start and end date and it returns the number of days between them that fall on workdays. It automatically excludes weekends, and you can create a holiday list that it will exclude as well. Very cool.

When you enter a number that is too wide for the cell width, Excel tries to help you by automatically widening the column to accommodate the number's length. Or at least it will if the column width has not been explicitly set. If it has, you get either an odd-looking thing that is your number in scientific notation (e.g., `1E+09`), or a series of repeating pound signs (#####). Just widen the column and the number will be displayed. Obviously, it would be far too dangerous and misleading if numbers were allowed to spill over adjacent blank cells or were truncated as text strings are.

New in Excel 97 is the ability to create conditional formats that let you control how a value is displayed depending on certain criteria you establish. For example, if either a value entered into the sheet or a formula returns a result and the result falls below a certain threshold, you can have it appear in bold and red. You can establish three separate conditions for the application of specific formatting. Formatting attributes can include fonts, borders, and patterns. (See Figure 4-20.)

Working with formulas

Formulas are the programming routines you write at the cellular level to define relationships between the constants entered into your sheet and to produce the calculated results you want.

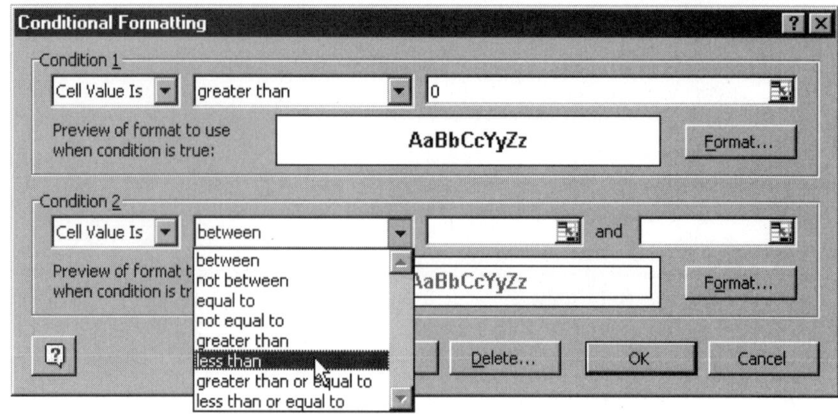

Figure 4-20: Creating conditional formats

You can write formulas using the basic math operators:

- plus (+)
- minus (-)
- multiply (*)
- divide (/)
- percent (%) (for example, `=A1*2%`)
- exponent (^)

the comparison operators:

- equal (=)
- greater-than (>)
- less-than (<)
- greater-than or equal to (>=)
- less-than or equal to (<=)
- not-equal-to (<>)

the reference operators:

- range (:)
- union (,) (for example, `=SUM(A1:A4, C5:F5)`)
- intersection operator ( ) The intersection operator is the space character (for example `=Rent Feb97` would return the cell where the Rent range intersects with the Feb97 range)

or the text operator you saw earlier:

- concatenation (&)

In addition to operators, you can use worksheet functions in your formulas. A function is a bit of built-in programming that generally takes an argument(s), and returns a result. For example:

```
=SUM(range)
```

This function takes an argument, in this case the *range* of cells to be summed, and returns as a result the sum of the values in the range argument. The union operator could be used in this function to sum several ranges at once:

```
=SUM(range, range)
```

Functions can be used with the various operators and even nested within other functions. We'll come back to formulas after we've covered some additional topics that will let us better utilize them.

Working with Data

In Chapter 1 we talked about becoming more efficient in our use of Excel both to save time and to reduce the general annoyance level. Extending this concept of efficiency, we'll take a look at entering data into your sheets. Excel has a number of very useful tools to speed up this tedious process—you just have to learn how they work and about some of their more interesting quirks.

We've mentioned how, in this version of Excel, the character limit for text entered into a single cell increased from 255 to 32,000. This, while generally hailed as a good thing, actually introduces an interesting problem all on its own. Consider Figure 4-21.

When you enter constants or formulas into a cell, the entry appears both in the formula bar and in the cell itself. You can turn off this in-cell editing feature (Tools ➤ Options, Edit tab, "Edit directly in cell") if this stereo effect annoys you.

As you type more into a cell, the formula bar expands to display all the contents on screen. The first problem is that the formula bar obscures the scroll bar. Often when editing long formulas, we like to scroll around the sheet to see the areas the formula refers to. Scrolling down is no problem, but it's tough to scroll up without the top of the scroll bar visible (unless you have an IntelliMouse as discussed in Chapter 2, *Excel as Workhorse*). And, as you can see from Figure 4-21, the entry itself

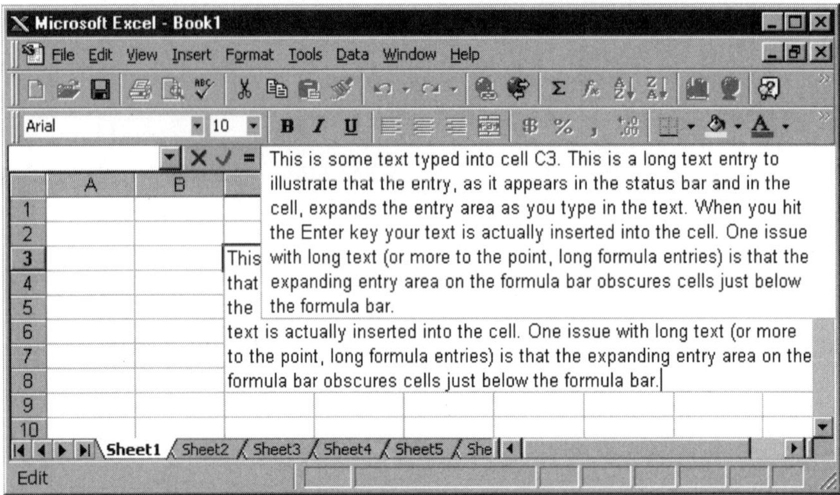

Figure 4-21: Those large text entries

hides a goodly portion of the sheet cells, which can make formula entry somewhat challenging. Once the visible display is full, you can keep right on pounding text into the cell until you reach the 32,000-character limit. There is no provision for scrolling the entry; you'll just have to use the arrow keys to move the insertion point up or down through the entry. Sheesh! For really long text entries, you might consider editing them in Word and then using cut and paste to get them into Excel.

AutoEntry

Excel allows you to set an option that will move the active cell up, down, left, or right, every time you hit the `Enter` key (Tools ➤ Options ➤ Edit). Annoying? Oh, you bet! This "feature" drives a number of us crazy—it never moves in the right direction for what we're doing at the moment. Most of us wind up just turning the bloody thing off. (See Figure 4-22.)

This can be a useful setting to speed data entry when crunching numbers in columns, assuming you're going to go with the flow, the flow being the direction in which Excel is set to move the active cell. As a bonus, pressing `SHIFT+ENTER` makes the active cell move in the *opposite direction*! This doubles the usefulness of this feature, which, under the right circumstances, can really speed up data entry. The Redmond Rangers have never given this feature a catchy name, so we've dubbed it AutoEntry just for reference.

Building on this notion of automatically having the active cell move whenever you hit `Enter`, we've come up with a trick we like to think of as

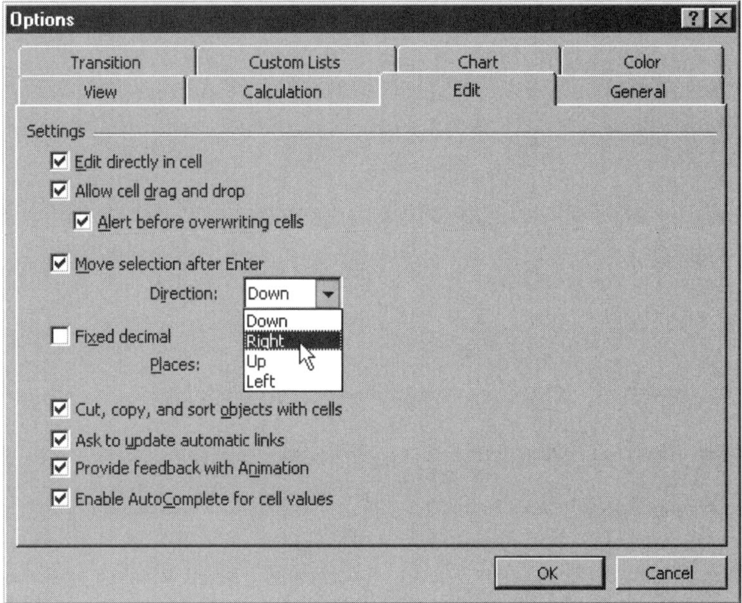

Figure 4-22: Setting the Move selection after Enter

SuperAutoEntry. It's a bit more work, but it deals nicely with the annoying trait of the built-in AutoEntry of just moving back and forth in one direction (up *or* down *or* left *or* right). Our technique will work in conjunction with whatever setting you've selected for AutoEntry, or even if you have it turned off entirely. (See Figure 4-23.)

	A	B	C	D	E	F	G
1	Total Sales by Product Line						
2		Jan-97	Feb-97	Mar-97	Apr-97	May-97	Jun-97
3	Product A						
4	Product B						
5	Product C						
6	Product D						
7	Product E						
8	Product F						
9	Total Sales						
10							
11							

Sheet1 Sheet2 Sheet3 Sheet4 Sheet5 She

Figure 4-23: SuperAutoEntry

In this example, you are entering numbers into a table, and we'll assume the AutoEntry setting is unchecked (turned off), as this gives you the greatest flexibility. The trick is to first select the data entry range as shown in Figure 4-23. If you normally like to enter data moving down a column, just key in your entry and hit the `Enter` key. The active cell is automatically moved to the next cell down the column. Make no entry and hit `Enter` to skip a cell. Every time you hit `Enter`, the active cell jumps down one cell. If you have to go back and correct something hold down the `Shift` key and press `Enter`. The active cell jumps up one cell. When the active cell reaches the last cell in the column and you hit `Enter`, the active cell jumps up to the top of the next column.

If you want to edit a cell that has content, you can either rekey the data and hit `Enter` to replace the content, or you can hit the `F2` function key, which lets you edit the contents of the active cell.

If you'd rather enter your data by row, just hit the `Tab` key instead of `Enter`, and the active cell jumps one cell to the right. To go back (left), use `SHIFT+TAB`.

The keys supported by SuperAutoEntry are shown in Table 4-2.

Table 4-2: SuperAutoEntry Keys

SuperAutoEntry Key	Moves the Active Cell Through a Selection
`ENTER`	Down by columns
`SHIFT+ENTER`	Up by columns
`TAB`	Across (left to right) by rows
`SHIFT+TAB`	Across (right to left) by rows

AutoFill

This feature can save you from untold annoyances when entering data into worksheets. It was built on the foundation of the old Data Series command from versions past. The Series dialog box (Edit ➤ Fill ➤ Series) lets you enter a series of values in a selected range. You can set the value to increment the series by (the Step value), and you can enter a value to stop at (the Stop value).

While the Series command still has its uses in Excel, this command really sings when it comes to entering data in a worksheet.

First, make sure the Tools ➤ Options ➤ Edit, "Allow cell drag and drop" check box is checked. Without this option being turned on, AutoFill is completely disabled.

AutoFill is used to quickly enter data into rows and columns.

In Figure 4-24 you can see the process of AutoFill using the fill handle. The value 100 was entered into cell A1. The mouse is positioned over the small square black box in the active cell's lower right-hand corner where

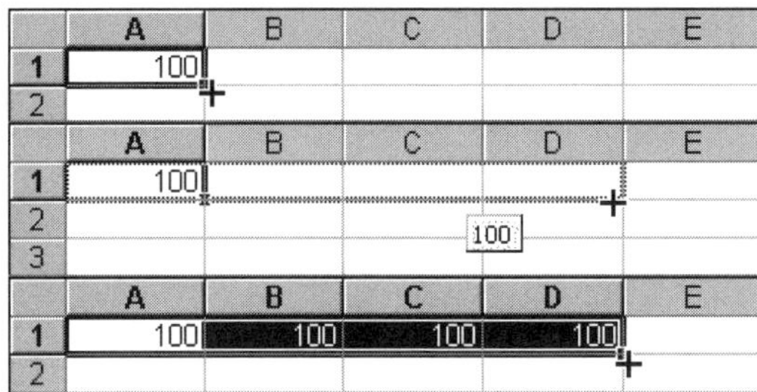

Figure 4-24: The amazing fill handle

it mutates into the fill handle pointer. Drag using the left mouse button, and you can extend and fill the entry in A1 into each cell in the range B1:D1.

Stepping the AutoFill

If you want to increment the values being filled, you can hold down the `Ctrl` key as you do your drag. The fill handle pointer gets a small plus sign appended to it to indicate that the values will be stepped as you drag. `Ctrl`+drag to the right (or down), and each cell's value will be incremented, in this case by one. Go up or to the left, and the value will decrement by one. As you drag, you get a visual indication of what value you are at. (See Figure 4-25.)

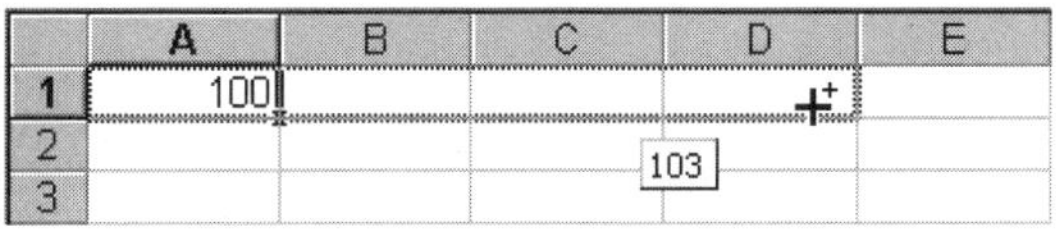

Figure 4-25: Stepping out with the fill handle

You can control the step value by simply entering two or more values and selecting them before you drag the fill handle. Using this method, you do not need to hold down the `Ctrl` key. The step value is calculated from the difference between the selected values. If you include a blank cell in your selection, the blank will be included in the fill. In Figure 4-26, for instance, cells A1:C1 were selected and AutoFill was used to extend the series out to F1.

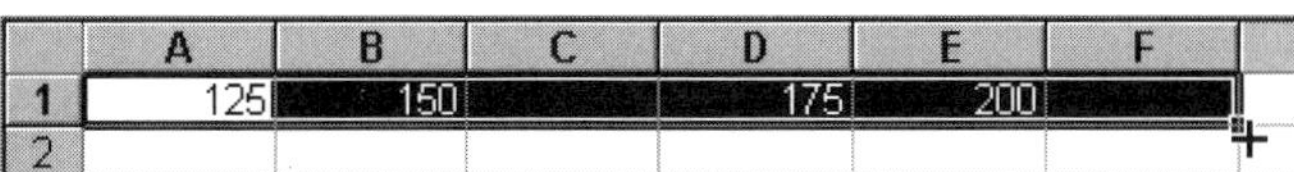

Figure 4-26: Stepping with a blank cell in the selection

You can, oddly enough, force the AutoFill *not* to increment or step when you have made a selection like this by holding down the `Ctrl` key. That can be very annoying if you are in the habit of using it to increment single values.

The AutoFill is very smart in that if you have labels with both text and numbers in them, the text remains static and the values step. Consider Figure 4-27. The labels in row 1 were entered manually and selected. Then the fill handle was dragged down to row 5. Notice that not only did the values step (without the use of the `Ctrl` key), but the ordinals in column C changed appropriately even to the extent of reverting back to the 1st Qtr on row 5. Pretty smart indeed.

	B	C	D
1	Year 1	1st Qtr	Rogue 5
2	Year 2	2nd Qtr	Rogue 6
3	Year 3	3rd Qtr	Rogue 7
4	Year 4	4th Qtr	Rogue 8
5	Year 5	1st Qtr	Rogue 9
6			

Figure 4-27: Stepping mixed labels

Enter **`Year 1997`** and **`Year 1999`** in adjacent cells, select both, and drag the fill handle and you'll get a two year step as you would expect. But there is one thing that's pretty annoying: say you have the values in cells A1:A4. You select them and, holding down the `Ctrl` key, you drag the fill handle to the right. Nothing steps. You just get the same values in column A entered in the range you drag across. We'll show you how to work around this annoyance by using the AutoFill shortcut menu in just a bit.

Custom list magic

AutoFill is the magic behind being able to enter a day of the week in a cell, drag the fill handle, and have the days increment. There is a gizmo called "Custom Lists," and the days of the week and months of the year (in spelled out and abbreviated forms) have already been entered into them. You can create your own custom lists very easily. Click Tools ➤ Options, and select the Custom Lists tab. (See Figure 4-28.)

In the Custom Lists tab, select the NEW LIST item, then just click in the "List entries" list box and type in your list, separating each item by hitting the Enter key, or select an existing series from a worksheet and click on Import. Then click on Add and you're done. Oh, while the dialog box calls this a custom list, you won't find anything listed in the Help file under that term; you have to look up "Custom fill series." Custom lists are

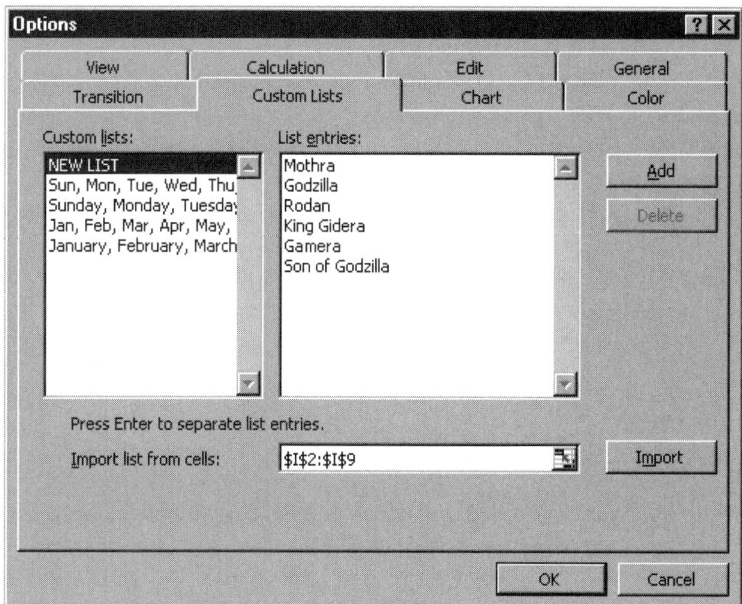

Figure 4-28: Creating a custom monster list

stored along with toolbar customizations in the *username8.xlb* file, which usually resides in the *C:\Windows* folder.

Tricks with the double-click

If you double-click on the fill handle of a non-blank cell, any of several things may happen depending on the contents of the adjacent columns. Consider Figure 4-29.

	G	H	I
2	Monday	1	100
3	Tuesday	5	110
4	Wednesday		120
5	Thursday		130
6			140
7			150
8			160

Figure 4-29: Automating the AutoFill

In this example, if you double-click the fill handle of the current selection (H2:H3), you'll get an AutoFill extending down to row 5, the last row containing a value in column G, with a step value of 4. But if column G, the column to the left of the fill column, were empty, then double-clicking on the fill handle would extend the series to row 8, the last row on which column I has contents. If neither the column to the left nor right of the fill column had contents, you could click on the fill handle all day and nothing would happen.

Be careful with this technique, because when the series is extended, it has the annoying habit of overwriting any cell contents that may be in the cells being filled. No warning, just blip! and your cells are overwritten.

Double-clicking on a fill handle automatically extends a selection:

- If the column to the left of the selection has contents, the selection is extended down to a row even with the last cell with contents in the column on the left.
- If the column to the left does not have contents and the column to the right of the selection has contents, the selection is extended down to a row even with the last cell with contents in the column on the right.
- If neither the column to the left nor right of the selection has contents, the selection is not extended.

AutoFill shortcut menu

The AutoFill techniques work fine for most data input needs, but there is one more trick that gives you maximum flexibility and control over your fills. It is simple, and you may decide to use this method to the exclusion of the others we've discussed.

Use the right mouse button when you drag the fill handle. That's all there is to it.

When you right-click-and-drag the fill handle, you get the shortcut menu shown in Figure 4-30. From this menu, you get all of the options we've discussed so far and then some. You can copy, fill a series (stepping), just copy the cell formats, or fill the values (fill without stepping). If you have a numeric value selected that has been formatted as a date, the fill days, weekdays, months, and years options become available. You also have access to linear or growth trends. Finally, if none of the other options are adequate for your needs, you can pop up the Series dialog box itself, as shown in Figure 4-31.

Data Validation

You carefully craft your spreadsheet, checking the formulas and clearly labeling the input areas. Then you distribute it to your department, and someone immediately renders your work useless by entering invalid data hither and yon with wild abandon. Text where values should go, numbers

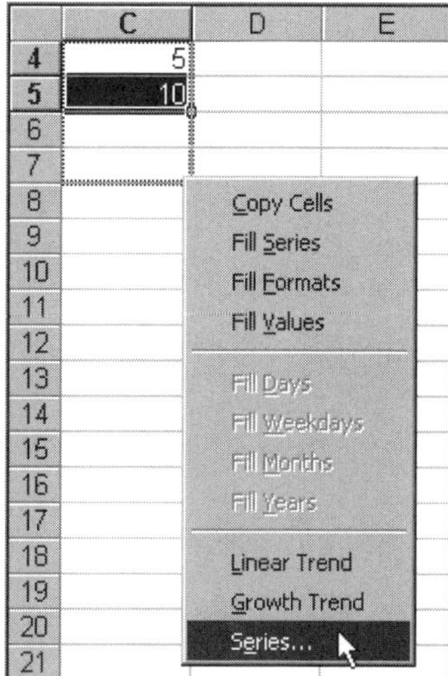

Figure 4-30: The powerful AutoFill shortcut menu

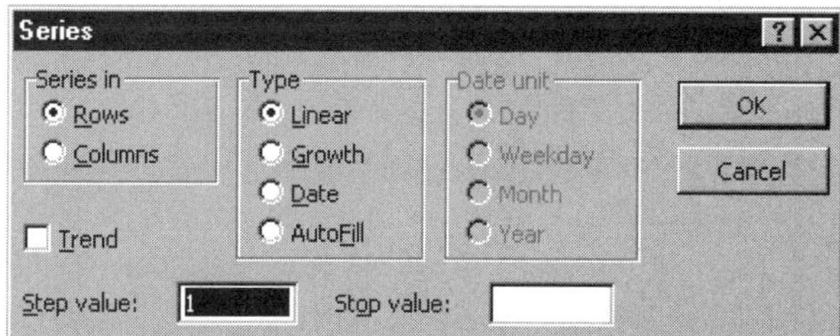

Figure 4-31: The Series dialog box

where you expect to be grabbing text to concatenate, zeros where you need to have divisors, thereby making your sheet break out with #DIV/0 errors like it had the measles. Talk about annoyances! Fear not.

Along with the methods discussed for getting data into your worksheets, Excel 97 provides some industrial strength tools to ensure that the data you want is the data you get.

For the first time, you can establish validation rules for entries made into specific cells in your worksheet. Select the target cells—from a single cell to an entire range—and then choose Validation from the Data menu. Excel 97 displays the Data Validation dialog shown in Figure 4-32.

You get fairly wide-ranging control over the type of data that a cell will accept. You can indicate, for instance, that whole numbers, decimals, and dates should lie within a specified start and end range, or you can restrict the length of a text entry to a minimum or maximum length, to name just a few of the dialog's options and features. If you started off with a range

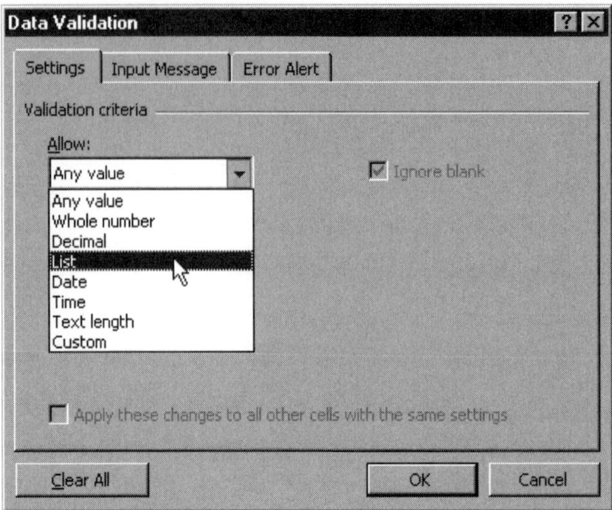

Figure 4-32: Setting up validation rules for data entry

selected, any rules you establish are applied to each cell within the range when you click OK.

This technique of adding validation rules is so important to ensuring a spreadsheet's integrity that you really should fully explore this feature. Once you have established validation on a cell, you can copy that cell and then do a Paste Special on a destination cell to paste just the validation rules. This makes applying existing rules to new cells and ranges of cells very easy.

You can also set up an Input Message—sort of like a custom cell tip—that pops up when the target cell is selected. This is massively useful, since you can create an Input Message for a cell whether you validate any information or not. This lets you have instructional messages appear whenever certain cells are activated.

One of the best methods of validating data is to allow the user to choose from a predefined set of values; this is precisely what an interface object like a drop-down list box does. Excel 97 allows you to create such a list box without using a form or an external control. The List validation shown in Figure 4-33 warrants a bit of discussion. You create a list of valid entries on a sheet. Select the List choice in the Allow drop-down list box in the Data Validation dialog. Then click in the source box and highlight the valid entries in your worksheet. Click OK. There is now a drop-down list associated with the target cell that only appears when that cell is selected. Very nifty indeed. Well, perhaps one minor annoyance—you can't pick a default value. If the user does not make a selection, the cell is blank.

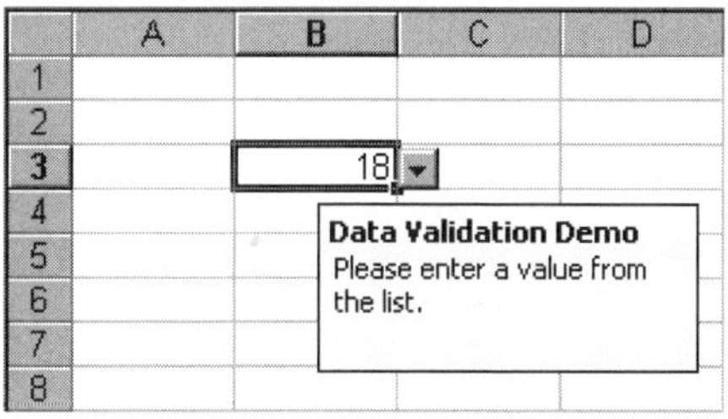

Figure 4-33: Pop up instructions when a validated cell is selected

Last but not least, you can create your own error alert message that gets displayed when an attempt is made to enter a value outside of the specified parameters, as Figure 4-34 shows. You can control the dialog's icon, caption, and message text by providing the appropriate information in the Error Alert tab of the Data Validation dialog.

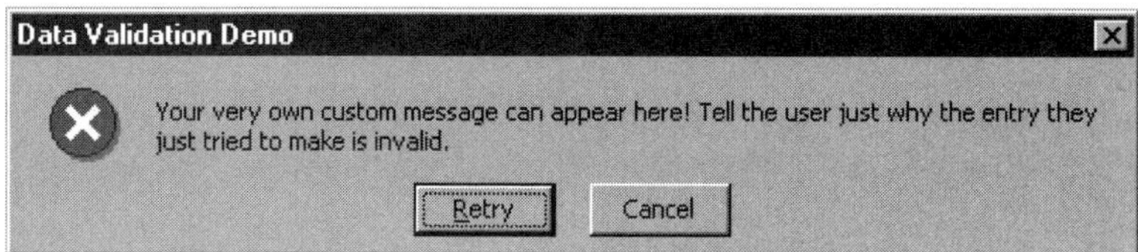

Figure 4-34: Your message here

One minor annoyance is that once you have associated validation rules with a cell, you don't have any visual clue that you've done so unless you select the cell and see that it has an Input Message. What you can do is pull up the Go To dialog box (press the F5 function key) and click the Special button. In the next dialog box, click the "Data validation" button and then the OK button. All cells with rules will then appear as a noncontiguous selection on the sheet. Use the `Tab` key to cycle through all the selected cells.

We'll talk more about the Go To Special dialog when we discuss auditing techniques in Chapter 6, *Excel Strategies*.

The Editing Room

Not all of your work involves entering nice new data into crisp shiny worksheets. Often you work and rework existing worksheets that are already chock full of data. Or you create your worksheet and then decide that you need to redesign it. This brings us to editing extant data, moving and copying cells already full to the brim with contents. And therein lies the rub, or at least a few annoyances.

Clearing and deleting

Because this is a confusing topic that can have profound impact on your models, let's nail down the difference between deleting a cell and clearing a cell. Without an understanding of the difference, someone meaning to clear a cell could delete it instead and instantly wreck a model by shifting all the rows or columns out of alignment.

When you select a cell with contents and hit the `Delete` key on your computer's keyboard, you are *not* deleting the cell. You are clearing the cell. You are only clearing the cell's contents; any formatting or comments remain unscathed. To get the full range of choices for the things you can clear from a cell, you need to go to the Edit menu and select the Clear option (see Figure 4-35).

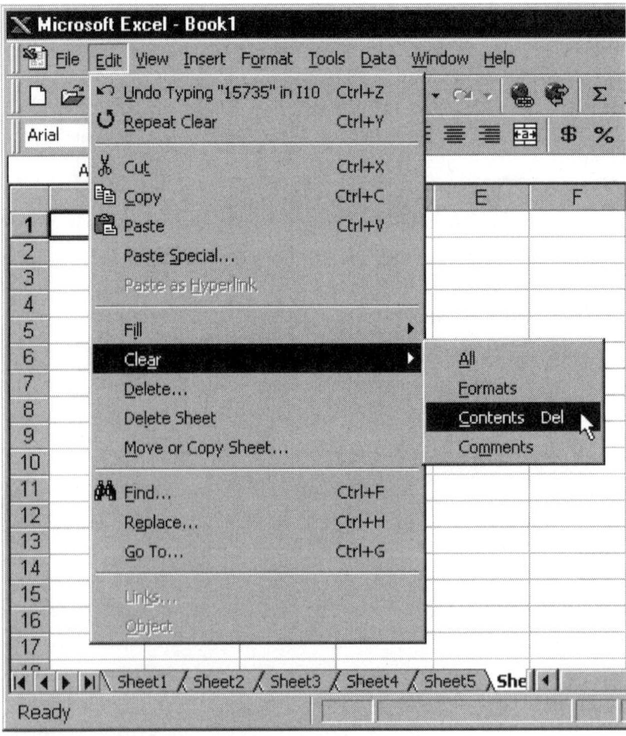

Figure 4-35: Edit ➤ Clear's cascading menu

You can clear comments from a cell, the cell's contents (this is the default you get via your keyboard `Delete` key), any formats that have been applied to a cell, or all of the items just mentioned. You can also clear contents from the shortcut menu that appears when right-clicking on a cell or range.

Deleting is an entirely different kettle of fish. Deleting a cell is the equivalent of punching that cell right out of the matrix and shifting all cells to the right of the deleted cell left or all cells below the deleted cell up. You can perform a true delete from the Delete option on the Edit menu or the cell shortcut menu.

When you click on the Delete option, you have to tell Excel if you want to shift cells up or left (see Figure 4-36). This is because you cannot have a worksheet in any shape other than a table containing 256 columns and 65,536 rows. Every cell shifts and a new empty cell is magically created from the void and is added to column IV or down at the last row in the sheet. The same principle applies to the deletion of entire rows or columns.

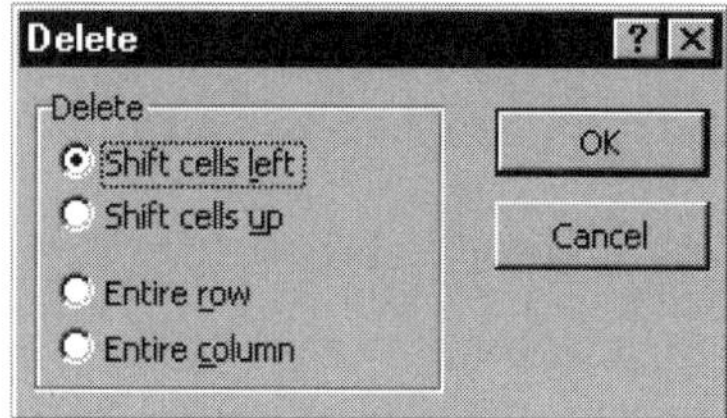

Figure 4-36: Deleting cells, rows, and columns

As you might imagine, shifting every cell below or to the right of a cell that you are deleting can have a profound effect on your model. You must exercise caution that such a shift does not play hell with your model and its reported results.

Rearranging data the old way

There are two ways to take some cells with contents from *here* and put that content or the cells themselves over *there*.

First, there is the traditional cut-and-paste technique that you've probably used for years. You select some cells, choose Copy (if you are looking to copy the data) or Cut (if you are looking to move the data), select the target cell or range, then choose Paste. You can access these commands from the toolbar or from the Edit menu or the cell shortcut menu.

Excel's implementation of Cut, Copy, and Paste is exceedingly annoying because it's completely contrary to the way almost every other Windows program ever written works. The clipboard is a temporary repository of whatever was last cut or copied from your current application, so you can fuss around and when you're ready you can paste the contents of the clipboard into your application. But Excel clears the clipboard at the conclusion of the Paste operation.

NOTE A word of caution when using Cut, Copy, Paste, and especially Paste Special in Excel. When you cut or copy, Excel puts a marquee (the marching ants) around the range you have placed on the clipboard. You can select your destination and perform Paste. If you paste by hitting the `Enter` key, no problem. The contents of the clipboard are pasted and the clipboard is cleared. But if you paste via any other method (paste button, shortcut menu, etc.) the clipboard is not cleared, and if you then hit the `Enter` key, the clipboard is dumped to the active cell. Get in the habit of hitting the `Escape` key after a cut, copy, or paste operation to clear the clipboard and end the operation.

You can get even more mileage with Cut and Paste in Excel if you avail yourself of the Paste Special command. You can initiate a Paste Special from the Edit menu or from the cell pop-up menu. (See Figure 4-37.)

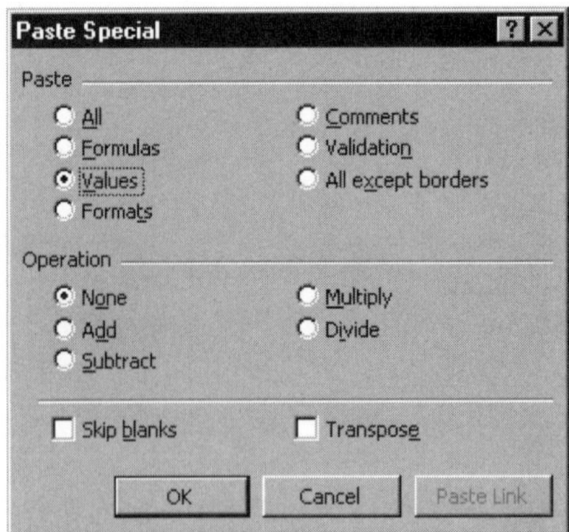

Figure 4-37: The Paste Special dialog box

You can use this dialog box to paste just a formula (sans formatting) or the value of a cell instead of the formula it might contain. The Paste Values option is one of our favorites. You set up a column, use a formula to do some interim calculations, copy the range, and paste it back on itself with Paste Special Values. You get the values as constants and not formulas.

You can also perform operations where, for example, you might copy some constants and have them added to the constants in the destination cells. This dialog is also where you go to copy data validation rules between cells, as we discussed earlier.

NOTE While the mouse techniques we're going to cover in the next few sections have their application, if you are going across sheets or across workbooks, you might want to use the old tried-and-true Cut, Copy, and Paste from the Edit menu or the toolbar buttons. As often as not, the time spent arranging sheets and workbooks to allow using a mouse to drag-and-drop negates the time saved.

Drag-and-drop mouse tricks

When you are working with data that you need to quickly move or copy from one area on your sheet to another, and these areas are reasonably close by, the mouse is your best tool.

Start by selecting a cell or contiguous range of cells, and touch the mouse pointer to any edge of the selection (except the fill handle). The mouse pointer will change from the selection cross hair to the northwest mouse pointer shape when you are right on the selection edge. With this pointer, you can click and hold down the left mouse button and drag the selection to a new location (see Figure 4-38). Notice that the destination coordinates are shown on-screen as you drag the selection.

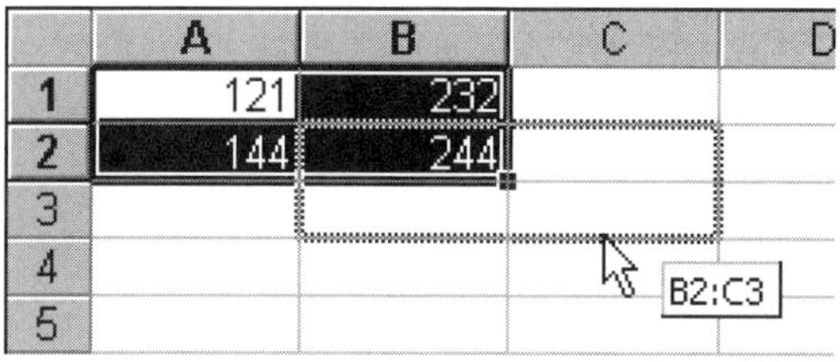

Figure 4-38: Dragging a selection with the mouse

When you release the mouse button, the selected cells are moved to the new coordinates. Most users are first introduced to this technique accidentally when they have a selection and are trying to select a different range. The mouse touches a selection edge and before they know it, they've moved the original selection and are wondering why Excel hates them. This technique is the equivalent of a cut-and-paste operation.

If you hold down the `Ctrl` key while you perform the drag-and-drop in Excel, you will copy the cells instead of move them. The northwest pointer takes on the little plus symbol denoting that you are now doing a copy operation.

NOTE A word of caution to all the Word users out there: in Word, when you drag-and-drop selected text *with the mouse,* the clipboard is bypassed. This is handy because anything you have captured to the clipboard stays there even though you are moving text around in your Word document (and in most Windows applications in general). But in Excel, when you drag-and-drop with the mouse, Excel runs the selected content through the clipboard and the clipboard is cleared at the end of the operation. You can't rely on any content remaining on the clipboard.

Hold down the `Shift` key when you do a drag-and-drop, and when you release the mouse button, Excel performs an insert paste as opposed to a plain paste. This inserts your selection at the drop point, pushing cells down or right. (See Figure 4-39.)

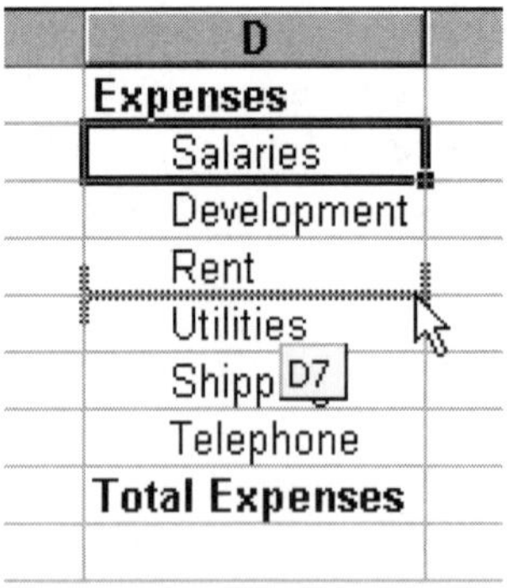

Figure 4-39: Drag-and-drop with the Shift key down

Excel displays a gray indicator showing you where the data will be inserted and what the destination address will be. In this example, all the entries shift to accommodate the new location of the Salaries label. If you have data all the way out at the end of the column (or row), this technique won't work, since Excel will never shift data off the worksheet and into the void.

Hold down both the `Ctrl` and the `Shift` keys when you drag-and-drop, and you'll get a copy operation combined with an insert paste.

Now all you have to do is memorize which key does what when you do a drag-and-drop on your sheet with the mouse, right? Well, you certainly can if you want to. Table 4-3 summarizes the different combinations.

Table 4-3: Drag-and-Drop Keyboard Combos

Drag-and-drop with this key combination	Performs this operation
`CTRL` key	Copies the contents of the source range to the destination cell(s). Dropping on a cell(s) with contents overwrites the destination cell(s).
`SHIFT` key	Performs a cut operation on the source cell(s) and an insert paste (Insert ➤ Cut Cells from the menus) operation on the destination cell(s).
`CTRL+SHIFT`	Performs a copy operation on the source cell(s) and an insert paste (Insert ➤ Copied Cells from the menus) operation on the destination cell(s).

There is another technique that gives you the most flexibility and does not require you to memorize any keyboard+mouse combinations.

Just use the right mouse button when you click-and-drag. When you drop the selection, you'll get a pop-up menu that lets you choose from a number of options on how to complete the operation. (See Figure 4-40.) You can decide if you want to move, copy, shift, or not shift cells in the destination range, and you can create links (a formula reference back to the source) or a new hyperlink (a shortcut back to the source).

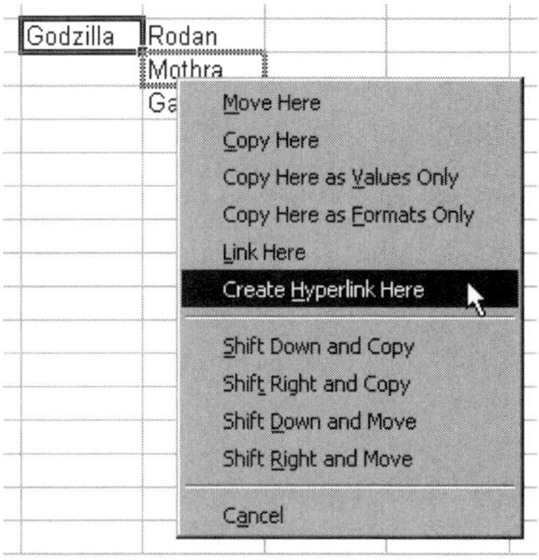

Figure 4-40: The ultimate drag-and-drop choices

If you open the current workbook in a separate window (Window ➤ New Window) and arrange them both on-screen (Window ➤ Arrange All), you can drag-and-drop between different sheets in the same book. Ditto for going between workbooks. Just get both windows displayed on-screen. Annoyingly enough, you can't drag across a split screen in Excel 97; however, you can in Word.

Working with Names, Formulas, and Functions

Formulas are the crux of developing your spreadsheet model. Formulas are the little mini-programs that define the relationships between cells and calculate your results. In your formulas, you can utilize any of over 300 built-in functions that Excel provides. These are preprogrammed calculation engines that you provide information to and that, in turn, return a result.

To lend power and sanity to your formulas, you have the range name in your arsenal of development tools. In this section we'll work through the basics of formula building.

Range Names and Labels

Individual cells or groups of cells can be given text descriptions called *names*—plain English descriptions made up of letters, numbers, periods, and underscore characters. If you are not using names, it's high time you start. Take a look at Figure 4-41.

	B	C	D	E	F
1					
2	Income	500	25	Expense	498
3					
4		500	25	Expense	498
5					
6			=Income		=Expense
7					
8					

Figure 4-41: A study in Excel's natural language names

No cells were explicitly named in this example, yet we can use the names "Income" and "Expenses" in formulas within the sheet. This is because of the new Label feature in Excel 97 that lets you use what the Redmond PR machine calls "natural language" in your formulas. That's a new moniker for an old concept, the named range. But in this case it's Excel that is assigning the names automatically. Here's how it works.

Excel uses whatever labels are handy and applies those names to the appropriate rows and columns. The formulas in cells C4, D4, and E4 are all identical: `=Income`. Excel has applied the name "Income" to cells C2:E2. You won't find a named range if you look in the Insert ➤ Name ➤ Define or in the Go To dialog, but you can use the name in a formula just the same. So the `=Income` in C4 returns 500, the value from cell C2.

D4 returns the value 25, which it reads from cell D2; the formula in E4 returns the string "Expense," the value from cell E2. Columns are also affected. If there were no value in C2 but you had a value in B4, the formula in C4 would return the value from B4. On row 2, the Income name stops where the Expense label appears in column E row 2. The formula in F4 then, `=Expense`, returns 498 from row 2.

Confusing? More like annoying. The names that Excel is assigning don't show up in the defined names list, so you can't check what name refers to which range. Overall, it's nice of Excel to go to all this trouble, but we strongly recommend you explicitly name your ranges so this issue of "What cell will it return, the row or the column?" does not arise.

In Figure 4-42, cell C2 has been named Income (Insert ➤ Name ➤ Define) and C3 has been named Expenses. This makes using the names in a formula very straightforward since there is only one cell each name could refer to.

SUM =Income-Expense

	A	B	C	D
1				
2		Income	500	
3		Expenses	498	
4		Net Income	=Income-Expenses	
5				

Figure 4-42: Names created by the user

A name can be up to 255 characters and can be made up of letters, numbers, periods, and the underscore. It must begin with either a letter or underscore and cannot look like an actual cell reference (example: A1 or R1C1). You can use uppercase and lowercase letters to make the name more readable, but case is ignored by Excel (i.e., you can't have Sales and SALES as two different names in the same sheet).

In the rest of the book, we'll use explicitly named ranges.

The Name box

The quickest way to add a named range to a sheet is to select the cell or cells to be named and then click on the Name box. Type the name and press the Enter key. This creates the name and associates it with the selected cell(s). (See Figure 4-43.)

The Name box displays names in alphabetical order. You can't use the Name box to redefine a name, since the box also lets you select or type in a range name, and when you hit `Enter`, that range is automatically selected. This makes it impossible to use the Name box to rename some-

Gizmos = 109

Doohickeys
Gizmos
Qtr.1
Qtr.2
Qtr.3
Qtr.4
Widgets

	B	C	D	E	F
	Division Sales				
		Qtr.1	Qtr.2	Qtr.3	Qtr.4
	ts	98	101	112	75
	ckeys	110	92	98	75
6	Gizmos	109	86	104	79
7	Totals	317	279	314	229
8					

Figure 4-43: Using the Name box

thing, since instead of associating a new range with an existing name, the old range is selected when you press the `Enter` key.

Define names

Pull down the Insert menu, click on Names, and choose Define from the cascading menu. This displays the Define Name dialog box. (See Figure 4-44.)

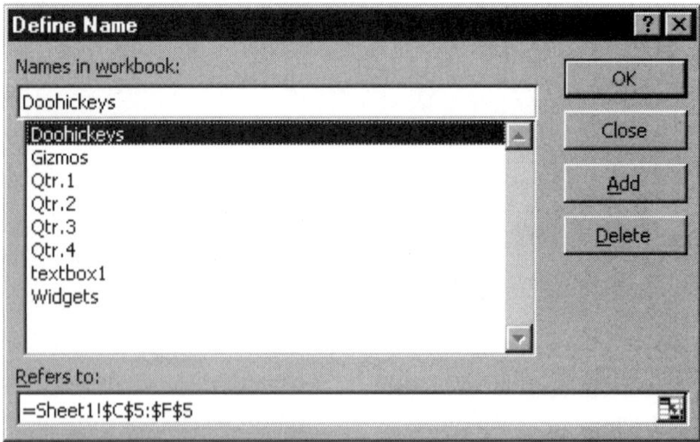

Figure 4-44: The Define Name dialog box

You type in the name, and in the "Refers to" text box you can enter a reference, select one with the mouse, or you can type in a formula. The current selection in the current sheet is the default entry in the "Refers to" box. Click Add if you want to create another name, or OK if you're done. The Delete button deletes the selected name, but there is no warning or confirmation message, so be careful with this command. If you realize your error, you can use the Edit Undo command to restore the name.

One potential annoyance: the "Refers to" text box suffers from a limit of 255 characters, so if you have a very complex set of range coordinates, you might exceed this limit. Excel just truncates your reference without warning, so beware!

Name an entire row or column by just selecting the rows or columns (or both) you want and creating the name. This is how Excel keeps track of print titles, those rows and/or columns that are printed on each page of a report. Excel just takes the coordinates you enter into the Sheet tab of the File ➤ Page Setup dialog, and creates a range name for the current sheet called Print_Titles. There are several names that have special meaning to Excel like Print_Titles, Print_Area, Database, Criteria, Data_Form, Extract, Consolidate_Area, Sheet_Title, and a slew of names beginning with the prefix Auto_ that are used in triggering macros when specific events occur—like opening a particular workbook.

By default, the cell references in the "Refers to" text box are entered in their *absolute* form (note the dollar signs in the cell reference). We'll discuss relative and absolute cell references shortly and revisit their effect on range names at that point.

Create names

Excel has some nice features that make creating names a snap. If you highlight a cell or a range of cells, you can ask Excel to create names for you based on any labels in certain locations within the selection. (See Figure 4-45.)

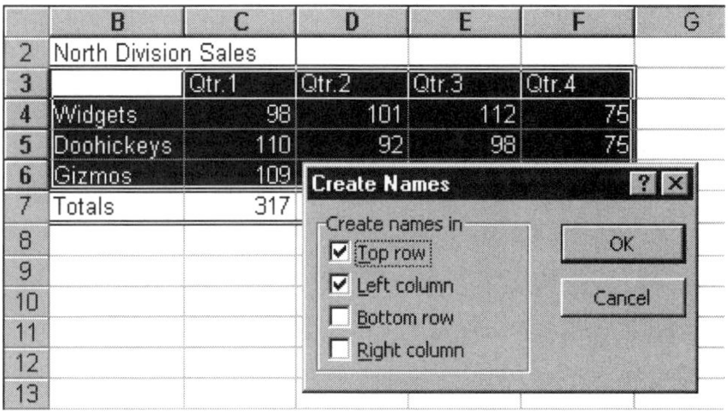

Figure 4-45: Creating names based on text labels

The table in this example was first selected. Then we clicked on Insert ➤ Names ➤ Create and got the dialog box shown in Figure 4-45. Excel has done some guesswork and offers to use the top row and left column as range names for the selected cells. If these defaults are accepted and OK is clicked, the range names shown in Table 4-4 are created.

Note in this case that both column and row ranges were named simultaneously, and that the cells containing the labels are not part of the defined "Refers to" range. Because we knew that Excel does not like spaces or names that begin with numerals, we stacked the deck in our favor by the way we named our columns, i.e., Qtr.1, with the text prefix "Qtr" first, and a period instead of a space between the text and the number.

Table 4-4: Range Names from Figure 4-45

Range Name	Refers to
Widgets	C4:F4
Doohickeys	C5:F5
Gizmos	C6:F6
Qtr.1	C4:C6
Qtr.2	D4:D6
Qtr.3	E4:E6
Qtr.4	F4:F6

Had we used something perhaps more typical, like "1st Qtr," where a number is first and a space is in the label, Excel would have adjusted by changing the label in the associated range name. "1st Qtr" would have become the name "_1st_Qtr" with a leading underscore and an underscore replacing the space. This is actually a good thing, so don't let it annoy you the first time you run into it.

Book-level names

All the examples you've seen so far are book-level names. A book-level name is a defined range that refers to the same range and sheet, no matter which sheet you might reference that name from. Name cell B12 on Sheet1 "Lobster," and no matter what sheet in the workbook you are in when you use the name (say in a formula), you'll get the contents of cell B12 from Sheet1.

A book-level name has a context global to the workbook. From any sheet, Lobster appears in the Name box, and you can use the Name box to jump to that referenced range.

NOTE In the examples where we refer to individual sheets within a workbook, we'll use the default names, Sheet1, Sheet2, etc., but if you rename your sheets, you would just substitute the actual names. This is where a convention mentioned earlier comes into play: that of not using spaces in sheet names. It's a lot easier to use sheet names in formulas and range names if you don't use spaces in the names.

Sheet-level names

A sheet-level name only exists in the context of the sheet on which it is located. If you have a locally defined name on Sheet2 and Sheet1 is the active sheet, the name on Sheet2 will not appear in the Name box at all. But make Sheet2 the active sheet, and the name appears.

You create sheet-level names by preceding the range name with the sheet name. A sheet-level name of Lobster referring to cell B3 on Sheet2 would be named "Sheet2!Lobster." You separate the sheet name from the actual name with an exclamation point (referred to in conversation as a "bang"). Using sheet-level names, you could use the same name on every sheet (and confuse the hell out of yourself and any other poor person who had to work with that workbook). Assume we set up a workbook with the following names:

Name	Physical Location
Lobster	Sheet1, cell B12
Sheet2!Lobster	Sheet2, cell B3

The formula `=Lobster`, entered on any sheet in the workbook *except* Sheet2, would return the value in Sheet1, cell B12 (book-level Lobster). But the same formula on Sheet2 would return the value in cell B3 of that sheet (sheet-level Lobster).

If you wanted to refer to the book-level Lobster on Sheet2, you would have to reference the range name like this (assuming the workbook has the default name of Book1 and has not been saved):

```
=Book1!Lobster
```

This would return the value in Sheet1, cell B12, even though there is a local sheet-level reference to Lobster. If the workbook had been saved under the name "Crustaceans," you would need to include the filename, `=Crustaceans.xls!Lobster`.

To reference the sheet-level name, Lobster, on any sheet *other* than Sheet2, you would just include the sheet name:

```
=Sheet2!Lobster
```

That said, take our advice and don't duplicate names for both book-level and sheet-level names. In fact, consider carefully if you really need to use sheet-level names at all.

3-D names

A 3-D (three-dimensional) name is a range name where the range spans more than one sheet. The selected cell(s) must be the same for all of the sheets to be included in the range name.

You must use the Define Name dialog box to create a 3-D name, and they only appear here as well. You won't see a 3-D name in the Name box or the Go To dialog. To create a 3-D name, do the following:

1. Open the Define Name dialog box and enter the name **`Snout`**.
2. Select the contents in the "Refers to" text box and type an equal sign (**=**).
3. Now, click on the tab of the first sheet to be included in the reference.
4. Hold down the `Shift` key and click on the last sheet (sheets must be contiguous).
5. Select the cells in the active sheet to be named.
6. Click on Add or OK.

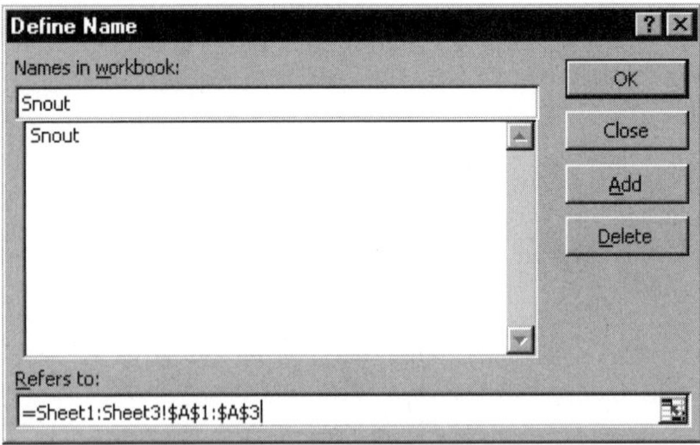

Figure 4-46: Creating a 3-D range name

You could, of course, just type in the correct range reference in the "Refers to" box yourself and not bother with selecting the sheets and ranges with the mouse.

In our example, creating a formula like `=SUM(Snout)` returns the sum of all values in cells A1, A2, and A3 on Sheet1, Sheet2, and Sheet3. (See Figure 4-46.)

How Cut, Copy, and Sort affect names

There are some aspects of naming cells that you have to be aware of, or your annoyance level will skyrocket.

First, remember that you are naming a cell and not that cell's contents. Adding or deleting cells, rows, and columns—in effect, any operation that shifts the physical location of cells around—causes the range names to shift as well. The exception to this rule is 3-D names. The 3-D named range on any local sheet doesn't shift when you add or delete cells, causing the cells in the sheet to shift around in relation to the named range. If a particular value in cell B5 is part of a 3-D reference and you delete row 1 on that sheet, the value in B5 shifts up one row. B6 is now B5 and this new B5 value becomes part of your 3-D reference.

If you copy a cell, you are copying the cell's contents, not the range name associated with it. But *move* the cell, and you are moving the cell itself, and the range name follows along (the caveat for 3-D names applies here as well).

Things get really annoying when working with sheet-level names. Follow us through this example. You create a sheet-level name on Sheet1 in cell B3 named "ImLost." Enter a value in B3 then cut the cell to the clipboard. Switch to Sheet2, cell D5 in the same workbook and paste. You now have a sheet-level name on Sheet1 that refers to a cell on Sheet2. On Sheet1 the formula `=ImLost` returns the value from Sheet2 cell D5. Pull down the Name box on Sheet1, click on ImLost and you'll jump to Sheet2, cell D5. But enter the formula `=ImLost` on Sheet2, and you'll get a #NAME error since no sheet other than Sheet1 groks the range name. Be careful or be annoyed.

Using names

Using names in your spreadsheet models is like eating peanuts. Once you start, it's difficult to stop, and that's a good thing. You do have to be mindful of typos when entering names into your formulas, and Excel gives you the Paste Name dialog to eliminate that major annoyance.

You can pop-up the Paste Name dialog via the toolbar button we added earlier or by clicking on the Insert menu, choosing the Names option, then the Paste option on the cascading menu. (See Figure 4-47.)

This is most useful when you are building formulas. While entering or editing a formula, just pop up the Paste Name dialog box, select the name you want, and click OK. The name is dropped right into your formula without any chance of a typographical error.

The names appearing in the Paste Name dialog box are all the book-level names and any sheet-level names on the active sheet. To paste a sheet-level name from another sheet, just start entering/editing the formula,

Figure 4-47: Avoid typos when entering range names

switch to the sheet with the local sheet-level name you want, pop up the Paste Name dialog, and paste the local name.

To get a list of all names in the current book (and any sheet level names for the active sheet), select an empty area of the sheet, pop up the Paste Name dialog box, and click on Paste List. This creates a two-column list with the names on the left and the corresponding cell coordinates on the right. Beware that this operation overwrites any cells that are in the way with no warning whatsoever.

You can also substitute range names for cell references in existing formulas. (See Figure 4-48.)

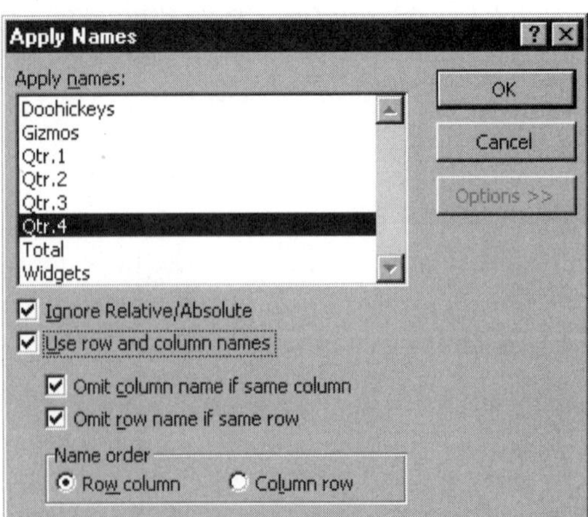

Figure 4-48: Applying names to existing cell references in formulas

Select a single name in the list, and wherever a cell reference in a formula matches the coordinates of a named range, the name replaces the cell reference in the formula. This list is multi-selectable, so you can select the names you want applied. Don't select any, and they're all applied. The "Use row and column names" check box allows Excel to use implied intersection (discussed in detail later) where an explicit name for a given cell is not available. The Omit options also allow the use of implied intersection instead of having to include a column or row name where the formula cell is the same column or row as the cell being referenced. The Name order tells Excel whether to use the row name or the column name (this does not affect the results of the formula, just the order of the names).

Formulas as names

Excel lets you enter a formula or a constant as the content of a range name. Think of this as naming a constant that you can use anywhere in your workbook. This has several applications, the most common being where you want to use a constant or a formula throughout a workbook, but don't want them explicitly entered into a sheet.

Just pop up the Define name dialog and enter a name like "Overhead." In the "Refers to" box type in your constant, say `=3%`. Then in your worksheet you could create a formula that utilizes the name Overhead:

```
=14000*(1+Overhead)
```

This would return 14,420. Names like this (Overhead) do not appear in the Name box or in the Go To dialog since they do not represent physical locations on a sheet that can be jumped to.

Named formulas can be quite complex (limited primarily by the 255 character limitation of the text box you have to enter them into) and can reference other named formulas or named ranges or cell references on the various sheets in the workbook.

Formulas and Functions

Now that you're thoroughly grounded on names, we can take on formulas and functions at the cellular level. This is where you actually program your spreadsheet model and automate the calculations that it will perform when it updates.

Formulas are limited to 1,024 characters, so in some circumstances you may need to break up a calculation into several smaller parts, run each in a different cell, and reference these in a summarizing formula. But all in all, there are few annoying things about Excel's implementation of formulas. And Excel now traps some of the more common formula entry errors automatically with a feature called AutoCorrect (what else?)—things like using a semicolon where a colon should be used for a range separator, beginning a formula with two equal signs, etc. Very nice.

Absolute vs. relative addresses

Cell references, or range names for that matter, can be either absolute, relative, or mixed (a combination of both absolute and relative references), and you'll never get out of the minor leagues of spreadsheet building until you are completely comfortable with the difference between these terms.

A1 is a relative address. $A$1 is an absolute address.

What's the difference? An absolute address only refers to a given cell; in this case $A$1 only refers to the cell that is at the intersection of column A and row 1. Type this reference into any cell you want, copy it to any other cell, and you'll always get column A, row 1.

But A1 is a horse of a different color. Type `=A1` into a cell on a worksheet. Now copy it one cell to the right of the cell you entered the formula into originally. Is the formula still `=A1`? No, it isn't. It now reads `=B1`. The cell reference changed *relative* to the new location of the formula. You moved the formula one cell to the right so it now references the cell one cell to the right of the original reference.

Annoying? No, definitely not. This is by design, and it enables many of the wonderful things we use spreadsheets for. You have columns of numbers, you create a formula adding up the first column, and you use the fill handle to drag and copy that formula across the bottom of the other columns. The formula changes (well, it *appears* to change) so that each column is totaled, courtesy of relative referencing.

To understand what's going on and why a dollar sign denotes an absolute reference, you have to realize that this business of having column letters is just an elaborate fiction. Excel thinks in terms of row and column *numbers*! Let's see how this works by changing the reference style to R1C1:

1. In cell B2 enter `=A1`.
2. In cell B3 enter `=$A$1`.
3. Now, from the Tools menu click on Options.
4. In the General tab, check the "Reference style" check box.
5. Click on OK.

Your formulas should now look like Figure 4-49.

The first thing you notice is that the columns are now numbered, not lettered. This is how Excel really thinks, in terms of both row numbers *and* column numbers. The formula in cell R2C2 (that's B2 in the old nota-

R3C2 = =R1C1

	1	2
1		
2		=R[-1]C[-1]
3		=R1C1
4		

Figure 4-49: The difference between relative and absolute

tion) looks pretty odd until you get comfortable with this type of notation. Reading the formula from left to right it says: "*From this cell up one row, from that cell one column to the left.*"

NOTE In this section we're more concerned with the formulas in the cells than with the result of the formulas. The result is what Excel displays by default. But you can do what we call *flipping* the sheet, making the formulas be displayed in the cells instead of their result. Hold down the `Ctrl` key and press the back apostrophe key (`). To flip it back, just press this key combo again.

R stands for row, C for column, and numbers in brackets tell you what direction and how far to travel to find the referenced cell. The minus sign means up or left. Positive numbers mean down or right. Easy.

The formula in cell R3C2 is an absolute reference. It refers to the intersection of row 1, column 1. That intersection never changes no matter where you copy this formula.

Here's another example. Switch the notation back to A1 notation. Then enter the formula `=B6+B7` in your worksheet into cell B8. Now, use the fill handle to copy this formula to C8 and D8. Your formulas look like those in Figure 4-50.

B	C	D
=B6+B7	=C6+C7	=D6+D7

Figure 4-50: Adding the two cells above, in A1 referencing

The individual formulas changed (well, they *appeared* to have changed) as you copied them into the adjacent cells. This is because the original formula was entered using relative references. This type of reference is meaningful only in the context of the relative positions of the cells. In this case all three formulas are identical. They look different, but they are all identical to Excel. To see this, just flip the R1C1 notation style back on. (See Figure 4-51.)

2	3	4
=R[-2]C+R[-1]C	=R[-2]C+R[-1]C	=R[-2]C+R[-1]C

Figure 4-51: Same formula adding the two cells above only in R1C1 notation

Each formula is identical, as we said. Each formula says, in effect, "*Start from this cell and go up two rows but stay in this column, and add that value to the value in the cell up one row from this cell, in this same column.*" And each formula says exactly the same thing. Drag any of the formulas to any spot on the sheet, and it will try to add the two cells directly above the current cell. If you try to reference a cell location that is off the sheet (say, by copying this formula up to row 1), you'll get a #REF! error.

An absolute reference in R1C1 notation style is quite simple. Just the R(ow) and C(olumn) coordinates. No brackets.

You can create a mixed formula that contains both absolute and relative references:

```
=R1C[3]
```

This formula refers to row 1 (absolute) and three columns to the right relative to the cell containing the reference. Flip back into A1 notation and you get something like this:

```
=E$1
```

The column reference (E) is relative. The row number $1 is absolute. The dollar sign denotes absolute referencing in the A1 style.

If you really want to get a feel for what formulas are all about, turn on the R1C1 reference style for a month or so. You may never turn it off.

Relative range names

By default, range names are created as absolute references. This is as it should be. But you can do some nifty stuff with relative range names. Try this:

1. Select cell A4.
2. Create the name ThreeCellsUp (Insert ➤ Name ➤ Define).

3. Use the Tab key to select the "Refers to" box (the contents of that box must be highlighted).
4. Use the mouse to select A1 in the current sheet and click-and-drag down to cell A3.
5. Press the F2 function key. This lets you edit the formula in the "Refers to" box.
6. Delete the dollar signs, thereby making the reference relative.

You can then use this range name in a formula. (See Figure 4-52.)

SUM =SUM(ThreeCellsUp)

	A	B	C	D	E	F
1	North Division Sales					
2		Qtr.1	Qtr.2	Qtr.3	Qtr.4	Total
3	Widgets	98	101	112	75	386
4	Doohickeys	110	92	98	75	375
5	Gizmos	109	86	104	79	378
6	Totals	=SUM(ThreeCellsUp)		314	229	1139
7						

Figure 4-52: Relative range name in a formula

The ThreeCellsUp range name refers to the three cells directly up from the relative position of the cell containing the reference.

Range Finder

Excel provides some excellent tools to make building and maintaining formulas a snap. New in Excel 97 is the Range Finder. The Range Finder is a feature that visually displays the cells being referenced by a formula when the formula is being edited.

Range Finder assigns each reference in a formula a color and then outlines the referenced cells in the same color. In the formula shown in Figure 4-53, the reference B6 is blue and that cell is bordered in blue on the sheet. C6 is in green, and E3 is in purple. To edit a formula just select the cell and hit the F2 function key, or double-click on the cell.

	A	B	C	D	E
1	North Division Sales				
2		Qtr.1	Qtr.2		
3	Widgets	98	101	COGS per unit	$3.98
4	Doohickeys	110	92		
5	Gizmos	109	86	Total COGS	=B6+C6*E3
6	Totals	317	279		
7					

Figure 4-53: Range Finder in action

The Formula Palette

Formulas in Excel always begin with an equal sign (=). Start a formula by selecting a cell and pressing the equal sign key or by clicking on the equal symbol located on the Formula Palette. The Formula Palette is also a new feature in Excel 97. This feature is primarily designed to help you enter functions into your formulas, but it offers numerous features for formula construction.

In Figure 4-54, the equal symbol at the left of the formula bar was clicked and a simple formula was entered, one that adds the values in two cells. The formula bar is modeless, meaning you can have it active and still click on cells, pull down menus, switch workbooks or applications, etc. Cell B6 in the active sheet was selected, the plus symbol was typed, and cell C6 was clicked on.

Figure 4-54: Clicking on the equal symbol activates the Formula Palette

The Palette displays the result of the formula at this point (Formula result = 596), a Help button on the left, and an OK and Cancel button on the right. Click on the OK button (or the little checkmark symbol to the left of the equal symbol), and the formula is entered into the active cell. Click on the Cancel button (or on the X next to the checkmark symbol), and the formula is discarded and no changes are made.

Excel has over 300 built-in functions. You can peruse them by pulling down the Insert menu and clicking the Function option, which calls up the Paste Function dialog. You can also access this dialog from the Palette by pulling down the drop-down list of functions. This list tracks the last 10 functions you used in formulas, and at the bottom is an option for More Functions which calls up the Paste Function dialog (see Figure 4-55).

In the Paste Function dialog, functions are grouped by categories. Select a category and then the function name. At the bottom of the box, the function is shown along with all the arguments that it accepts (always within parentheses). Below that is a description of the function itself.

In programming terms, a function is a series of instructions that return a value. In Excel a function may return a numeric value, a string of text, or a logical value like TRUE or FALSE. We'll refer to any of these things as values in the context of a function.

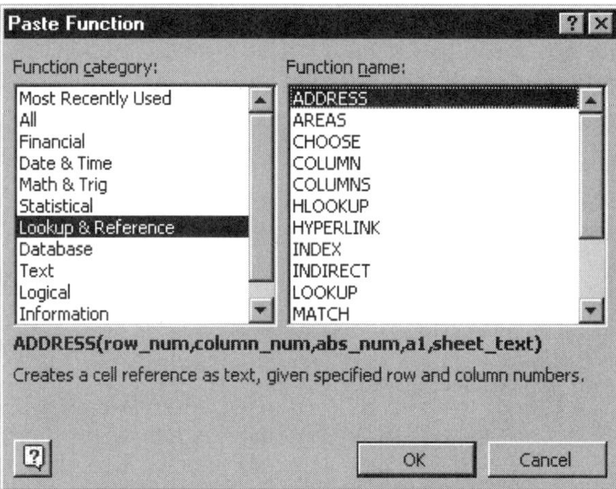

Figure 4-55: The Paste Function dialog box

Functions usually accept arguments, which is any piece of information you give a function so it can return a value. Think of it like this:

```
=BUILD_A_HOUSE(Nails, Lumber, Tools)
```

The function name determines what the function will do, the arguments (Nails, Lumber, and Tools) are what the function uses to determine the result. An argument can be a numeric value, equation, range reference, text string, logical value, logical comparison, error value, or even another function.

The Formula Palette replaces the clunky Function Wizard of versions past. In Figure 4-56, the IF function was selected from the drop-down list in the Palette, which provided us with information about the function and the arguments that it accepts. The IF function lets you perform a logical test—in this case we're checking to see if the totals of several columns are equal to the totals of the rows, called a crossfoot. It then returns one result if the logical test is TRUE, or a different result if the test is FALSE.

The Palette is truly a mind-bogglingly useful implementation of the Wizard concept. Note the buttons at the end of the input boxes. They cause the Palette to roll up out of your way while you look at the sheet or make selections with the mouse.

AutoSum and propagating formulas

There is no requirement to use the Formula Palette; you can type your formula directly into the formula bar, and for most formulas that is probably the fastest, most efficient way. But when you are working with

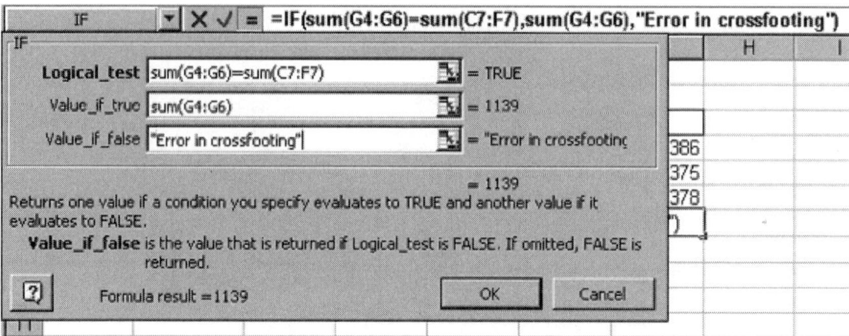

Figure 4-56: Entering functions with the Formula Palette

functions that you are not completely familiar with, the Palette is worth its weight in gold.

The most commonly used function is the `=SUM(range)` function. You can include multiple ranges in the argument by using the union operator (,) as in `=SUM(range, range, range)`. Excel even offers a one-click AutoSum button on the toolbar for quickly entering this function. AutoSum looks at the active cell's immediate surroundings and makes some educated guesses as to what range you probably want to sum, and it builds a sum formula for you using that range. (See Figure 4-57.)

=SUM(C2:C4)

B	C	D
Ixpob	90	
Znarff	22	
Rav'dat	375	
	=SUM(C2:C4)	

Figure 4-57: Excel's AutoSum in action

The cell at the bottom of a column of three values was selected in this example, and the AutoSum button on the toolbar clicked. You can also invoke AutoSum from the keyboard via `ALT+=`, and it's not a bad idea to commit this key combo to memory. Excel looks around the sheet and decides you probably want to sum the three values above the active cell. The formula is built, a marquee is placed around the range Excel has decided you want to sum, and you are left in edit mode for this formula.

If Excel did not guess correctly, you can reselect the range (two blank cells will make it truncate the selection, sometimes it will include a label or blank row you don't want, etc.). Hit the `Enter` key and the formula is entered. This technique can be extended to enter multiple relative sum formulas simultaneously. For example, if you have a table of figures and you want to add them down and across you can enter all the necessary formulas in one operation. (See Figure 4-58.)

	2	3	4	5	6
1		Qtr.1	Qtr.2	Qtr.3	Total
2	Ixpob	90	37	155	
3	Znarff	22	15	18	
4	Rav'dat	375	299	100	
5	Totals				
6					

Figure 4-58: AutoSum down and across with one click

One click on the AutoSum button, and you'll get a formula using the `=SUM` function adding each column down (`=SUM(R[-3]C:R[-1])`) and each row across (`=SUM(RC[-3]:RC[-1])`). Select just the columns, and you'll only get formulas adding down. Extend the selection to include the empty column to the right of the constants, and you'll just get the formulas adding the rows across. AutoSum is so clever, it can even handle multiple selections and subtotals and grand totals correctly.

You can enter a constant or a formula into a range of cells by first selecting the range, typing in the formula, and then instead of pressing the `Enter` key, press `CTRL+ENTER`. This is a slick way to propagate constants or formulas quickly. Say that you were building the table in Figure 4-58, but the constants had not yet been entered. Select R5C3:R5C6, type in **`=SUM`**, select the range R2C3:R4C3, then press `CTRL+ENTER`.

Evaluating formulas

When building and troubleshooting formulas, there are several tips and tricks that can make the experience a lot less annoying. The Range Finder we discussed earlier is one of these tools, and in the next chapter we'll talk about the dynamite auditing tools that Excel offers.

One often overlooked trick is using the `F9` function key (used to force a recalculation of the active sheet) to calculate the result of *a part of a formula*. Edit the formula, highlight the portion of the formula that you want to resolve, and press the `F9` function key. But be careful! If you hit the `Enter` key, the selected portion of the formula is instantly changed to the resultant value and your formula permanently changed. (See Figure 4-59.)

=SUM(B4:B7)*Projected_Increase

=SUM({123;425;362;125})*Projected_Increase

Figure 4-59: Resolving a portion of a formula on the fly

This is a useful, albeit dangerous technique. In a complex formula that is not working correctly, you can evaluate a function, see what a range is really returning, see the value underlying a range name, or look at the logical results of functions or conditional statements. Fast, easy—just be careful when you use it.

Another trick deals with Excel's annoying habit of not letting you enter a formula that has an error in it. And errors happen. Miss a parenthesis or blow an argument, and Excel hits you with an error message and forces you to fix the formula before it'll let you back into your worksheet. (See Figure 4-60.)

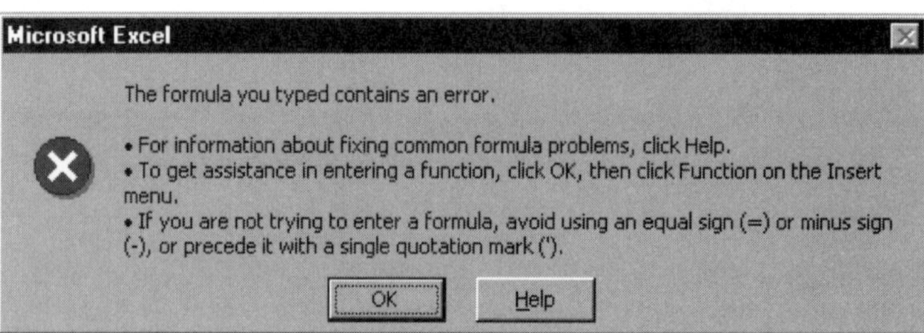

Figure 4-60: The formula you typed contains an error, d'oh!

Often your formula is just hanging on some minor snag, and the majority of what you just spent the better part of 20 minutes typing in works great. But you need to study the problem a bit and maybe look over your data (perhaps on another sheet) to track down the flaw. Do you just scratch what you've entered so far and start over? No, you hit the OK button on the error message, which dumps you back into your formula, hit the `Home` key, then type an apostrophe. Hit `Enter` and your formula is entered into the cell, intact but as text. This lets you study the problem without having to reenter everything. It's a very handy technique, and one that the error message hints at in its last bulleted item.

Implied and explicit intersection

The intersection operator is the space character. This is used primarily in formulas involving range names and is used to reference the cell at the intersection of two ranges. This is usually done explicitly using the syntax:

```
=range1 range2
```

with the range names separated by a space. This is why long-time Lotus users, who used to *blank* cells by putting spaces in them, have to break that old habit. Leaving intersection operators lying about hither and yon is not a good spreadsheet practice.

Implied intersection is where you refer to a single range name. If Excel does not have the second name to use to plot the intersection point, it looks to see if the specified range intersects the row or column containing the active cell. If it does, it uses that *implied* intersection point to determine the cell to reference (see Figure 4-61).

D8 = =Widgets

	B	C	D	E
3		Qtr.1	Qtr.2	
4	Widgets	98	101	
5	Doohickeys	110	92	
6	Gizmos	109	86	
7	Totals	317	279	
8			101	#VALUE!
9				

Figure 4-61: Implied intersection

The shaded area (C4:D4) has been given the range name Widgets. In cell D8 and E8, the formula `=Widgets` has been entered. The range Widgets intersects with column D, so in D8 the implied intersection is D4, which is what the formula returns. But Widgets does not intersect with column E at all, so the formula in E8 returns a value error.

In this case an explicit intersection must be used. If the range D4:D6 had the range name "Qtr.2," you could refer to cell D4 anywhere on the sheet using the formula:

```
=Widgets Qtr.2
```

The range Widgets intersects with Qtr.2 at cell D4.

5

In this chapter:
- *Jump Start*
- *The VBA/Excel Editor*
- *Writing VBA Programs*
- *Controlling Excel*
- *Hooking in to Excel*

Using VBA to Customize Excel

As we said earlier in the book, simply by using Excel—developing formulas, establishing relationships between cells, etc.—you've been programming. Even if you couldn't care less about the difference between a bit and a byte and break out in hives at the thought of becoming A Programmer, you owe it to yourself to read through this chapter.

Why? Because the VBA/Excel macro language lets you get so much done that you'll quickly wonder how you ever lived without it. Besides, if you have a pretty good handle on how Excel works, you've already figured out the hard part. Picking up a little Basic and poking around a programming editor pale in comparison.

Think of macros as leverage, a near-exponential increase in your Excel prowess. When you made the transition from green multi-column dead-tree ledger sheets to Excel, you should've seen a huge boost in the quality and quantity of models you were producing. By learning how to create macros, you'll take even greater control over Excel and boost the quality and quantity of the models you produce even farther. Furthermore, VBA—along with the user interface customization techniques we've shown you in previous chapters—is your most powerful weapon in fighting off the annoyance horde. Absolutely any Excel behavior that you find annoying can be reprogrammed your way using VBA. Remember that annoyance is a relative term. An outright bug is annoying, but so is having to click more times than you'd like in order to activate a feature you frequently use. Case in point: it takes five clicks to toggle R1C1 reference style on or off, and after enough toggling you'll wonder if there's a better way. With VBA, you betcha! In Chapter 6, *Excel Strategies*, we provide a seven-line macro that gives you a one-click toggle for R1C1 reference style. One very small VBA macro makes a very big difference in your daily use and enjoyment of Excel.

Jump Start

The macro language that lives inside Excel is called *Visual Basic for Applications*. It was first introduced in Excel version 5.0 (Office 4.x), and at that moment, Excel earned the distinction of being Microsoft's first Office application to use VBA.* When referring to the specific dialect of VBA that comes inside Excel, we usually speak of *VBA/Excel*. Microsoft insists that the VBA inside Excel is the same VBA that's inside Word, PowerPoint, and Project, and to a point that's true. Still, a program written in VBA/Excel usually won't run, unchanged, in its sibling applications, so we'll continue to draw the distinction. (By *program* we mean a macro or procedure that calls upon application-specific components or behaviors. It's certainly true that a general-purpose VBA procedure—say, one that hot-swaps a marker in a string variable with incoming replacement text—could be written in VBA/Excel and also be used unmodified in Word/VBA. It's a subtle but important distinction.)

What's the neatest part about VBA/Excel? You don't have to buy anything. It's sitting right there inside Excel, waiting for you to bring it to life. All it takes is a little learning and a little gumption, and we hope to give you a good dose of both in this chapter.

Once you're under way, the major conceptual hump involves understanding Excel. Not to worry. We'll take you by the hand and show you all the important parts.

The Concepts

Anything you can do in Excel, you can do with a VBA/Excel program.† Many things you *can't* do in Excel, you can do with a VBA/Excel program. Indeed, anything you can accomplish with a program in

---

* Both Excel 5 and Project 4 simultaneously released VBA to the world, but since Project has never been part of the official Office family, we give the vote of pioneering distinction to Excel.

† You can call 'em macros if you like, but they're really full-fledged programs. We'll use the terms "macro" and "program" interchangeably throughout the book. Technically, in VBA a "macro" is a subroutine with no parameters. In practice, self-impressed bit twiddlers use macro as a term of derision, e.g., "Oh, it's just a *macro*! I thought you had a program going." Those of us who have been working with macros for many years know better: "Oh, it's just a *program*? I thought you guys knew how to write real *macros*."

Windows itself can be done in a VBA/Excel program. The full range of Windows programming—from simple offerings for the Windows Gods, to complex delving into Windows' innards—is at your beck and call from a simple (or not so simple!) VBA/Excel program. Mind boggling.

Now we have VBA in Word, Excel, PowerPoint, and Project (although Project isn't a member of the official Office nuclear family). They're the epitome of programmability. Access has something that Microsoft likes to call VBA, and there are some familial similarities, but Access hasn't come up to speed just yet. Internet Explorer and Outlook both limp along with a severely stunted macro language (VBScript, a subset of VBA). They don't come close. VBA, at this point, is the cat's pajamas. It's as good as it gets.

Microsoft has licensed VBA to other companies: Visio, for example, was the first company outside Microsoft to come up with a full implementation. Lots of companies are or will be jumping on the VBA bandwagon. In fact, Microsoft itself has actually swiped the VBA programming editor from the Office group and stitched it into the latest version of Visual Basic. It's that good.

What does that mean for you? You only need to learn VBA once. The skills and tips (and bugs and workarounds) you learn in VBA/Excel transfer over, nearly intact, to Visual Basic, VBA/Word, VBA/PowerPoint, VBA/Visio, and many others. Sure, you have to learn the application—in Excel you're looking at cells and ranges; in Word it's paragraphs and sentences; in PowerPoint it's slides and wipes; in Visio it's shapes and connectors—but the structure that holds all the macros together stays the same. That's leverage on a grand scale.

Recording Macros

Excel, like most Windows applications, lets you "record" macros.

The mechanism for macro recording is pretty simple, and it's virtually identical in every computer application. There's a macro Record Start command, not unlike pressing the Record button on a tape recorder or VCR. Once you start, VBA/Excel watches what you do and stores away your actions in a program, er, macro.

When you're done, you press a Record Stop button, and VBA/Excel stops recording your actions. Then you can play back (we would say Run) the recorded program by pushing a Play button. It's very simple. Let's give it a shot.

NOTE Why would you want to record a macro? In some very limited situations, you may be able to record a macro to solve a particular problem—after all, macros were originally conceived as a way to automate repetitive tasks. If you need to repeat the same keystrokes over and over again, a recorded macro may save you some time.

Our intentions, though, are not so pure. We want you to record a macro so you can see what a macro looks like, and so you have something hanging around later to dissect when we start building more capable macros. We'll get you started recording a macro, primarily for demo purposes. But in the end, all we're really doing is constructing a guinea pig for you to play with a bit.

Macro recording, for us, is a means, not an end.

Start with a new, blank workbook and the active cell A1 on Sheet1. To keep this example simple, we ask that you temporarily turn Excel's "Move selection after Enter" feature off—Tools ➤ Options ➤ Edit, make sure the "Move selection after Enter" box is not checked (if it is, before clearing it make a mental note of the Direction setting, as we'll have you reset this momentarily), click OK.

Click on Tools, then Macro, then Record New Macro. You should see a dialog box like that in Figure 5-1.

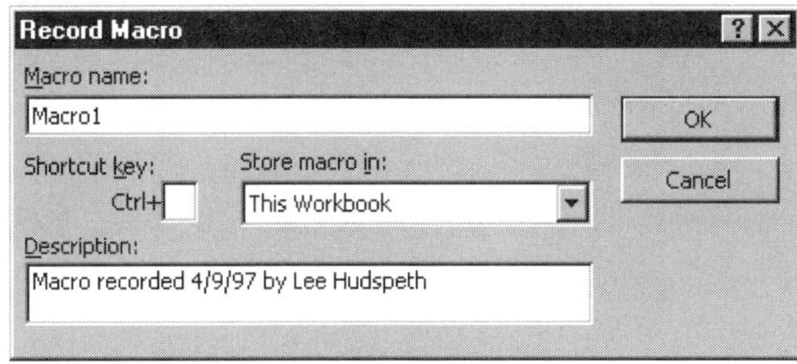

Figure 5-1: Start the macro recorder

Click OK. Doing so informs Excel that you want to record a new macro (or program) called Macro1, and that you want the recording to begin right now. You'll see the Stop Recording toolbar pop up (you can't read the full title of the toolbar, but it's shown in full in the Customize dialog's Toolbars list). The recorder is on, so you need to do something. Next, click on the Stop Recording toolbar's right-most button (ToolTip "Relative

Reference", which we'll explain momentarily), so that it looks as though it is pushed in. We typed

```
VBA is oh so cool!
```

in cell A1, pressed Enter, used Format ➤ Cells ➤ Font to set the font to Comic Sans MS at 26 points blue, then pressed the down arrow key to end up in cell A2. When you're done doing whatever you wanted to do, click the Stop Recording button on the Stop Recording toolbar—the button with the square on it that's supposed to look like a VCR Stop button. (The second button, with the ToolTip "Relative Reference," tells Excel whether to use absolute or relative references while recording. By default, the macro recorder interprets cell addresses as absolute, so we clicked on the Relative Reference button to have VBA move the active cell cursor down one row from wherever the active cell is when you start the macro later, instead of always going back to the absolute address $A$2.)

Congratulations. You've just written your first VBA/Excel program.

Want to see how it works? Easy. Activate a different cell, say, C3. Click Tools ➤ Macro ➤ Macros. Click once on Macro1, and click Run (see Figure 5-2). Your program will play back—run, if you will—and insert the text all over again.

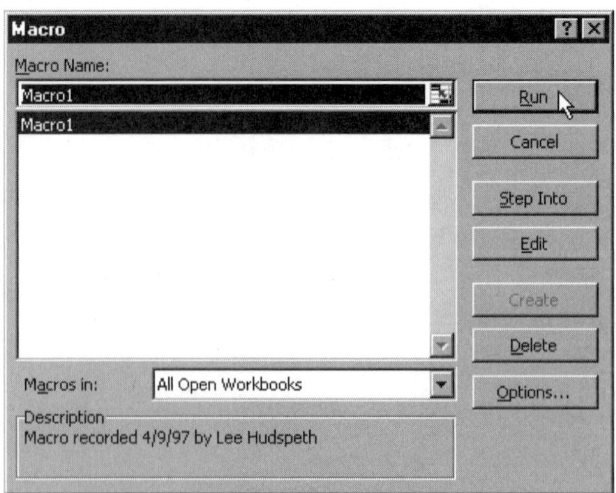

Figure 5-2: Run your first VBA/Excel program, er, macro

You can repeat that as many times as you like. Each time you run the program called Macro1, you'll insert the formatted label into the current cell and select the cell one row down. Nothing to it.

If you want to return Excel's "Move selection after Enter" setting back to its prior state, do so now.

> ### *Help in VBA/Excel*
>
> When you set up Office (or Excel), you have to specifically tell the installer that you want to include VBA Help. If you go into the VBA/Excel Editor and hit `F1`, the Office Assistant should be ready to answer your VBA questions. If it isn't, insert the Office or Excel CD, and reinstall. (This can be done easily using the Add/Remove Programs option from the Control Panel.) This time, make sure you click on Custom, and click the Online Help for Visual Basic box.

The VBA/Excel Editor

NOTE Now we've got you hooked. You have a recorded macro sitting in front of you that you can now dissect. This is where we start introducing you to the macro surgeon's tools: the scalpels, clamps, and sutures you'll use to create your own macros, very soon. No need to get squeamish. We'll take you through the gore, step by step.

Curious to see what your program looks like? Good. Click Tools ➤ Macro, then Visual Basic Editor. The window that will appear before your eyes (see Figure 5-3) looks very, very complicated. For good reason. It is. Remember the first time you saw Excel in all its glory? Well, the VBA/Excel Editor window, in its own way, is every bit as complicated as the Excel window. Relax a bit, though: once you get into it, the Editor itself—the part behind this intimidating window—is nowhere near as complicated as Excel. It just looks that way.

Let's start by navigating the various parts of the VBA/Excel Editor.

Project Explorer

Starting in the upper-left corner, you'll see something called the Project Explorer—a fancy name for something that's very simple once you understand the history of the blasted befuddling terminology. (See Figure 5-4.)

This Project Explorer window, probably more than any other single part of VBA/Excel, illustrates what happens when Microsoft worlds collide.

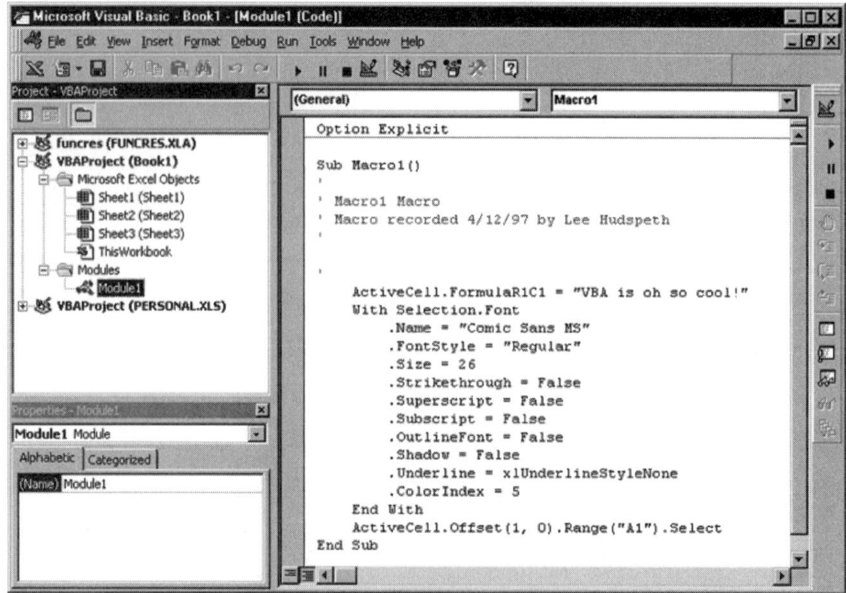

Figure 5-3: Your first program in the VBA/Excel Editor

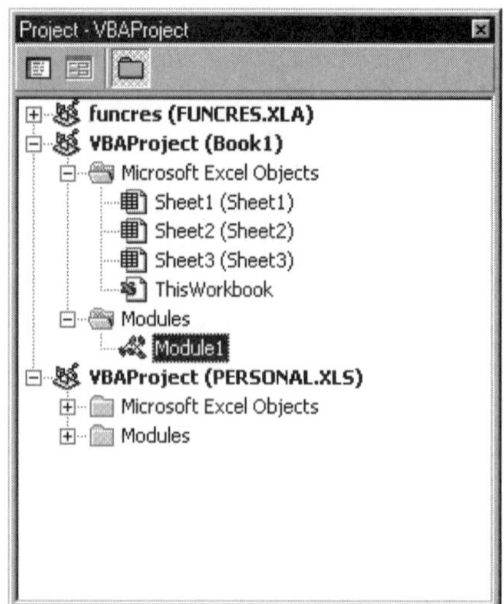

Figure 5-4: The Visual Basic Editor's Project Explorer

On the one hand, the people who built Excel started out more than a decade ago with workbooks and sheets. On the other hand, the Visual Basic people—who work in a division of Microsoft that, until recently, was completely separate from the Excel group—speak in terms of projects. A *project* is simply a bunch of programs, custom dialog boxes and the like which, taken together, form what most people would call an *application*. More or less.

Then the Excel world melded with the VB world. The VB folks had to figure out a way to stick their projects inside Excel workbooks. At the same time, the Excel folks had to figure out a way to meld their workbook-oriented way of looking at things into the project-oriented scheme of the VB group. The compromise they reached is embodied in the Project Explorer.

One Toolbar Button's Worth a Thousand Clicks

The Project Explorer window is different from other Explorer-like windows in that you can't open a new project directly in the window, or even in the Visual Basic Editor, for that matter. If you want to have a new project listed in the Project Explorer window, you must go *out to Excel itself*, and open the workbook that contains the desired project. That's weird, it's annoying, but that's how it works. (Tip: you can toggle between the Visual Basic Editor and its Excel host with the tried-and-true `Alt+Tab` technique, but it's even faster to click the "View Microsoft Excel" button on the editor's Standard toolbar; not surprisingly, this button has the classic Excel icon on it.)

It probably won't surprise you that given this nice one-to-one correspondence, the groups decided that each Excel workbook would contain one, and only one, VBA project. Microsoft essentially equated the concepts of workbook and project. So in the Project Explorer, Figure 5-4, VB people will think, "I'm looking at a list of all the projects currently available to me," while the Excel people will think, "I'm looking at a list of all the workbooks that are currently open." In fact, the two different points of view are both entirely accurate: the Project Explorer lists all open workbooks—or, if you prefer, all projects that are open.

Actually, there's a bit more to the list of workbooks (projects) revealed by the Project Explorer at any given time. Obviously, any workbooks you've opened appear in the project list. Any workbooks in the *\Xlstart* folder—and your alternate startup folder, if you've defined one—appear in the Project Explorer project list, even if the workbooks are hidden. This means you'll see the special *Personal.xls* workbook that Excel handles for you. (*Personal.xls* is a workbook that Excel creates for you as a general-purpose macro repository; this special file is stored in the *\Xlstart* folder, and Excel keeps it hidden by default.) You'll see some but not necessarily all add-ins (workbooks that have been compiled with an .XLA extension) that are currently loaded. Such add-ins could be add-ins you've loaded manually with the Add-in Manager (Tools ➤ Add-Ins) or that auto-load by virtue of being installed to auto-load themselves.* Typically, although not always, an add-in will be protected, in which case if you try to view its properties in the Project Explorer, you'll be prompted for its password.

If you're looking for the VBA/Excel program you just recorded, navigate in the Project Explorer window to "VBAProject (Book1)." Then move down to the place where all program code is stored, the Modules folder. Finally, move down to the module called Module1 and double-click on Module1.

Before we do anything else, let's save the workbook we've been practicing in—Book1 if you've been following along—and use it from here on out. By the way, we're choosing not to put these macros into your *Personal.xls* in the event that your working PC is in an office environment where *Personal.xls* is managed—in spite of its name—by your Information Systems protocols or staff.† Let's save this workbook as *Intro to VBA.xls.*

Properties Window

Directly below the Project Explorer sits the Properties Window. Whenever you click on an object, the object's properties appear in the Properties Window. In the case of Figure 5-5, the object is the project attached to the workbook called *Intro to VBA.xls.* The only property of this project is its name, which happens to be, uh, VBAProject.‡

Unless you do something to change it, the default name for all projects is "VBAProject," and that name appears in the Properties Window. You can change it by simply selecting the name in the Properties Window and typing in a new name. Although a project does have other properties—like Description, Help File, etc.—only its Name property is exposed in the Properties Window. That's annoying. If you want to change these other properties, you can't use the Properties Window; instead you have to right-click on the project in the Project Explorer tree, choose VBA-Project Properties (Tools ➤ VBAProject Properties also works), and change them in the dialog box (see Figure 5-6). Go ahead and do this

* Being installed to auto-load without user intervention would be common for a third-party or custom Excel solution delivered as an add-in.

† Recall that *Personal.xls* is the door XM.Laroux uses to gain a toehold and infect a system.

‡ Remember Major Major Major Major in *Catch-22*? We're absolutely certain he wrote the specs for default project names in the Office implementation of VBA.

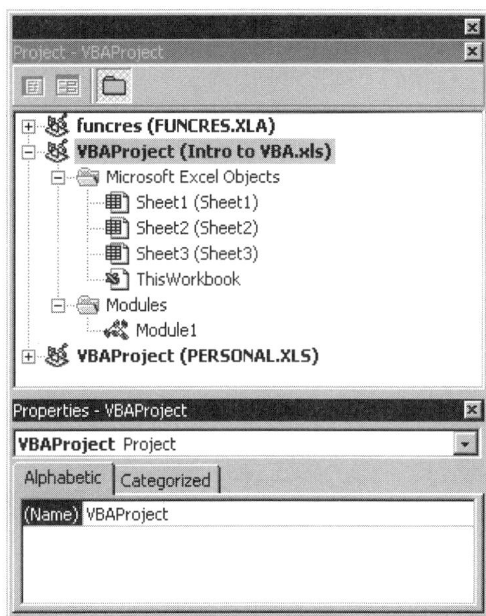

Figure 5-5: The Properties Window, shown docked to the bottom of Project Explorer

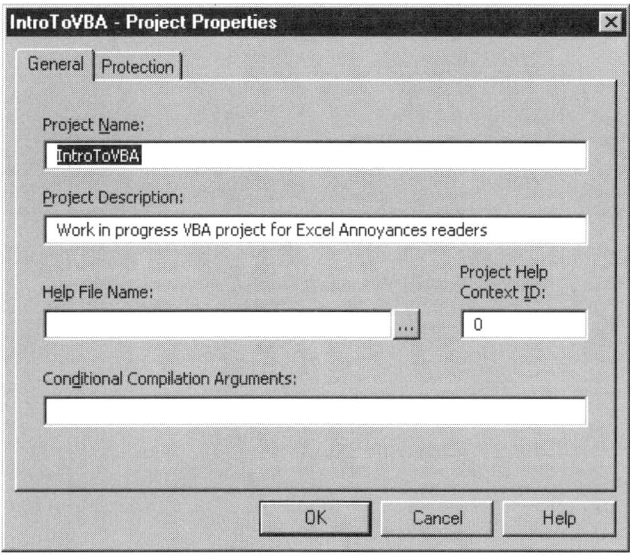

Figure 5-6: The Project Properties dialog box

now: change the name to *IntroToVBA* and add descriptive text as shown in the figure. Note that project names must begin with a letter and can include up to 40 characters (letters, numbers, and underscores are all legal). Instead of the VB Editor's user interface, you could use VBA code to change, say, the description for this project, along with some other properties that are *not* exposed in the Project Properties dialog box. A line of code like:

```
ThisWorkbook.VBProject.Description = _
    "Work in progress VBA project for Excel Annoyances readers"
```

does the trick.

NOTE Annoyance alert! In Excel and PowerPoint, the default name for all projects is "VBAProject." In Word, the default name for projects attached to templates is "TemplateProject," and for projects attached to documents, "Project." The name of the VBA property in the Office object model that returns a VBA project for a particular workbook, template, document, etc. is "VBProject" in Excel, PowerPoint, and Word. Go figure.

We'll be seeing a lot more of the Properties Window when we hit things that have more properties.

NOTE You should get into the habit of changing the name of a project from its default *before* you start working on the workbook. This is a good habit to get into because you'll save yourself grief down the road if the project is referenced by other projects.* Word in particular is a real pain about this. Due to an extraordinarily annoying (read: dumb) design decision, Word "loses" custom settings for a document or template when its project name is changed. Your toolbar changes, keyboard assignments, and the like get the deep-six when you change the name of the project attached to a document or template.

---

* By changing an Excel VBA project name from the default, you'll avoid the "Name conflicts with existing module, project, or object library" error that occurs when there are several open projects with the name VBAProject and VBA is unable to distinguish between them. You'll also avoid the compiler error "Variable not defined" that occurs when code that worked previously is disrupted by a change in the name of the project that owns a called procedure.

Code Window

NOTE Now we're ready to go beyond the window dressing, into the heart of the matter: the program code itself. Don't be overly concerned if you still haven't figured out exactly what the Project Explorer and Object Window do; you'll have a chance to see it all work together once we dig into the code.

The Code Window is where you'll be doing most of your work (see Figure 5-7). It takes up the right side of the VBA Editor window and contains (*mirable dictu!*) your code.

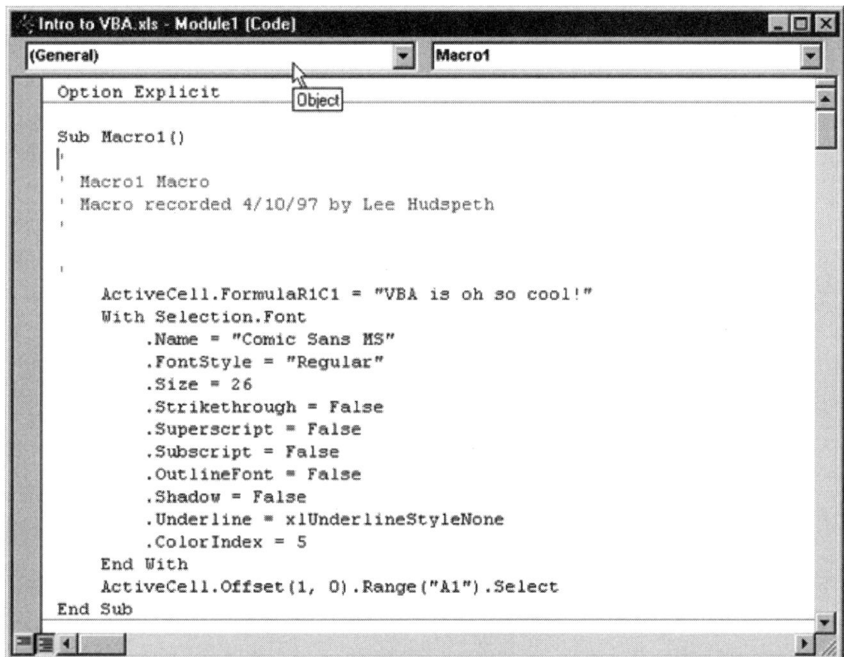

Figure 5-7: The Code Window—Home Sweet Home

A brief grand tour:

- The Code Window's title bar has all the controls you'd expect of a title bar, but there's a subtle—and annoying—difference between them in Excel and Word. In Excel the title bar always *includes* the project filename's extension (see Figure 5-7). In Word the title bar always *omits* the project filename's extension (see Figure 5-8). Why, we ask? And there's more. Compare the Project Explorer listing for

Excel and Word and you'll discover two differences. First, Word's project listing omits the parenthetical filename listing when the root filename and the project name are exactly the same *and* the file is a global template (whether that global template is open or not), whereas Excel's project listing always shows the parenthetical filename even when the root filename and project name are exactly the same. Second, Word's project listing never displays a project filename's extension, and Excel's always does. Again, we ask why? More of Microsoft's little mysteries.

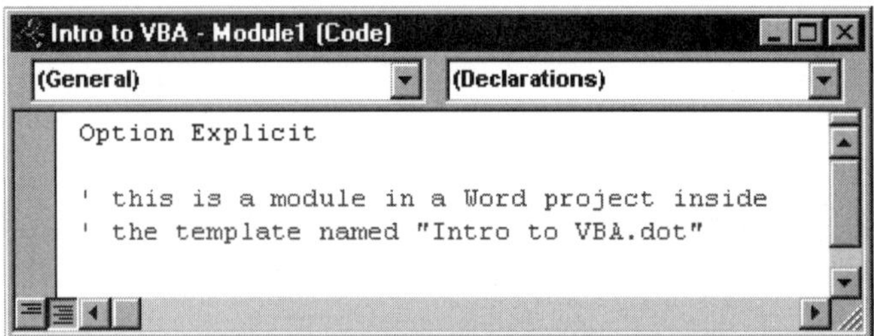

Figure 5-8: Word's Code Window oddly drops the project filename extension

- In the upper-left corner is the Object box, an area where you can pick one of those mysterious objects, in this case objects that can have subroutines or functions* attached to them.
- In the upper-right corner sits the Procedure box, which contains a list of all the subroutines or functions available in the object shown in the Object box.

  If you're looking at the Module1 module of the *Intro to VBA.xls* project (read: the collection of programs called Module1 that's stuck in *Intro to VBA.xls*), the General Object (read: the main collection of programs) should have two procedures. The subroutine you just recorded is a procedure called Macro1. And the other procedure is kind of a miscellaneous catch-all thing called (Declarations).
- The stripe down the left side lets you control the way the VBA/Excel Editor runs your program, shows you which line of the program is currently running, and lets you set *breakpoints*—lines where VBA is supposed to stop running and wait for you to figure out what's going on. It can come in very handy, as you'll see momentarily.

---

* A *subroutine* is just a program: it's a bunch of VBA/Excel code that does something. A *function* is just like a subroutine, except that when it's done, it produces a value. For example, a subroutine might print a document, whereas a function might print the same document and return the number of pages that were printed. The distinction is largely academic and tends to become much clearer when you start working with programs.

- The two buttons in the extreme lower-left corner control whether you see just one procedure at a time (this is called *procedure view*) or if the VBA/Excel Editor shows you all the code from all the procedures (arranged alphabetically) that can fit in the window (termed *full module view*).

Believe it or not, you're looking at one of the most sophisticated programming environments available for any programming language. Grown men and women who struggle with wimpy programming editors every day have been known to cry at the sight of this marvel. Imagine. All that attention lavished on us lowly macro programmers!

Docking

If you click-and-drag the window title (the blue part) of the Project Explorer or the Properties Window, you'll see that both windows will detach themselves from the Editor. You can put them outside the VBA/Excel Editor window, drag them to different corners, even dock the two of them together outside the Editor. So many choices. Nice of Microsoft to offer them.

NOTE You can precisely control which of the Visual Basic Editor's windows are dockable. Select Tools, choose Options, click the Docking tab, and check or uncheck at your discretion. (We recommend you leave all these docking options checked except Object Browser, which we find is easier to use if not dockable.)

Furthermore, there is a dragging trick—at least we found it to be tricky at first—to getting a window to dock. Let's say you want Project Explorer to be left-docked. If it's floating aimlessly in the middle of the Visual Basic Editor display space, grab it by the title bar and start dragging it left. Often, its "in motion" frame will suddenly attach itself—for no apparent reason—to the bottom of the screen, then suddenly undock. Very disconcerting. Just hold on and keep dragging. *When you've left-dragged the window such that about two-thirds of its entire real estate is off the left edge of the screen* (you'll see the thick gray "in motion" frame become a thin gray frame), let go, and it will be left-docked.

But when it comes right down to it, most of the time the Project Explorer and Properties Windows only amount to giant annoyances. Yes, when you're switching around between projects, the Project Explorer comes in handy. Yes, when you're setting properties (particularly when you're designing custom dialog boxes), the Properties Window is indispensable. But when you're really hunkered down writing VBA/Excel programs, you rarely need either.

We recommend that you hide them both, by clicking on the X in the upper-right corner of each window. When you need them, calling them back takes just a click on the VBA Standard toolbar. We'll show you how.

Toolbars

The VBA/Excel Editor, like Excel, has a handful of toolbars. When you first start the Editor, you'll see the two most important ones: Standard, and Debug (see Figure 5-9 and Figure 5-10). Surprisingly, there's a substantial amount of overlap between the two. Not so surprisingly, some parts of both toolbars are very poorly designed.

Figure 5-9: The Editor's Standard toolbar

We won't go into a lot of detail about customizing the VBA/Excel toolbars, except to note that it can be done—if you know the trick. Word, Excel, and PowerPoint let you change toolbars by clicking on Tools, then Customize. Not so the Editor. You'll have to right-click on a toolbar, pick Customize, then click and drag from that point.

Figure 5-10: The Editor's Debug toolbar

NOTE Don't bother trying to get that huge "Ln X, Col Y" button off your Standard toolbar, or to shorten it. The button won't come off, and you can't make it any smaller. You can drag the Standard toolbar anywhere you like—make it float, dock it on the left, do whatever you can—and that gargantuan, ugly button stays put. Man, talk about annoying. You'd think that Microsoft would put it down in the lower-left corner, to the left of the horizontal scroll bar.

The most important three buttons on both toolbars (so important they put 'em there twice!) are the right-wedgie Play button, the two-vertical-line Pause button, and the square block Stop button. Clicking on those buttons, respectively, play, pause, and stop execution of the current subroutine. For all you ToolTip-philes out there, these buttons' ToolTips read like this, though for semantic sanity we'll stick with the VCR-type terminology:

- Play—Run Sub/User Form (`F5`)
- Pause—Break (`Ctrl+Break`)
- Stop—Reset

The next important button is the one in the middle of the Debug toolbar that looks like a stack of pancakes with a loopy arrow. When you click on that button, VBA/Excel runs just the next line of your program. It's called a "Step Into" button because when you run programs with it, VBA/Excel "steps into" each subroutine and function that gets called.

Finally, you can bring back up the Project Explorer window by clicking the button near the end of the Standard toolbar that looks like a sheet of paper with squares and pills on top of it. (We call the picture "Portrait of Project with Descending Quaaludes," but your impression may vary.) The button immediately to its right—the one with a finger on a sheet of paper—brings up the Properties Window.

Some of the other buttons do nifty things—the three Debug toolbar buttons that look like sheets of paper invoke tremendously powerful debugging aids (the Locals Window, Immediate Window, and Watch Window, respectively)—but we'll limit our exploration in this book to the buttons mentioned. They'll get you started. You can strap on the warp drive later.

NOTE So much for the orientation. You've seen the macro surgeon's tools. Now let's put them to use.

Annoying Settings

Before you start using the VBA/Excel Editor, there are two sets of settings you need to fix.

First, everybody who uses VBA should click on Tools ➤ Options and under the Editor tab, check the box marked Require Variable Declaration. (See Figure 5-11.)

The mechanics behind this setting are unimportant, but the requirement outstrips all others. With this box checked, VBA/Excel will require you to

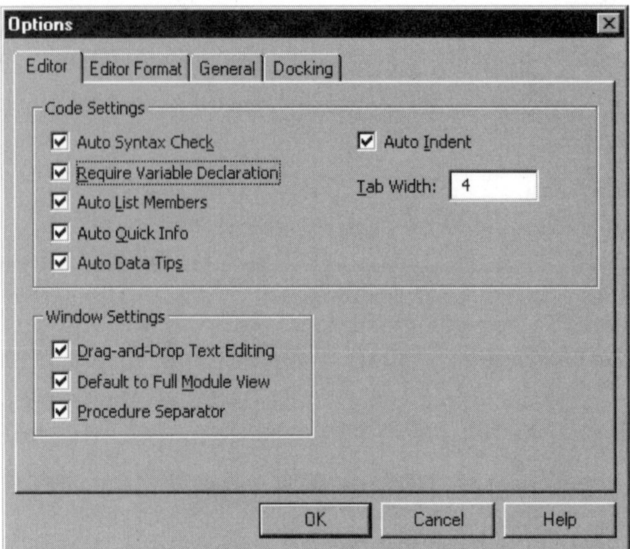

Figure 5-11: Always require variable declaration

declare any variable names before using them in code that you write. By forcing you to declare variables (you'll see how shortly), VBA/Excel effectively minimizes the number one source of programming bugs: misspellings.

NOTE To find out more about the data types supported by VBA, see the Help file topic "Data Type Summary."

Second, if you have installed any Office components, or any other applications that VBA/Excel will use, it's important that you tell VBA/Excel about them. Do so by clicking on Tools ➤ References and checking the box next to any programs you expect to be using with VBA, as shown in Figure 5-12.

If you plan to use VBA/Excel aggressively (and, hey, you paid for it—why not?), consider adding references to any programs you might want to control from Excel. We check all of the following:

- Microsoft Office 8.0 Object Library
- Microsoft Word 8.0 Object Library
- Internet Explorer Scripting Object Model
- Microsoft Access 8.0 Object Library
- Microsoft Binder 8.0 Object Library

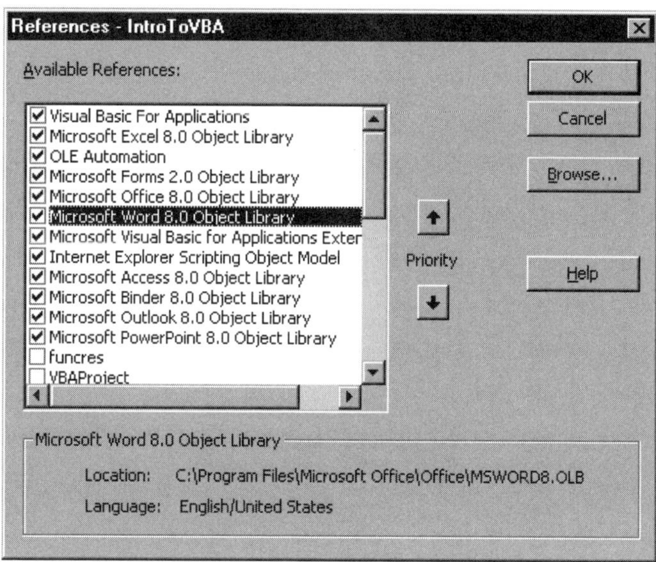

Figure 5-12: Add References

- Microsoft Outlook 8.0 Object Model
- Microsoft PowerPoint 8.0 Object Library
- DAO 3.5 Object Library (especially if you're going to use Access)

Adding each of these references entails a small amount of overhead. They can also lead to a bit of confusion when VBA asks questions like "Do you want to look at Help on the Windows collection for Excel or for Word?" But by and large it's much better to have these around should you need them.

Basic Functions

NOTE So far VBA/Excel is just a disembodied ghost, floating around in some promised land of milk and programmatic honey. Let's take a look at how the Visual Basic Editor works with Excel, and vice versa. We'll haul out that little recorded macro, just to give you a look-see.

Microsoft hooked the Code Window into Excel itself: you can run your program in the Code Window and watch the effects of your program over in Excel. We find it most useful to run Excel and VBA/Excel in windows that don't overlap, or overlap just a little bit, so we can see everything that's going on.

To get a feel for what's happening, arrange VBA/Excel and Excel itself so you can see both of them at the same time (see Figure 5-13). Make sure Macro1 is showing in VBA/Excel. If you have recorded more than one macro, put the cursor somewhere in Macro1.

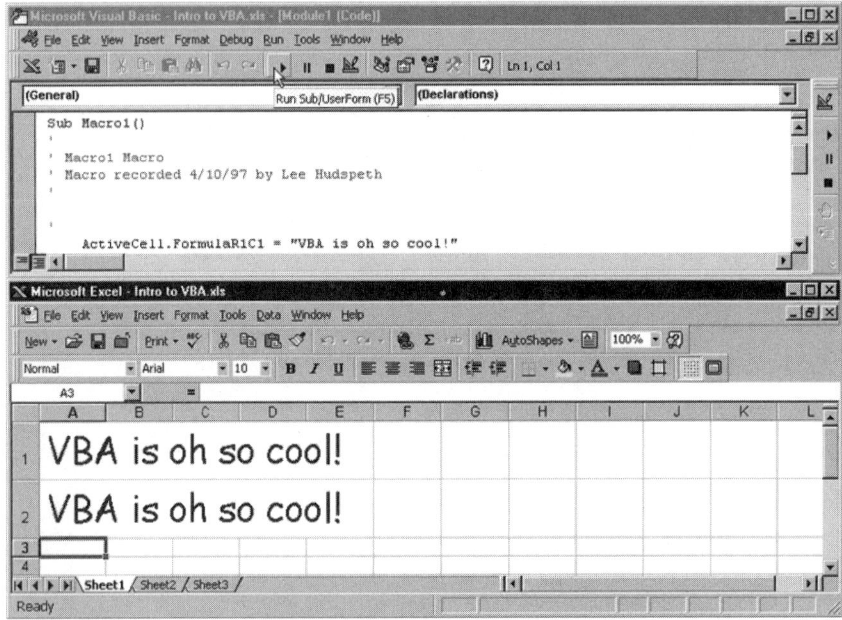

Figure 5-13: Testing VBA/Excel's interaction with Excel

NOTE Quick tip for precisely splitting your desktop between two application windows: minimize all applications (right-click the taskbar tray and choose Minimize All Windows), right-click the taskbar icon of the first application and choose Restore, right-click the taskbar icon of the second application and choose Restore, then right-click the taskbar tray and choose Tile Horizontally (or Tile Vertically).

Now click the right-wedgie Play button a few times. See how VBA/Excel puts text in successive cells (moving down one row at a time) in the blank worksheet?

To put it all under a microscope, here's what's happening:

1. You push the Play button. VBA/Excel runs the program called Macro1.
2. VBA/Excel sets the contents of the active cell to the formula—in this case a text label—comprised of the text "VBA is oh so cool!"

3. VBA/Excel applies all the properties you set while in the Font tab of the Format Cells dialog (font name, font style, size, and so on).
4. VBA/Excel selects the cell that is in the same column but one row down from where the active cell was when you started the macro.

If you then push the Play button again, everything starts all over at step 1.

Try playing with this a bit. Change the text in Macro1 to, oh, "Excel is the King of Spreadsheet Hill!" Click the Play button a few times. Do something different. Change the font to be even more outlandish or plain vanilla or whatever, activate some random cell, and click the Play button again. See how that works? Pretty straightforward.

Are you curious about that last expression, the one that reads:

```
ActiveCell.Offset(1, 0).Range("A1").Select
```

Here's an explanation:

1. The `ActiveCell.Offset(1, 0)` part of this expression returns a Range object that is offset from the specified range (in this case, the range defined by `ActiveCell`). The offset is 1 row positive (read: 1 row down) and 0 columns (read: same column), meaning, one cell directly down from where you started.

   So, if the active cell was cell A1, `ActiveCell.Offset(1, 0)` refers to cell A2.
2. The expression `.Range("A1")` is a relative expression—and, it turns out, superfluous, but the recorder put it in for reasons known only to the folks who wrote the recorder. It means "same column, same row," or in other words, no change to the range defined in step 1 above. How do we know this? Well, carefully read the last paragraph of the Help topic "Range Property (Application, Range, or Worksheet Object)" and you'll get the drift in the sentence, "For example, if the selection is cell C3, then `Selection.Range("B1")` returns cell D3 because it's relative to the Range object returned by the Selection property." Here, think of `Range("B1")` more like a relative reference of RC[+1] because B1 has a relative offset of one column relative to A1 (A1 is the upper-left corner or origin of any Excel worksheet), and B1 has a relative offset of zero rows relative to A1, and that's RC[+1].

   So, if the range resulting from step 1 above is cell A2, at the end of step 2 you're still at cell A2. Really!
3. The expression `.Select`, not surprisingly, selects the range defined by everything that went on so far in the VBA expression.

So, at the end of step 3 you've selected cell A2. Whew! Moral: when writing VBA code manually to accomplish this, drop the `.Range("A1")` part of this expression and simply say `ActiveCell.Offset(1, 0).Select`.

Writing VBA Programs

NOTE See how it all fits together? No, we didn't think so. Hang in there. The more you work with it, the more it'll make sense. Honestly. This is one humdinger of a programming environment.

Just so you understand where we've been and where we're heading: At this point, that recorded macro has served its purpose: it's given you something to play with on your way to VBA/Excel understanding. You can forget about it now. You're old enough to make your own toys, from scratch. With a little bit of help, of course.

Before we dive into the big, bad world of events and object models, let's take a few minutes to write and run a couple of simple VBA programs.* These won't cure any of Excel's annoyances, but they'll give you a fighting chance to ease into the VBA way of thinking.

Creating a New Program

Our first program puts a series of message boxes up on the screen that count from one to ten. (See Figure 5-14.)

Figure 5-14: The final message box

Start by ensuring that you're still working in IntroToVBA's Module1 module.

---

* We use the term VBA here because these programs rely on Visual Basic for Applications alone. In other words, they'll run precisely the same way in VBA/Excel, VBA/Word, VBA/PowerPoint, VBA/Visio, and probably any other VBA flavor you can find. They'll also run the same way in Visual Basic itself.

If You've Never Written a Program, Don't Panic

Computer languages, like human languages, don't unveil themselves immediately. You have to memorize little snippets—"Hello, how are you?" or "Where is the bathroom?" or "I can count to ten"—and then work on tying the snippets together.

Computer languages, like human languages, have all sorts of rules and conventions. There are phrases that "sound right," and there are phrases that don't quite go together, even if they do work.

You wouldn't expect to learn French in one sitting. It's amazing how many folks get frustrated because they can't learn Basic in one sitting. In many ways, Basic is more difficult than French. Of course, in other ways, it's considerably simpler.

If you concentrate on getting the feel of a language—again, human or machine—you'll often find that the nit-picky rules fall into place, sooner or later. You'll get better at it with practice. That's precisely the method we think you'll find easiest for learning VBA/Excel.

NOTE For simplicity's sake, from this point forward we're going to refer to a project by its project name as opposed to its filename. So when we say "put a new procedure in IntroToVBA's Module1 module" you'll know we're referring to the IntroToVBA project stored inside the file called *Intro to VBA.xls*, even though the Visual Basic Editor's title bar in Excel uses the filename, not the project name (unlike VBA/Word, which uses the project name, as we discussed earlier in this chapter).

If you can see Macro1 in the Code Window, you're in good shape. If not, bring up the Project Explorer (possibly by clicking the "Portrait of Project with Descending Quaaludes" button on the Editor's Standard toolbar), navigate to the project called IntroToVBA, then Modules, then double-click on Module1.

We're going to create a new program called *LoopPractice*. Start by clicking on Insert, then Procedure, as shown in Figure 5-15.

When the Add Procedure dialog comes up, type in the name **`LoopPractice`**. Leave the option buttons alone, and click OK, as shown in Figure 5-16.

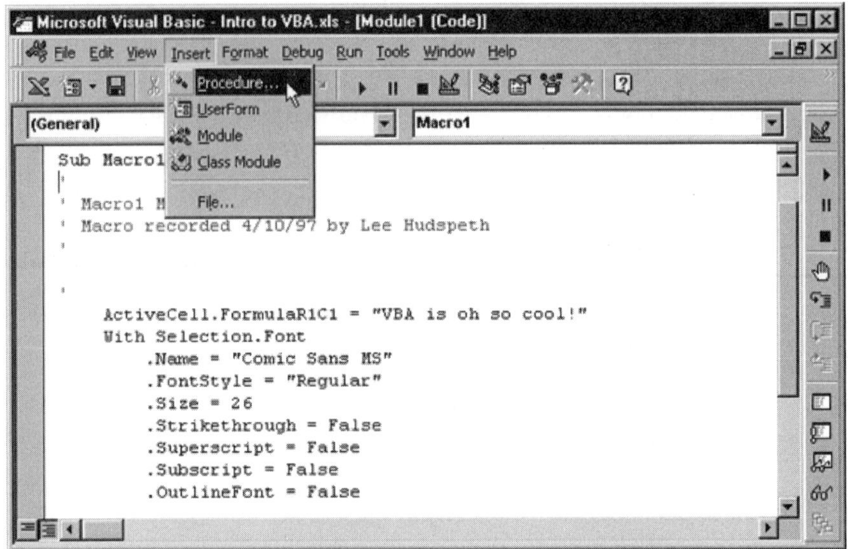

Figure 5-15: Put a new procedure in IntroToVBA's Module1 module

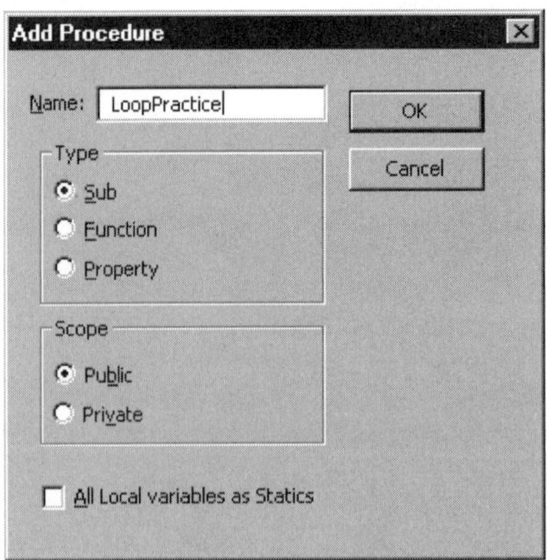

Figure 5-16: Create a subroutine called LoopPractice

VBA will create a new subroutine called *LoopPractice*, complete with `Sub` and `End Sub` statements, which mark the beginning and end of the subroutine. Your cursor is already in position for you to start typing your program. (If you're following along, it will be sitting at the beginning of the empty line following the `Sub` statement as shown in Figure 5-17).

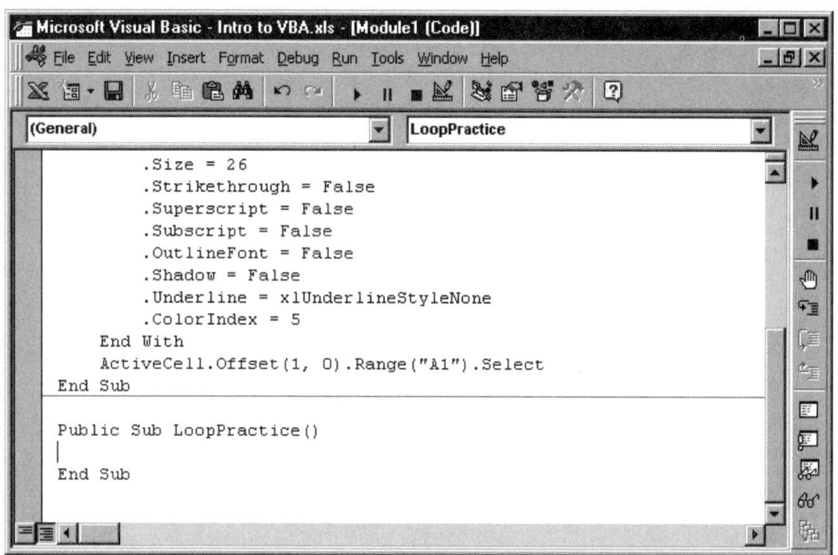

Figure 5-17: LoopPractice appears in the Code Window

Type the code shown in Example 5-1 (remember, VBA has already provided the first and last lines):

Example 5-1: The LoopPractice Subroutine

```
Public Sub LoopPractice()
Dim i As Integer
For i = 1 To 10
   MsgBox i
Next i
End Sub
```

NOTE Notice that we've indented code inside the `For...Next` loop construct by one tab stop. If you're new to programming, the practice of indenting code is a long-standing tradition and definitely makes your code more readable.

That's a fully functional VBA program. Translated into English, it goes something like this:

1. This is a subroutine called *LoopPractice* that's Public, i.e., other programs can use it.
2. Set aside room for a variable called *i*. It will hold integer values.
3. Do the following, with *i* first set to 1, then to 2, then to 3, etc., and finally with *i* set to 10.

4. Put a message box up on the screen that contains the current value of `i`.
5. Repeat with the next value of `i`.
6. This is the end of the subroutine called *LoopPractice*.

It probably won't surprise you too much to know that *LoopPractice* will put a series of ten message boxes on the screen, each with a number from one to ten. Verify that by running *LoopPractice*: simply push the Play button and watch what happens.

If you were watching closely as you typed in the program, you probably noticed little cheat boxes that popped up, offering to help you with your program. The first one (see Figure 5-18) listed all the different variable types that could go in a `Dim` statement. You wanted Integer.

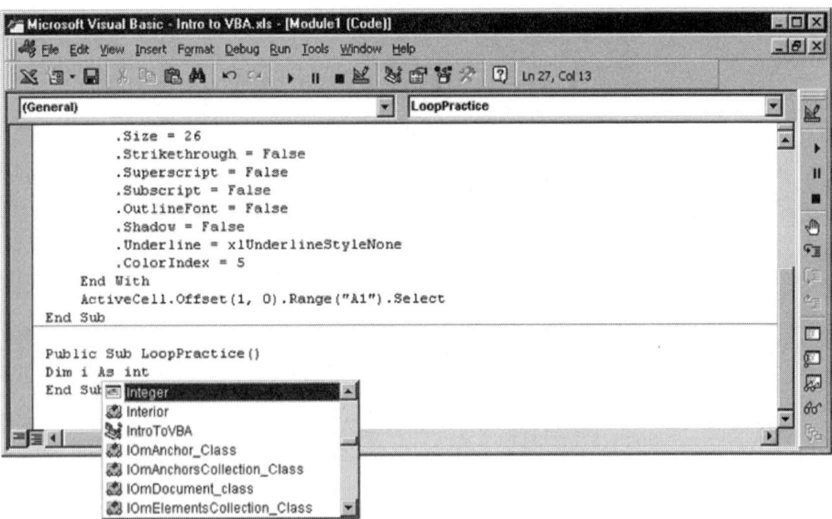

Figure 5-18: VBA offers valid variable types as Auto List Members

This capability, where VBA offers you a list of valid commands at a particular point in building a line of code, is called Auto List Members. You can scroll down the proffered list with the up and down arrow keys, or you can simply type more letters in the command to scroll down the list. Either way, when VBA has found the item you want, hitting the `Tab` key will automatically fill out the remainder of the command and leave the cursor on the current line. It's a wonderful feature.

NOTE Pressing the `Tab` key to accept the desired item in the list may feel awkward at first, but you'll get used to it. You can press `Enter` to accept the desired item in the list and start a new line.

The Auto List Members list will differ depending on the References you've defined for the current project. You'll recall from earlier in the chapter that we've thrown our References net fairly wide to include several other applications' object models.

The second cheat box that popped up (see Figure 5-19) listed the parameters that could go along with a message box function. You only used the first parameter, in this case the variable *`i`* in place of the ***`Prompt`*** parameter.

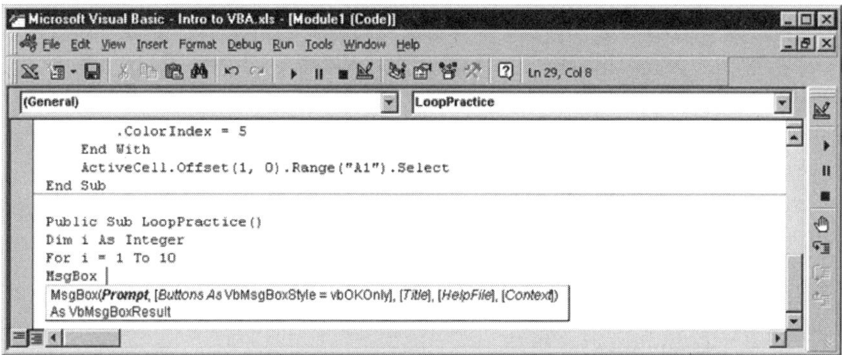

Figure 5-19: VBA offers valid parameters as Auto Quick Info

This capability, where VBA prompts you with the various parameters for a particular command, is called Auto Quick Info. It can come in very handy, especially if you're forever forgetting which parameters are available, and what sequence they come in. The shorthand VBA uses can sometimes grow cryptic, and VBA doesn't offer to complete commands for you as it does with Auto List Members. Still, you'll come to rely on this feature over and over again.

If you find type-ahead looking-over-your-shoulder features like these annoying—and some people do—you can turn them off by choosing Tools ➤ Options, Editor, and un-checking them individually or en masse as desired. For additional information about the Visual Basic Editor's settings, click this dialog's Help button.

NOTE Note that when you type the command form of a command—`MsgBox i`—instead of the function form—`rc = MsgBox(i)`—VBA's Quick Info pops up at different times. In the command form, you won't see Quick Info until you type a space character following the command. In the function form case, you'll see Quick Info as soon as you type the opening parenthesis of the parameter list.

Embellishment

The best way to learn about VBA is to play with it a bit. You have a great little sandbox here, so take advantage of it! Try these variations.

The `For` statement can do lots of things. Replace `For i = 1 to 10` with the following:

```
For i = 5 to 10
For i = 1 to 10 Step 2
For i = 5 to 1 Step -1
```

The *MsgBox* command has three commonly used parameters. The first parameter is just the message that appears in the box. The second parameter specifies the types of buttons (OK, Cancel, etc.) and the icon (none, exclamation mark, question mark, etc.) that appear in the box. The third parameter appears as the box's window title. (See Figure 5-20.) Try these in place of `MsgBox i`. In each case, try to guess what will happen before you run the program:

```
MsgBox i*10
MsgBox i, vbOKOnly
MsgBox i, vbYesNoCancel
MsgBox "The value of i is: " & i, vbExclamation, _
       "My Loop Practice Routine"
```

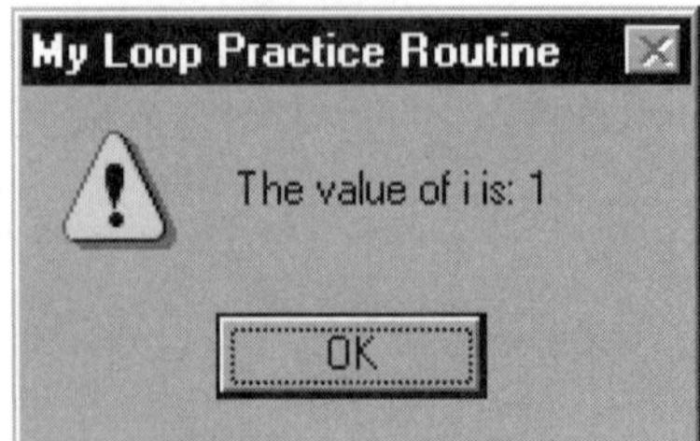

Figure 5-20: A fancier MsgBox

`vbOKOnly`, `vbYesNoCancel`, and `vbExclamation` are examples of VBA constants. They're numbers predefined by VBA and given relatively easy to remember names. For example, `vbYesNoCancel` is preassigned the value 3 by VBA. You could try to remember that the number 3 will produce Yes, No, and Cancel buttons on a VBA *MsgBox*. But you'll undoubtedly find it much easier to remember the constant `vbYesNoCancel`. Since these general-purpose constants are the same across all the Office applications that support VBA, your learning curve is lessened dramatically.

NOTE If you need help with a particular object, method, property, or function in your source code, right inside the Code Window simply click next to (or anywhere inside) the keyword you want help on and press `F1`.

A More Interesting Program

Let's try a slightly more complex program, and see if we can take advantage of several additional VBA features. Get VBA going, click Insert ➤ Procedure, type **`PowerOfTwo`**, and click OK. Then type in the program shown in Example 5-2.

Example 5-2: The PowerOfTwo Subroutine

```
Public Sub PowerOfTwo()

Dim iMax As Integer, i As Integer
Dim sMsg As String
iMax = InputBox("Enter a number between 1 and 32766", "Find Power")
If iMax > 0 And iMax < 32767 Then
    If iMax = 1 Then
        i = iMax
    Else
        i = 1
        Do
            i = i * 2
        Loop Until i > iMax
    End If
    sMsg = "The greatest power of two less than or equal to " _
         & iMax
    sMsg = sMsg & " is " & i & "."
    MsgBox sMsg, vbOKOnly, "Find Power"
Else
    MsgBox "You typed an invalid number.", vbOKOnly, "Find Power"
End If

End Sub
```

In English, the program goes more or less like this:

1. This is a subroutine called *PowerOfTwo* that other programs can use.
2. Set aside room for integer variables called `i` and `iMax`, and for a string called `sMsg`.
3. Ask the user to type in a number between 1 and 32766.* Set `iMax` to that value.
4. If the user typed a valid number, keep calculating progressively larger powers of two. Stop when you've reached a number bigger than `iMax`, and display in a message box the power of two that's closest to but less than `iMax`.
5. If the user didn't type a valid number, tell her so.
6. This is the end of the *PowerOfTwo* subroutine.

Look like a reasonable program? Good. Click the Play button and run it. The dialog in Figure 5-21 appears, asking you to enter a number between 1 and 32,766. Let's start by seeing how fast this program will go when it works on a significant problem. Feed it a big number like, oh, 20,000.

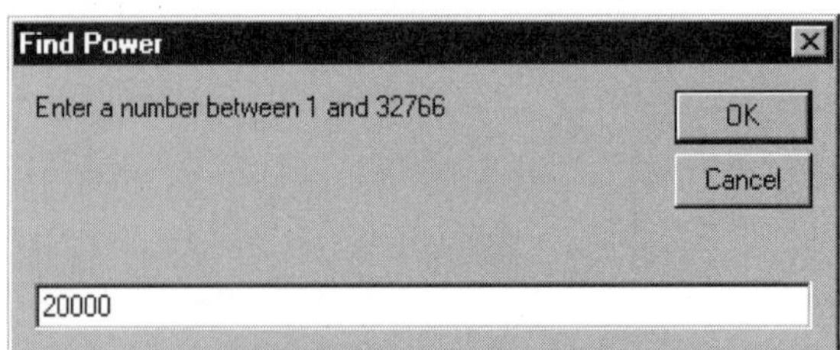

Figure 5-21: The PowerOfTwo Input Box

Oops. Something went wrong. You've hit an overflow—programmer's jargon for "the result you got when you did a calculation that is too blasted big to fit into the variable it's supposed to go into." (Click the Help button in Figure 5-22, and you'll see a somewhat less understandable description.) What went wrong? And why?

To help find out, click the Debug button in Figure 5-22. VBA will immediately highlight the line it was running when the error occurred. A yellow arrow appears in the vertical bar to the left of the line that was being executed. (See Figure 5-23.)

* Note that integer variables can only hold values up to and including 32,767. To learn that, hit `F1` and ask VBA Bob, "What is the maximum value of an integer?" After you've seen that he hasn't a clue what you're talking about, ask Bob "integer data type," then select the Integer Data Type topic.

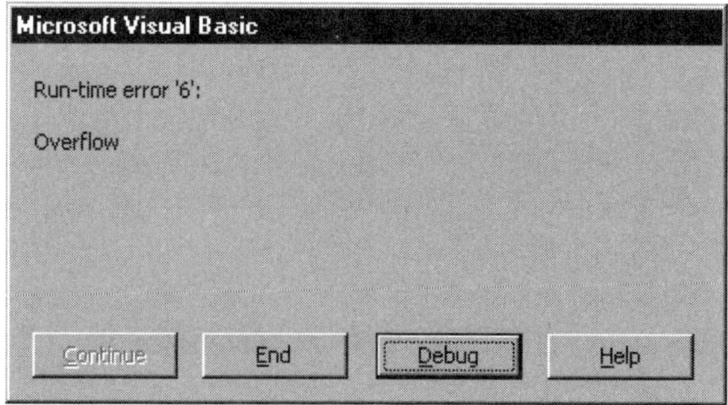

Figure 5-22: Run time error 6

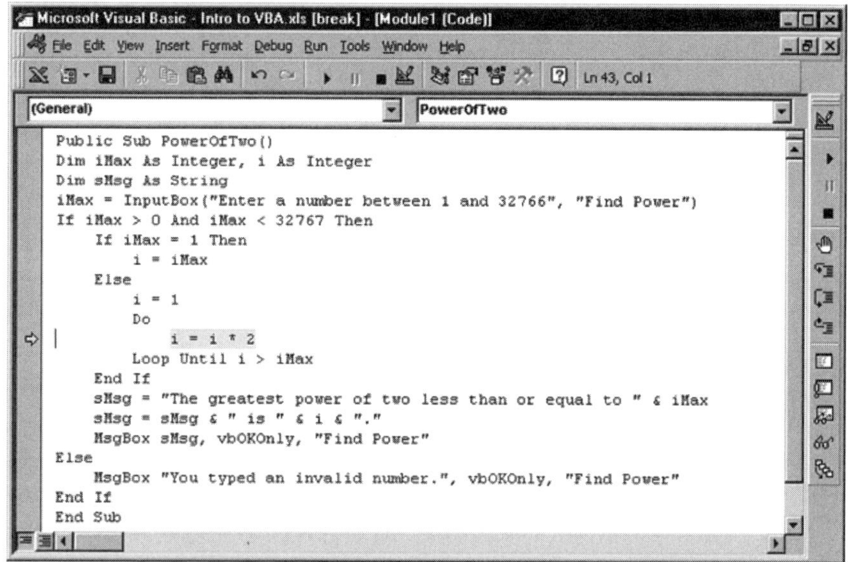

Figure 5-23: The offending statement

Somehow, the variable `i` is getting too big. (You'll also notice that if you enter a smaller value, say 4, the program reports a result that's larger than what you entered. This is obviously wrong. You'll see why and fix this bug in the ensuing paragraphs.) That's the only possible reason why you'd hit an overflow on that particular line. Let's use a couple of VBA's cooler features to track down the error.

While it's true that we could step through the program line by line by clicking on the Debug toolbar button that looks like a stack of pancakes, doing so could take a while—particularly if the program is calculating lots of powers of two. Let's take a different tack and insert a breakpoint in the program.

One of the most useful debugging tools, breakpoints tell VBA "Pause when you reach this line." Breakpoints don't affect the flow of the program, don't change any variable values, don't do anything but get VBA to wait while you look at how things are going. You can insert a breakpoint at the line that says `Do` by left-clicking at that point in the vertical bar on the left of the Code window, as shown in Figure 5-24. Do so now.

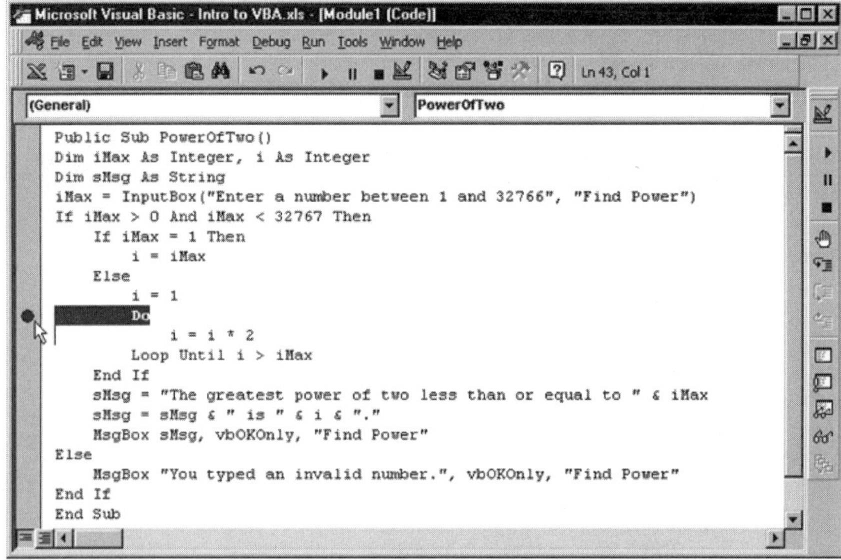

Figure 5-24: Breakpoint set at "Do"

Now, stop the program (click the square-box Stop button) and run the program again, using the Play button. Type in **20000** again when asked for a number between 1 and 32766. Click OK, and boom! VBA stops dead in its tracks when it hits the breakpoint. Note how nothing has changed: the program simply paused so you could take a look-see. (See Figure 5-25.)

Now simply hover the cursor next to any variable. See how its value appears, in a yellow box, as a so-called ToolTip? Amazing.

Once you've ascertained the value of *i*, hit the Step Into (`F8`) button again and again, until VBA triggers another overflow. Do you see where the problem lies?

There's a bug in the program. If you don't see it yet, click the Stop button then start the program all over again using the value 20000. Once you reach your breakpoint, keep hitting the Step Into (`F8`) button until the

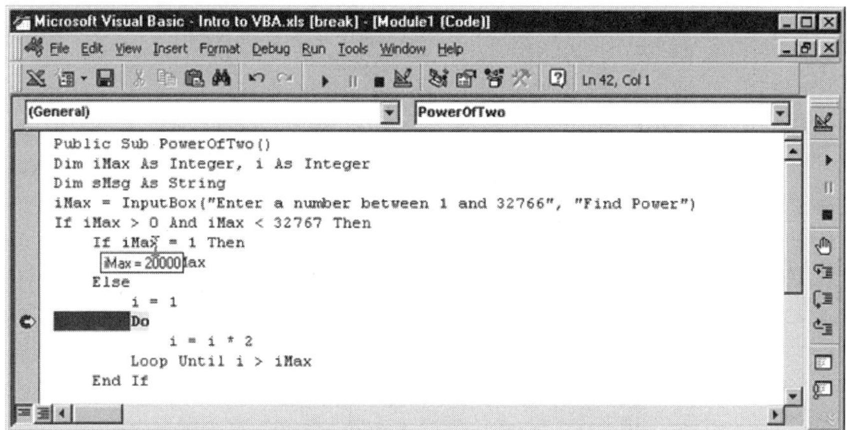

Figure 5-25: Variable value ToolTips—a to-die-for feature

value of *i* gets up to 16384, then pause reflectively. Aha! Your program is about to multiply 16384 by 2 again, and the resulting number, 32768, will trigger the overflow. It'll also send the value of *i* higher than the number that the user typed in. If you think about it a bit, you'll come to the conclusion that the `Until` part of the loop should stop at `iMax / 2`.

Okay. No need to let that little bug stop you. If the value of *i* is at 16384 and the yellow arrow is pointing to the `i = i * 2` line, you can skip farther down in the program by simply picking up the yellow arrow and sticking it on the next statement that you want VBA to execute!

```
    Else
        i = 1
        Do
            i = i * 2
        Loop Until i > iMax
    End If
    sMsg = "The greatest power of two less than or equal to " & iMax
    sMsg = sMsg & " is " & i & "."
```

Figure 5-26: Bypassing the bug

If you put the arrow on the first `sMsg =` line and click the Play button, as we've done in Figure 5-26, VBA will continue to run from that point on, and you can get on with your testing. Just don't forget to change the `Loop` line to say:

```
Loop Until i > iMax / 2
```

As we said, it's quite an editor. It's a treat to use, once you get the hang of it. And we haven't even scratched the surface of all its features. As you grow more proficient at VBA—and your programs get longer and longer, and buggier and buggier—you'll learn about the other editor debugging features, including:

- The Locals window, which lists all defined variables and their current values
- The Immediate window, which lets you run any VBA statement, manually, while a program is executing
- The Watch window, which lets you pause the program when a variable's value changes, and much more

Unfortunately, all of these topics are beyond the scope of this book, but a few hours spent kicking around the VBA Editor's Help file will reap big rewards. Most of all, you should come away with the belief that the VBA Editor is a world-class program editor—quite possibly the best ever created.

And it's at your beck and call.

PrintCbarControlsList: A Genuinely Useful Program

NOTE Congratulations on surviving your first VBA/Excel programming experience. Now may be a good time to take a break. From this point on, we're going to tackle a variety of problems, just so you can get some experience working with VBA/Excel and the Editor. There's no way we could squeeze a full introduction to VBA/Excel into this chapter, so we'll sacrifice completeness for broad exposure.

Even if you're thinking of picking up a VBA/Excel book or reference later (the *Mastering Office Development* CD produced by Microsoft is a good starting point), try wading through the remainder of this chapter. You'll have a chance to see VBA/Excel in action, solving real problems. If you follow along closely, you may pick up a number of tips and insights the other sources don't touch.

Besides, the *PrintCbarsControlList* program's pretty cool, and you won't find it anywhere else!

The best way to get to know VBA/Excel is to trace through working programs, trying to figure out exactly which commands accomplish what tasks. Just as there's no substitute for practice in a foreign language—and complete immersion works even better—diving head first into real, working VBA/Excel programs will give you a great opportunity to absorb the language and its nuances.

Back in Chapter 3, *Tales of the Toolbar and Other Aides-de-Camp*, we included figures that revealed some interesting control properties for Excel's Standard and Formatting toolbars. We used a VBA macro called *PrintCbarsControlList* to uncover those command bar control properties.

To create your own copy of the macro, bring up the VBA/Excel Editor (Tools ➤ Macro ➤ Visual Basic Editor). Make sure you're in the IntroToVBA project, navigate down to the Module called Module1, and add a new procedure to the module by clicking Insert ➤ Procedure, typing the name **PrintCbarControlsList**, and clicking OK. Then type in the program in Example 5-3. This is a rudimentary version of the macro, stripped down to make it easier to understand. For example, it doesn't gracefully deal with misspelled command bar names, and the formatting could be improved. For now, though, you should be able to step through the macro and see more or less what's going on.

Example 5-3: The PrintCbarControlsList Routine

```
Public Sub PrintCbarsControlsList()
    ' ----- Initializations/declarations
    Dim cbarControl As CommandBarControl
    Dim i As Integer
    Dim lngRowIndex As Long
    Dim rngHeadings As Range
    Dim strCBarName As String
    Dim strDefault As String
    Dim strPrompt As String
    Dim strTitle As String
    Dim strType As String
    strTitle = "ExcelAnnoy Command Bar Control Lister"
    ' ----- Main body
    strDefault = "Standard"
    strPrompt = "Please enter the name of the command bar " & _
        "you're interested in:"
    strCBarName = InputBox(strPrompt, strTitle, strDefault)
    ' don't bother with an empty string or Cancel from user
    If strCBarName = "" Then Exit Sub
    ' create a new sheet in the current workbook
    Sheets.Add Type:=xlWorksheet
    ' put the command bar name in A1
    Cells(1, 1) = "Command Bar name: " & _
                 Command Bars(strCBarName).Name
    ' starting in A2, add the column headings
    lngRowIndex = 2
    Set rngHeadings = Range(Cells(lngRowIndex, 1), _
                  Cells (lngRowIndex, 10))
    rngHeadings.Value = Array("Index", "BuiltIn", "Caption", _
        "DescriptionText", "Id", "OnAction", "TooltipText", _
        "Type (Value)", "Type (Name)", "Visible")
    rngHeadings.Font.Bold = True
    ' starting in A3, add the data
    ' On Error to avoid run-time error 438 on some .OnAction calls
```

Example 5-3: The PrintCbarControlsList Routine (continued)

```
    On Error Resume Next
    lngRowIndex = lngRowIndex + 1
    For Each cbarControl In CommandBars(strCBarName).Controls
        With cbarControl
            Cells(lngRowIndex, 1) = .Index
            Cells(lngRowIndex, 2) = .BuiltIn
            Cells(lngRowIndex, 3) = .Caption
            Cells(lngRowIndex, 4) = .DescriptionText
            Cells(lngRowIndex, 5) = .Id
            Cells(lngRowIndex, 6) = .OnAction
            Cells(lngRowIndex, 7) = .TooltipText
            Cells(lngRowIndex, 8) = .Type
                strType = "<<we'll calc this later>>"
            Cells(lngRowIndex, 9) = strType
            Cells(lngRowIndex, 10) = .Visible
        End With
        lngRowIndex = lngRowIndex + 1
    Next
End Sub
```

Translating that into English goes something like this:

1. This is a subroutine called *PrintCbarControlsList.*
2. Save space for one CommandBarControl object variable, one integer, one long integer, one Range object variable, and five strings.
3. Ask the user which command bar he wants a report on. If the user enters no command bar name, exit quietly.
4. Create a new worksheet in the current workbook.
5. Put the command bar name in A1.
6. Starting in A2, add the column headings.
7. Starting in A3, add the data.
8. Use the `For Each...Next` construct to walk through the CommandBarControls collection for this particular command bar, and put property values into cells in the current row.
9. *PrintCbarControlsList* ends here.

NOTE In object model lexicon, a *collection* is an ordered set of objects that you can refer to as a single item. You can also refer to its individual component objects.

To run the macro, put the cursor anywhere inside the subroutine, then click the Play button. See Figure 5-27 for a sample report.

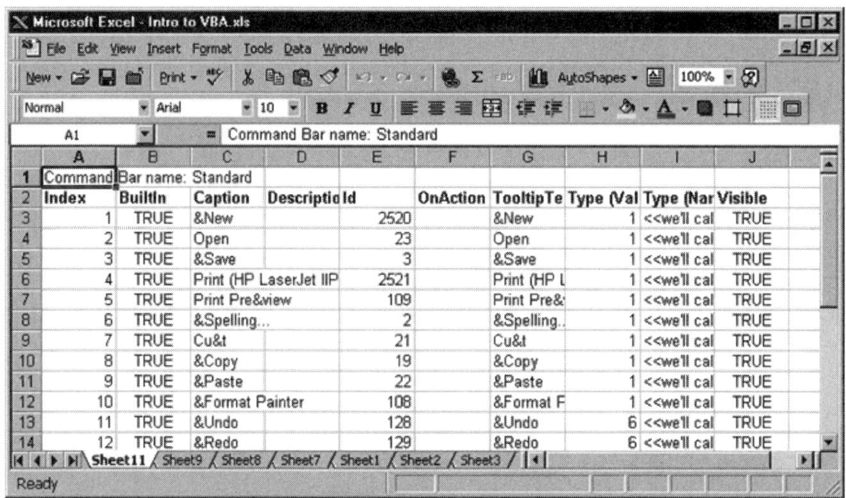

	A	B	C	D	E	F	G	H	I	J
1	Command Bar name: Standard									
2	Index	BuiltIn	Caption	Descriptio	Id	OnAction	TooltipTe	Type (Val	Type (Nar	Visible
3	1	TRUE	&New		2520		&New	1	<<we'll cal	TRUE
4	2	TRUE	Open		23		Open	1	<<we'll cal	TRUE
5	3	TRUE	&Save		3		&Save	1	<<we'll cal	TRUE
6	4	TRUE	Print (HP LaserJet IIP		2521		Print (HP L	1	<<we'll cal	TRUE
7	5	TRUE	Print Pre&view		109		Print Pre&	1	<<we'll cal	TRUE
8	6	TRUE	&Spelling...		2		&Spelling..	1	<<we'll cal	TRUE
9	7	TRUE	Cu&t		21		Cu&t	1	<<we'll cal	TRUE
10	8	TRUE	&Copy		19		&Copy	1	<<we'll cal	TRUE
11	9	TRUE	&Paste		22		&Paste	1	<<we'll cal	TRUE
12	10	TRUE	&Format Painter		108		&Format F	1	<<we'll cal	TRUE
13	11	TRUE	&Undo		128		&Undo	6	<<we'll cal	TRUE
14	12	TRUE	&Redo		129		&Redo	6	<<we'll cal	TRUE

Figure 5-27: PrintCbarControlsList output for the Standard command bar

---

NOTE Collections tip: There are two quick ways to call up a list of all 42 Excel collections in Visual Basic help. First, the Item topic: ask the Office Assistant "item" and choose the Item topic. Second, the "Add Method" topic: ask Robert "add method" and choose the "Add Method (Workbooks Collection)" topic, then click the See Also link and choose the second "Add Method" item in the list. The former lists all collections as jump topics (topics you can click on and go to immediately). The latter lists what happens when the Add method is applied to each collection, also with jump topics.

Fleshing Out VBA

NOTE Let's take a quick look at the other parts of VBA—valuable parts that you may want to exploit in your programs, somewhere down the line. As before, we won't even try for completeness. Instead our goal is to give you an idea of the major chunks of the language that are available, and how they all fit together.

That's the "Basic" part of VBA: a very powerful programming language, tied into a world-class programming editor and debugger. As you've seen in *PrintCbarControlsList*, the Basic part of VBA, all by itself, can do all sorts of things to Excel—and alleviate all sorts of annoyances. But the programming language itself is only part of the story and only one of the tools at your disposal to customize Excel to work for you and, if you develop custom Excel applications for others, your users.

The "visual" part of VBA consists of an enormously powerful kit for drag-and-drop construction of custom dialog boxes, plus built-in hooks to associate controls* on the dialog boxes—push buttons, text boxes, check boxes, spin buttons, and much more—with your program code.

Four kinds of hooks between the visual and the Basic—the dialog boxes and program code—come into play:

1. Your program can set many of the controls' characteristics. For example, you can write a program that changes the name that appears on a push button, or one that changes the color of the entire dialog box. These characteristics are called *control properties.*
2. Your program can retrieve controls' characteristics. For example, if you set things up so your custom dialog box can be resized, you can write a program that retrieves the dialog's current size or location on the screen. If you have check boxes on the dialog, your program can look to see if a particular box has been checked.
3. You can set up certain programs to be run when specific things happen to the custom dialog. For example, you can tell VBA/Excel "run the program called Foobar whenever the user double-clicks on this picture." The things that can happen are called *events.* We call the programs that handle events *event handlers.*
4. Finally, you can make your program trigger or fire events. For example, you can write a program to tell VBA/Excel, "behave precisely the same way you would've behaved if the user had clicked the OK button." Think of this as an invisible hand that you can manipulate from inside your programs. Sure, the user can click a Cancel button, but your program can click the Cancel button just as well.

Let's take a look at custom dialog boxes, how they're constructed, and what options are available to you. Then we'll tie together the visual and the Basic with a demonstration of event handlers.

* As far as we're concerned in this discussion of VBA, *controls* are simply the things that sit on a dialog box. In the larger Windows world, controls can sit in dialogs, Excel sheets, Word documents, on Web pages, and many other places. You can create your own controls with Visual Basic 5.0, Control Creation Edition.

Custom Dialog Boxes

VBA calls the dialog boxes you construct *User Forms* (code name Forms^3, pronounced "forms cubed"). The term *form* has come to be synonymous with *dialog box*. We'll try to stay consistent here and only refer to custom built dialogs, dialog boxes, or simply *dboxes*. (Note: if you develop any applications in Word, be aware that Word includes yet another type of Form, which is a particular kind of document (template) that has certain parts locked out so they can't be modified. A VBA User Form is decidedly not a Word Form.)

To see what's going on, let's construct a simple custom dialog box. If you're not in the Visual Basic Editor, click on Tools ➤ Macro ➤ Visual Basic Editor. Bring up the Project Explorer and the Properties Window by clicking on the two buttons on VBA's Standard toolbar. Navigate to the IntroToVBA project, which should have a Module called Module1 that contains the macros you worked on earlier.

To create a new custom dialog box, click on Insert ➤ UserForm. VBA/Excel will place a new dbox in the window that used to hold program code. It will call the new dbox UserForm1 and put UserForm1 in the dbox's title area (see Figure 5-28). At the same time, a window marked Toolbox will appear. It contains controls that you will probably want to paint on your dbox.

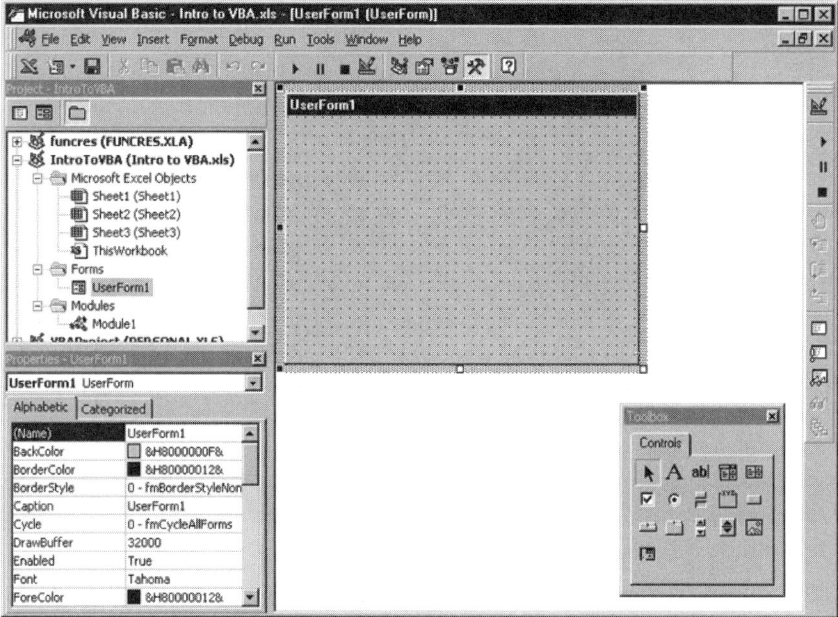

Figure 5-28: Creating a new custom dialog box

For starters, let's change the caption at the top of the dbox. To do so, locate the Properties Window, which probably sits just below the Project Explorer. The top of the Properties Window should say Properties—UserForm1, which is meant to inform you that you are looking at the properties of the thing called UserForm1. Underneath sits a drop-down list box that says UserForm1 UserForm, which repeats the name of the dbox, and informs you that the dbox called UserForm1 is a UserForm. Rocket science.

Look down in the body of the Properties Window and locate a line that says Caption. The Caption property of UserForm1 is nothing more or less than the text that appears in the title bar of the UserForm1 dbox. Change the Caption to, oh, "My Custom Dialog" and watch as VBA/Excel changes the title bar of UserForm1 while you type. (See Figure 5-29.)

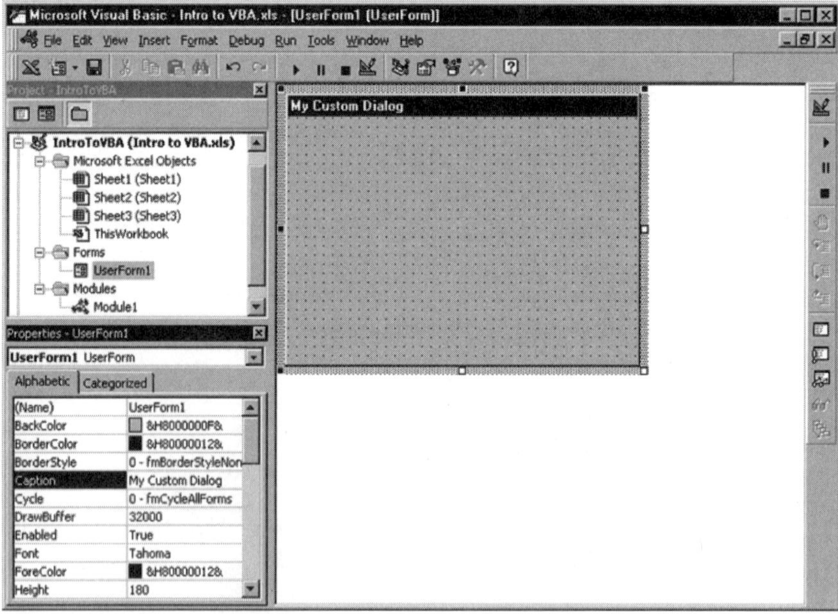

Figure 5-29: Changing the title (Caption) of the custom dialog box

For this simple exercise, we're going to place a single Command Button control on the dbox. To do so, first make sure the Toolbox is visible by single-clicking anywhere inside your custom dbox. Then locate the Command Button control in the Toolbox. It's the last control on the second row and has a ToolTip of "CommandButton." Click it once. Now click on the custom dbox and paint a Command Button on it. (See Figure 5-30.)

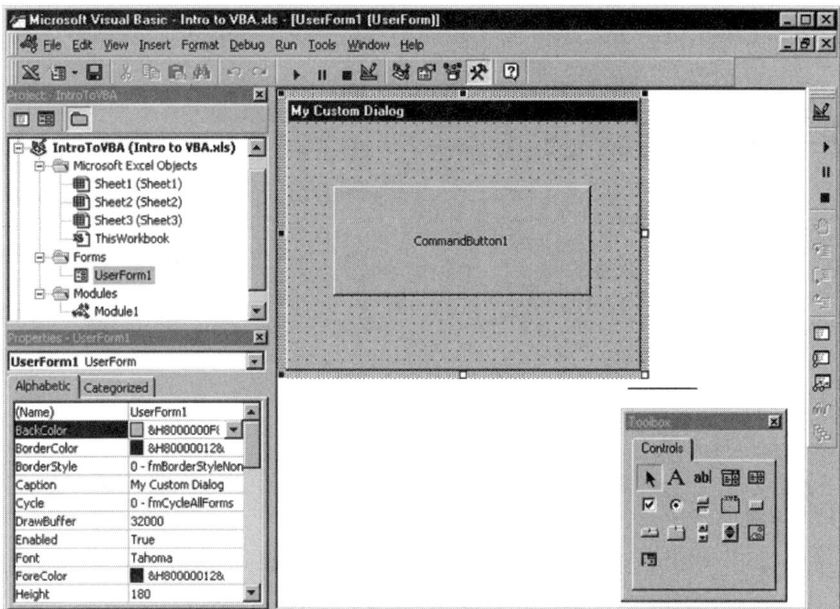

Figure 5-30: Painting a Command Button control on the custom dbox

We want the Command Button to say something slightly more intelligent than "CommandButton1". The text that appears on a Command Button face is simply the Caption property of the Command Button. Go over to the Properties Window, scroll down to Caption, and change it from CommandButton1 to "PUSH ME!" (See Figure 5-31.)

Congratulations. That's all it takes to build a custom dialog box in VBA/Excel. Granted, it doesn't do much just yet, but adding intelligence to a dbox remains the provenance of event handlers. For now, think of this nascent dbox as an exceedingly pretty face that can perform a few airhead tricks.

To see the entire UserForm1 repertoire, click the VBA/Excel Play button. Your custom dbox will spring to life as shown in Figure 5-32.

Note how you can push the Command Button, but it doesn't do much, aside from looking marvelous. You can also move the dbox around, placing it anywhere on the desktop. But that's about it. When you're bored (should take about two seconds), click the X in UserForm1's upper-right corner, and you'll return to VBA/Excel.

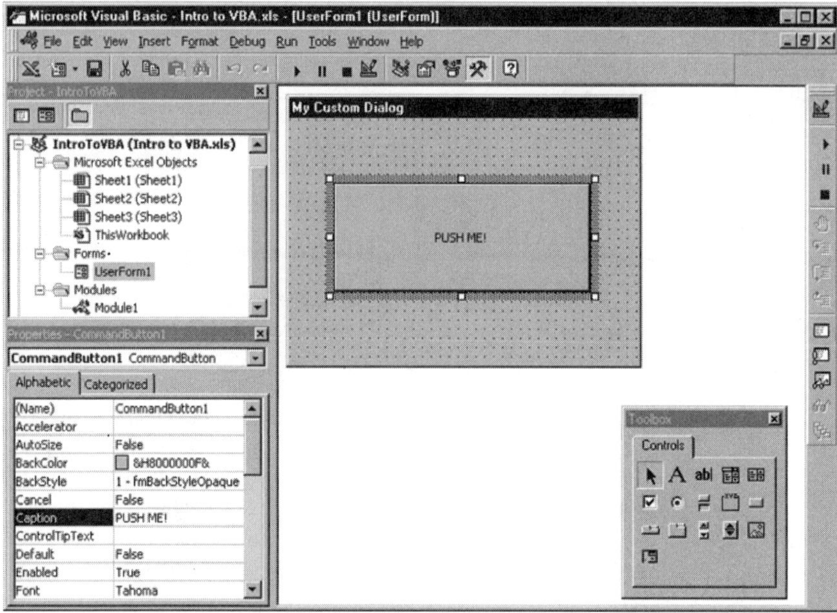

Figure 5-31: Changing the Caption property of CommandButton1

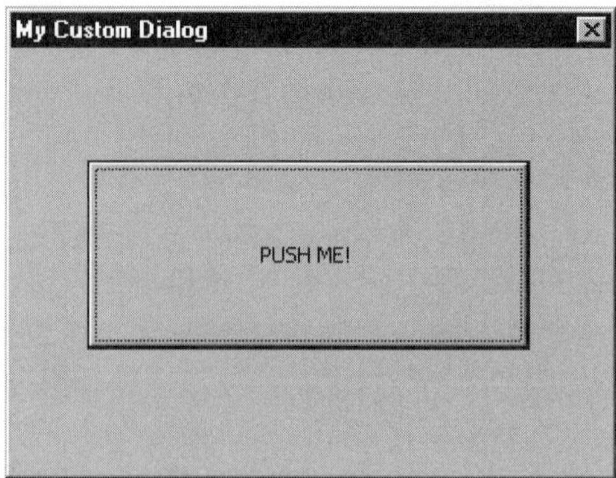

Figure 5-32: Run UserForm1

Events and Event Handlers

Let's write an event handler that will accomplish something when you push UserForm1's Command Button. While we won't try to create anything as fancy as *PrintCbarControlsList*, we think you'll be pleasantly surprised by how easy it is to make programs work with VBA/Excel custom dialog boxes and how little effort it takes to change those dboxes from inside a program.

We're going to write a program that runs whenever the user clicks the Command Button. In VBA/Excel speak, the program should run when the CommandButton1.Click event occurs (or fires). VBA/Excel's method of associating events with their event handlers is simplicity itself, and it relies on the names of the event handler subroutines. For example, when the CommandButton1.Click event fires, VBA/Excel looks for a subroutine called `CommandButton1_Click`. If that subroutine exists, Excel runs it. Easy.

So if we want to write a program that will run when the user clicks on CommandButton1—or, if you want to impress your boss, a "handler for the CommandButton1.Click event"—we apparently need to construct a subroutine called `CommandButton1_Click`. VBA/Excel makes that incredibly simple, too.

Design Time vs. Run Time

The official documentation makes a big distinction between *design time* and *run time*. No need for you to get hung up about it. The difference is really quite simple.

Sometimes you're writing a program. Other times you're running the program. That's the whole difference. When you're writing a program, design time, you don't expect things in the outside world to suddenly affect your program. When you're running a program, though, you expect it to respond to everything.

Since VBA/Excel gives you so many ways to run and stop programs—breakpoints, single-line stepping, and much more—sometimes it's hard to remember when you're running and when you're programming. The basic rule is this: if you click something or push something, and you don't get the response you were expecting, check to make sure you're in the mode you thought you were in. To move from design mode to run mode, just click once inside the VBA/Excel editor and hit `F5`, or click the right-wedgie Play button. To move from run mode to design mode, click the square-box Stop button.

Whenever you want to write an event handler for any control's most common event, you just double-click on the control and VBA/Excel will get the subroutine going for you. In this case, the Click event is far and away the most common event for a Command Button. So if you double-click on CommandButton1, VBA/Excel will get rid of the custom dialog box, move you into the code writing window, and start a subroutine for you that's called `CommandButton1_Click`.

We prefer to get rid of the Project Explorer and Properties Window as soon as we start writing code. You might want to do the same by clicking the X in the upper-right corners of each. The result is what you see in Figure 5-33.

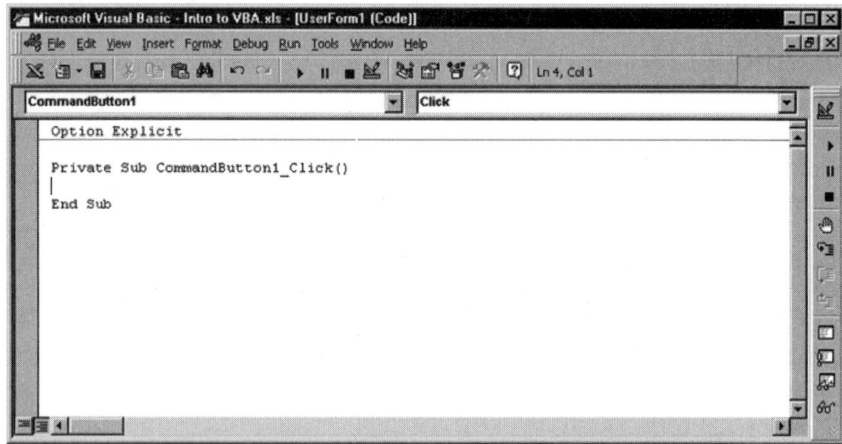

Figure 5-33: Double-click on the Command Button, and VBA/Excel sets this up for you

Type in the simple program shown in Example 5-4. (VBA/Excel has already supplied the first and last lines.)

Example 5-4: The CommandButton1.Click Event Handler

```
Private Sub CommandButton1_Click()
If CommandButton1.Caption = "PUSH ME!" Then
    CommandButton1.Caption = "Push Me AGAIN!"
Else
    CommandButton1.Caption = "PUSH ME!"
End If
End Sub
```

No doubt you can figure out what the program does without our help. It works by looking at and changing the text on the face of the Command Button. Or, in VBA/Excel-speak, it examines and sets the Caption property of the CommandButton1 control.

Once you're done typing in the code, you can run the whole thing by clicking on the right-wedgie Play button. Click on the Command Button a few times to make sure all is well (see Figure 5-34). Then click the X in the upper-right corner to flip back into VBA/Excel.

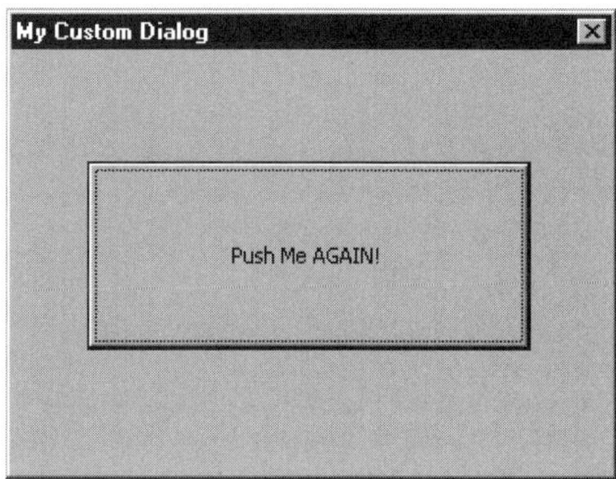

Figure 5-34: The CommandButton1_Click event handler in action

One last note before we start tying VBA/Excel into Excel itself. Back in the coding window, take a look at the Object and Procedure drop-down lists. On the left side you'll see a list of all the controls available in the current custom dialog box. On the right—as shown in Figure 5-35—there's a list of all the events associated with whatever control you've chosen. The enormous number of available events (e.g., MouseMove, which fires whenever the user passes the cursor over a Command Button) gives you unprecedented leeway in making custom dialog boxes work the way you want them to work.

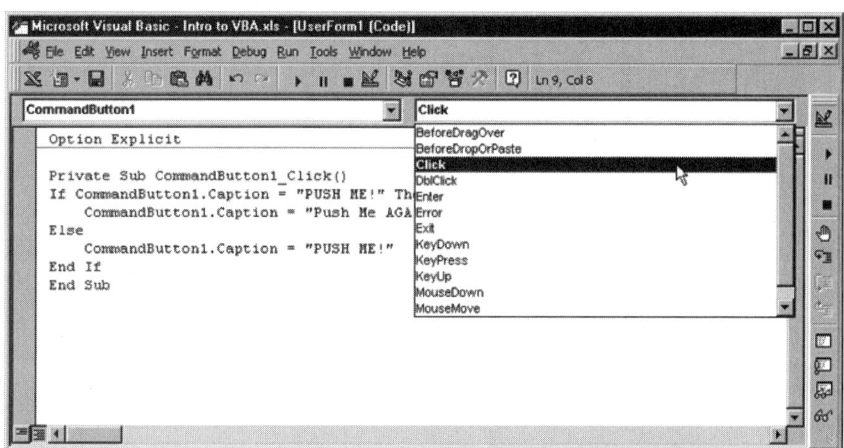

Figure 5-35: The events defined for the CommandButton1 control

NOTE As your VBA programs grow larger and more complex, you may find yourself longing for some guidelines on how to systematically name your variables, constants, controls, procedures, etc. There is a lot of material on this subject out there. In terms of what's readily accessible from Microsoft's Web site, you might want to start with the TechNet CD's article *Using Consistent Naming Conventions for Solution Development with MS Office.* Also check out the Microsoft Knowledge Base article Q110264 *LONG: Microsoft Consulting Services Naming Conventions for VB.* Wherever you turn for naming conventions, the payback for adopting a convention and using it consistently will be tremendous.

Controlling Excel

NOTE In this section, we'll delve into the Excel Object Model—the set of hooks that let you write programs to control the way Excel behaves. What does the Excel Object Model have to do with annoyances? Just about everything. The Excel Object Model defines (and limits!) precisely how your programs can manipulate Excel. If you've never hit an Object Model before, the concept can be a bit confusing. Not to worry. We'll take you through step by step, give you a handful of examples, and then turn you loose to try it for yourself.

So much for the whirlwind introduction to VBA, its programming environment, and the way VBA influences—and is influenced by—custom dialog boxes. Much of what you've seen so far in this chapter is applicable to VBA/Word, VBA/PowerPoint, VBA/Visio, and even Visual Basic itself. Once you've spent a few hours learning VBA/Excel, a substantial portion of what you've discovered will be immediately useful in any of those other programming languages.

Now let's turn to the ways in which VBA can control Excel workbooks, and Excel itself. It's not an exaggeration to say that you can write a VBA/Excel program to do just about *anything* in Excel.

Objects, Properties, Methods

Buzzwords, buzzwords.

Wherever you look in VBA land, you'll find references to objects, properties, and methods. They constitute the ruling triumvirate of the VBA party. You'll see the terms mentioned so often that you might be tempted to believe they represent some sort of cosmic truth. That they're a literary shorthand for The Fundamental Concept Behind VBA, Life, the Universe, and Everything. That somehow understanding the difference between an object, property, and method will bestow instant transcendental illumination on your road to VBA enlightenment.

Ha.

NOTE Chances are good that you're reasonably well versed in the tenets of grammar. If so, here's what you need to know: an object is a noun, a property is an adjective, and a method is a verb. That's it.

Fortunately, object modeling hasn't yet descended to the level of adverbial clauses and the subjunctive mood. But those days are coming.*

Objects are things. In Excel, that includes workbooks, sheets, cells, ranges, shapes, built-in dialog boxes, and much more. One of the most fundamental objects in Excel is the range—a conglomeration of cells that could be a single cell, an entire column or row, a selection of cells that includes one or more contiguous blocks of cells, or a 3-D range. In VBA itself, programs are considered to be objects, as are custom dialog boxes and controls on the boxes. Whenever you're tempted to point at something on the screen and call it a "thing," chances are very good VBA/Excel considers it to be an object.

Properties refer to the characteristics of objects. You've worked with the Caption property in custom dialog boxes and Command Buttons. It probably won't surprise you to learn that Font is a property of Range or that Name is a property of Workbook.

---

* Quick question to you object modelers out there—and I know you're reading this. What do you call a property of a property? (Grammatically, that's an adverb.) How long before you draw a distinction between methods that operate directly on associated objects, changing the object itself, and methods that merely change the contents or appearance of an object? (Akin to the distinction between transitive and intransitive verbs.) Better brush up on your Latin, guys.

Methods do things to objects. For example, the Add method applied to the Workbooks object (a collection object, actually) adds (creates) a new workbook. The Delete method applied to a Sheet object deletes the specified sheet.

In modern parlance, the difference between nouns, adjectives, and verbs has blurred somewhat: nouns take on the appearance of adjectives, verbs become nounified, and so on. The same is true of objects, properties, and methods—in some cases it isn't completely clear if a property should in fact be a method, or vice versa. Only the most anally retentive grammarian would deny this blurring in modern language. Only the most anally retentive object modeler would deny the blurring in VBA.

This can lead to a great deal of confusion. For example, in Excel, Find is a method (or verb), and this is the way most people would think of it. But in Word, Find is an object (or noun). In Excel, Zoom is a property (or adjective), but in Word, Zoom is an object.

Don't get too hung up in the terminology, and don't be overwhelmed by the huge number of objects, properties, and methods available in VBA/Excel. The terminology ultimately comes to make some sense. And your work will commonly concentrate on a small subset of all the available objects, properties, and methods.

Is This Object Oriented Programming?

Most Office users, upon learning that VBA/Excel works with things called objects, want to know if VBA/Excel actually incorporates Object Oriented Programming (or OOP).

In a word, the answer is no.

While the precise definition of OOP has seen more changes than Michael Jackson's nose, most OOPers (OOPophiles?) agree that a true Object Oriented language must provide solid support for techniques with odd sounding names—encapsulation, inheritance, polymorphic operators, and such. While VBA 5 has built-in support for some aspects of those features, typically via Class Modules, in fact VBA is still a long, long way from the OOP ideal.

The Excel Object Model

If you're using VBA/Excel for the first time with Excel 97, then the following note will only be of passing, historical significance to you (that is, unless you ever inherit someone's pre-Excel 97 VBA code, so maybe you'd better read the note anyway). If you used VBA/Excel in Excel 95 or VBA/Excel in Excel 5, then stop everything you're doing, study Figure 5-36, and then go read and print out hard copies of the eight relevant Help topics.

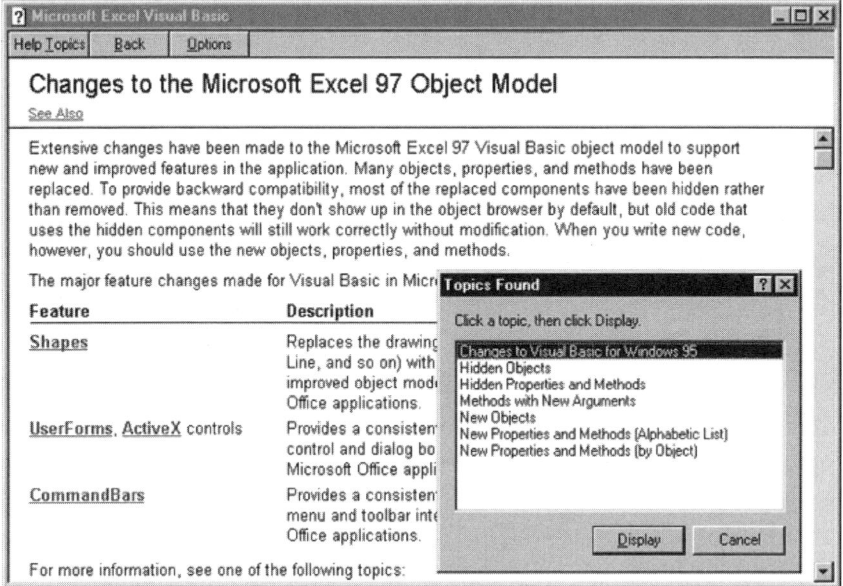

Figure 5-36: The crucial Help topic "Changes to the Microsoft Excel 97 Object Model"

NOTE The Excel Object Model has changed in Excel 97. Changes have been made to support the application's new features. For backward source code compatibility, older components have been hidden. For example, you wouldn't refer to a Line object any longer, but rather the Shapes collection, the Shape object, or the ShapeRange collection and their relevant methods and properties. You can unhide these hidden components in the Object Browser by right-clicking on the Excel Application class and then choosing the Show Hidden Members menu item; hidden components are shown in light gray type. (A complete list of these hidden components appears in the Help topics "Hidden Objects" and "Hidden Properties and Methods.") Pre-Excel 97 VBA code still runs fine in Excel 97 in most cases. You should use (and benefit from) the new components unless your code needs to run unmodified across multiple versions of VBA/Excel.

Sooner or later almost every computer program has to interact with the outside world. Very simple, old-fashioned DOS programs interacted with the user by waiting for the user to type something and then acting on whatever key was typed. They interacted with a printer by writing lines, one at a time, to the printer's port. They interacted with floppy disks by reading or writing a record of data at a time.

As these old program became more sophisticated, they rarely interacted with the user directly. Instead, they took advantage of the programs built into DOS so they didn't have to muck around with nitpicking details: the location of a particular file on a hard drive; whether the user hit a backspace to delete the preceding character; spooling output to a print file so the program didn't have to check constantly whether the printer was busy. Gradually, programs shifted from working with the user to working with the operating system. By and large, that was A Good Thing. Sure, the programmer had to learn how to call the operating system, but the additional hassle of figuring out operating system calling conventions far outweighed, say, building your own print spooler from scratch.

Then came Windows, and all hell broke loose. Windows insulated programs from the user very effectively—so effectively that very few programs attempted to bypass Windows and interact directly with the user. Instead, programmers learned how to use Windows routines—learned how to "call the Windows Application Programming Interface" or Win API—to get things done. The Windows API just describes all the routines that can be called by Windows programs, along with a definition of variables to be passed to the routines, and the meaning of the values that should be returned. While it was, and is, very difficult to write a solid Windows program, much of the complexity was tamed by setting the Windows API in concrete and forcing programmers to work through the Win API.

Object Models in general, and the Excel Object Model in particular, take this abstraction one step farther. Where an API defines the routines a program can use, along with their parameters and values, an Object Model defines the things—the objects—a program can manipulate along with valid operations on the objects. It's a subtle distinction, but one we've found useful for thinking about the Excel Object Model.

Hidden here is a fundamental secret behind the Excel Object Model: it makes every nook and cranny of Excel available to you for manipulation in your VBA/Excel programs, and it does so in a very nonprocedural (no, we won't say "object oriented") way. Microsoft has gone to great pains to ensure that the Excel Object Model describes all the things inside Excel (objects), along with characteristics of those things that you can change (properties), and activities you can perform on the things (methods). It's a significant step forward in the evolution of macro programming languages.

The Excel Object Model doesn't look like an API, like a set of procedures and their parameters. In VBA/Excel the emphasis focuses strictly on objects, properties, and methods.

Lots and lots and lots of objects, properties, and methods.

Using VBA to Answer Common Excel Dilemmas

When you're controlling Excel with VBA, you're eventually going to need Excel to tell you what condition it's in or what it's doing. In this section, we'll use VBA to answer the following common Excel questions:

- Are any workbooks open?
- How many workbooks are currently visible? (Yes, this is a trick question.)
- What is the fully qualified filename (path included) for each saved, open workbook?
- What's the name of the active workbook?
- In the active workbook, what's the index and the name of the active sheet?
- List the current workbook's sheet names in either their positional or alphabetical order.

To solve these Excel dilemmas, we'll explore frequently encountered Excel objects, methods, and properties, and at the same time we'll provide some more exposure to VBA/Excel.

NOTE In each of the following sections, first we show the source code for the procedure being discussed, followed by a short block of code that demonstrates how to use the procedure. To download the code go to *ftp://ftp.ora.com/published/oreilly/windows/excel.annoy* and then search for *Intro to VBA.xls.*

First let's add three new modules to the IntroToVBA project to help organize our test procedures, function procedures, and subroutine procedures. In the Project Window, right-click on the IntroToVBA project, choose Insert, choose Module, then change the name of the new module in the Property window to `modDemosC5` (select the module in the Project window, then in the Properties window type the new name). Repeat these steps for two more new modules—`modFunctions` and `modSubroutines`.

There are two issues you should bear in mind as you study the ensuing source code:

1. We're focusing on Excel 97-only solutions and are not concerning ourselves with code running across multiple versions of VBA/Excel (remember, Excel introduced VBA to the world at large two versions ago in Excel 5.0), a subject worthy of a book all its own.
2. For ease of presentation in a book format, we include all the local variables and constants each procedure needs to run independently; however, we encourage you to identify all variables or constants that are used by macros in different modules throughout the project and move them into a separate module (we use one called `modGlobals` for this purpose) all earmarked as `Public`. For more information about variables, where they live and how long they survive (a phenomenon called *scope*), see the Visual Basic Reference Help topic "Understanding Scope and Visibility."

NOTE The first remark statement in each code listing shows which module of *Intro to VBA.xls* the procedure belongs to.

Open that workbook kimono

Are any workbooks open? In Excel, a workbook can be either open and visible, or open and hidden. In the latter case, a reference to the Active-Workbook object returns the special value `Nothing`. The ActiveWorkbook object is a handy VBA keyword that refers to the current active workbook. An example of a workbook that's open but hidden is your *Personal.xls* workbook.

The custom function *fblnNullMenuState* (see Example 5-5 and its demo program in Example 5-6) returns a Boolean TRUE if Excel has no active workbook, and it returns FALSE if there is an active workbook. No active workbook visible amounts to the pre-Excel 97 condition known as "null menu mode," except that in Excel 97, the primary menu bar retains all its commands—instead of showing only File and Help—and disables most drop-down items since they won't work without an underlying workbook to operate upon. To see what null menu mode looks like in Excel 97, simply close all open workbooks and begin clicking on the various menu bar menus. Most items in these menus are disabled when no workbooks are open and visible.

Example 5-5: The fblnNullMenuState Function

```
' Stored in the module modFunctions
' ------------------------------------------------------------------
' Purpose:  Indicates whether Excel is in "null menu" state
'           (no visible workbooks and primary menu bar commands
'           mostly disabled).
'
' Inputs:   None.
'
' Returns:  Boolean.
'
' Updated:  04/17/97 (PCG) - validated for Excel Annoyances
'           04/24/97 (BM)  - simplified to test for no active
'                            workbook
' ------------------------------------------------------------------
Public Function fblnNullMenuState() As Boolean _
    fblnNullMenuState = ActiveWorkbook Is Nothing
End Function
```

Example 5-6: Demo Program for fblnNullMenuState

```
' Stored in the module modDemosC5
' ------------------------------------------------------------
' demo procedure - 04/17/97 (PCG)
' ------------------------------------------------------------
Public Sub sAnybodyHome()
    If fblnNullMenuState Then
        MsgBox "Excel is in null menu mode."
    Else
        MsgBox "Excel is not in null menu mode."
    End If
End Sub
```

How many workbooks are visible?

How many workbooks are currently visible? (Yes, this is a trick question.) If you count the number of workbooks with the expression `Workbooks.Count`, you might be surprised. If you have a *Personal.xls* that is hidden (the default in Excel), then even if only one workbook appears in your Window list, the expression returns 2. That's because there's one hidden workbook and one unhidden (visible) workbook, for a total of two workbooks. This is correct and appropriate behavior by the Excel Object Model. Two workbooks are *open*, but we're interested in *visibility*.

This assignment is a classic Excel brain teaser. You can't just stand there and point to a Workbook object and ask it if it's hidden (coy little devils). That's not really surprising, is it? When you hide or unhide a workbook you select Window ➤ Hide. It's a Window object, not a Workbook object, that's hidden. And a single workbook can have more than one window. So the challenge is to produce a list of the workbook names for those whose windows are *all* hidden. You can scan through the Windows collection of each workbook checking for any visible windows; if none are visible, then you have a completely hidden workbook. As an added feature, the function *fintWorkbookCountHidden* (see Example 5-7 and its demo program in Example 5-8) returns one argument that's an array of the hidden workbook names.

Example 5-7: The fintWorkbookCountHidden Function

```
Workbooks.Count - fintWorkbookCountHidden(strArray())

' Stored in the module modFunctions
' ---------------------------------------------------------------
' Purpose:  Count the number of open hidden workbooks (not
'           necessarily the same as the number of hidden windows).
'
' Inputs:   strHiddenWorkbookNames() - returns packed with any
'                                      hidden workbook names
'
' Returns:  Integer.
'
' Updated:  04/17/97 (PCG) - validated for Excel 97
'           04/24/97 (BM)  - modified to deal with writable window
'                            captions
' ---------------------------------------------------------------
Public Function fintWorkbookCountHidden(strHiddenWorkbookNames()
                  As String) As Integer
    ' ----- Declarations
    Dim intHidden As Integer
    Dim blnHidden As Boolean
    Dim wnd As Window
    Dim wrk As Workbook
    ' ----- Main body
    ' make array big enough for all
    ReDim strHiddenWorkbookNames(Workbooks.Count - 1)
    ' number of hidden workbooks found so far
    intHidden = 0
    For Each wrk In Application.Workbooks
        ' set blnHidden False if wrk has any visible windows
        blnHidden = True
        For Each wnd In wrk.Windows
            If wnd.Visible Then
                blnHidden = False
                Exit For
            End If
        Next wnd
        If blnHidden Then
            ' all windows of wrk are hidden
            ' add to array and to count
            strHiddenWorkbookNames(intHidden) = wrk.Name
```

Example 5-7: The fintWorkbookCountHidden Function (continued)

```
            intHidden = intHidden + 1
        End If
    Next wrk
    ' excise any dangling unassigned elements
    If intHidden > 0 Then
        ReDim Preserve strHiddenWorkbookNames(intHidden - 1)
        fintWorkbookCountHidden = intHidden
    Else
        ' disallow redim to -1
        ReDim strHiddenWorkbookNames(0)
        fintWorkbookCountHidden = 0
    End If
End Function
```

Example 5-8: Demo Program for fintWorkbookCountHidden

```
' Stored in the module modDemosC5
' -------------------------------------------------------------
' demo procedure - 04/17/97 (PCG)
' -------------------------------------------------------------
Public Sub sPeekABoo()
    Dim i As Integer
    Dim intCountHidden As Integer
    Dim strArray() As String
    Dim strPrompt As String
    intCountHidden = fintWorkbookCountHidden(strArray())
    strPrompt = "fintWorkbookCountHidden() returns " & _
        intCountHidden
    MsgBox strPrompt
    If intCountHidden > 0 Then
        ' if there are some, output their names
        For i = 0 To UBound(strArray)
            MsgBox strArray(i)
        Next i
    End If
End Sub
```

To find out how many open workbooks are *not* completely hidden, simply do the algebra.

Are you fully qualified?

What is the fully qualified filename (path included) for each saved, open workbook? The custom function *fvntWorkbookNames* (see Example 5-9 and its demo program in Example 5-10) creates a list of the full names of all the currently open, unique workbooks. The list includes the names of hidden and visible workbooks. This function returns a Variant (a general purpose variable type that supports a wide variety of other data types, including arrays), so it's easy to call the function (you don't have to pass a string array as an argument). The disadvantage is that you can't refer to the Variant function name itself inside the function body *as an array*. If you do, you get a run-time error.

Example 5-9: The fvntWorkbookNames Function

```
' Stored in the module modFunctions
' -------------------------------------------------------------
' Purpose:  Provide an array of the full names (path plus 8.3 name)
'           of all open (hidden and unhidden) workbooks.
'
' Inputs:   None.
'
' Returns:  Variant.
'
' Updated:  04/17/97 (PCG) - validated for Excel Annoyances
' -------------------------------------------------------------
Public Function fvntWorkbookNames() As Variant
    ' ----- Declarations
    Dim i As Integer
    Dim strTemp() As String
    Dim wrk As Workbook
    ' ----- Main body
    If Workbooks.Count <> 0 Then
        ReDim strTemp(Workbooks.Count - 1)
        i = 0
        For Each wrk In Workbooks
            strTemp(i) = wrk.FullName
            i = i + 1
        Next wrk
    Else
        ' handle case where count is 0 (don't allow ReDim to -1)
        ReDim strTemp(0)
    End If
    fvntWorkbookNames = strTemp()
End Function
```

Example 5-10: Demo Program for fvntWorkbookNames

```
' Stored in the module modDemosC5
' -----------------------------------------------------
' demo procedure - 04/17/97 (PCG)
' -----------------------------------------------------
Sub sWhatsYourName()
    Dim i As Integer
    Dim intUBound As Integer
    Dim vntTemp As Variant
    vntTemp = fvntWorkbookNames
    intUBound = UBound(vntTemp)
    For i = 0 To intUBound
        MsgBox vntTemp(i)
    Next i
End Sub
```

Workbook names, the long and the short of it

What's the name of the active workbook? What we really want to know is, "What's the name of the workbook with the focus (the active workbook), and give it to me either as a filename only (no path information) or in its fully qualified format." The custom function *fstrActiveWorkbookName* (see Example 5-11 and its demo program in Example 5-12) provides an argument to determine which format is returned. This function assumes the caller has already checked to determine if Excel is in null menu mode. If the active workbook hasn't been saved (for example, is in the form "Book1") then the function returns just that.

Example 5-11: The fstrActiveWorkbookName Function

```
' Stored in the module modFunctions
' ------------------------------------------------------------------
' Purpose:  Provide the active workbook's filename only or its
'           fully qualified filename depending on input.
'
' Inputs:   intPathName
'           =  0 indicates return filename only
'           <> 0 indicates return fully qualified
'                filename (complete with path)
'
' Returns:  String.
'
' Updated:  04/17/97 (PCG) - validated for Excel Annoyances
' ------------------------------------------------------------------
Public Function fstrActiveWorkbookName(intPathName As Integer) _
                As String
    If intPathName = 0 Then
        fstrActiveWorkbookName = ActiveWorkbook.Name
    Else
        fstrActiveWorkbookName = ActiveWorkbook.FullName
    End If
End Function
```

Example 5-12: Demo Program for fstrActiveWorkbookName

```
' Stored in the module modDemosC5
' ------------------------------------------------------------
' demo procedure - 04/17/97 (PCG)
' ------------------------------------------------------------
Public Sub sHeyYouWithTheFocus()
    MsgBox fstrActiveWorkbookName(0)
    MsgBox fstrActiveWorkbookName(1)
End Sub
```

The active sheet

In the active workbook, what's the index and the name of the active sheet? Answering this question doesn't require writing a custom procedure, just two simple expressions. To determine the active sheet's unsorted position in the Sheets collection, use the Index property—`ActiveSheet.Index`. To determine the active sheet's name, use the Name property—`ActiveSheet.Name`.

Could I see your sheet names?

List the current workbook's sheet names in either their positional or alphabetical order. The custom subroutine *sActiveWorkbookSheetNames* takes two arguments: a string array that returns the list sorted as you requested, and an integer to indicate whether you want the list of sheet names back in positional order (0) or alphabetical order (not 0). *Positional* order means as they appear in the Sheets collection (right-click on the worksheet tab bar's scrolling buttons to see this). The returned list mixes sheets of all types. (*sActiveWorkbookSheetNames* and its accompanying sorting routine, *sShellSort*, are shown in Example 5-13, while the demo program appears in Example 5-14.)

Example 5-13: sActiveWorkbookSheetNames and sShellSort Subroutines

```
Option Explicit
Option Compare Text

' Stored in the module modSubroutines
' ---------------------------------------------------------------
' Purpose:   Returns a list of all the active workbook's sheet
'            names, either in positional (collection) order,
'            or sorted alphabetically.
'
' Inputs:    strArray() - array to pack with the names
'            intOrder   - if = 0 then leave in positional order
'                         if <> 0 then sort alphabetically
'
' Updated:   04/18/97 (PCG) - validated for Excel Annoyances
' ---------------------------------------------------------------
Public Sub sActiveWorkbookSheetNames(strArray() As String, _
            intOrder As Integer)
    ' ----- Declarations
    Dim i As Integer
    Dim intSheetCount As Integer
    ' sht *must* be declared as a generic Object
    Dim sht As Object
    ' ----- Main body
    intSheetCount = ActiveWorkbook.Sheets.Count
    ReDim strArray(intSheetCount - 1)
    i = 0
    For Each sht In ActiveWorkbook.Sheets
        strArray(i) = sht.Name
        i = i + 1
    Next sht
    If intOrder <> 0 Then
```

Example 5-13: sActiveWorkbookSheetNames and sShellSort Subroutines (continued)

```
        ' sort in alpha order, else do nothing
        modSubroutines.sShellSort strArray()
    End If
End Sub

' ---------------------------------------------------------------
' Purpose:  Sort a string array. Ported w/ permission from WOPR 2's
'           ShellSort, © 1991-92 Pinecliffe International.
'
'           CRITICAL - Option Compare Text must be set in the
'           current module. This sub will not behave properly
'           if the default  Option Compare Binary is used.
'
'           A fast, practical sort routine based on Donald L.
'           Shell's technique (CACM 2, July 1959, pp 30-32), as
'           adapted by Don Knuth ("The Art of Computer
'           Programming, Vol 3, Sorting and Searching",
'           Addison-Wesley, 1975, pp 84-87); see Knuth for
'           a detailed description.
'
' Inputs:   strArray() - target string array (ASSUMED TO BE 0-BASED)
'
' Updated:  04/18/97 (PCG) - validated for Excel Annoyances
' ---------------------------------------------------------------
Public Sub sShellSort(strArray() As String)
    Dim i As Integer
    Dim j As Integer
    Dim n As Integer
    Dim s As Integer
    Dim strKey As String
    n = UBound(strArray)
    s = Int(n / 2)
    If s < 1 Then s = 1
    While s > 0
        For j = s + 1 To n + 1
            i = j - s
            strKey = strArray(j - 1)
ShellNext:
            If strKey >= strArray(i - 1) Then GoTo SortNext
            strArray(i + s - 1) = strArray(i - 1)
            i = i - s
            If i > 0 Then GoTo ShellNext
SortNext:
            strArray(i + s - 1) = strKey
        Next
        s = Int(s / 2)
    Wend
End Sub
```

Example 5-14: Demo Program for sActiveWorkbookSheetNames

```
' Stored in the module modDemosC5
' ---------------------------------------------------------
' demo procedure  - 04/18/97 (PCG)
```

Example 5-14: Demo Program for sActiveWorkbookSheetNames (continued)

```
' -----------------------------------------------------------
Sub sMyKingdom()
    Dim i As Integer
    Dim strArray() As String
    sActiveWorkbookSheetNames strArray(), 1      ' alpha
    For i = 0 To UBound(strArray)
        MsgBox "Alpha order ... " & strArray(i)
    Next i
    sActiveWorkbookSheetNames strArray(), 0      ' positional
    For i = 0 To UBound(strArray)
        MsgBox "Positional order ... " & strArray(i)
    Next i
End Sub
```

In the statement `For Each sht In ActiveWorkbook.Sheets`, since any individual object in the Sheets collection could be any of four types—a chart sheet, a dialog sheet (for Excel 5/95 backward compatibility), a macro sheet (for Excel 4 backward compatibility), or a worksheet—you can't declare `Dim sht As Worksheet`. Instead, you must use the generic `Dim sht As Object`. This avoids a run-time 13 "Type mismatch" error.

The Object Browser

We've spent several pages introducing you to various components of the Excel Object Model and VBA. Since the Excel Object Model contains more than 150 objects and collections of objects along with innumerable properties and methods, you might get the impression that we've only scratched the surface.

You'd be right.

Your closest source of information (it's free, too) on the Excel Object Model is something called the Object Browser. It's a frequently overlooked component of the VBA editor. (See Figure 5-37.)

The Object Browser displays all the valid objects, properties, and methods accessible to your programs. It also has very good hot links from the objects, properties, and methods to the on-line Help screens for each of them (right-click an item in any of the browser's many panes and choose Help). If you learn to use the Object Browser as your reference of first resort, you'll stand a fighting chance of writing programs that actually work.

To get into the Object Browser, go into the VBA editor and click View ➤ Object Editor (or simply hit `F2`). The interface is decidedly nonstandard and a bit obtuse, but stick with it and the entire Object Model is at your fingertips. If you want to copy the named arguments list for a particular

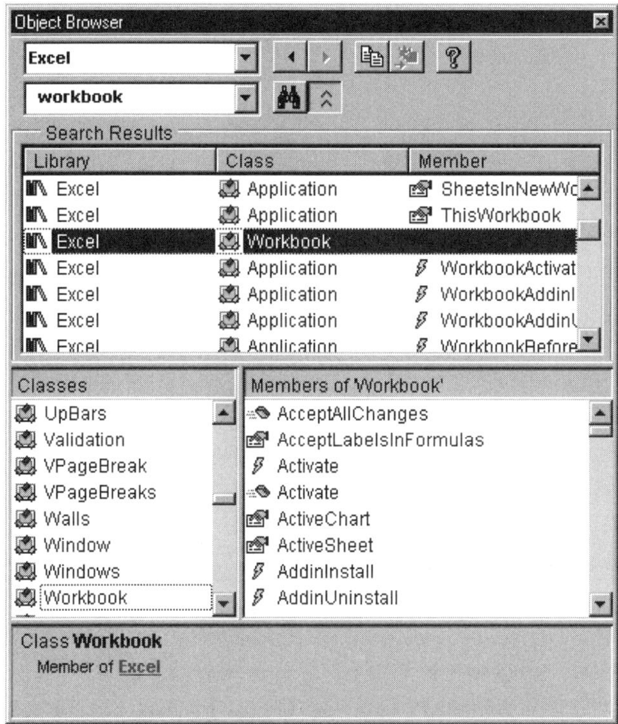

Figure 5-37: The VBA Object Browser

method (including custom procedures in any of your own projects), once that method is displayed in the Display Pane (the pane at the bottom of the browser), highlight it with your mouse and copy it to the clipboard as shown in Figure 5-38.

NOTE Be ever vigilant. No program documentation is ever complete—or completely accurate—and the VBA on-line Help is no exception. Some of the descriptions are just plain wrong. Some of the code samples don't work. And many, many "gotchas" are left unexplored. Still, if you take the documentation with a small grain of salt, you'll find an enormous amount of important information there. And the easiest way to get to the information is via the Object Browser.

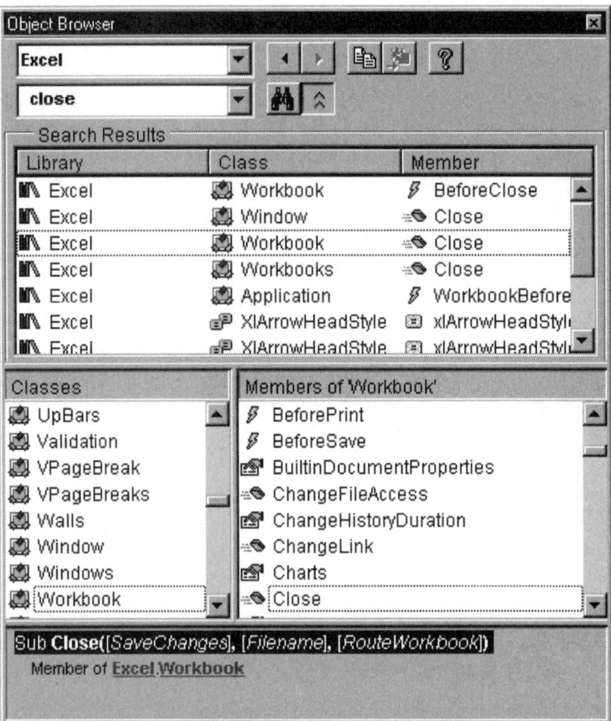

Figure 5-38: Use Object Browser to grab the named arguments for the Workbook object's Close method

Hooking in to Excel

So much for our introduction to the Excel Object Model. We hope you've seen enough to get a feel for the nouns, verbs, and adjectives that your programs can use to harness Excel's power and turn it to your own devices. Let's turn our attention now to the way you shoehorn programs into Excel, so they look and feel like they're part of Excel itself. After all, you may come up with a great way to solve an annoying Excel problem, but it won't mean much if you can't make it easy to use.

Even if you never write a custom macro or program a single lick, this information is important because it will let you tie other peoples' solutions into your own copy of Excel.

All of these macros are nice, of course, but they aren't very useful if you can't make them run from inside Excel itself. Let's take a look at all the different ways you have to weave your programs into the fabric of Excel.

Where to Put Macros

In Excel, you can store macros in several different project locations if you want them available every time you start Excel:

- The special *Personal.xls* workbook
- A workbook that is always loaded by virtue of being in the *Xlstart* folder or your alternate startup folder, if you've defined one
- An add-in that is always loaded by virtue of its presence in the Add-In Manager's internal tables

Using *Personal.xls* is convenient, but as we mentioned earlier, this special workbook is an easy target for macro viruses; this makes it a less useful candidate for storing macros. Auto-loading workbooks is the solution we suggest in the context of this book (with a qualification we'll discuss momentarily), primarily because you won't be saddled with the complex and Byzantine behavior of Excel add-ins. The trick is to finish the workbook's feature set and then hide it; this way it auto-loads but isn't visible when you start Excel. Furthermore, although hidden, you can still edit its macros from the Visual Basic Editor as you would any other open workbook.

Excel add-ins offer greater protection capabilities and an entire set of behaviors that you may find helpful, especially if you're developing custom Excel solutions for more users than just yourself. Since we could write an entire book on this topic, for our purposes here we'll use *Intro to VBA.xls* as an auto-loading workbook to demonstrate hooking up your macros to Excel. Here are the steps:

1. Activate *Intro to VBA.xls.*
2. Save *Intro to VBA.xls* in the Xlstart folder (typically *C:\Program Files\Microsoft Office\Office\Xlstart*).
3. Select Window ➤ Hide.
4. Exit Excel and respond Yes when prompted if you want to save changes to *Intro to VBA.xls.*

Assign to Toolbar Button

You can put your VBA/Excel programs, er, macros on Excel toolbars with a few simple clicks. Whenever the user clicks on that particular toolbar button, your macro gets run. Here's how: click on Tools ➤ Customize ➤ Commands tab. On the left, scroll down to Macros. On the right, choose either the Custom Menu Item or Custom Button control, then drag and drop it onto the toolbar of your choice. Now right-click the new control, choose Assign Macro, choose This Workbook in the "Macros in" list, scroll down to the *PrintCbarsControlList* macro, and click OK. (In Figure 5-39 we used a name of "Print Controls List" and the button image from the Format ➤ AutoFormat control.) As you learned in Chapter 3, you can easily change the name and button image if you want. Now click Close.

From this point on, the button you just put on the toolbar will run the macro you chose. In this case, clicking on the button will run the *Print-CbarsControlList* macro in the Module1 module in the IntroToVBA project. As Figure 5-39 shows, Excel even picks up a ToolTip that's the same as the name you give the control (not necessarily the same as the underlying macro name, by the way).

Figure 5-39: The button is ready

Assign to Menu Bars

The method for assigning macros to locations on Excel's menu bars resembles the toolbar procedure and was covered in Chapter 3.

Assign to Keyboard

When it comes to assigning keyboard shortcuts to Excel macros, there's good news, annoying news, and more annoying news.

First the good news—you can actually assign a keyboard shortcut. But even the good news is a bit annoying—you can assign any keyboard combination you want as long as it is `Ctrl` plus some other key. Meaning, you can't do `Alt+` or `Shift+` or combinations thereof; the key combination must always begin with `Ctrl`.

Annoyingly, to assign a shortcut key, you must be in Excel (not the Visual Basic Editor) and click Tools ➤ Macro ➤ Macros. Select the macro you want from the displayed list and click the Options button. (See Figure 5-40.) You should also be able to do this from the Visual Basic Editor but you can't, and that's a real disappointment.

Figure 5-40: The Macro Options dialog box assigns shortcut keys and a macro description

Here you can select a key to use in combination with the `Ctrl` key, as well as type in a description of the macro. This is where you hit another major annoyance—if you use a key combination that you've already assigned, the new assignment overwrites the old without any warning whatsoever.

Workbook Events

Excel possesses rich event-handling capabilities. You can associate code with application object events, but to do so requires that you write a class module. Class modules are beyond the scope of this book, but you can read about them in Excel's on-line Help, *Mastering Microsoft Office 97 Development*, and various books on Visual Basic 4 and 5. The relevant Excel Visual Basic Help topic is "Using Events with the Application Object." Associating code with workbook, worksheet, and chart object events doesn't involve class modules. You can write macros that are associated with any of 17 workbook events, as shown in Figure 5-41. (For more information about other Excel objects that support events, see on-line Help.) Here's what happens when the two most common workbook events fire:

- The `Workbook_Open` subroutine runs when the workbook is opened.
- The `Workbook_Close` subroutine runs before the workbook closes (if the workbook has changed, this event occurs before the user is asked to save changes).

To see how to construct these event handlers, open up a convenient test workbook. (We used one called *test.xls*.) In the VBA editor's Project Explorer, navigate to the Microsoft Excel Objects folder and double-click on This Workbook. On the left, in the Code Window's Object box, pick

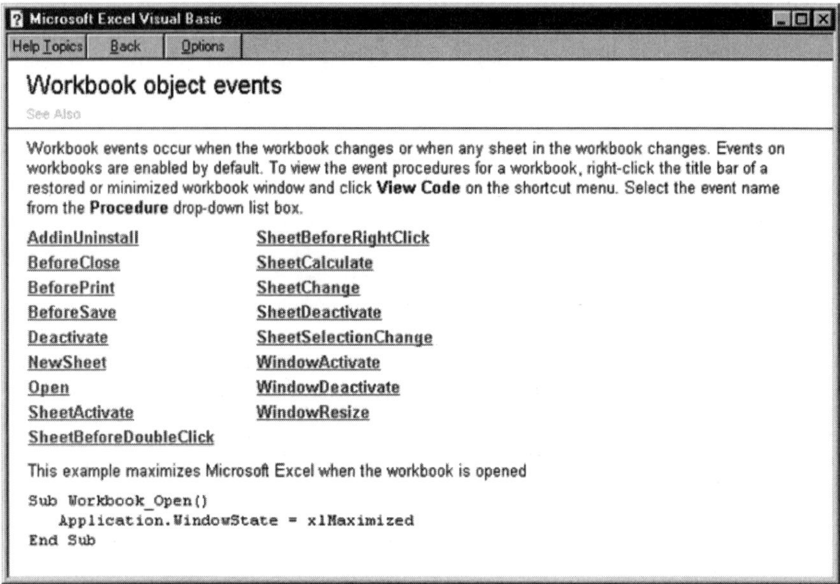

Figure 5-41: Excel supports 17 workbook object events

Workbook. By default, the editor creates an empty, private `Workbook_Open` subroutine as shown in Figure 5-42. (If you want a different event, you would choose from the list on the right.)

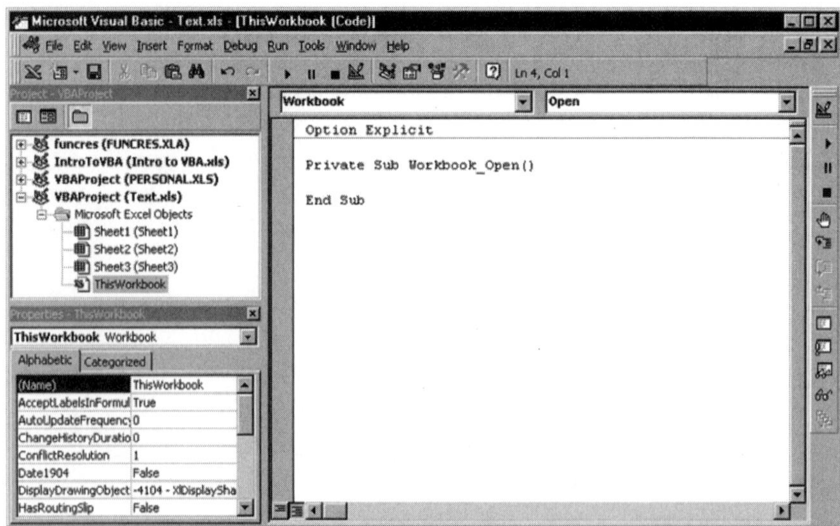

Figure 5-42: Setting up the Workbook_Open event handler

Now type in the simple program in Example 5-15. Close your test workbook. Yes, you want to save changes.

Example 5-15: Defining a Workbook.Open Event Procedure

```
Private Sub Workbook_Open()
MsgBox "Opening test.xls"
End Sub
```

Now open the test workbook. Excel will greet you with its "Virus warning" message. Click Enable macros. As soon as you clear the "Virus warning" message, Excel fires the Workbook.Open event. VBA/Excel goes looking for an event handler, and finds one in *test.xls* called `Workbook_Open`. The result is a message box on the screen as shown in Figure 5-43.

Figure 5-43: The Workbook.Open event handler kicks in

NOTE Here's an annoying bug that afflicts Word but *not* Excel. As soon as you set up a document event handler in a Word document, *every* time you open that document, you'll trigger the Virus warning message. Even if you delete the document event handler macros entirely, Word continues to believe that there are macros attached to the document, and continues to bedevil you with that warning message. Since there's no way to delete the Microsoft Word Objects component, there's no way to completely clean the document once it's been soiled. Your only option is to copy the entire contents of the document to a clean new document, and refrain from writing event handlers! *We repeat—this bug does not occur in Excel.*

6

Excel Strategies

In this chapter:
- *The Virus Threat*
- *The Audit Trail*
- *Self-Monitoring Error Traps*
- *Auditing Tools*
- *Formulas vs. Results*
- *Go To Special*
- *Excel's Internet Connection*
- *Presentation Strategies*
- *Maps! Data Meets Geography*
- *Charts—Numbers as Pictures*
- *Hard Copy!*

Excel is a powerful and feature-rich development tool, meaning you can pretty much build anything you can think up. But with any tool as powerful and flexible as Excel, you have to have a plan or strategy behind your development or your model will be difficult to use, difficult to maintain, and prone to errors. Troubleshooting strategies, automatic error detection procedures, input and presentation views, visual presentations of numeric data, report printing . . . all need to be considered and implemented, *as you build your model—not just as an afterthought!*

This introduces an annoyance of a different and more subtle variety. Because spreadsheets have proven to be so vastly superior to the manual systems that they replace, and since Excel makes it so easy to jump in and start building models, there's a temptation to skip over the planning part of your modeling project. Perhaps the ultimate annoyance isn't when the software doesn't work as you expect, but when your spreadsheet is inaccurate because an error in construction occurs, you haven't thought through the model, or you have made it possible for someone using your model to introduce an error.

In this chapter we'll look at these issues and more. What must you do to deal with the macro virus threat? How should the new Internet features in Excel be implemented in your model building strategy? What about the many choices for formatting and data presentation? Are Maps really useful? Should you chart everything in sight? What are the best strategies for generating reports?

Let's find out.

The Virus Threat

As of the time of this writing, there are (depending on which industry list you last checked) between 300 and 500 known Word macro viruses. You can argue about how many are truly "in the wild" and how many have never been outside the labs of the antivirus companies and the interested parties who track these things. Any way you slice it, that's a passel of nasty creepy-crawlies. Stop by some of the web sites where anyone with a browser can download a hundred or so working versions of these little nightmares—to say nothing of a complete do-it-yourself virus creation engine—and you'll stop arguing and start reaching for the aspirin bottle.

There's good news and bad news as far as Word 97 is concerned. The good news is that very few of the Word 95 WordBasic macro viruses are capable of infecting Word 97 since it switched to VBA as its macro language. The bad news is that the first of the Word 97 specific VBA macro viruses have been identified. Epidemic to follow.

What does the sorry state of Word's virus situation have to do with Excel? In a nutshell: XM.Laroux, XM.Robocop, XM.Legend, XM.Sofa, and XM.Delta, just to name a few.

Concept, the first Word macro virus, inspired someone to develop Laroux, the first macro virus written in Excel/VBA. Like Concept, Laroux is relatively benign—it just replicates itself and is massively annoying, but it does not delete data or wipe out your hard drive. Also like Word, there's good news and bad news.

The good news is that of the half dozen or so Excel macro viruses floating around (also downloadable from sundry sites on the Web), most are based on the original Laroux strain and are merely annoying, not catastrophic. The bad news is that this is changing. XM.Delta, for example, is capable of deleting **.ini* files and the odd cell in your worksheets. It's only a matter of time before something really nasty comes along in the form of an Excel specific virus. So what can you do about this?

Excel 97 ships with a built-in brick wall virus protection feature. As we touched on briefly in Chapter 1, *Required Reading*, many people hate this annoying warning dialog, the one that pops up whenever you try to open a workbook that contains macros (see Figure 6-1).

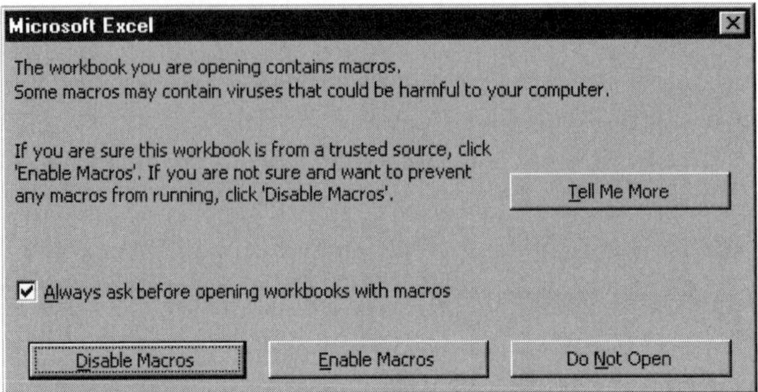

Figure 6-1: Your last line of defense; don't turn it off!

Don't confuse this with what the Excel Help file calls its "New in 97—Virus search and removal" feature (Choose Security from the "What's new in Microsoft Excel 97?" topic). *There isn't one.* The reference to the Virus Search add-in is bogus. There may have been one on the Redmond drawing boards, but it didn't make it into the Excel 97 release. There is the *Xlscan.xla* for Excel 95 (available at *http://www.microsoft.com/excel/productinfo/vbavirus/add_in.htm*) that works for Excel 95 and only eradicates Laroux. There is an Excel 97 version of the same (Laroux only) utility, *Xlscan97.xla*, also available from Microsoft. Again, these are Laroux-specific and are not going to protect you from other Excel viruses that are running around.

In Excel 97 what you get is the dialog box shown earlier in Figure 6-1, which isn't a virus checker at all. It doesn't look for viruses, it doesn't identify viruses, it doesn't eliminate viruses, and it doesn't do a whole lot to protect you from virus infection. Still, when you get the "Warning" message in Figure 6-1, you need to sit up and pay attention. Nine times out of ten, the workbook you're trying to open won't be infected. But that other one time can ruin your whole day.

Whatever you do, don't uncheck this "Always ask before opening workbooks with macros" check box or, equivalently, the "Macro virus protection" check box in the Tools ➤ Options ➤ General dialog. Even if you think the Warnings are annoying, they could save your tail some day. Trust us. This "Warning" message is not an annoyance. It's a last line of defense.

On the other hand, don't get the notion that this Macro virus protection setting is the only Excel virus defense you'll need. This dialog only lets you open the file with macros enabled (something you should only do if you *know* the file is clear of potential viri), open the file with the macros disabled, or forget the whole thing and not open the file at all. The better option is to run a real virus checker on the suspect file.

For this you must buy, use, and frequently update a good antivirus software package that's capable of dealing with Excel macro viruses. There are many to choose—from the biggies like Norton AntiVirus from Symantec (*www.symantec.com*) and McAfee's VirusScan (*www.mcafee.com*), to the smaller AV manufacturers like FRISK Software, who make F-PROT (*www.datafellows.fi/vir-info/index.htm*).

Rather than recommend any one package, we suggest that you check the latest reviews from any of the major PC magazines, including *PC Computing* (*www.pccomputing.com*) and *Office Computing* (*www.office-computing.com*), and choose one that you fancy. Then use it.

The Audit Trail

Internal Revenue Agents like to tell this joke . . .

Q: *"What do you get for the man who has everything?"*

A: "An audit."

Then they laugh uproariously. This could be why the word *auditing* makes most of us break out in a cold sweat. But when it comes to spreadsheets, auditing is a good thing. Honest. The first step to safe spreadsheeting is to blaze an audit trail as you work on your (or someone else's) model.

Spreadsheets tend to take on a life of their own, especially where you inherit a model that was developed way back when, by person or persons unknown who may no longer even work for your company. Every time the model was tweaked, poked, prodded, modified, spun, folded, and mutilated, there was a reasonable chance that an error was introduced. The annoying part is trying to find it.

Design Notes

Whether you are working with a spreadsheet that you alone built just yesterday, or a model that's been handed down from user to user over the years, if it is not documented, *stop what you are doing and document it now!* Would you want to use a computer program that had no Help file, no manual, and no documentation? No, and as we pointed out in Chapter 2, *Excel as Workhorse*, Excel is a programming environment that you program spreadsheets in.

Anyone who has had to try to fix a spreadsheet that's suddenly gone belly up can appreciate the need to document the design. We've been called into this situation many times, and unfortunately the usual response when we ask who was the original author of the spreadsheet is, "Oh, Joe doesn't work here anymore." Next we ask when the workbook in question was last audited. For this we either get blank looks or some hemming and hawing with lots of long contemplative gazes up at the ceiling. This, of course, leads to the most uncomfortable question of all, "How do you know it works?"

Or doesn't work, for that matter. At a minimum you need to record the following information for every workbook you create:

- **Author**—the original author of the model, its primary designer. If there's a team that is responsible for the model, each person should be listed along with what section of the model they designed/built. If the model was built from an external specification, that document should be referenced here.
- **Purpose**—write down the purpose of the model. What does it do? What's involved? Where does the data come from? Who gets the generated reports? This might just be an overview with a reference to see the on-line Help file, or it might include the detailed instructions. It depends on the complexity of the model.
- **Date of origin**—the date that the model was created.
- **Design notes**—details on the basic construction, how the various sheets and sections fit together. How are the various pieces of the model linked? Are any formulas dependent on tables of data that require periodic updating?
- **Date of last change**—a running list of dates on which the model was modified.
- **Description of modification**—the details on each change made to the model. Who made the change, why, and what was done? This becomes your map when a model that was working suddenly starts causing trouble.

Where and how you track this information is up to you. A separate sheet for documentation is a good idea. You could type the data right into cells on the sheet, use the text box drawing control, or even embed a Word document. You should also consider providing full instructions and a usage overview in an on-line Help file.

Comments (the Feature Formerly Known as Notes)

Excel has had a *Notes* feature for years. It was one of those buried treasures that was always there but few knew about or used effectively. In Excel 97, this feature has been renamed *Comments* and has some nifty new abilities. A note, or comment, to use the new lexicon, is used to tack on a remark, question, or explanation to a given cell.

Excel lets you control whether you have the comments themselves displayed or just the comment indicator, which is a small red triangle in the upper right-hand corner of the cell containing the comment. In the Tools ➤ Options dialog, select the View tab, and in the Comment group are three option buttons. You can have neither the indicator nor the comment displayed, just the indicator, or both the indicator and the comment. We generally set this to display indicators (see Figure 6-2).

	B	C	D	E	F	G
2	North Division Sales					
3		Qtr.1	Qtr.2	Qtr.3	Qtr.4	Product Total
4	Widgets	98	101	112	75	386
5	Doohickeys	110	92	98	75	375
6	Gizmos	109	86	104	79	378
7	Totals	317	279	314	229	1139
8						

Figure 6-2: Comment indicators are small red triangles

Providing you have not set the comment display under Tools ➤ Options, View tab to None, you can cause a comment to be displayed by simply placing the mouse pointer over the cell containing the comment. All the comments in a workbook can be displayed by choosing Comments from the View menu (this forces the setting on the Tools ➤ Options, View tab to both indicator and comment). (See Figure 6-3.)

	B	C	D	E	F	G	H	I
2	North Division Sales							
3		Qtr.1	Qtr.2	Qtr.3				
4	Widgets			112				
5	Doohickeys			98				
6	Gizmos			104				
7	Totals			314				
8								
9								
10								

T. J.: 4/08/97
This product line was added due to the by-products generated by the Gizmo development

Lee: 4/11/97
This figure was phoned in by Gale at the plant and has not been confirmed as of this date.

Woody: 4/02/97
The formula in this cell verifies the crossfoot totals down and across.

Figure 6-3: All comments displayed

We could not find the stated maximum character count in either the Excel Help file or the Office Resource Kit, but you can take our word for it, it's

32,767 characters. In any event, we've never had a real-world note run more than a couple of hundred words when documenting a very complex formula. But we've created notes over 3,000 characters in experiments. Suffice it to say that you probably won't be running out of room.

Enter a comment by selecting the cell and choosing Comment from the Insert menu—or just hit the `SHIFT+F2` keyboard shortcut. Gone is the old Cell Note dialog box. Now you get the on-screen comment graphic, and you can type directly into that.

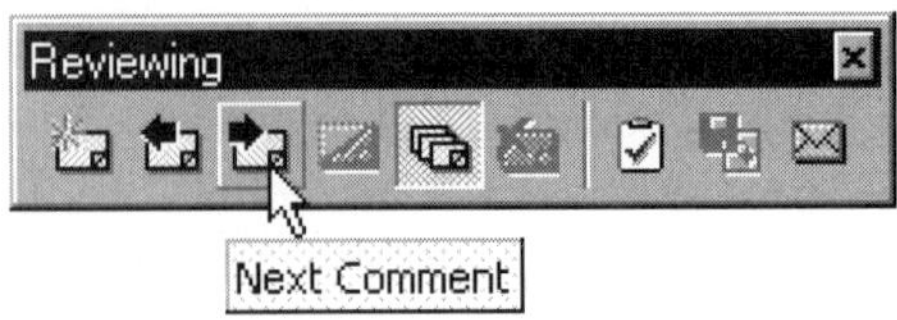

Figure 6-4: The Reviewing toolbar

To more effectively work with comments, display the Reviewing toolbar (View ➤ Toolbars) shown in Figure 6-4. The first button on the left lets you add a comment to the active cell. The next two buttons jump you to the previous or next comment (moving left to right, top to bottom). These can make your work easier when auditing a worksheet. Turn on the comments and use the previous/next buttons on the Reviewing toolbar to check each and every comment in the sheet. The old Cell Note dialog (in versions prior to Excel 97) actually let you see a list of all cells in the active sheet that had notes, and you could review the notes without having to leave the dialog or scroll around the sheet. It's annoying that this functionality was not preserved in Excel 97.

Use comments to explain where a constant came from, if a number needs to be updated, to explain the logic of complex formulas. You can also use comments for pop-up instructions. There are lots of uses for comments—please get the in habit of using them.

Sheet Layout

When you build a spreadsheet model, you wind up knowing your way around it like you do your own living room. But have you ever tried to figure out a complex sheet that someone else built? Stuff gets dropped in over *here*, tables built *there*, and you can waste tons of time wandering around a sheet looking for all the goodies. Don't waste time.

There are several strategies for quickly getting the layout of a given sheet that revolve around the effective use of Excel's ability to zoom the size of the sheet in and out. Next time you're trying to find out what's where on a sheet, try this:

1. Pull down the View menu and choose Full Screen.
2. Press `CTRL+END` to move the active cell to the end cell (i.e., the last row and column intersection for the right-most column and the bottom-most row in the sheet that contain data).
3. Press `SHIFT+CTRL+HOME` to select from the end cell back to cell A1. This effectively selects the area of the current sheet that has content.
4. Pull down the View menu and click Zoom.
5. In the Zoom dialog box, select the Fit Selection option button and click on OK.

This procedure shrinks the selected area so that it is all displayed on screen (within Excel's 10% to 400% magnification limits). See Figure 6-5.

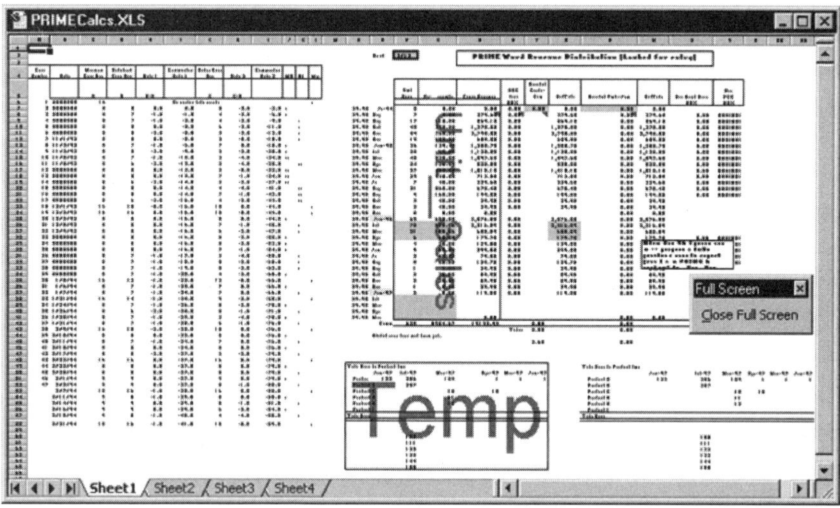

Figure 6-5: Getting the bird's-eye view of the current sheet

Granted, you can't read anything useful at this magnification, but you can see how the sheet is laid out. Now, select the general area you want to review with the mouse (you may be off a row or column but that won't matter) and View ➤ Zoom ➤ Fit Selection again. This brings up a specific selection in a size you can work with. After you've reviewed that area, zoom out and select another area for review. This technique is a big time saver.

Self-Monitoring Error Traps

As annoying as it is when a formula blows up when you're building a spreadsheet, it's worse when the error slips past you and winds up in your final model. When programmers develop applications, they write error-trapping routines into their code to let them know when something goes wrong. You should adopt this practice for your spreadsheets to let your model help you maintain its integrity by monitoring values and results, and warn you or the model's users when an error occurs.

This is not as difficult as it might sound. Excel provides some great tools for error trapping, and with a little imagination, you can whip up a spreadsheet that'll do everything automatically . . . except start the coffee in the morning!

Conditional Results

The most powerful tool in your trap setting arsenal is the conditional statement, which in Excel is the `=IF` function. In programming circles, we call this `IF THEN ELSE`. `IF` something compared to something else is true, `THEN` return this, `ELSE` (the comparison was false) return something else.

For example, the formula `=IF(A1=B1, 100, "Lobster")` returns the value 100 if the contents of cell A1 equals the contents of B1. If A1 is not equal to B1, the formula returns the string Lobster. The contents of the two cells being compared (A1, B1) could be text, values, or even blank. A blank A1 is equal to a blank B1.

You can use this trick to make labels change based on the value of the adjacent cell. You might have an Income Statement that uses a formula to return a label like this:

```
=IF(G96<0, "Net Loss", "Net Income")
```

Here's a more practical example. Consider a simple table of values that you have added down each column and across each row. The sum of each row total should be equal to the sum of each column total, unless there's an error. To check this crossfoot scenario, you could build a formula like that shown in Figure 6-6.

This formula compares the sum in C7:F7 (the totals of the columns) to the sum of G4:G6 (the sum of the rows), and if they are not equal, you get a warning message as the returned value (a string in this case). If they are equal, you get the sum of the columns as the returned value. Very neat.

= =IF(SUM(C7:F7)<>SUM(G4:G6),"Crossfoot error!",SUM(C7:F7))

B	C	D	E	F	G
North Division Sales					
	Qtr.1	Qtr.2	Qtr.3	Qtr.4	Product Total
Widgets	98	101	112	75	386
Doohickeys	110	92	98	75	375
Gizmos	109	86	104	79	378
Totals	317	279	314	229	1139

Figure 6-6: A comparison of values determines the returned result

---

NOTE For the examples in this chapter we'll use cell references in our formulas for demonstration purposes instead of range names (which would be more appropriate for the real world). Also, due to the limited space we have for screen displays, we'll use very brief examples in which the errors may be more apparent than in models containing hundreds of rows and columns.

Conditional statements can be nested up to seven levels deep, which lets you build a decision tree for complex comparisons.

Error Tables

Using Excel's `=IF` function to make comparisons and return error messages right in the various tables scattered around your sheet is a first step in the right direction. But to take it to the next level, you need to build a separate table or sheet that does nothing but check for errors or values above or below the anticipated results of your calculations.

Figure 6-7 shows part of a simple error table that performs a number of tests and shows the results all in one location. Conditional formatting (discussed next) was used to make anything unexpected stand out. Handy hyperlinks in the adjacent column let you jump with one click to the sheet/cell where the error occurs.

= =DivisionSales!F6

B	C	D
Test Description	**Result**	**Hyperlink**
Test for table crossfoot	Error!	DivisionSales!F6
Test for table crossfoot	375,421	DivisionCosts!H35
Test for value in range	Okay	DivisionSales!C37
Test for value in range	UnderMin	DivisionCosts!P13

Figure 6-7: Gather all error results into one location

Custom/Conditional Formats

In Figure 6-7, cells in column C that return errors (Error! and UnderMin) are shaded in bright yellow so you can look at the error sheet and immediately see where problems are occurring in your model. The setting of conditional formats controls this shading.

Prior to Excel 97, we used to do something similar to this using custom formats. Custom formats are still around, and you can create formats like the following:

```
[Blue][>1000]#,##0;[Red][<-1000]#,##0;[Green]#,##0
```

A cell formatted with this custom format displays values greater than 1,000 in Blue, less than negative 1,000 in Red, and from 1,000 to –1,000 in Green. Custom formats can return text strings as well:

```
#,##0;[Red]"Error"
```

This format returns the string "Error" (in red text) if a value entered is negative.

While custom formats are nice and still have their uses, the new conditional formatting capabilities in Excel 97 take this concept to an entirely new dimension. To create a conditional format, select Conditional Format from the Format menu.

When you first display the dialog box shown in Figure 6-8, it lets you set a single condition. If you click the Add button, you can add a second. Click Add again, and you can set a third (as shown here). You can test the value of a cell (Cell Value Is), or you can enter a formula that evaluates to TRUE or FALSE. This latter ability is very powerful, letting you change the formatting of cells based on what's happening in other cells on the active sheet or on other sheets in the workbook.

Formats you can specify are font, borders, and patterns (shading). A minor annoyance is that you can't adjust the weight of borders. Also, like the regular Format ➤ Cells ➤ Borders, you aren't able to specify a color for the border settings. Oh, you can choose one, but it won't appear—Microsoft's version of "any color you want, as long as it's black."

Conditional formats are a dynamite way to build in visual cues as to what is happening in your model.

Auditing Tools

It's amazing the faith and trust people put in the printed spreadsheet. "It came off the computer so it must be right." Hah! Don't you believe it.

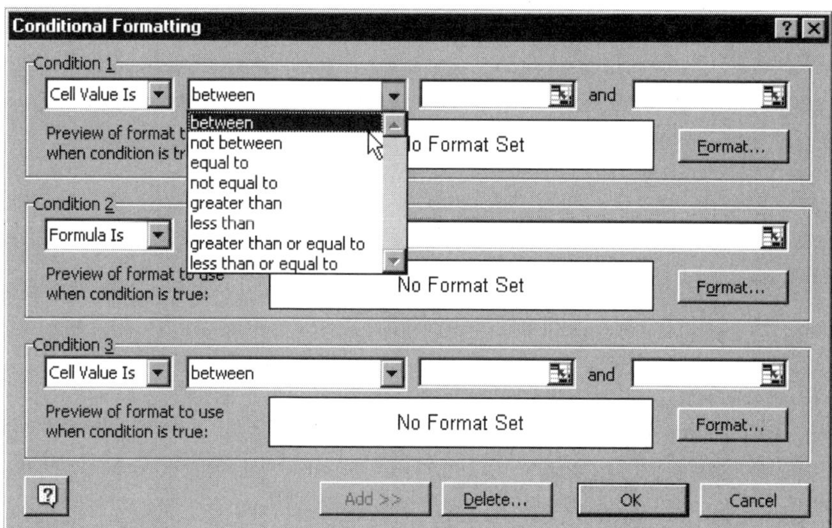

Figure 6-8: Set up to three conditional formats

You need to maintain a constant vigil for little errors in logic, arithmetic errors, the odd row that gets left out of a =SUM formula, and on and on.

One of us used to audit spreadsheets as part of his job as a CPA. You'd be amazed how often significant errors show up. Not just faulty or unrealistic assumptions used to project income (which could be a book in itself); no, we're talking plain old "Oops, now how did that formula get overwritten with a constant?" and "Hmm, 2 + 3 = 6 does look a little odd, doesn't it?" type errors.

Display the Auditing Toolbar

Be it your own spreadsheets or the spreadsheet that someone is using to try to convince you to invest your IRA funds into perpetual-motion, hydroponics-powered, space-based cattle feed lots—audit them. Time was when all we had was our trusty 10-key adding machine to crunch the numbers. Fortunately, Excel provides us with some outstanding auditing tools that are easily accessed from the Auditing toolbar. (See Figure 6-9.)

Figure 6-9: The Auditing Toolbar—don't spreadsheet without it!

We feel pretty strongly about the need to check your work (and the work of others) and think you should have this toolbar displayed at all times. Annoyingly enough, it's not on the normal toolbar list (View ➤ Toolbars or right-click any visible toolbar). No, that would be too easy. In Excel 97, you have to drill down to View ➤ Toolbars ➤ Customize to find it or look over on the Tools menu. No matter, we recommend you force this toolbar to be displayed every time you start Excel. Create the routine shown in Example 6-1 in the *Personal.xls* workbook* and the Auditing toolbar will always be on when you fire up Excel.

Example 6-1: Using the Workbook.Open Event Handler to Display the Auditing Toolbar

```
Private Sub Workbook_Open()
'
' Workbook_Open Macro to display the Auditing Toolbar
' Written xx/xx/xx by YourNameHere
'
    If Not Toolbars("Auditing").Visible Then
        Toolbars("Auditing").Visible = True
    End If
End Sub
```

The first two groups of buttons allow you to trace precedent and dependent cells and to remove the trace arrows after you've reviewed everything. The fifth button lets you wipe out all trace arrows with one click. The yellow traffic sign button with the exclamation point on it is the Trace Error button. To its right is the Comment button (a duplicate of the one on the Reviewing toolbar mentioned earlier), and then you have a group of two buttons used to circle invalid data and to clear the circles.

Trace precedents

Let's take a simple example where we have a small table whose conditional statement error trap informs us that there is an error in crossfooting. Select the cell returning the bogus results and click once on the Trace Precedents button. (See Figure 6-10.)

The precedent arrows show the cells that impact the total in G7. Thin lines denote a single cell; the thicker lines (shown in this example) show that a range is precedent to the active cell. But we're no closer to finding the problem than we were before. Click on the Trace Precedents button again to drill down to the next level of precedent cells. Excel beeps,

* For the sake of simplicity we'll use *Personal.xls*, but, as noted in the last chapter, you might want to create a hidden workbook of your own in the *Xlstart* folder using a different name for storing these utility type macros.

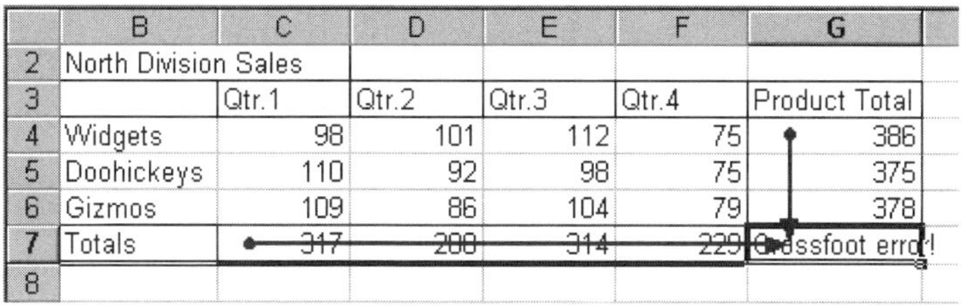

	B	C	D	E	F	G
2	North Division Sales					
3		Qtr.1	Qtr.2	Qtr.3	Qtr.4	Product Total
4	Widgets	98	101	112	75	386
5	Doohickeys	110	92	98	75	375
6	Gizmos	109	86	104	79	378
7	Totals	317	288	314	229	Crossfoot error!
8						

Figure 6-10: Tracing the precedent cells

meaning all cells with values impacting the current cell have now been traced. (See Figure 6-11.)

Lo and behold! The error jumps up in column D where the total in D7 isn't being added down properly. Most likely, a constant was inadvertently entered, overwriting the formula in D7. Like all the trace operations, if you correct, modify, or change the spreadsheet, you should remove all arrows and rerun your trace.

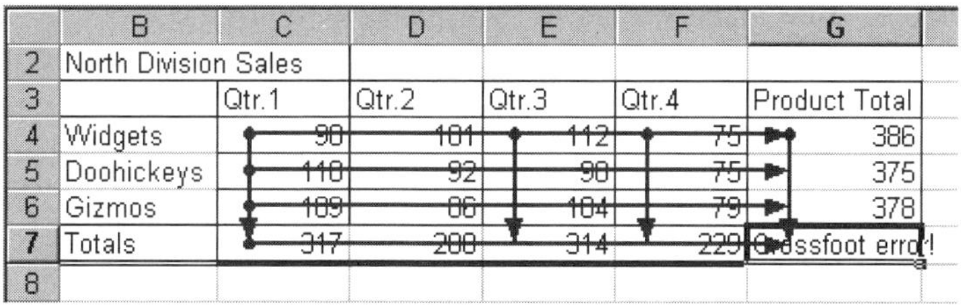

	B	C	D	E	F	G
2	North Division Sales					
3		Qtr.1	Qtr.2	Qtr.3	Qtr.4	Product Total
4	Widgets	98	101	112	75	386
5	Doohickeys	110	92	98	75	375
6	Gizmos	109	86	104	79	378
7	Totals	317	288	314	229	Crossfoot error!
8						

Figure 6-11: All precedent cells traced

Trace dependents

Dependents are cells that are impacted by the contents of the current cell (the arrows point from your source cell to the dependent cells). In our example you can select a constant like F5 and click on the Trace Dependents button until you hear the beep, indicating all dependent levels have been traced. (See Figure 6-12.)

These examples are very compact for display purposes, and you will often have arrows shooting off to distant locations on your sheet. Never fear! You can easily navigate the trace arrows. Double-clicking on the circle (originating cell) shoots the active cell to the next cell in that trace (the cell where the arrowhead is). From there you click on the circle in that cell and off you go on the next leg of the trace. Navigate upstream by double-clicking on the arrowhead. In Figure 6-12 you see that D13 is dependent on D10, which is dependent on G7, which is dependent on both G5 and F7, which are both dependent on F5. *Whew!* Using the

	B	C	D	E	F	G	H
2	North Division Sales						
3		Qtr.1	Qtr.2	Qtr.3	Qtr.4	Product Total	
4	Widgets	98	101	112	75	386	
5	Doohickeys	110	92	98	75	375	
6	Gizmos	109	86	104	79	378	
7	Totals	317	200	314	229	Crossfoot error!	
8							
9							
10	North Division Sales		Crossfoot err				
11	Central Division Sales		1141				
12	South Division Sales		1032				
13	Total Sales		2173				
14							

Auditing

Figure 6-12: Tracing the elusive dependent cell

proper terminology you'd say that G5 and F7 are *directly* dependent on F5 while the rest of the cells in the trace are *indirectly* dependent on it.

Note the black dashed arrow leading from D13 to the small worksheet icon. This indicates that a cell on another sheet is indirectly dependent on F5. This sheet may be in the current workbook or in another workbook entirely. Double-click on the black arrow, and you'll get the Go To dialog box with the address for the dependent cell in the other sheet listed (see Figure 6-13). Just click on it, click OK, and off you go. Once you get to the destination, you'll have to click on the Trace Dependents button again to continue the trace.

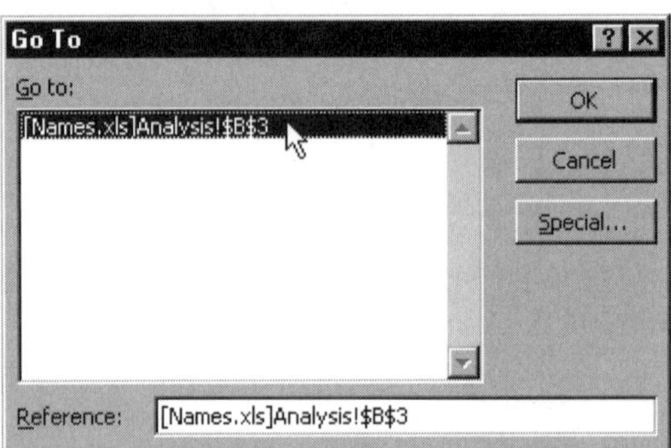

Figure 6-13: Fast trip to the external reference

Trace errors

The Trace Errors button is used when you have a formula that returns an error (`#VALUE`, `#N/A`, or the ever common `#DIV/0` divide by zero error), that is caused somewhere in a cell that the current cell is dependent upon. A single divide by zero error can make a spreadsheet break out in errors like it has chicken pox. Clicking once on this button traces the entire upstream chain of precedent cells using *red* arrows to cells with error values and blue arrows beyond them to cells in the chain that don't generate errors, such as cells containing constants.

You can use the standard Trace Precedents button on a cell displaying an error, and you can trace upstream one level at a time using the red arrows. But you have to go level by level and deal with entire ranges if they are in the trace path. Using Trace Error with existing trace arrows in the path causes Excel to pop up a message box warning you to remove all arrows and try again, so hit the Remove All Arrows button before doing a Trace Error operation.

New comment

This button lets you create a new comment for the active cell (or edit an existing one). Since we pretty much covered that ground earlier, we won't say anything more other than to admonish you once more to comment the heck out of everything. Document, document, document!

Invalid data

The last button group on the Auditing toolbar concerns invalid data. Back in the section "Data Validation," in Chapter 4, *How Excel Works*, we discussed how you can set up validation parameters for cells that govern what you can enter into them. You might restrict valid data to only positive numbers, or numbers between a set of minimum and maximum values. Text strings, decimals, date, time—all can have parameters set to define what a valid entry is. Custom formulas can be entered that evaluate to TRUE or FALSE, and you can control whether a blank entry is to be considered valid or not.

There are three levels of validation (what Excel calls styles of error messages): Information, Warning, and Stop. (See Figure 6-14.)

The default is Stop and prevents the user from entering anything outside the defined parameters. If invalid data is entered, the user sees a message box (you specify the title bar and the message text) with the halt symbol and only a Retry or Cancel button on the box. Retry leaves them in edit mode, while Cancel aborts their entry. (See Figure 6-15.)

You might be leaning towards just going with Stop for any validation rules you impose and forget about the other levels (which can permit a user to enter invalid data). But keep in mind how draconian this is. If a clerk is pounding in data that someone has given him and that data has an entry that is outside the valid range, his work comes to a screeching halt. The spreadsheet will not accept the entry. Maybe it's an error, or

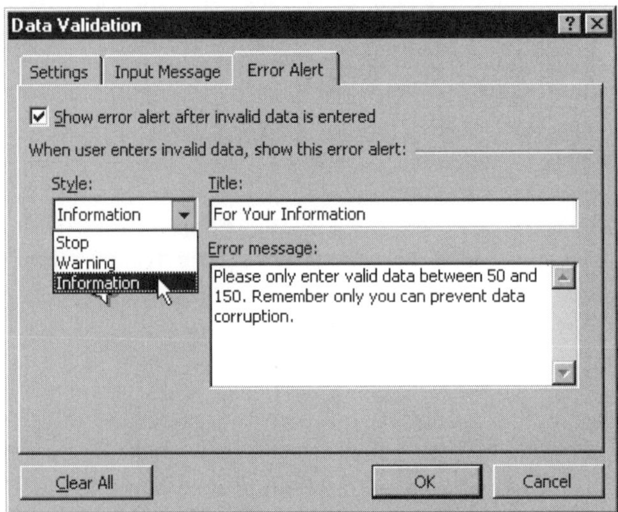

Figure 6-14: Setting the Error Alert determines the user's range of actions

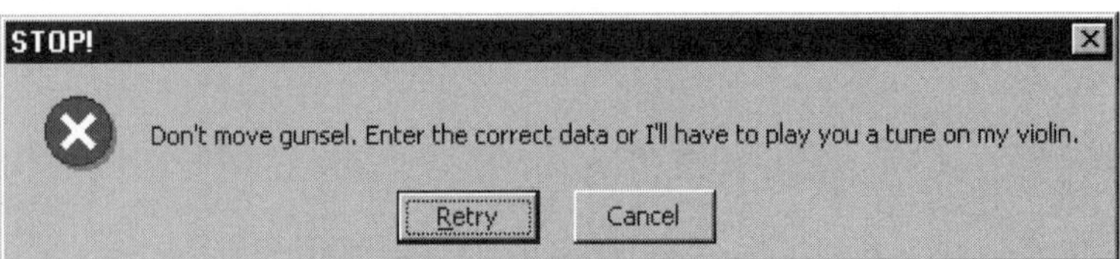

Figure 6-15: The Stop message prevents invalid data entry

maybe there was some kind of adjustment made that month that, while outside the normal range, is nevertheless valid. Do you want to halt the process there or run a validation check later? Read on!

Defining the Error Alert as Warning presents the user with a message box that sports a Yes, No, and Cancel button. Yes causes the invalid data to be accepted by the sheet. No puts you in edit mode so you can change the entry, and Cancel aborts the entry. (See Figure 6-16.)

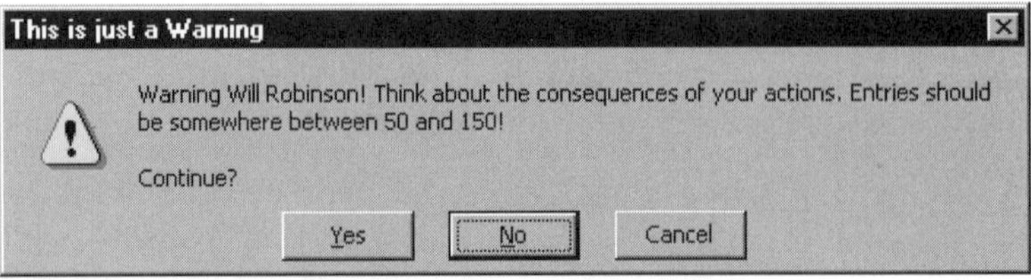

Figure 6-16: Just fire a warning shot over their heads

Finally, the Information error setting presents your message and the standard OK and Cancel buttons. Select OK and the data is entered; select Cancel and the entry is aborted. (See Figure 6-17.)

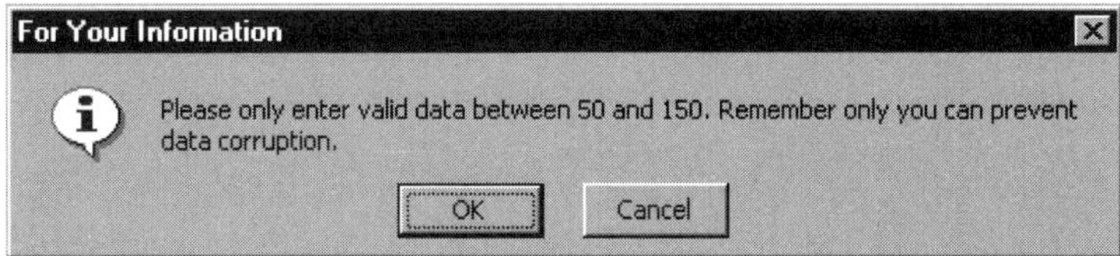

Figure 6-17: The friendly "invalid data" message

It may seem as if we've gone down a rabbit hole since we began talking about the Auditing toolbar and its last two buttons on the right—Circle Invalid Data and Clear Validation Circles. If you always set all your data validation error levels to Stop, you won't ever have to deal with these buttons. But if you use the Warning and Information levels, it's possible to enter data that falls outside the validation parameters.

In a review process, the Circle Invalid Data button can be clicked, and any invalid entries are circled in red (see Figure 6-18).

	B	C	D	E	F	G
2	North Division Sales					
3		Qtr.1	Qtr.2	Qtr.3	Qtr.4	Product Total
4	Widgets	98	101	112	75	386
5	Doohickeys	110	92	98	75	375
6	Gizmos	109	86	104	79	378
7	Totals	317	279	314	229	1139
8						
9						
10	North					
11	Central Division Sales		1141			
12	South Division Sales		1032			

Auditing

Circle Invalid Data

Figure 6-18: Invalid entries circled in red really stand out

The circles are a bit ephemeral and can disappear when you least expect it, like if you save or close the current workbook. They can be turned off manually with the Clear Validation Circles button as well (last button on the right of the Auditing toolbar).

Data validation . . . extremely useful no matter how you implement it.

Formulas vs. Results

A cell can contain a number or text (constants), or a formula. But what you *see* in a cell may not be what was entered into a cell. Formatting can control what you see in a cell. For example, 34547 formatted as a date might display as Aug-94. The formula `=3+5` displays as 8.

There are two faces to a sheet, what a cell really contains, and what the cell displays. Normally, Excel shows the results of formatting and calculations. We'll call this the *results* side. What was really entered into the cells we'll call the *formula* side, since the actual formula and not the formula's result is what we're really interested in here.

Changing a sheet display from results to formulas is called "flipping the sheet," and is an incredibly useful strategy for testing and reviewing spreadsheet models.

Flipping Sheets

You can flip the entire sheet by going to the Tools ➤ Options ➤ View dialog tab and checking the Formulas check box under the Windows option group, or you can press `CTRL+`` (hold down the `Ctrl` key and press the back apostrophe key). This keyboard shortcut will toggle the flip state between results and formulas.

Consider the example shown in Figure 6-19.

	A	B	C	D	E
1	Central Division Sales				
2		Qtr.1	Qtr.2	Qtr.3	Qtr.4
3	Widgets	98	101	112	75
4	Doohickey	110	92	98	75
5	Gizmos	109	86	104	79
6	Totals	317	289	314	229
7					

Figure 6-19: A sample table showing the results side

At first glance everything looks okie-dokie. But flip the sheet and surprise! (See Figure 6-20.)

	A	B	C	D	E
1	Central Division Sales				
2		Qtr.1	Qtr.2	Qtr.3	Qtr.4
3	Widgets	98	101	112	75
4	Doohickeys	110	92	98	75
5	Gizmos	109	86	104	79
6	Totals	=SUM(B3:B5)	289	=SUM(D3:D5)	=SUM(E3:E5)
7					

Figure 6-20: Same table flipped to its formula side

It appears that the expected formula in cell C8 has been overwritten with a constant. Admittedly, this is a simplistic example, but this technique can really help you audit and/or troubleshoot a spreadsheet!

Formula/Results flipper button

We feel this strategy of flipping sheets as you build and work with them is so compelling that we recommend you add a button to your Auditing toolbar that lets you toggle the formula/results state with a single click.

Open Module1 in your hidden *Personal.xls* and enter the code from Example 6-2.

Example 6-2: The Formula_Flipper Routine to Attach to a Toolbar

```
Sub Formula_Flipper()
'
' Formula_Flipper Macro to flip the worksheet display
'    between formulas and results
' Written xx/xx/xx by YourNameHere
'
    On Error GoTo EndMacro
    ActiveWindow.DisplayFormulas = Not ActiveWindow.DisplayFormulas
EndMacro:
End Sub
```

Now, add a button to the Auditing toolbar and hook it up to this code:

1. Pull down the View menu and choose Toolbars.
2. In the Toolbars dialog box, click on the Customize button.
3. Click the Commands tab, then choose Macros from the Categories list.
4. Drag the Custom button to the first position on the Auditing toolbar.
5. Right-click the happy face button.
6. Change the Name to Formula_Flipper.
7. Select Change Button Image and choose a pre-designed button face, or choose Edit Button Image and try your hand at designing your own image.
8. Right-click on the button again and click on Assign Macro. Choose the Formula_Flipper macro.
9. Right-click on the Trace Precedents button (the button to the right of the Formula_Flipper) and click on Begin a Group.
10. Click on Close in the Customize dialog box.

When you're done, your Auditing toolbar should resemble the one in Figure 6-21.

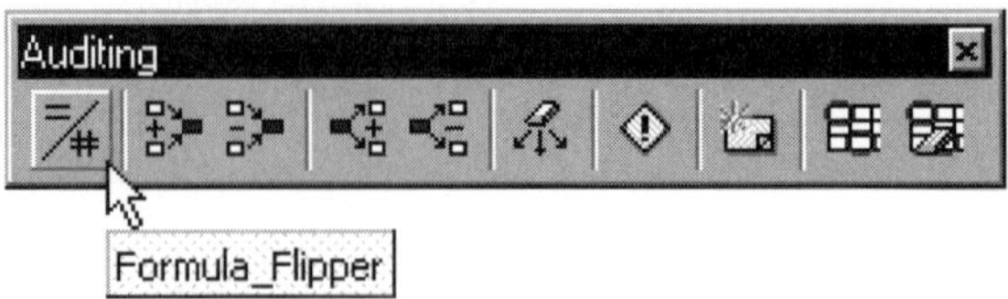

Figure 6-21: Custom Formula_Flipper button on the Auditing toolbar

R1C1 Reference Style

We've already talked about the differences between absolute and relative references and introduced the R1C1 reference style that Excel actually thinks in, as opposed to the A1 reference style that Excel displays and that most spreadsheet users are familiar with. The R1C1 reference style is good for more than just getting comfortable with absolute/relative referencing. It is an invaluable troubleshooting and auditing strategy.

A formula that gets overwritten can be readily discovered using the formula_flipper technique discussed in the previous section. But formulas that are off just a bit—they're harder to ferret out, and this is where R1C1 can help.

In Figure 6-22, we've shown the same column of formulas in R1C1 style on the left and in A1 style on the right. The formulas use relative referencing, meaning that each formula is identical under R1C1. Which style is it easier to spot the error in?

6	6
=RC[-4]-RC[-3]*RC[-2]	=C4-D4*E4
=RC[-4]-RC[-3]*RC[-2]	=C5-D5*E5
=RC[-4]-RC[-3]*RC[-2]	=C6-D6*E6
=R[1]C[-4]-RC[-3]*RC[-2]	=C8-D7*E7
=RC[-4]-RC[-3]*RC[-2]	=C8-D8*E8
=RC[-4]-RC[-3]*RC[-2]	=C9-D9*E9
=RC[-4]-RC[-3]*RC[-2]	=C10-D10*E10
=RC[-4]-RC[-3]*RC[-2]	=C11-D11*E11
=RC[-4]-RC[-3]*RC[-2]	=C12-D12*E12
=RC[-4]-RC[-3]*RC[-2]	=C13-D13*E13
=RC[-4]-RC[-3]*RC[-2]	=C14-D14*E14
=RC[-4]-RC[-3]*RC[-2]	=C15-D15*E15

Figure 6-22: R1C1 versus A1 reference style

Yes, we agree. The error (fourth from the top) is easier to spot in R1C1 style, no doubt about it. Combined with the other strategies in this chapter, this technique is worth its weight in furry ferrets for finding anomalies in formulas.

Rounding out your Auditing toolbar tools is a one-click reference style flipper. Open Module1 in your hidden *Personal.xls* and enter the code from Example 6-3.

Example 6-3: The Style_Flipper Routine to Attach to a Toolbar

```
Sub Style_Flipper()
'
' Style_Flipper Macro to switch between R1C1 and A1 reference style
' Written xx/xx/xx by YourNameHere
'
    With Application
        If .ReferenceStyle = xlA1 Then
            .ReferenceStyle = xlR1C1
        Else
            .ReferenceStyle = xlA1
        End If
    End With
End Sub
```

Add a second button to the Auditing toolbar and hook it up to this code:

1. Pull down the View menu and choose Toolbars.
2. In the Toolbars dialog box, click on the Customize button.
3. Click the Commands tab, then choose Macros from the Categories list.
4. Drag the Custom button to the second position on the Auditing toolbar (to the right of the Formula_Flipper).
5. Right-click the happy face button.
6. Change the Name to Style_Flipper.
7. Select Change Button Image and choose a pre-designed button face, or choose Edit Button Image and try your hand at designing your own image.
8. Right-click on the button again and click on Assign Macro. Choose the Style_Flipper macro.
9. Click on Close in the Customize dialog box.

Your Auditing toolbar should now resemble the one shown in Figure 6-23 (except, of course, that our icons are certain to look worse than yours).

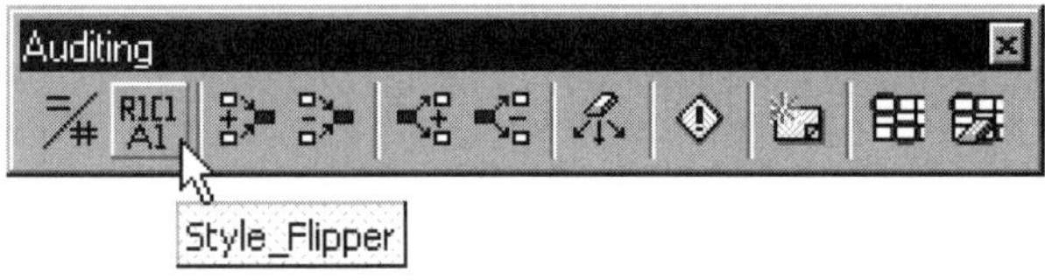

Figure 6-23: Style flipper ready for action

In checking and troubleshooting formulas, don't overlook the technique we discussed in Chapter 4 under "Evaluating formulas." You can evaluate any portion of a formula in the formula bar (the Formula Palette must not be activated). Select the cell with the formula, select just that portion of the formula you want to evaluate in the formula bar, and press the `F9` function key. Highlight a range and you'll see all the values contained therein. Select a range name and see what it evaluates to. Just remember to hit the `Escape` key when you're done, or you will permanently change (and damage) the formula.

Go To Special

We've talked about the Go To dialog box as a major aid to navigating the sheets of a workbook. But the Go To dialog hides one of Excel's great hidden treasures. The Special button on the Go To dialog (Edit ➤ Go To, or `F5`) calls up another useful tool for your troubleshooting toolbox. (See Figure 6-24.)

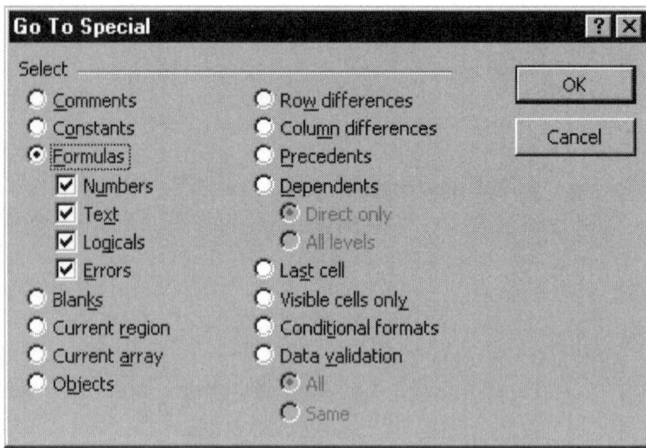

Figure 6-24: The Go To Special dialog box

Go To Special allows you to select a number of cells in the active sheet simultaneously. You specify the criterion for the selection by checking the appropriate option button in the dialog.

Select only a single cell in the current sheet, and the entire worksheet is searched. But select a range of cells, and only that range is searched for matching cells. This ability to limit the search to a given range is the strength of this technique. Zoom out, select a range, Zoom to fit selection, and start testing the selected range for cells of a specific type.

Let's walk through the options as they're listed in the Go To Special dialog box.

Comments, Constants, Formulas, and Blanks

These are the big four, the most useful of the Go To Special selection criteria overall. (No wonder they come first!) We'll go through them individually. Remember, once you have selected all the cells in the sheet that match your criteria using Go To Special, you can jump through the cells by using the `Tab` key. An outstanding way to review a group of cells scattered throughout the sheet.

Comments

Checking this option button and clicking on OK allows you to select every cell in the current sheet that has a note attached. You can achieve pretty much the same effect by using the Previous Comment/Next Comment buttons on the Reviewing toolbar. But the Previous/Next methodology selects the notes, not the cells containing the notes. To actually jump from cell to cell (useful if you want to review the actual content of each commented cell), first display all the comments in the sheet, then use the Go To Special ➤ Comments trick.

Constants

When you select the Constants option button, you can further refine your criteria by checking (or unchecking) the Numbers, Text, Logicals, or Errors check boxes. This lets you zero in on constant numeric values as opposed to text strings. You can under certain circumstances have a Logical or Error as a constant in a cell. The layout of this set of controls—the way the checkboxes are indented below the Formulas button but also apply to Constants—is annoying and confusing.

This is another technique that can find errant constants that have overwritten formulas.

Formulas

Conversely, Formulas can return Numbers, Text, Logicals, and Errors, so not only are all the check boxes available, they actually work to filter the selected cells.

Blanks

A blank cell is one that does not have *any* contents, and this option lets you find them, or verify them, as not every cell that *appears* blank really is. A lot of us old Lotus users learned to blank a cell by hitting the spacebar. But in Excel the space is the intersection operator. Scattering them liberally around a sheet can cause you a number of assorted problems. Select a range and run this option. Anything not selected is not really blank, no matter how it looks.

Another old trick is to create a custom format of `;;;;` to hide cell contents. Nothing appears, but the cell is not really blank.

Current Region

The current region is, *ahem*, "the range of cells around the active cell bounded by any combination of blank rows and columns." In other words, all the cells in a rectangle, including the current cell, that are not empty rows and columns. That is not to say that blank cells may not be included in the current region—it depends on the layout of the adjacent cells that are not empty. Pick a cell that is surrounded by empty cells and that one cell alone is the current region all by itself.

Play around with this one, and while the definition still won't make any sense, you'll quickly figure out what's what with the current region.

Once you have the current region selected, you can search through it using the other Go To Special options.

Current Array

Select a cell with an array-entered formula (a formula that acts on a group of cells all at once) and run this option. The entire range of cells containing the array formula are highlighted.

Objects

This option lets you select every graphical object on the current sheet's drawing layer. The Objects option cannot be limited to a selected range of cells since the drawing layer floats above the cells themselves. It's an all or nothing affair.

We're talking all graphical objects. AutoShapes, connectors, text boxes, embedded pictures, charts, circles, arrows, you name it. Oh, the audit trace arrows and the data validation circles are not considered graphical objects, so this does not select them, but that's all that gets excluded.

This option is great for finding what objects exist in a sheet. Run this, and then tab your way through the entire collection. And since the objects are all selected when you first run this, it's great for instantly grouping everything, for moving all the objects a few pixels one way or the other, or even for deleting them all at once if you want to.

Row and Column Differences

We've discussed how easy it is to spot something rotten in Denmark, er, in relative formulas by using the R1C1 style and then flipping the sheet to formula mode. Anything not right stands out like a full moon. But that technique works best with small selections and tables. For huge spreadsheets that span hundreds of rows or columns, you need a more industrial-strength strategy.

Row and Column differences are just such a strategy. You select all the formula entries in a row or column. Make sure that the formula in the active cell of the selection is kosher and run the applicable differences option in Go To Special. Each formula in the selection is compared to the base formula (the one in the active cell of the selection), and any cells that do not match are highlighted. It's amazing to see in action. It does not matter if you are in R1C1 or A1 notation; anything that does not match is found.

Precedents and Dependents

These two options are holdovers from the olden days before the tracing features were added to Excel. They work in a similar manner, only they're not as elegant, merely highlighting the precedent or dependent cell(s) of the current cell. Our advice is to stick with the tracing tools on the Auditing toolbar.

Last Cell

Remember the last cell, also known as the end cell? That's the last row and column intersection for the rightmost column and the bottommost row in the sheet containing data.

Selecting Edit ➤ Go To ➤ Special ➤ Last Cell ➤ OK does exactly the same thing as pressing `CTRL+END`. Only `CTRL+END` saves you about eight keystrokes or three mouse clicks. Guess which way we recommend for finding the last cell in a worksheet?

Visible Cells Only

Ever selected a couple of cells, copied them, then pasted them in another sheet? Then, instead of only the cells you selected, you get a ton of stuff you didn't expect? All the contents of cells from hidden rows and columns get copied if your selection extends across the hidden cells. Yuck!

Visible Cells Only to the rescue! Select your range, then pop up the Go To Special dialog and click on the Visible Cells Only option. Hit OK and proceed with your copy; *only the cells visible on the sheet are copied to the clipboard.*

Conditional Formats and Data Validation

This is how you can quickly find all the cells in your sheet that have conditional formats applied to them. Ditto for cells that you have applied some data validation to.

With either option, you can use the All or Same suboption. Choose All and all the cells matching your criteria (conditional formatting or data validation) are selected. The Same option finds only those cells that match the format or validation rules for the active cell.

Adding Go To Special to Your Toolkit

As you can see, the Go To Special dialog box is chock full of useful tools for troubleshooting errant spreadsheets. The major annoyance is that you have to drill down to the Go To dialog box, then choose a button on that dialog to get to the Go To Special dialog. The solution is to add another custom button to your ever-displayed Auditing toolbar.

Enter the code shown in Example 6-4 into Module1 in your *Personal.xls,* and add a third button to your Auditing toolbar.

Example 6-4: The EditGotoSpecial Macro to Open the Go To Special Dialog

```
Public Sub EditGotoSpecial()
'
' EditGotoSpecial Macro to pop-up the Go To Special dialog
' Written xx/xx/xx by YourNameHere
'
    If TypeName(ActiveSheet) = "Worksheet" Then
        On Error GoTo EndMacro
        Application.Dialogs(xlDialogSelectSpecial).Show
    Else
        Beep
    End If
    Exit Sub
EndMacro:
    If Err = 1004 Then
        MsgBox "No cells (or objects) found.", vbExclamation
    End If
End Sub
```

You know the drill by now for adding a button to a toolbar, so we won't bore you with it again. Your Auditing toolbar should now be fully tricked out and ready for anything Excel can throw at you! (See Figure 6-25.)

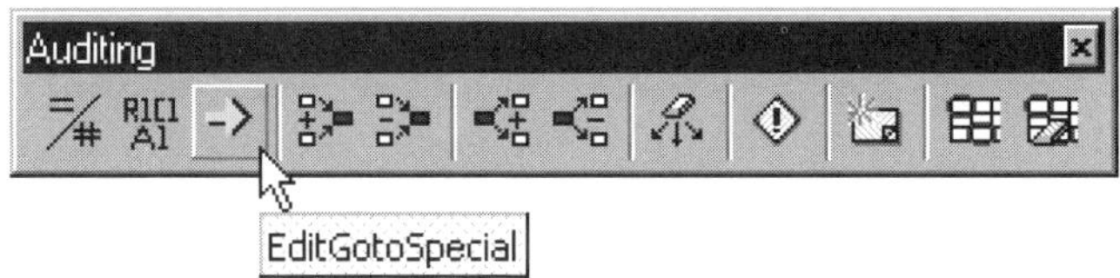

Figure 6-25: The fully accessorized Auditing toolbar

Excel's Internet Connection

Everything these days has to somehow be tied into the Internet, the über-buzzword extraordinaire. Not to be left behind by the hyperbole media machine, Excel 97 has its share of Web and Internet features. These features range from the useful to the "that's very interesting, but why would anyone want to do that?" variety. Ah well, the Marketing Suits seem to have taken over. It's not that we're knocking the Internet as a strategy, we're just not sure how much you need your spreadsheet application tied into it.

Still, there are some nuggets to be mined from the sluice-box of Internet/Web hype.

FTP to and from the Internet

Should you find yourself wanting to open a file from your web or FTP (File Transfer Protocol) site in Excel, you'll be pleased to know that you can now FTP right from within Excel. From the File ➤ Open dialog box, pull down the "Look in:" drop-down and take a peek at the bottom of the list. You'll find a resource called "Internet Locations (FTP)." Below this resource is an option, "Add/Modify FTP Locations," that lets you add new sites or modify existing FTP locations. Finally, all the locations that have already been set up are listed. (See Figure 6-26.)

The Internet Locations (FTP) resource appears in the File ➤ Save As dialog as well, letting you save files directly to an FTP site.

You'll have to have either a direct connection to the Internet or be able to connect via modem. Select a site that you've set up and you'll see the files located on that site appear in the Open or Save As dialogs. You must have read/write privileges on the FTP site, which at first glance seems to make this feature best suited to internal company intranets. But read on.

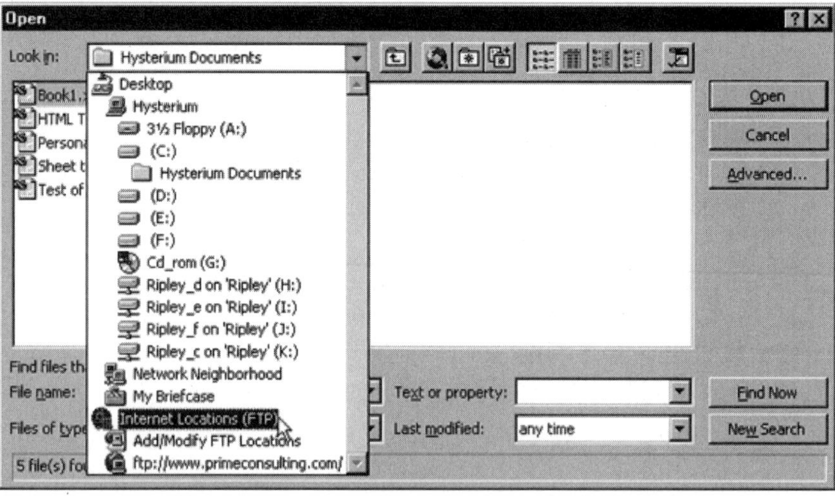

Figure 6-26: Access the Internet from Excel

Your own FTP site

If you work on spreadsheets both at work and at home, there is a practical application of the built-in FTP access that you might want to consider. Many of you have access to the Internet from work and also have your own ISP (Internet Service Provider) so you can surf the Net from home.

Check to see if your ISP provides free web site space on their server. Many ISPs give you web space as an incentive to use their service, and you can FTP to and from your personal web space. Create a worksheet at home and save it right to your web site. Open it directly into Excel from the office. Forget about having to schlep floppies back and forth between home and office. Get to your files from anywhere you have Internet access. The other applications in Office also have this ability to FTP.

One potential annoyance you'll encounter when using FTP from within Office applications—you are summarily dumped into the root directory of the destination server instead of your home or target folder. This forces you to do quite a bit of navigating to get where you want to go today. Depending on how many files and folders you have to wade through, this can be a real time waster. The good news is that there is a workaround. Select, but don't open, the folder that is your ultimate goal in the File Open or File Save As dialog box, right-click on it, and choose Create Shortcut. You'll get a message box telling you that you can't create the shortcut there (in the server folder) and suggesting that the shortcut be created on your desktop. Click Yes, and a shortcut to your target folder is created. Move the shortcut from your Desktop to whatever folder you favor, and the next time you want to FTP to that folder, click on that shortcut in your dialog. This takes you straight to your target folder, bypassing all points in between.

Security is paramount

There are, however, some serious caveats to this idea of using the Internet as an extension of your computer's hard disk. The Internet is not the most secure place to go storing the company payroll spreadsheets, or the projections for that megabuck hostile company takeover you've been planning. Web sites occasionally get broken into, so use some common sense:

1. Don't trust truly vital data out on the Net. That said, how many of your spreadsheets are so sensitive to entice someone to spend the effort to try to find them?
2. Password protect the Excel files that you store on the Net. True, the protection offered by Excel's encryption feature can be circumvented, but it is still a good precaution to take. Remember, you won't be telling anyone at work where you're keeping your files, so your only real exposure is that some hacker randomly stumbles onto your site and decides to go to the trouble to break in.
3. If you are using a web site to house your files, create an innocuous looking *Index.html* home page about collecting string or some such interesting topic. If you don't have an index page, anyone accessing your site from a browser (like Netscape Navigator or Microsoft Internet Explorer) sees a list of the files stored in that folder.
4. Don't store your files in the root folder of your site space. Create a folder tree and stick your files in an out-of-the-way branch, three or four levels deep.

There are some other things you can do, depending on the services offered by the ISP that hosts your site. Rather than discuss all the possibilities here, just ask your ISP what you can do to further secure a particular folder on your site.

URLs in Formulas

Hyperlinks are a new name on an old feature, that of linking information between documents. A new wrinkle to links in Excel 97 is the ability to link across (you guessed it!) the Internet. Again, this is a feature that really is quite useful on an intranet, where data is stored on a Web server on your local network and where your connection is always active.

The following formulas use the new hyperlink feature to link to external data using HTTP and FTP:

```
=[http://www.somewhere.com/Afile.xls]Sheet1!A1
```

The preceding formula returns the contents of cell A1 from a sheet named Sheet1 in a workbook named *Afile.xls* in the root folder of the *www.somewhere.com* domain. The next formula returns the contents of the range name "MyNamedCell" from the sheet named AnamedSheet in the *Bfile.xls* workbook in the *stuff* folder on the *ftp.server.somewhere* FTP site:

```
=[ftp://ftp.server.somewhere/stuff/
Bfile.xls]AnamedSheet!MyNamedCell
```

Excel as HTML Generator

A handy Internet Wizard comes with Excel 97. To use it, you have to make sure you installed the Internet Assistant Wizard when you installed Excel or Office. Kick things off by opening the workbook you want and selecting a specific sheet to be converted to HTML code. Select "Save as HTML" from the File menu, and the Wizard appears. (See Figure 6-27.)

The Wizard automatically lists the current selection and any embedded charts in the "Ranges and charts to convert" list box. It's mildly annoying that named ranges don't appear in the list. Still, you can click the Add button, which rolls up the Wizard dialog and lets you select a range in the current sheet manually.

What you wind up with is a table (what else?) in HTML code. The Wizard lets you choose between a standalone HTML file, and having the selected range or chart injected into an existing HTML document. The trick is to first open the existing document and add `<!--##Table##-->` at the point in the code where you want the Excel information inserted. The Wizard replaces that string of text with the table data or chart graphic reference from Excel.

Charts are converted into GIF images, which means you have to deal with two files, the HTML page and the GIF file that it references.

The tables and charts, once converted, are not linked to the original spreadsheet data, so don't expect anything like dynamic updating of information. Font formatting is preserved when a table is converted to HTML, as are cell background color and merged cells. This makes Excel one great table generator for those of you who have to crank out Web pages.

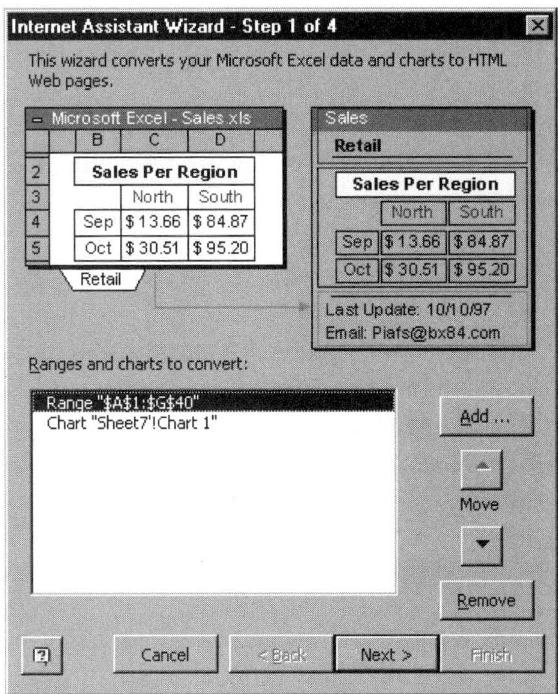

Figure 6-27: Excel's Internet Assistant Wizard

Web Queries

Choosing Data ➤ Get External Data ➤ Run Web Query will let you select a query to run against some Web page. Query files are text files that contain instructions on what page to access on the Web and what data to extract once there. Excel 97 comes with several sample queries (*C:\Program Files\Microsoft Office\Queries*). (See Figure 6-28.)

Once a query has been selected, you are prompted for how you want the incoming data dealt with by Excel. You can designate the cell that is to define the upper-left corner of the incoming information, or you can have Excel create a new sheet in the current workbook. See Figure 6-29.

You may be prompted for additional information depending on how the query is constructed. A sample query file (with an *.iqy* extension) might look like this:

```
WEB
1
http://webservices.pcquote.com/cgi-bin/exceldow.exe?
```

Queries are text files with an *.iqy* extension. The *Microsoft Office 97 Resource Kit* includes detailed instructions on how queries work and how

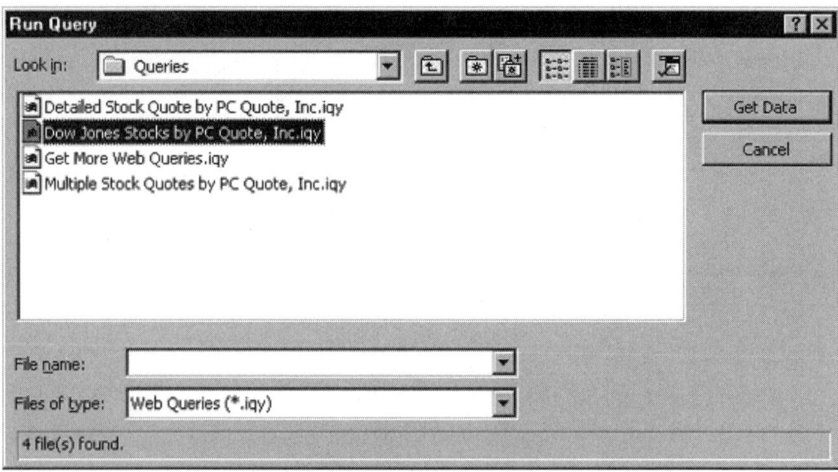

Figure 6-28: Choosing a Web query to run

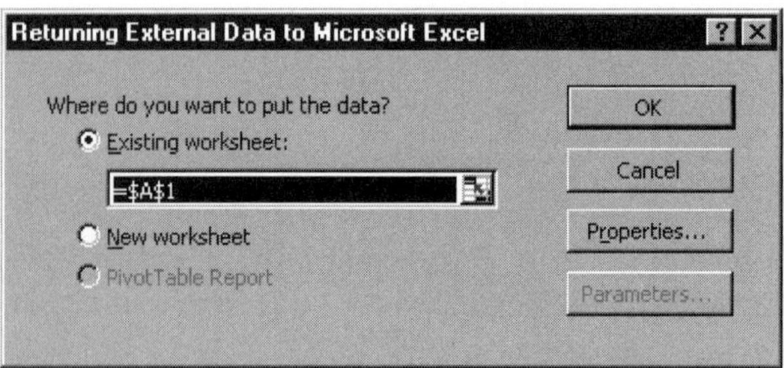

Figure 6-29: Where do you want the incoming data to go?

to construct them. Syntax, post, static, and dynamic parameters are all covered for the Webmasters among you. Highly recommended.

Web Form Wizard

Excel 97 lets you use workbooks as Web Forms to collect information from users who fill out the forms from within their browsers. This requires the Excel program to be available on the user's computer (the Microsoft Excel Viewer does not support data input). Collected information can be saved to any of several different formats on the server. The Web Form Wizard automatically creates the scripts necessary to save the data to a database file.

Web Forms are best suited to internal intranets, and you can quickly get bogged down in Perl, ISAPI, CGI, ASP, IDC, and other scary sounding acronyms. Again, the *Microsoft Office 97 Resource Kit* has the information you'll need to get started with Web Forms.

Web Toolbar

The Web Toolbar is the first salvo in the barrage to soften us up for the next step in making everything on your computer look like a web browser. With this toolbar, it's possible to pretend you are running a browser (something designed to let you look at things) instead of a super-powerful spreadsheet application. Oh joy—NOT!

Making believe Excel is a *user-friendly* (and we use the term loosely) browser becomes annoying in short order. Consider the toolbar in question (see Figure 6-30).

Figure 6-30: Excel in Internet Explorer clothing

From left to right, you have your Forward and Back buttons, the Stop button, and the Refresh, Home, and Search buttons. Then your Favorites menu list (same as you have in MSIE), ditto for your Go menu. The last button before the drop-down history list is the Show Only Web Toolbar that switches off all your other visible toolbars. It toggles, so just click it a second time, and the other toolbars become visible again.

You can type a standard path and filename to an Excel file in the Address list box (shown on the right in Figure 6-30), and up pops the file. Oddly enough, if you want to open an HTML file inside Excel, you have to use the plain old File Open dialog. Trying to type in a URL or a path to an HTML file inside the Web Toolbar Address box will fire off your default browser, and the Web page is loaded there. This is just as well because even though Excel makes a valiant attempt to display HTML files, the formatting leaves much to be desired. But this is not really Excel's fault. Excel is a spreadsheet program. If you want to surf the Web (Internet or intranet), use a browser.

When using Excel as browser, if you open a workbook via the Web toolbar, and then you open a second workbook (again, with the Web toolbar), the first workbook is closed (unless you made a change to it, in which case you're prompted to save it before it's slammed closed) in keeping with a browser's "display one file at a time" paradigm. This is progress? If you don't know the path, you can browse for it. Click Go on the Web toolbar, click Open, in the Open Internet Address dialog box click on the Browse button, and you finally get to where you would have been had you just clicked on Excel's Open button. Sheesh!

The day may be coming when we'll be forced to pretend the world is a giant web site and all our software is a browser, but until then, forget the Web Toolbar. Use Excel as Excel and get a browser to work the Web.

Presentation Strategies

Before we launch into all the various and sundry ways that Excel provides for formatting and making your information look spiffy, let's take a time out for a reality check. Better you jot down meaningful numbers on a matchbook cover than to present bogus numbers that look great with reverse shading, embedded charts, bells, whistles, and maybe some sound and animated graphics thrown in. Your mantra should be *substance over form!*

That said, once the numbers have been crunched, the formulas formulated, and the results thoroughly audited, then and only then should you give some consideration to the presentation of your spreadsheet.

Formats Galore

At first blush it would seem that formatting cells in Excel is simplicity itself. You select the cell or range of cells to format, and apply the formatting attributes you want. What could be easier?

The trick is in dealing with the plethora of formatting options that are available. Select some cells and choose Cells from the Format menu. You get the multi-tabbed dialog box shown in Figure 6-31.

More Number formats than you can shake a bundle of sticks at. A double handful or so of Alignment options—including the very cool orientation attribute that lets you rotate the contents of a cell—Fonts, Border, Patterns, and Protection attributes. While it's great that you have this amount of formatting control, you can spend a lot of time applying all of the various options over and over to your sheets.

We've already discussed some tricks for data entry that can help with formatting. The trick wherein you select several sheet tabs then enter data on all the sheets at once can be used for formatting. Select several tabs, highlight some cells, and apply formatting attributes. The formatting is applied to all the selected sheets.

You are not limited to the Format ➤ Cell dialog box for applying formatting attributes. The ExcelAnnoy Formatting custom toolbar (as well as the default Formatting toolbar) sport Font Color and Fill Color buttons for formatting, as well as a Borders button. These buttons display palettes of

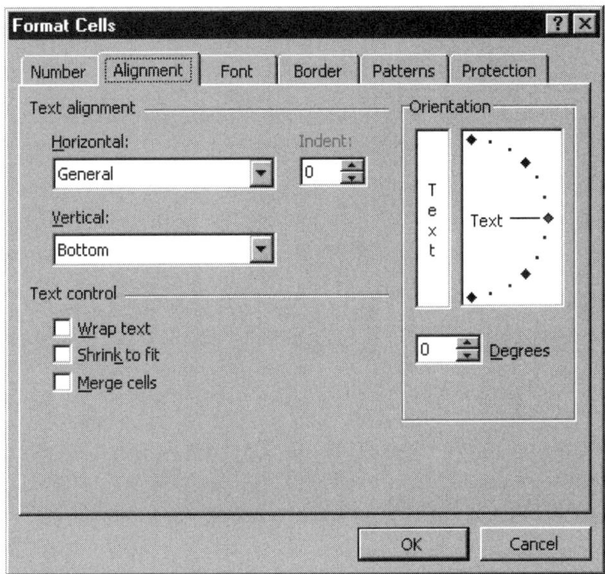

Figure 6-31: The possibilities are nearly endless

choices you can click on to select formatting on the fly. These palettes can be torn off the toolbar and become freestanding floating mini-toolbars. Very nice when doing some complex manual formatting. (See Figure 6-32.)

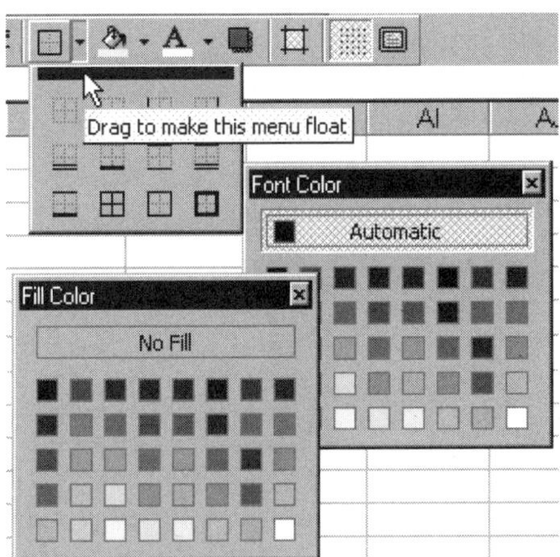

Figure 6-32: Tear-off tool palettes for formatting

Autocratic AutoFormat

To help make formatting on a large scale easier, Microsoft came up with AutoFormat. This feature works best with tables of numbers, which is good, since that is what comprises most spreadsheets. Select your table and choose AutoFormat from the Format menu. The AutoFormat dialog box is displayed. (See Figure 6-33.)

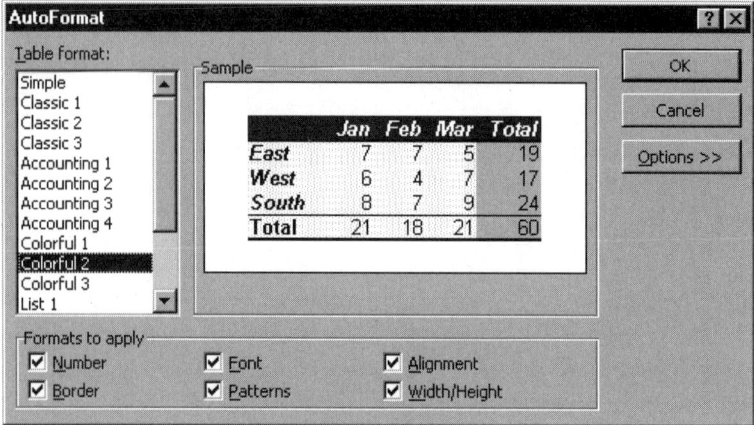

Figure 6-33: AutoFormat preset formatting options

Choose a table format from the preconfigured list and click OK. All of the formatting options displayed in the Sample window are instantly applied to your table. In Figure 6-34 you can see the same table of data both before and after applying the preset Colorful 2 table style via AutoFormat.

B	C	D	E	F	G
Central Division Sales					
	Qtr.1	Qtr.2	Qtr.3	Qtr.4	Total
Widgets	101	117	90	65	373
Doohickeys	131	109	115	95	450
Gizmos	90	80	77	71	318
Totals	322	306	282	231	1141

Central Division Sales					
	Qtr.1	Qtr.2	Qtr.3	Qtr.4	Total
Widgets	101	117	90	65	373
Doohickeys	131	109	115	95	450
Gizmos	90	80	77	71	318
Totals	322	306	282	231	1141

Figure 6-34: AutoFormat—before and after

The good news is that the AutoFormat feature works as advertised. The annoying news is that you are limited to what the Excel programmers have provided as collections of preset table formatting attributes. And some of these presets are just plain awful.

What's needed is a way to create and store your own custom AutoFormat presets. Ah, well, we've had this on our wish list since Excel 5 . . . maybe in Excel 98.

You can mitigate this limitation somewhat by using the check boxes at the bottom of the AutoFormat dialog. To display these check boxes (as shown in Figure 6-33), you have to click on the Options button. By unchecking these boxes, you can selectively eliminate certain attributes from the preset collection. Say you like everything in Colorful 2 but the number format. Format the numbers in your table the way you want them, then uncheck this box before applying the preset. You'll get everything but the Colorful 2 number attributes. In our example we unchecked the Width/Height check box to preserve the column widths of our original table.

Still, if you have to resort to manually applying formatting, the value of AutoFormat is greatly reduced.

Formatting with Styles

If you use Word 97 (and have read O'Reilly & Associates' *Word 97 Annoyances*), you're probably very cognizant of styles, which are fundamental to power word processing. A *style*, for all you spreadsheet jockeys out there who rarely venture outside Excel, is a collection of formatting attributes that can all be applied simultaneously by simply applying the style name that represents the collection of attributes to a selection on the worksheet.

A style can be applied to a single cell or a range of cells and can contain any and all of Excel's formatting attributes. Figure 6-35 shows a table that was formatted using styles.

	B	C	D	E	F	G
9	**South Division Sales**					
10	*Product*	*Qtr.1*	*Qtr.2*	*Qtr.3*	*Qtr.4*	*Total*
11	*Widgets*	$102	$120	$98	$80	$400
12	*Doohickey*	85	101	77	79	342
13	*Gizmos*	97	65	73	55	290
14	Totals	$284	$286	$248	$214	$1,032
15						

Figure 6-35: Formatting with styles

Not as fast as AutoFormat, but you get exactly the formatting you want. The table was first created without regard to formatting—you want to devote all your attention to making the numbers and calculations accurate and meaningful—then styles were applied. (See Table 6-1.)

Table 6-1: Styles Used in Figure 6-35

Style Name	Figure 6-35 Range	Formatting Attributes
TableName	B9:C9	Bold, white, left right top borders, shaded
ColHead	B10:G10	Horizontal centered, italic, left right top bottom borders, shaded
RowLabels	B11:B13	Left (1 indent), italic, shaded
Num1stLine	C11:G11	$#,##0_);[Red]($#,##0), shaded
NumLine	C12:G13	#,##0_);[Red](#,##0), shaded
NumTotLine	B14:G14	$#,##0_);[Red]($#,##0), top bottom borders, shaded

The easiest way to create styles is to format a cell or range manually. Once you have it looking just the way you want, click once in the Style drop-down control that we added to your ExcelAnnoy Formatting toolbar. Type in the name that you want to use for this collection of formatting attributes and hit the `Enter` key. It's as easy as that!

When creating style names, keep them short, describe how the style is used (`RowLabels`), and *do not* describe the attributes (`BoldItalic$`), since you may change the attributes over time for a particular style name. You can use spaces in style names, but we opt for no spaces and use capitalization for readability.

To apply styles (once created) you highlight the range and choose the appropriate style name from the Styles drop-down list on the ExcelAnnoy Formatting toolbar.

You can further refine your styles by using the Format ➤ Style dialog box.

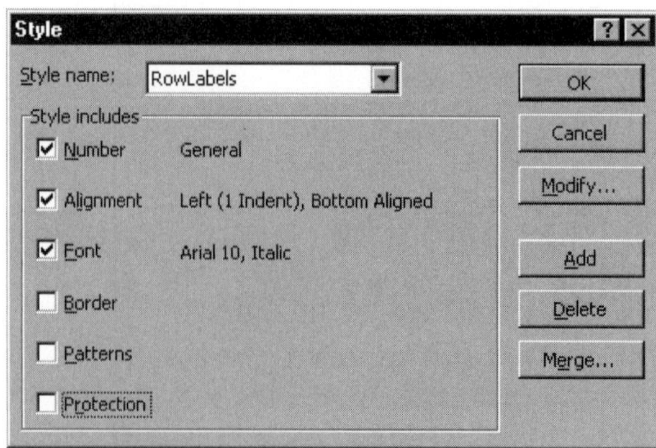

Figure 6-36: Controlling style attributes

In Figure 6-36 the RowLabels style has been modified so that it will now ignore any local formatting (formatting already applied to the current selection) as far as Border, Patterns, and Protection go. A style may deal with all categories of attributes, a subset of the categories, or even a single category.

Until we get a customizable AutoFormat feature, styles are the next best thing.

Custom Views

Another underutilized gem in Excel's strategic arsenal is the Custom Views facility. This used to be an add-in but now is a native Excel 97 feature.

A custom view is like a style in that it allows you to store a number of view attributes in a collection. By selecting the custom view, you apply all of those attributes simultaneously. So what kinds of attributes can you store in a custom view? For starters, you can store all of the settings in the Tools ➤ Options ➤ View dialog box tab.

As you can see in Figure 6-37, you can store Show, Comments, Objects, and Window option attributes in a custom view. In addition, the current sheet within a workbook, the current selection within a sheet, and split screen and freeze pane settings can all be stored. This is very handy for creating different views of the same sheet, one for presentation, one for data entry, one for auditing, etc.

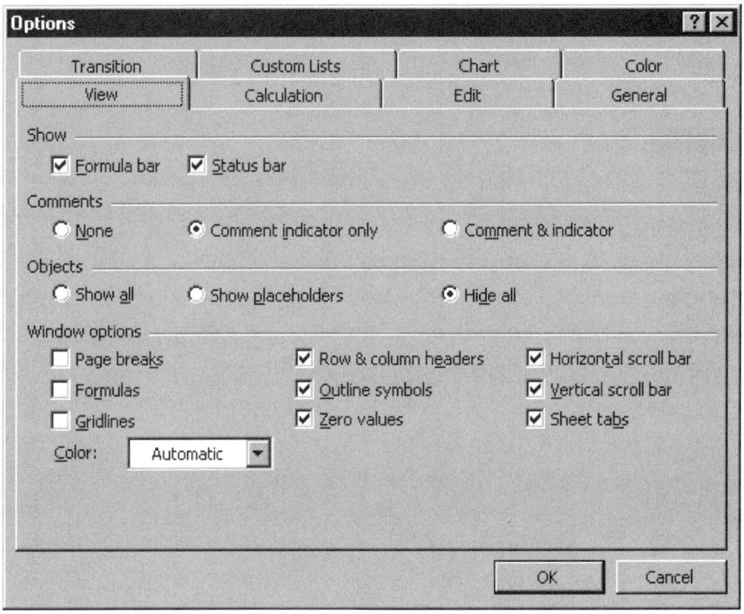

Figure 6-37: Custom View attributes

Set up the attributes you want for your custom view and select Custom View from the View menu. (See Figure 6-38.) These custom views are from a workbook that contains a single sheet.

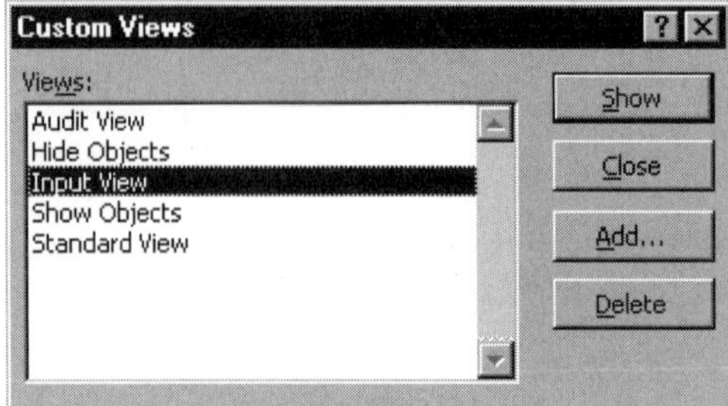

Figure 6-38: Selecting your Custom Views

To create a custom view click on the Add button. A dialog box appears, letting you name your view. (See Figure 6-39.)

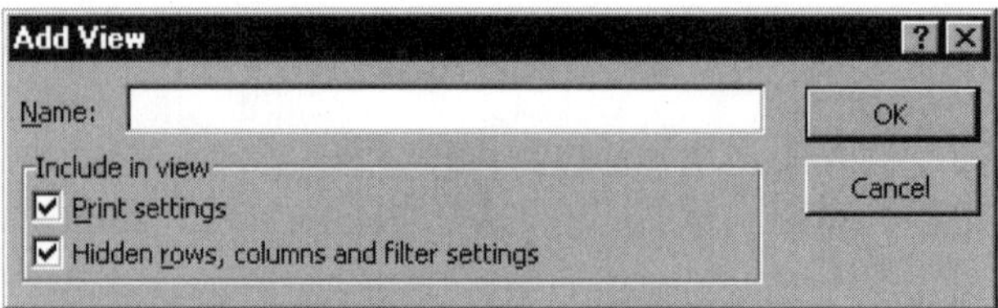

Figure 6-39: Adding a view

Since the view defines the current worksheet within the workbook, you'll want to include the sheet name in the view name for multi-sheet books.

Note that hidden rows, columns, and filter settings can also be saved as attributes of a custom view. This is handy for creating views that display columns that are usually hidden for presentation purposes.

The ability to include print settings lets you develop multiple print set-ups for the same sheet. Very, very handy for creating a summary report, a detail report, and an audit report, all for the same worksheet. Print settings include anything you can set in the Page Setup dialog and its assorted tabs: Page, Margins, Header/Footer, and Sheet.

The power of Custom Views is the ability to switch between different views with just a few keystrokes or mouse clicks, and once you start using them, you'll wonder how you got along without them.

That is not to say, however, that Custom Views are without their annoying little gotchas! There is no way to determine what view you are in at any given time. Whenever you click View ➤ Custom Views, the dialog appears with the first view name selected. Not even a hint of what the current view (if any) is. And updating a view is a tricky proposition as well. To update a view, you have to wind through the following steps:

1. Switch to the Custom View that is to be updated.
2. Make the desired changes to the view, page setup, and/or hidden row and column settings.
3. From the View menu select Custom Views.
4. From the Custom Views dialog click on the Add button.
5. Type in the name of the existing view. *Match this name exactly*!
6. Click on OK.

If you're lucky you'll see a message box telling you that this view already exists and asking if you want to delete it. By selecting Yes, the old view is deleted and a new view with the same name is created. Pretty annoying, huh? (See Figure 6-40.)

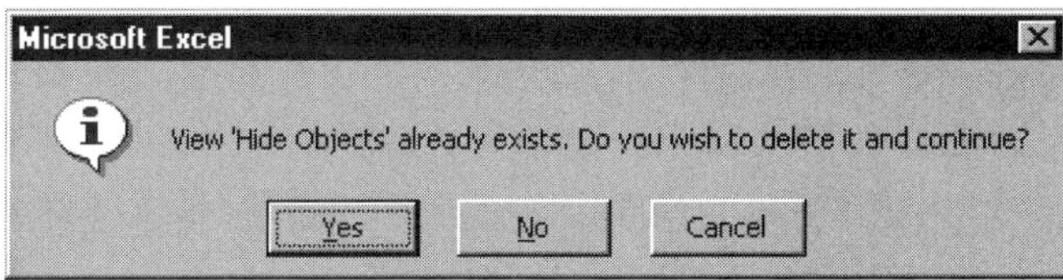

Figure 6-40: All this to update a Custom View

Maps! Data Meets Geography

In Excel 97 Microsoft has bundled in some technology from a company called MapInfo (we're assuming this based on the amount of advertising for map add-on products that you'll find in the Excel Help file when looking up information on this feature). If the Map component has not been installed, you can install it from the Office CD. Microsoft Map is very nice if you have any kind of data you'd like to visually present that ties to one of the provided geographical maps. You get maps for the following geographical areas:

- Australia
- Canada
- Europe
- Mexico
- North America
- Southern Africa

- UK and ROI Countries
- United States (AK & HI Inset)
- World Countries

Creating a map is easy. If you want data linked to the map (which is one of the main benefits of this feature), you select the range containing your figures—at least one column must contain geographical data, such as the names of the countries or states—select Maps from the Insert menu, and click-and-drag to create an embedded map object in the drawing layer of the current sheet.

The map appears, and you are left with the Map object active. This means you're really in an OLE application, you have a special map menu, and the Microsoft Map toolbar is displayed. If you are linked to data in the sheet, the Microsoft Map Control panel appears as well. (See Figure 6-41.)

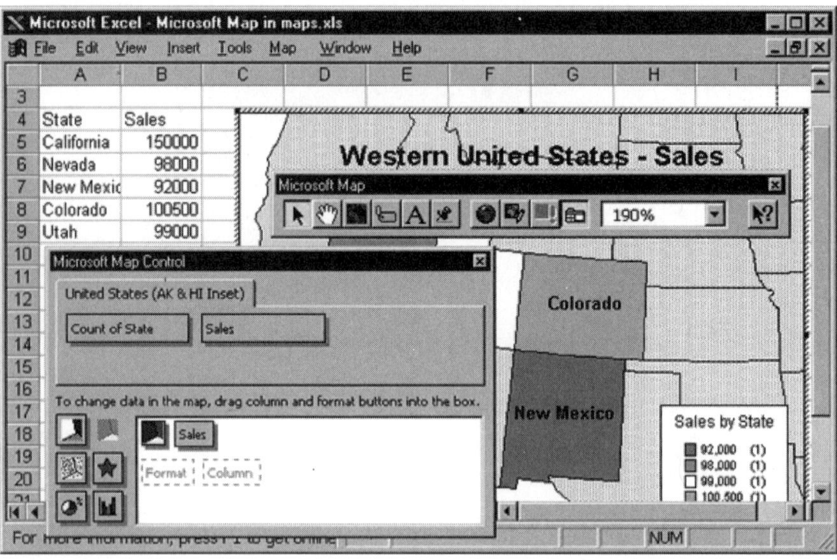

Figure 6-41: Creating Maps in Excel 97

Working with maps is a lot like working with Excel charts in that you can create labels and legends, you can control how data is represented on the map, etc. Like charts, we could write an entire book on the ins and outs of maps and presenting numeric data visually.

The relatively few maps that come with Excel is not as limiting as it sounds. You can, for example, create a map using the United States (AK & HI Inset), which gives you all 50 states. Then you can center the map on a particular state and zoom it in until just the area you want is displayed.

The Map applet is resource intensive, meaning that it'll gobble up a fair amount of your system resources and a whole bunch of your GDI resources. In our labs, if resources got low, we had trouble updating the map when we changed the underlying numeric data. By default, maps need to be updated manually—you change the data in your sheet, double-click the map to activate it, and click on the Map Refresh button on the Microsoft Map toolbar (see Figure 6-42).

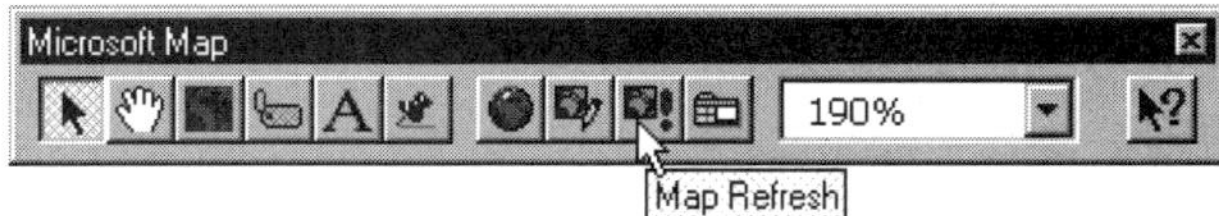

Figure 6-42: Manually updating a map when the linked data changes

This button is grayed out until the linked data changes. When we ran low on available resources in our tests, this button stayed grayed out even though the data had changed. At one point we had to shut down and reboot one of the test systems in our lab to get our map to update properly.

To make the update automatic, you first activate the map then choose Options from the Tools menu. Figure 6-43 shows the various options you can set for your maps. Under Data Refresh, you can switch from Manual to Automatic. Check the "Use as default for new maps" box to force the setting to apply to all new maps you generate.

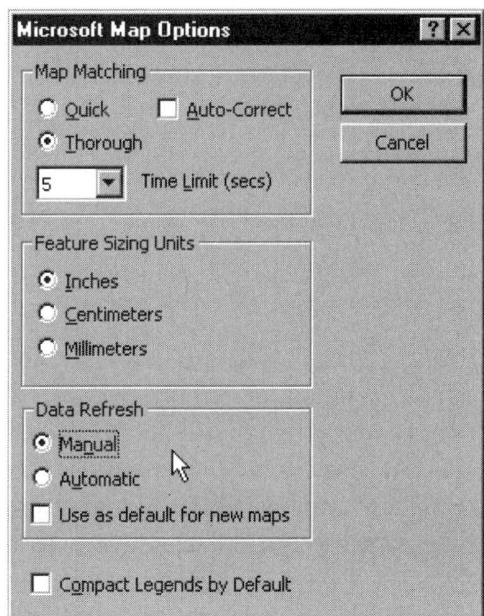

Figure 6-43: Microsoft Map options

Unlike charts, you don't have access to anything that resembles a data series formula, so adding data to a map is more involved. A new row of data can just be inserted, and the map refreshed. A new column is a bit more involved: you add the new column of data to your sheet, then activate the map. Select Data from the Insert menu. When prompted, select the geographic region column first, then the new numeric data (this might require you do a non-contiguous selection using the mouse and the `Ctrl` key). Click OK, and the Map applet does the rest. Use the Map Control to fine-tune the presentation.

Overall, maps are a bit of a niche feature but will be most welcome to those of you whose data lends itself to a geographical presentation.

Charts—Numbers as Pictures

Charts (or graphs, as we called them in grade school) are about taking boring numeric data and, by using some creative symbolic representations, presenting this data in a manner that shows some relationship between the numbers. The idea behind the concept of charts is that through the use of pictures you can make the relationship instantly recognizable (read: easier to figure out). A good chart should make the relationship clear without the reader having to analyze the underlying quantitative data.

This topic is a science unto itself, and entire books have been written on this subject—one of the definitive works being *The Visual Display of Quantitative Information* by Edward Tufte (Graphics Press). If you're really going to get into charting, you'll have to learn about data-ink ratios, non-redundant display of data-information, and other strange terms that are the meat and potatoes of charting.

New and Improved Chart Wizard

Charts in Excel all start with the Chart Wizard. Whether you kick off the process from the Chart Wizard button on the toolbar or by right-clicking on a sheet tab and choosing Insert ➤ Chart, the Wizard controls the process.

First thing to note in the Wizard's Step 1 (see Figure 6-44) is that there are several new chart types. The Bubble chart type we found interesting, and the new Cone and Pyramid types are pretty nifty. But the watch words in creating charts are clarity, precision, and efficiency, not wild, bizarre, and goofy-looking, so choose your chart type with care.

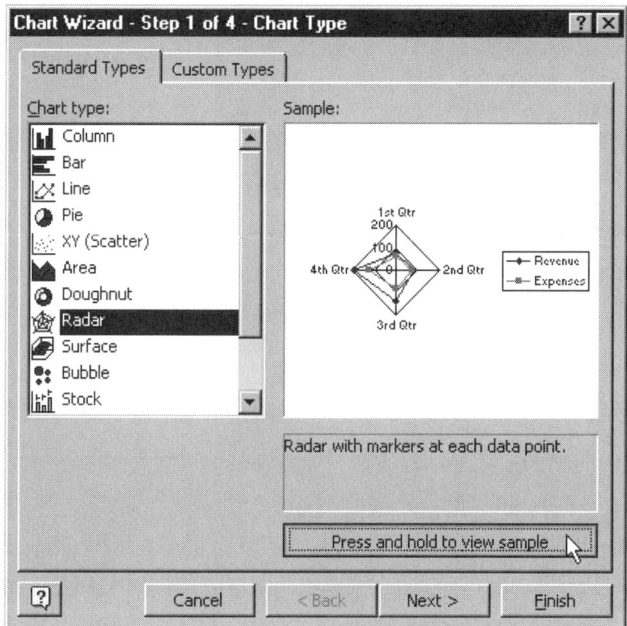

Figure 6-44: Improved Chart Wizard's Step 1

A very nice feature is the "Press and hold to view sample" button. This shows you, for example, just how really bad an idea it is to try to use the Radar chart type for data that does not lend itself to that type of charting. Always use this option to take a peek before deciding on the chart type you want.

WARNING There's a bug in Excel 97 that may not have a fix available by the time this book gets into print. When we created the ExcelAnnoy Formatting toolbar, we put the extremely useful Light Shading button on it. But there is a bug in Excel that caused the program to experience a General Protection Fault when you run the Chart Wizard with this button displayed. If you have either the Light Shading or Dark Shading buttons visible, you *must* turn off the toolbars on which they reside *before running the Chart Wizard.*

Step 2 of the Wizard (see Figure 6-45) lets you tweak the data range or the series information.

In the third panel of the new Chart Wizard, you can really exercise some control over the final look of the chart. You can tweak the titles (chart, X, Y, and Z axes), determine how to handle the displayed axes (including

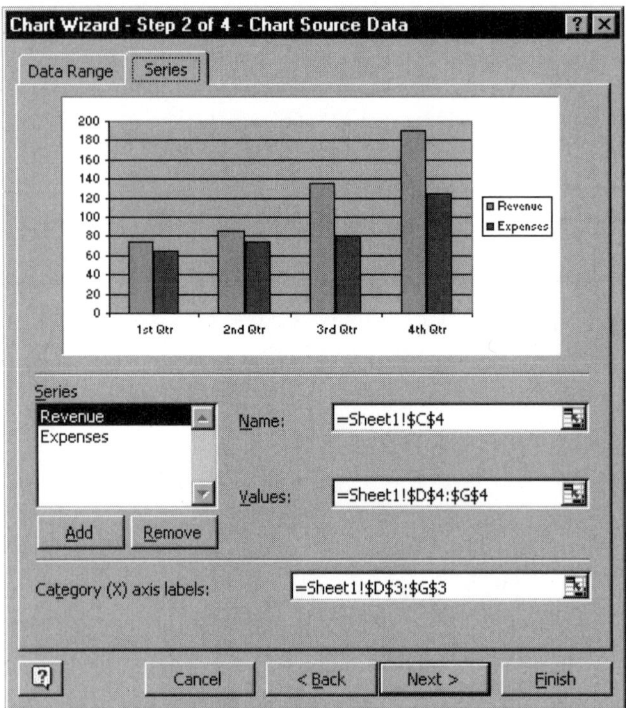

Figure 6-45: Step 2 of the Chart Wizard

the new Time Scale axis type), set gridlines, control legend display and placement, set data labels, and take advantage of a new feature—Data Table (shown in Figure 6-46)—that displays the underlying numeric data that the chart is based on, as part of the chart graphic.

The last step (see Figure 6-47) is to determine if the chart is to be embedded in the current sheet as an object or created on a separate chart sheet within the current workbook. Embedded charts are now activated with a single click instead of the double-click that was previously required.

Please keep in mind that the single most important step of charting takes place before you even start the Chart Wizard. You make or break it when you select the numbers to be charted. Select numbers that make sense and that create a visual display that gets your point across.

A Plethora of Points

For those of you who work with massive sets of scientific or financial data, you'll be pleased to know that Excel 97 ups the number of data

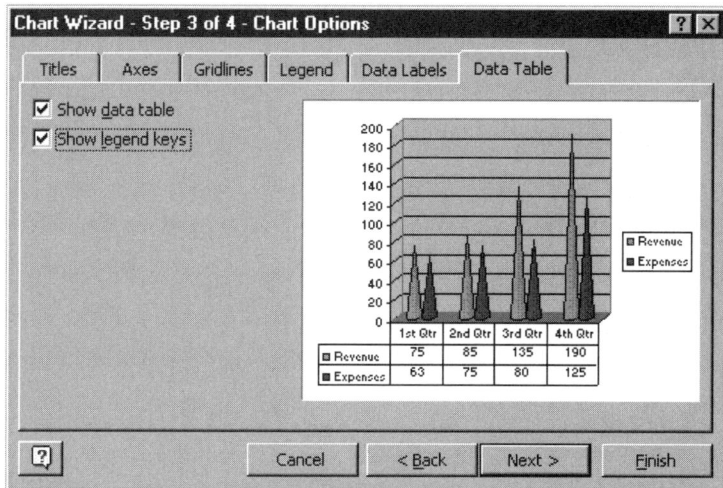

Figure 6-46: Step 3 of the Chart Wizard

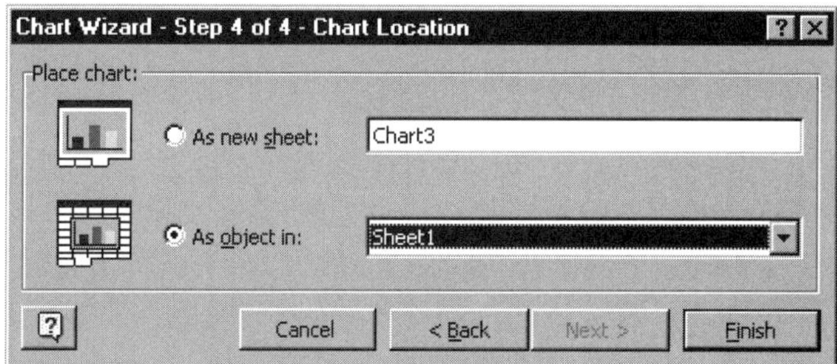

Figure 6-47: Step 4 of the Chart Wizard

points per series in 2-D charts from 4,000 points per series to 32,000 points per series.

Better Editing with Chart Tips/Chart Objects List

The various chart elements now display chart tips (like the ToolTips on the various toolbars), so you know exactly what you are about to click on when selecting objects in a chart for editing. (See Figure 6-48.) You can also select chart objects from the Chart Objects List, which is found on the Chart toolbar. (See Figure 6-49.)

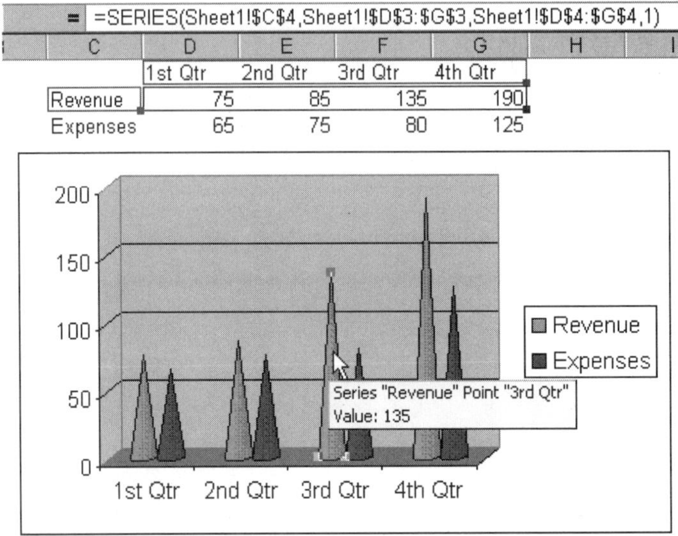

Figure 6-48: Range Finder at work

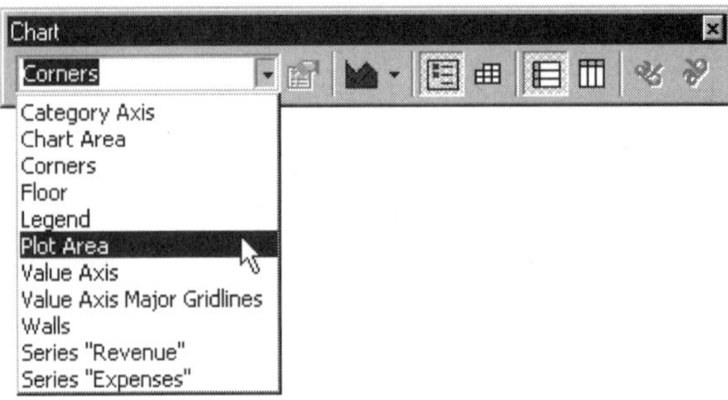

Figure 6-49: Chart Objects List on the Chart toolbar

Range Finder in Embedded Charts

Like the Range Finder feature we discussed in "Working with Names, Formulas, and Functions," in Chapter 4, when you activate an embedded chart, the data and labels in the sheet that are linked to the chart are outlined in color. You can actually change a data range by dragging the color border to include new data. This is a very slick feature, and you can watch the series range in the formula change dynamically as you drag the border.

Chart Printing Caveat

There's a bug that you need to be aware of in the Hewlett-Packard PCL printer language. If the chart you have embedded on a sheet should wind up over cells with content, those cells, while not visible on the sheet, print out *on top of your chart* when you print the sheet. This bug applies to Maps and other objects in the drawing layer and can be most annoying, so beware!

Hard Copy!

We'll assume that you're familiar with Excel's print functions and won't go into any detail on the basics. They've been around a long time and have not changed much over the versions.

Excel prints out the active sheet from row 1 column 1 to the end cell—and all cells in between—unless you define a specific print area via the Set Print Area command (File ➤ Print Area or via the Print menu pull-down on the ExcelAnnoy Standard toolbar). All Set Print Area does is define your current selection as a range name called `Print_Area`. You can do the same yourself. Just select your cells (even a non-continuous range) and define a name of `Print_Area`.

The same principle applies to rows and columns you want printed on each page; they are simply named `Print_Titles`.

Print Trick with Range Names

You can use Excel's affinity for range names to do the following trick, which prints several ranges from a single worksheet:

1. Give a unique range name to each range in the sheet to be printed. Assume the range names `Lobster`, `MainReport`, and `Godzilla` for this example.
2. Create a range with the name `Print_Area` (Insert ➤ Name ➤ Define).
3. In the "Refers to" edit box for `Print_Area` enter the following formula (assume Sheet2 is the sheet name):

```
=Sheet2!Lobster,Sheet2!MainReport,Sheet2!Godzilla
```

Your ranges will print out in one of two ways depending on how you define the range `Print_Area` in Step 3. We stumbled on this rather annoying inconsistency in our labs while testing this technique. If you define `Print_Area` by typing in the information in Step 3 and clicking the OK button in the Define Name dialog box, each range will start on a separate page. If instead you click the Add button then the Close button, the ranges do not start on separate pages.

For example if you have defined A1 as `Lobster`, B3 as `MainReport`, and C5 as `Godzilla`, clicking OK generates 3 separate pages (one range per page), but Add, Close prints all three ranges on a single page.

Report Manager

By far, the best way to handle complex printing is via the Report Manager. The Report Manager is an add-in, so if it does not appear on the View menu, you'll need to add it (see Tools ➤ Add-Ins, or search the help index for Report Manager).

You access Report Manager from the View menu. (See Figure 6-50.)

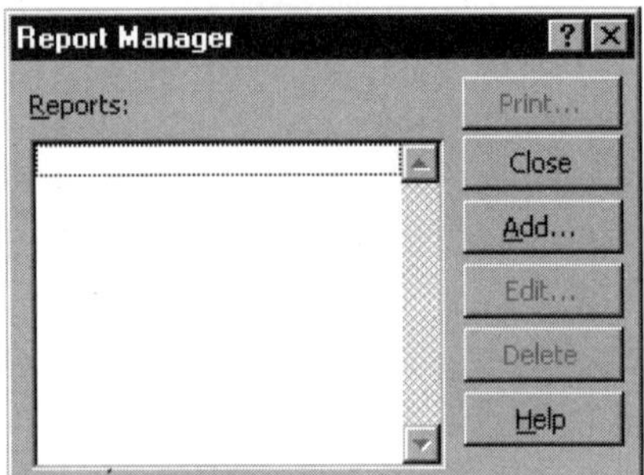

Figure 6-50: Report Manager—major timesaver!

The Report Manager is similar in function to the Custom View feature discussed earlier in this chapter. Like Custom View, it can save you huge amounts of time once you get everything set up.

Click on the Add button, and you can begin to create your report. You should have already created your various Custom Views, since these are used to great effect by the Report Manager.

In Figure 6-51, you see the various attributes you can set for a report. Keep the report name short (20-25 characters), since the display space in the Report Manager dialog is limited.

In a report, you specify various *sections*. A section consists of a given sheet in the current workbook. That sheet's `Print_Area` (if one is defined) is printed. If no `Print_Area` is defined, you get the default A1 to end cell. Each section is printed starting on a new page.

Where this really comes together is that you can specify a Custom View to be used for that sheet, and as discussed earlier, each Custom View can store a complete set of Page Setup settings. You can combine several views from a given sheet and have each printed out separately. If you

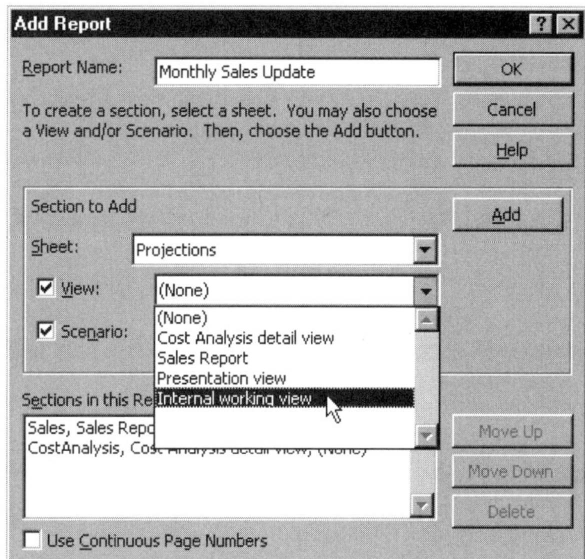

Figure 6-51: Details of an existing report

have set up any Scenarios, you can specify which one to use for each section as well.

Select each sheet scenario, view (in any combination), and click the Add button to create a new section to the Report. Note the check box in the lower left-hand corner, Use Continuous Page Numbers. Checking this box sequentially numbers each section so various pages from different sheets are all numbered as though from a single sheet. Now, this is the way to print complex reports!

NOTE Scenarios are created via Tools ➤ Scenarios. You define cells that have different values for each scenario. This lets you quickly switch between several "what-if" versions of your sheet.

On the annoying side, you can't edit an existing section's parameters. Your only recourse is to delete the section you want to change and add it back with the new settings. While the Use Continuous Page Numbers setting works (it will number each page of the report sequentially), it does not work properly with the "Page 1 of ?" built-in footer option. The page number itself increments properly, but the calculated total of all pages evaluates to the total number of pages *in each separate section of the report!* For example, take a three section report, section 1 consisting of two pages and sections 2 and 3 of one page each. The "Page 1 of ?" footer setting would print the following page numbers at the bottom of each page:

Section number	Physical page of section	Report page number
Section 1	Page 1	Page 1 of 2
Section 1	Page 2	Page 2 of 2
Section 2	Page 1	Page 3 of 1
Section 3	Page 1	Page 4 of 1

Pretty annoying, we'll grant you, but overall we find the Report Manager to be an excellent way to handle report printing.

In this chapter:

- *Launching Excel*
- *Excel Templates in the Office*
- *Protection in the Office*
- *Annotations, Comments, and Review*
- *Managing Lists*
- *Data Analysis with Pivot Tables*

7

Excel in the Office

In this chapter, we look at how you can use Excel down in the trenches—in the battles you fight every day in your office. We'll show you how to make Excel jump through some hoops every time you start it up and how to use the often overlooked power of templates to eliminate annoying repetitive busy-work and to manage styles effectively.

In day-to-day spreadsheet development, you want to be aware of the various means and methods by which you can protect your Excel files from unauthorized access or annoying accidents. Office life is fraught with perils of this sort just waiting to pounce on your unsuspecting spreadsheet. Protection is the watchword, and we show you precisely how to maximize your safety and minimize the annoyance of restricted access.

Finally, we touch on how to manage a review cycle of a spreadsheet model and then move on to two of the most powerful but underutilized Excel features available to the modern office: lists and pivot tables. Don't panic! We keep your annoyance level to a minimum as we examine these incredible tools that Excel provides, either of which alone is worth the price of Excel.

Launching Excel

Windows 95 introduced the shortcut file—sort of a Windows version of a short batch file. Shortcuts are a handy way to start your applications. When you start Excel via the Start menu, you're using a shortcut in the *C:\Windows\Start Menu\Programs* folder. If you start Excel from the standard Office Shortcut Bar, you're using a shortcut in the *C:\Program Files\Microsoft Office\Office\Shortcut Bar\Office* folder.

Shortcuts make it very easy to use the several startup switches to control what happens when Excel is first launched. Table 7-1 lists the switches you can use with Excel.

Table 7-1: Excel Startup Switches

Switch	Function
`/r` or `/R` *`c:\path\file-name.ext`*	This switch is used in conjunction with a fully qualified path and workbook name (enclose long filenames inside double quotation marks) to specify a particular workbook you want Excel to open upon loading. The switch causes the designated workbook to be opened as *read-only*.
`/p` or `/P` *`c:\path`*	This switch is used in conjunction with a fully qualified path to designate a particular folder to be used as the working folder for that session of Excel. This setting overrides the default file location set in the Tools ➤ Options ➤ General tab (if any).
`/e` or `/E`	This switch is used to prevent Excel from opening a default workbook when it loads.

You can create a number of shortcuts for starting Excel and have different switch settings for each one. In Figure 7-1 you can see that the `/e` switch has been used in conjunction with the `/p` switch to make *D:\Data* the working folder.

This shortcut starts Excel without a default workbook and using *D:\Data* as the working folder.

Excel Templates in the Office

Most of you who have used Microsoft Word are familiar with the concept of templates. A type of *master document* that contains all of the page setup settings, styles, boilerplate text, macros, and sundry stuff that you base new documents on.

A document based on a template inherits all the settings and attributes of the template. This is a major boon to word processing—letting all memos share a common look and feel, all letters be stylistically identical, and in general saving huge amounts of time by not having to reinvent the document wheel, as it were, every time a new document it created.

What most of you may not know, or have not considered, is that you can do the same thing in Excel. Instead of opening last month's expense

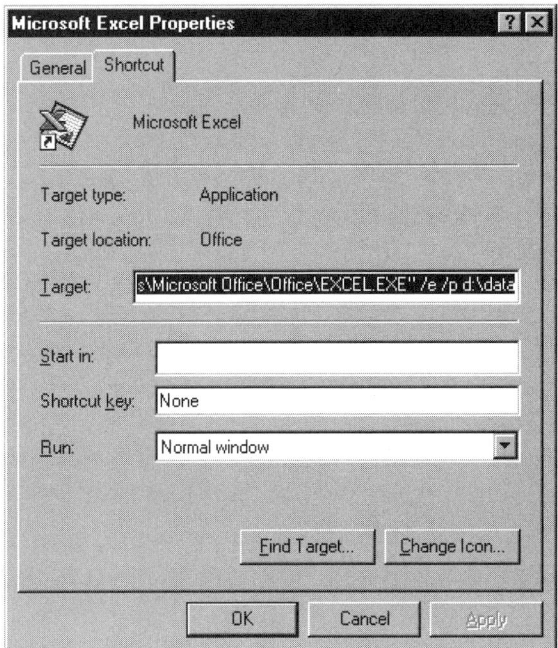

Figure 7-1: Setting the properties for a shortcut to Excel

worksheet, deleting the old data and the old formulas by accident (oops), and then remembering to save it under a new name so you don't wipe out last month's figures forever (oops again!), you can create an *Expense Report.xlt* template.

An Excel template can contain all the attributes of a spreadsheet—a given number of sheets, specific sheet names, text, numbers, formulas, formatting, styles, macros, the works! Unlike a Word template, once an Excel workbook has been created based on a template, that's the end of the relationship.

A Master Template

Templates, especially useful when combined with some of the other things discussed in this chapter like cell protection, can be created for any spreadsheet that you regularly have to create. Or you might consider templates for general development work where you standardize sheet names, or provide specific sheets/areas for recording the information that you should track on every spreadsheet (discussed in earlier chapters).

Let's work through an example. Say you want to create a generic template that all new workbooks will be based on:

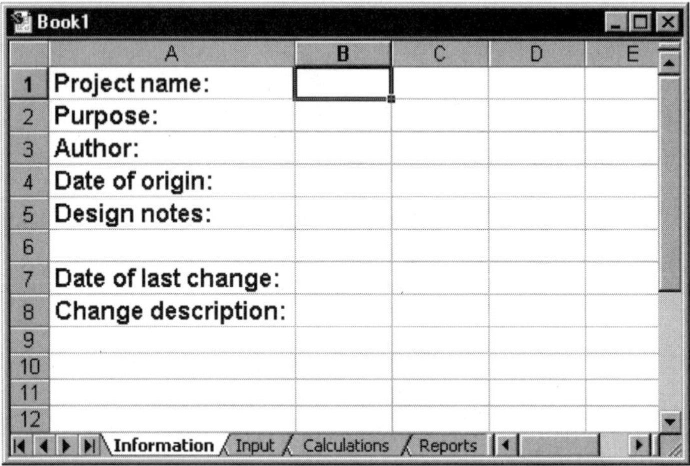

Figure 7-2: Creating an Excel template

1. Create a new book like the one shown in Figure 7-2.
2. Enter any boilerplate content that you want to appear in every new workbook. In this case we've opted for simplicity, but you could set specific headers/footers, print information, row and column widths and/or headings, cell protection, conditional formats, etc. Oh, and don't forget styles!
3. From the File menu click on Save As.
4. In the "Save as type" list, choose Template (**.xlt*). This will automatically give your filename the extension *.XLT*. You are also switched to the Template folder. Change folders to the Xlstart folder (usually *C:\Program Files\Microsoft Office\Office\Xlstart*).
5. Since this will be the default template (the template that will be used for a new workbook when you choose the New option from the ExcelAnnoy New menu), name it *Book.xlt*.
6. Close the *Book.xlt* workbook. Close and then restart Excel.

From here on out, when you create a new workbook, you'll get a workbook with the attributes of *Book.xlt*. To make this the default workbook, it has to be named "book" and it must be saved in the *Xlstart* folder. Actually, you could have saved it in the Alternate startup file location (ASFL) as defined in the Tools ➤ Options ➤ General tab and you'd get the same result. This is important if you are running Excel on a network and don't have access to the *Xlstart* folder on the server. Also, keep in mind that the ASFL takes precedence over the *Xlstart* folder. If you have different *Book.xlt*s in each folder, the one in the ASFL is what Excel actually uses, ignoring the one in *Xlstart.*

Multiple Templates

Create templates for each type of spreadsheet document that needs to be created. Other than the default workbook from the previous example, you can name your templates whatever you want. Just be sure to set the "Save as type" to template and save the file in the Template folder (this is the default folder when you set the "Save as type" to Template (*.xlt)).

Create a new workbook and type some text into it so you can differentiate it from the default *Book.xlt* you created in the last example. Name it *Lobster.xlt.*

When you choose New... from the New menu on the ExcelAnnoy Standard toolbar, you'll see something like the following (see Figure 7-3).

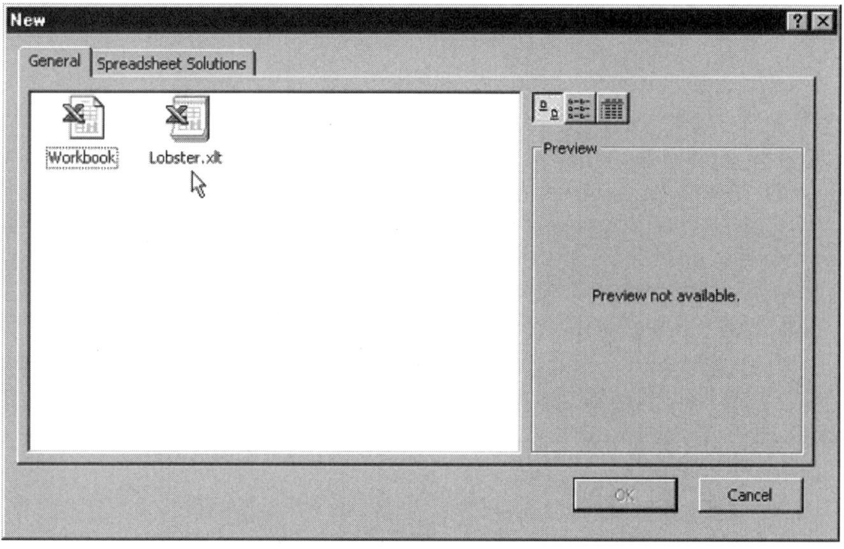

Figure 7-3: File ➤ New with custom templates

Because of the *book.xlt* you created earlier, if you click on Workbook, you get a new workbook based on your new custom default template. Use *Lobster.xlt*, and you get a new workbook with the default name of Lobster1 and based on the *Lobster.xlt* template.

Here is where things start to get annoying. If you're working in a workbook and you want to insert a new sheet by right-clicking on a sheet tab and selecting Insert..., you find your custom templates listed in the Insert dialog box. (See Figure 7-4.)

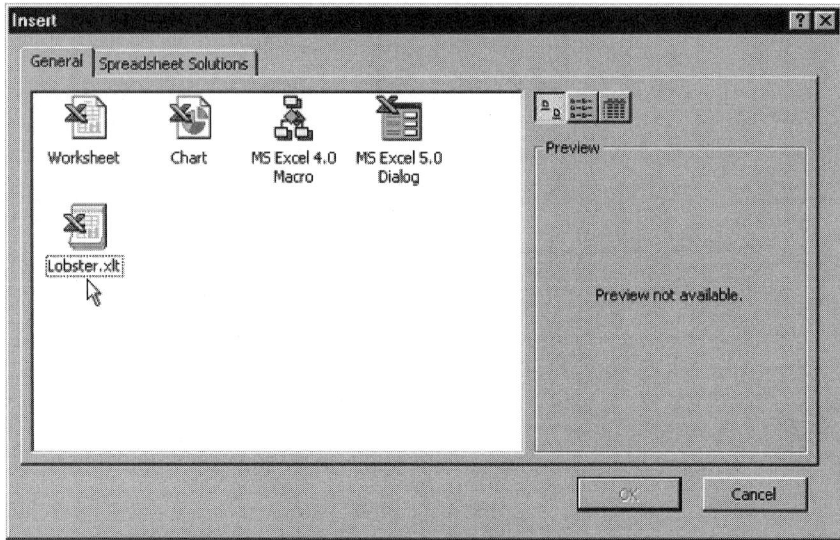

Figure 7-4: Inserting a new sheet

Where you'd expect to get only a single sheet inserted into the current workbook, you get a full-blown template. Choose *Lobster.xlt*, and you get all the sheets that are in the Lobster template dumped into the current workbook. Very annoying, but since it has worked this way since Excel 5, don't look for a fix anytime soon. Either be very careful when inserting sheets, or else create a new folder just below the Templates folder. Store all the custom templates you create in that folder, and they won't appear on the same panel as your standard Worksheet, Chart, MS Excel 4.0 Macro, and MS Excel 5.0 Dialog when you insert a sheet using the right-click on a sheet tab method.

On the other hand you can turn this quirk to your advantage. You can create templates that contain a single special-purpose sheet—one that may contain special tables of figures used in certain calculations, logos, prebuilt Autoshape diagrams, or whatever. Store these templates in the Templates folder so that when you insert a sheet into an extant workbook (using the right-click on a sheet tab method), you can have a choice of a plain vanilla sheet or one of your own custom sheets.

To create a new default sheet, just create a single sheet template named *Sheet.xlt*, and put it in the *Xlstart* folder.

Merging Styles Between Templates and Workbooks

When you start working with templates, you'll want to gather together the styles you've been using in your workbooks. A template is the perfect place to store your styles so that each new document you create starts off with the styles you use most often. It's actually pretty easy to manage and merge styles between workbooks and templates:

1. Open the workbook or template that contains the styles you want to merge. This would be the source file.
2. Create a new workbook or template (or open an extant file) that you want to copy the styles into.
3. Make the destination workbook or template the active file.
4. From the Format menu choose Styles.
5. In the Styles dialog box, click the Merge button. (See Figure 7-5.)
6. Choose the file from the list to use as the source for the merge.

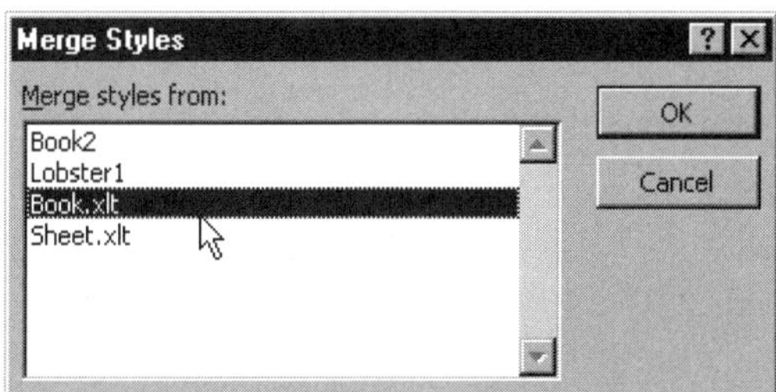

Figure 7-5: Choose the file to merge styles from

All the styles in the source file are copied to the destination file. If you have used the same style name in both the source and destination files, the destination style is overwritten.

Protection in the Office

Whether your spreadsheet is to be used only by yourself or by thousands of users throughout your division, you need to ensure that your model has integrity and is as easy to use as possible. We've covered many of the development practices you can utilize that let you maintain and modify a model long after the initial development work is done. But what about defensive measures to prevent someone from carelessly modifying the model and perhaps invalidating the spreadsheet altogether?

In this section we'll discuss the protective measures you can implement to keep your spreadsheets humming after they've left the safety of your hard disk.

File Protection Levels

The first protection method you can utilize is at the file level. When you save a workbook (either for the first time or from the Save As command), you can click on the Options button in the Save As dialog to set file-level protection passwords. (See Figure 7-6.)

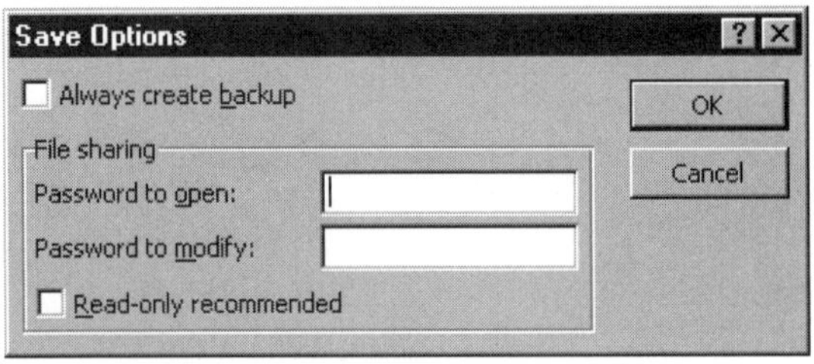

Figure 7-6: Setting file level protection options

Microsoft has gone a long way in eliminating some of the confusing terminology that plagued previous versions. Let's look at each of the options available under Save Options.

Always create backup

The "Always create backup" check box does not really have anything to do with passwords but is worthy of consideration—especially when developing a model. Check this box and then save your workbook as usual (for discussion purposes we'll assume you have saved the workbook as *Protection1.xls*). You make additional changes and save the workbook again. Here's what happens:

1. The file on disk (as was originally saved, not containing the subsequent changes you've made) is renamed as *Backup of Protection1.xlk* and stored in the same directory as the original version of *Protection1.xls.*
2. The current file in memory is written to disk as *Protection1.xls.*

You now have your workbook, *Protection1.xls,* and a one-generation-old backup copy, *Backup of Protection1.xlk.* The *.xlk* extension identifies this file as a backup file. This backup option can be used alone or in conjunction with the other Save Option settings.

Password to open

You can enter a "Password to open," which essentially locks the file, making it inaccessible to anyone who does not have the password. Passwords can be up to 15 characters long and are case sensitive. You must be very careful when you use passwords, as Excel provides no mechanism to regain access to the file if you forget the password or if you enter the password incorrectly. The case sensitivity is what causes users the most problems.

You type in your password (which appears as a series of asterisks in the edit box control so no one can read it over your shoulder as you type it) and you are then asked to confirm that password by typing it in a second time. (See Figure 7-7.)

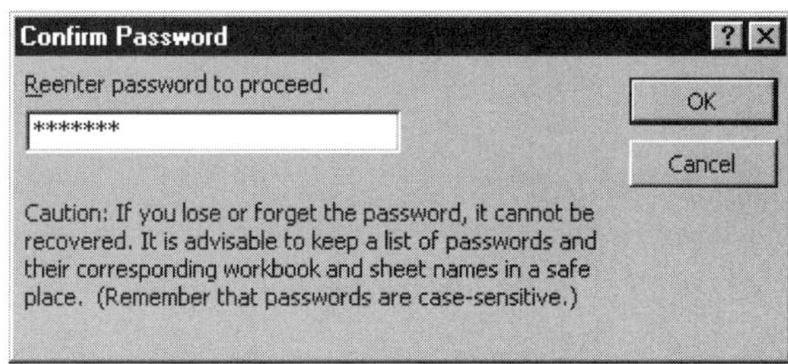

Figure 7-7: Confirming an entered password

If you protect a file in this manner, anyone opening the file is presented with this dialog box that requests him or her to enter the password. (See Figure 7-8.)

Figure 7-8: Opening a password-protected file

All you see are asterisks when you type in this control as well, so you must type carefully.

Password to modify

You also have the option of using a password to modify the file you are protecting. Again, you can use a case-sensitive password of up to 15-characters, and you'll be asked to confirm it.

For "modify" think *read-only.* This level of security requires a user to enter the modify password if they want to be able to modify the file (more on this term in a moment). Failure to enter the modify password *does not prevent the user from opening the file!* It just prevents them from saving any changes to the file under the same file name.

Users see the dealog box in Figure 7-9 when a file has a modify password. If they don't have the modify password, they can click on the Read Only button and open the file.

Figure 7-9: Excel prompts for the Password to modify

They can then change, modify, fold, spindle, and mutilate to their heart's content; they just can't overwrite the original file. They can, however, save the file under a new name.

Last but not least, you can have both a password to open *and* a password to modify. When opening the file, you must have the open password. Once you supply that, you are prompted for the modify password. The only annoying thing about setting up a file with both types of passwords is that when you are prompted to confirm the passwords, the confirmation dialog does not let you know which password you are confirming. Just remember, the first confirmation box is for the open password, the second for the modify password.

Read-only recommended

The last check box in the Save Options dialog is labeled "Read-only recommended." This is the gentlest level of protection imaginable. Check this box, and when a user tries to open the file, they are greeted with the message shown in Figure 7-10.

Figure 7-10: Read-only recommended

The user is admonished that she should opt for a read-only copy of the file unless she really, really needs to change it. This is perhaps a better option to use when you just want to remind yourself that a file should not be messed with. It will probably just confuse most users who encounter it out in the field.

Workbook, Sheet, and Cell Protection Levels

In addition to the protection available at the file level, you have additional protection at workbook, sheet, and cell levels. Using these settings, you can prevent sheets from being added to a workbook or renamed, and you can protect the contents of selected cells or entire sheets.

This gives you complete control over your models. Formulas can be protected against getting overwritten or changed, and sheet names can be counted upon not to change, all very important to the model builder.

Workbook-level protection

When you protect a workbook, you are locking up either the *structure* of the workbook, the *windows* within it, or both. This workbook protection is independent of file protection—you don't need to protect the file to protect the workbook. The structure protects the integrity of the physical structure of the sheets. Sheets cannot be renamed or moved to different positions in the book, nor can you copy or move entire sheets between workbooks.

To illustrate, first protect a workbook. From the Tools menu select Protection. From the cascading menu, click on Protect Workbook. You'll see the dialog box shown in Figure 7-11.

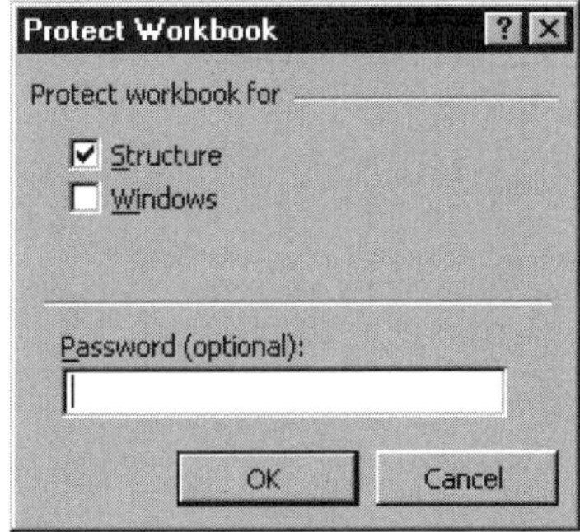

Figure 7-11: Protecting a workbook

The password is optional. You can omit the password and protect the workbook to prevent careless mistakes in the development cycle. If you protect without a password, you are not prompted to enter one when you unprotect the workbook. Providing a password works the same way as we discussed when protecting the overall file.

After protecting the workbook structure, if you right-click on a sheet tab, you'll notice that most of the options are no longer available. (See Figure 7-12.) As you can see, Insert, Delete, Rename, and Move or Copy are grayed out.

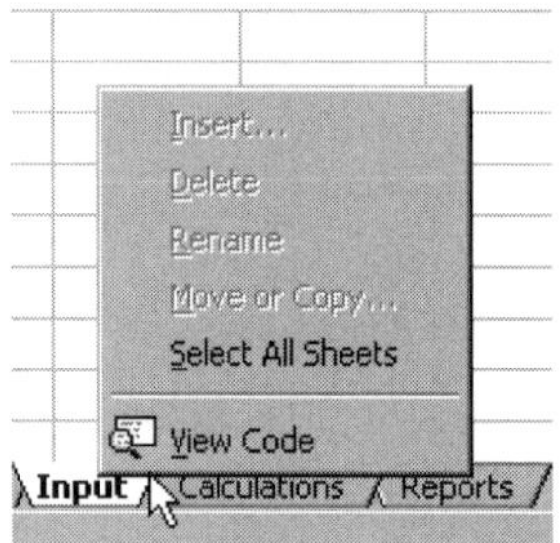

Figure 7-12: Workbook protection in action

The Windows check box protects the windows of the workbook from being resized, having the screen split, maximized, minimized, moved—the works. The control buttons on child windows disappear when this option is used.

Sheet-level protection

Protection at the sheet level is completely independent of workbook or file-level protection. Sheet protection deals with the contents of cells (preventing changes to certain cells), the objects embedded in the sheet's drawing layer, and different scenarios that you may have set up for that sheet. (See Figure 7-13.) Table 7-2 indicates what's protected by each of the three sheet protection options.

Figure 7-13: Setting the Protect Sheet options

As with workbook protection, a password is optional. You can protect a sheet just to prevent accidental changes, forcing you to explicitly unprotect a sheet to make changes. As in the workbook level examples, if you type in a password, you'll be prompted to confirm the password by keying it in again.

Table 7-2: Worksheet Protection Options

Protection Option	Protects the following
Contents	Protects individual cells in the worksheet from being changed (you cannot enter anything into a protected cell or modify extant contents); also protects items in charts from being changed or modified.
Objects	Prevents any graphic object in the drawing layer from being deleted, moved, edited, or resized, whether on a worksheet or a chart.
Scenarios	Protects all scenario definitions from being changed or modified.

Often, we'll leave a sheet protected for Contents and Scenarios, but not for Objects. This way, someone can review and test models while making comments right on the sheet, using text box objects or Excel's Comment feature. With a sheet protected for Objects, you cannot enter a Comment in a cell or create a drawing object like a text box.

The primary reason to protect a sheet is to protect the content of specific cells from being changed. But protecting the sheet only *activates* cell protection. An attribute of each cell in the spreadsheet controls whether that cell is protected or not.

Cell-level protection

Protection at the cellular level is controlled via a formatting attribute. Pull down the Format menu and click Cells. The last tab on the right of the Format Cells dialog is Protection. (See Figure 7-14.)

By default, the cell protection attribute is set to Locked. If you switch on sheet level protection, every cell in the sheet is then protected and you can't enter anything. The Hidden attribute does just what you'd think—it hides the contents of a cell, providing sheet level protection is turned on.

The way to implement cell level protection is to turn off the locked attribute on every cell that you want a user to be able to enter data into. Leave everything else set to the default of Locked, then protect the sheet. Only unlocked cells will accept entries. If someone tries to edit a locked cell or enter a number into one, he gets a message telling him he cannot. (See Figure 7-15.)

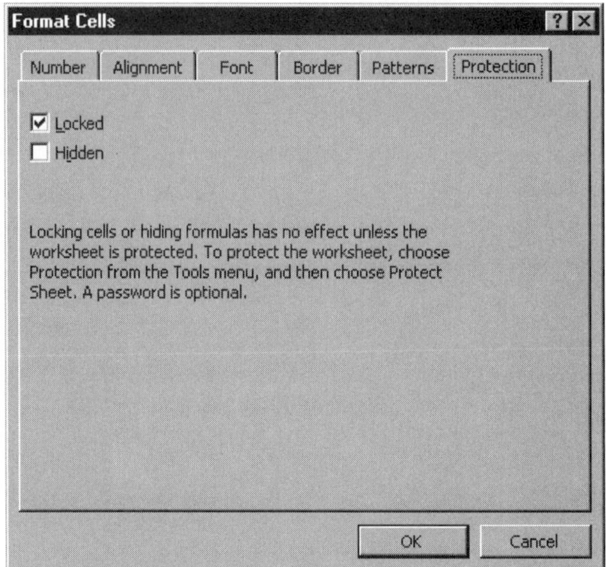

Figure 7-14: Setting the cell protection attribute

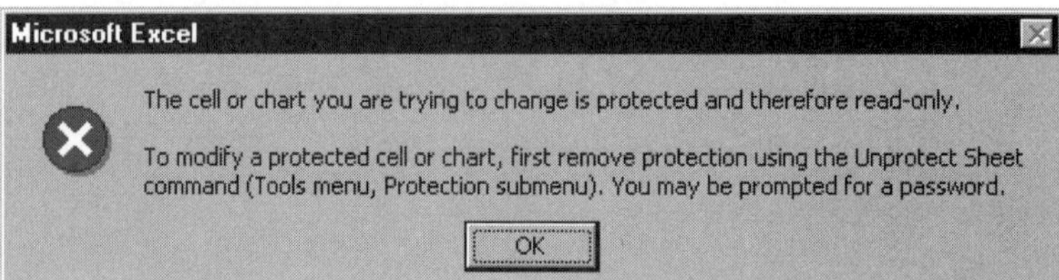

Figure 7-15: Try to edit a locked cell in a protected sheet, and this is what you get

A bonus of this technique is that you can easily move from unlocked cell to unlocked cell by just pressing the `Tab` key. This makes data entry a snap and prevents any accidents with formulas getting overwritten.

Circumventing Passwords

Passwords can be broken. Not just by clever cryptographers who can guess what you most probably used for a password, but by anyone with a utility designed specifically for breaking passwords in Microsoft Excel. There are reputable companies that sell password crackers for Word, Excel, and most of the major software products around today for just a couple of hundred bucks. The Internet can no doubt supply free utilities of varying effectiveness as well.

But the very fact that passwords are breakable should give you more confidence to use them, not less. Most business applications that you'll be developing are more in danger from an accidental mishap on the keyboard than from someone with the knowledge, ability, and motivation to break through your passwords. Password protection is just the ticket to prevent accidents from happening.

The decrypting technology just ensures that if you accidentally lock yourself out of your own model, you can find a skeleton key and get back inside. Should someone in your group be a bit unhappy that they were just tagged in the latest round of downsizing cuts, and assign random passwords to every model in the department, you can undo the damaging deed.

We've used the tools provided by AccessData (*http://www.accessdata.com*) on a number of occasions and find their tools to be first rate and the company to be very willing to work with developers who need to make their spreadsheets secure even against utilities like the ones that AccessData sells.

Annotations, Comments, and Review

In our shop, most models go through at least one review cycle. The user interface is critiqued, custom views reviewed, and changes are recommended, implemented, and tested. To this end, Microsoft has implemented a feature called Shared Workbooks.

Shared Workbooks lets multiple users on a network change, annotate, and update spreadsheets simultaneously. Each set of changes is recorded for review later. While we laud Microsoft on the concept, we find the 1.0 release of this feature to be wanting (although the way it handles multiple comments is pretty nice), at least as far as our own work style goes. Your mileage may vary. Check out this interesting feature in the Help file and see if it's a good fit for you. Ask the Office Assistant in Excel about "shared workbooks."

For quality reasons, we like to have only one person be responsible for changes in a given model at any one time. Workbooks are usually protected, so no one but the responsible author can make changes at the sheet level to cell content and at the workbook level to the structure of the workbook.

But we don't protect the workbook for objects. This lets a reviewer add Comments, add text boxes and make notes, and use AutoShapes to add circles, arrows, callouts, and related drawing objects. The reviewer can thus annotate, make suggestions, ask questions, and mark up a spreadsheet until the cows come home without actually changing anything in the various sheets themselves.

One annoying aspect is that the auditing utilities don't work on a protected sheet, and all your graphical objects are subject to the PCL printer bug discussed in "Chart Printing Caveat" in Chapter 6, *Excel Strategies*. If your annotation object is placed over cells with content, that content is printed *on top* of the graphic object.

Managing Lists

It's surprising how many things in an office are basically lists. Items needed for a project. Customer mailing lists. Sales records. A lot of time is spent futzing around with lists, from tracking things via the yellow sticky around the edge of the monitor method, to building complex Access applications. But it's often overlooked how Excel, well, excels at managing lists of information. A list, you see, is just a database waiting to happen.

Excel has long enjoyed an intriguing database feature, one that has been given a surprisingly soft peddle from the Redmond marketeers. Even its name is unassuming—lists. Not AutoList, AutoDatabase, or Auto anything. Just lists. But don't let that fool you. Lists—and a wide array of list-related features—are very powerful indeed.

Ask the Office Assistant "list," then choose the "About using a list as a database" topic. This Help topic defines a list as "a series of worksheet rows that contain related data, such as an invoice database or a set of client names and phone numbers. A list can be used as a database, in which rows are records and columns are fields." You could spend an inordinate amount of time in search of a more refined definition, but this one really does say it all.

Academically speaking, databases come in two flavors: flat file and relational. In a flat file database there's no relationship between individual records—simply rows and columns of information lumped together in one table. The *Microsoft Press Computer Dictionary* formally defines a relational database as a "type of database . . . that stores information in tables—rows and columns of data—and conducts searches by using data in specified columns of one table to find additional data in another table." If you need a relational database application, check out Microsoft Access.

A list in Excel is a flat file database. It's that simple.

How do you tell Excel what clump of cells you want to act as a list? Read on.

Excel Already Knows Your List Is a List

Intriguingly, the answer is that Excel already knows it's a list! Any contiguous range of rows and columns is a list. You can save yourself lots of time and trouble by adhering to a few simple rules governing lists:

- *The first row of a list should always contain column labels.* A column label is simply a field name, for example, "Company Name" or "Street Address." Excel looks at the first physical row in a list and figures out if that first row contains column labels or data and reacts accordingly. If it thinks the first row is data, not labels, it then proposes generic column labels like "Column A" and so on. It's best to apply a format to column labels that's different from the raw data. Use common sense when assigning field names. Use normal capitalization, for example, "Ship Region" instead of "ship region." There's no need to avoid spaces because Excel doesn't object to them. To improve readability, consider restricting a field name's length to 30 characters or less.
- *A list should never contain blank rows or columns.* Although in some cases Excel's list management features may be able to properly handle blank rows or columns inside a list, it's simply a bad idea and you're just tempting fate. Don't do it.
- *Use only one list per worksheet.* It is physically possible to have more than one list on a worksheet, but since AutoFilter can only be active for one list at a time, and to avoid confusion, it's best to limit yourself to one list per worksheet. If for some reason you must have multiple lists on a single worksheet, separate each list from the others with at least one blank column and row. This produces lists that are offset from each other in a down-and-to-the-right diagonal arrangement.
- *Give your list a name.* As with any range of cells, applying a name to the range makes it easier to refer to.
- *Understand how field content affects sorting and searching.* Field content has a direct impact on sorting and searching. There are three issues: capitalization, formulas, and leading spaces. Capitalization only affects sorting if you explicitly tell the sort to be case sensitive (Data ➤ Sort, click the Options button, select the Case Sensitive check box, click OK, then continue specifying your sort parameters).

Formulas in a list are sorted based on their return values. Leading spaces at the beginning of text in a cell are legitimate characters and affect sorting. If you need an indented appearance, use Format ➤ Cells ➤ Alignment ➤ Indent.

NOTE If you do select Case Sensitive for a sort, Excel retains this setting for the current worksheet only. When you switch to a different worksheet in the current workbook or a different workbook, be sure to respecify this setting if you need case sensitivity.

Using Forms to Enter Data in Lists

Excel supports four different types of form-based data entry. We list them here in order of increasing complexity and difficulty. Keep in mind that with increased complexity among these different types of forms you get the benefit of increased flexibility and customization:

- Excel's built-in data form feature (we'll call this feature *data form*)
- The Template Wizard with Data Tracking add-in
- An Access form that works with an Excel list (first you have to build the Access form)
- A form built on an Excel worksheet (we'll call this feature *workbook form*)

Before we can explore Excel's list features any further, we need a robust list to work with. Throughout this chapter, we use an Excel list based on the Northwind Orders table that ships with Access. Here are the steps to get this data from the Access table into an Excel list using Microsoft Query.

1. Create a new workbook, save it as *Lists.xls*, and select cell A1 in Sheet1.
2. Select Data, choose Get External Data, choose Create New Query, make sure the "Use the Query Wizard to create/edit queries" check box is selected, in the Databases file card select "<New Data Source> " then click OK.
3. In the Create New Data Source dialog box, type **`Northwind Orders Table`** in field 1 (the "What name do you want to give your data source?" field). Tab down to field 2, choose the Microsoft Access Driver (*.mdb), then click Connect.

4. In the ODBC Microsoft Access 97 Setup dialog box, click the Select button and browse until you locate *Northwind.mdb* (typically in the *C:\Program Files\Microsoft Office\Office\Samples* folder), select it, and click OK to dismiss the Select Database dialog. Click OK again to dismiss the ODBC Microsoft Access 97 Setup dialog.

NOTE These steps assume you have Microsoft Query installed. If you did a Typical setup of Office, Microsoft Query was *not* installed. For information on how to install Microsoft Query, ask Office Assistant, "install Microsoft Query."

Microsoft Query may be installed on your PC but not necessarily active as an add-in. To activate it, select Tools, Add-Ins, locate "MS Query Add-in for Excel 5 Compatibility" in the list, check it, then click OK.

---

5. In field 4 of the Create New Data source dialog, choose the Orders table, then click OK.
6. In the Choose Data Source dialog (Northwind Orders Table should be selected in the list now), click OK.
7. The Query Wizard—Choose Columns dialog box appears now, and Orders should be selected in the tree listing on the left (Available tables and columns), so click the > button to put all the Orders table's columns (read: fields) in your query. Click the Next> button.
8. In the Query Wizard—Filter Data dialog box, click Next>.
9. In the Query Wizard—Sort Order dialog box, click Next>.
10. In the Query Wizard—Finish dialog box the Return Data to Microsoft Excel radio button should already be selected, so click Finish.
11. Back in Excel, a few seconds later you'll see the Returning External Data to Microsoft Excel dialog box, indicating the data should pour in to the current sheet starting in cell $A$1. Perfect. Click OK.
12. Once the data has arrived, change Sheet1's name to Northwind Orders, save *Lists.xls*, and you're done.

Excel's built-in data forms

Data forms are by far the simplest way to work with Excel lists. A data form is a dialog box produced automatically by Excel that contains your list's column labels (fields), a text box for each field, and a complete set of controls for viewing, adding, changing, deleting, and searching for records. In *Lists.xls*, select Data, then choose Form. That's all it takes to produce a data form for the Orders list. (See Figure 7-16.)

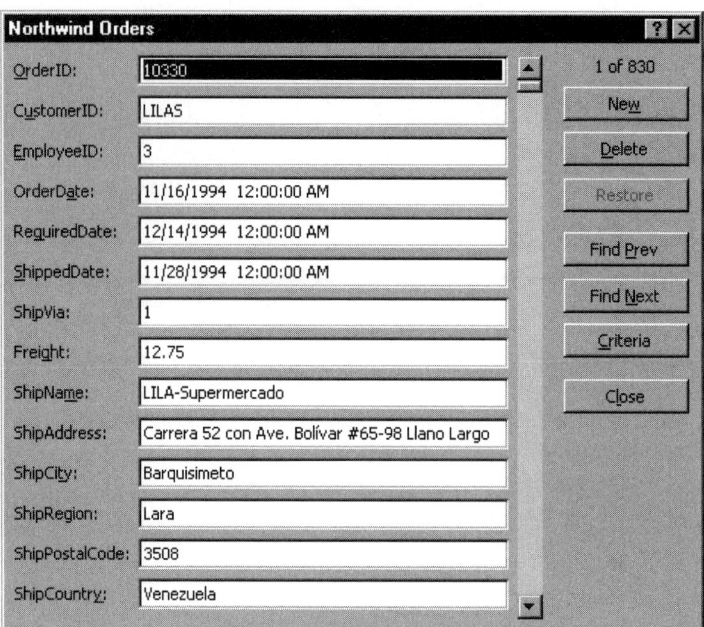

Figure 7-16: Instant data form for the Orders list

A data form can display a maximum of 32 fields. The content of editable fields appears in text boxes. Calculated values and protected fields also appear on the data form, but they aren't editable.

To view records, click Find Next or Find Prev, or use the form's scroll bar. To add a record, just click New (alternately, drag the scroll box to the bottom of the scroll bar; this clears all fields and sets the record counter to "New Record"). To delete a record once selected, click Delete.

To search for records that match some search criteria: click Criteria, enter the desired search criteria, then click Find Next or Find Prev to locate the next matching record. To clear all criteria and return to the last record displayed, click Criteria, click Clear, then click Form. When using search criteria in a data form, Excel will accept an exact search value for a numeric field, and you can enter simple comparison expressions (like > 0). If you want an exact match on a text field, enter the exact text (unquoted); wildcards also work with text searches. (Excel does not distinguish between lowercase and uppercase when doing these searches.)

NOTE Data forms behave annoyingly when you find the last match in a list but don't know it. Try it. Perform a search that returns at least one record. Now specify new criteria guaranteed to return *no* matching records and click Find Next. The data form beeps and displays the very last record you looked at in your previous search, implying that this record matches your current criteria, which it decidedly does not. A message box should appear indicating that no matching records could be found.

Changes are permanently saved when you press Enter, click New, click Close, or move to another record via the scroll box. *Before* you take any of these actions, if you want to restore the record to the way it was originally, click Restore.

Template Wizard with data tracking add-in

To demonstrate the Template Wizard, let's create a very small list in a workbook named *Subscription list.xls*, as shown in Figure 7-17.

	A	B	C	D
1	Journal	Subscriber Info	Type	URL
2	PC Computing	http://subscribe.p	PC General	http://www.pccomputing.com
3	PC Magazine	303-665-8930	PC General	http://www.pcmag.com
4	PC Week	609-786-8230	PC General	http://www.pcweek.com
5	The Surfer's Journal	714-361-0331	Fun	None
6	Visual Basic Programmer's Journal	303-684-0365	Programming	http://www.windx.com
7	Wired	415-276-5200	Digital General	http://www.wired.com
8				

Figure 7-17: A simple subscription list database

The logic behind using the Template Wizard to work with a list is as follows:

- You've already got a list in an Excel workbook somewhere. If you haven't already created *Subscription list.xls* as shown in Figure 7-17, do so now. (You can work with a wide variety of other databases, but let's concentrate on Excel list databases for now.)
- You need a form to input your data, and a plain vanilla data form won't cut the mustard for whatever reason. The Template Wizard

helps you create a template (think of it as the "parent form") from which you can quickly spawn new workbook forms, *each one of which contains an individual record destined for the list database.* Yes, this approach amounts to lots of disk space overhead and file clutter—one workbook form for each new record entered this way. But this approach offers a customizable interface (remember, a data form can't be customized, but a form template can) and—this is important—allows you to use the wizard to edit a record later by opening the record's associated workbook form instead of the list itself.

- It's easier to work with the Template Wizard if you let it take control from the beginning of this process. Although it can deal with a case where you created a template before invoking it, save yourself some heartache and start with a fresh unsaved workbook rather than an extant template.

NOTE Excel Help confusingly uses the term *worksheet form* when describing what we think is best called a *workbook form.* Although it is certainly possible to have more than one form in a single workbook (since obviously you can have multiple worksheets in a workbook), it's difficult to imagine a rationale for such an awkward approach.

The general process of creating a form template is as follows (we provide detailed, step-by-step instructions shortly): Starting with a fresh unsaved workbook, add some data entry labels and provide any formatting for specific fields if you want (the Template Wizard won't do any of this for you). Then save the workbook, run the Template Wizard, link the input cells to the list field names, and the Template Wizard will save the current workbook as a data tracking form template (read: the *.xls* will be saved as an *.xlt*). The next time you create a new workbook form based on the form template and then save the workbook form, the new data will be automatically added to your list.

Follow these steps to have the Template Wizard create a form template you can then use to work with your subscription list.

1. Close *Subscription list.xls* if it's currently open.
2. Create a new empty workbook.
3. In Sheet1, enter the labels **`Journal`**, **`Subscriber Info`**, **`Type`**, and **`URL`** in cells A1 through A4 respectively (no special formatting is required, but you can embellish them if you wish), select column A,

and click Format ➤ Column ➤ AutoFit Selection. (Note: it's important that you use cells A1 through A4 specifically in order to follow along with subsequent steps.)

NOTE These steps assume you have the Template Wizard with Data Tracking add-in installed. If you don't see the menu item Template Wizard on the Data menu, then you need to install it (see the Help topic "Use add-in programs of Microsoft Excel").

---

4. Save this workbook as *Subscription list (form template).xls*. (Note: this is still a workbook, not a template.)
5. Select Data, then choose Template Wizard. By giving this workbook the same root name you want for the form template, you're expediting the wizard, so just click Next> in the Step 1 of 5 dialog. Note that by default the wizard saves the form template to your main Office templates folder (typically *C:\Program Files\Microsoft Office\Templates*). (See Figure 7-18.)

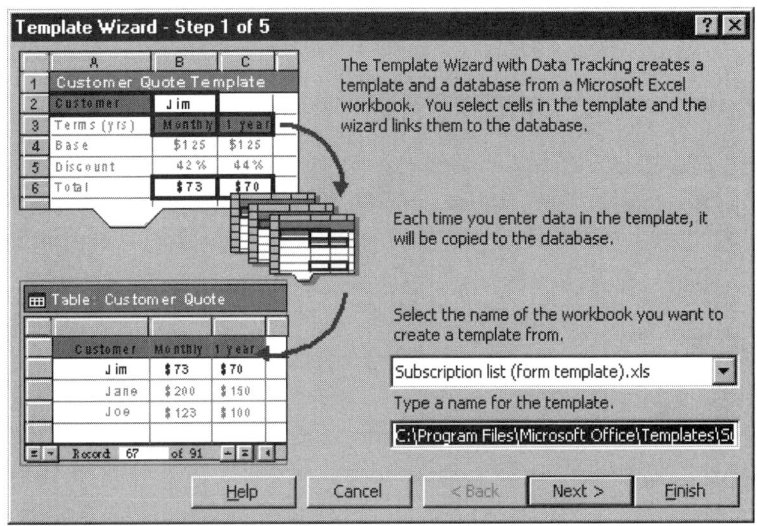

Figure 7-18: Template Wizard's Step 1 of 5 dialog box

6. In the Step 2 of 5 dialog, choose Microsoft Excel Workbook as the type of database you want the wizard to create, and ignore its misleading use of language implying you're about to create a database even though you have already created it. Then—if it's not already displayed in the text box—browse for the location of the *Subscription list.xls* workbook and click Next>. (See Figure 7-19.)

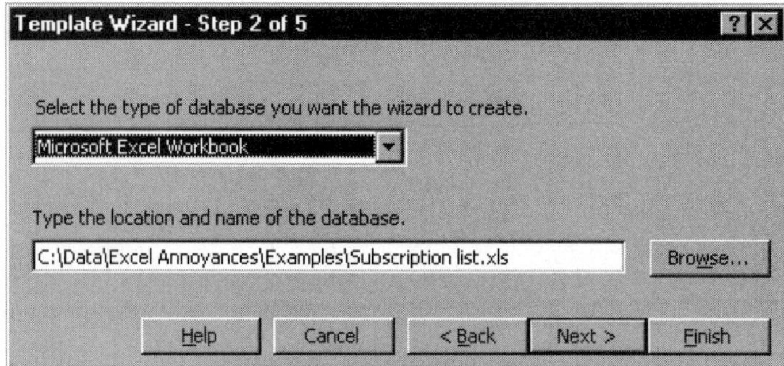

Figure 7-19: Template Wizard's Step 2 of 5 dialog box

WARNING If you don't manually browse for the extant database workbook (*Subscription list.xls*), then the wizard creates a new empty database with a filename comprised of your database workbook's root filename plus the word Database.

---

7. In the Step 3 of 5 dialog, select cells $B$1, $B$2, $B$3, and $B$4 on Sheet1 for the four matching fields then click Next>, as shown in Figure 7-20.

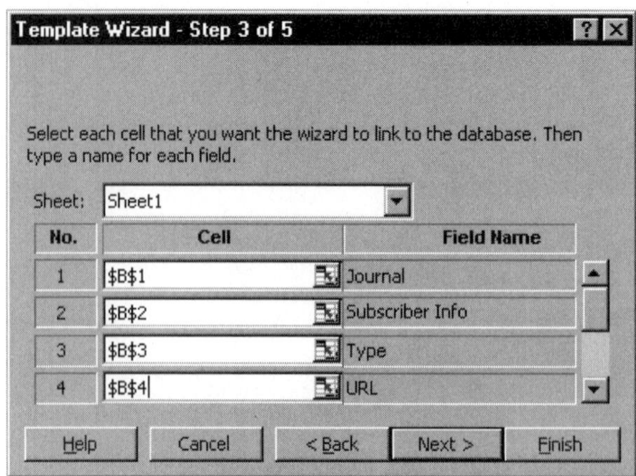

Figure 7-20: Template Wizard's Step 3 of 5 dialog box

8. The Step 4 of 5 dialog helps in the case where you want to add existing data to the database, a cool feature but one that we'll skip in this demonstration, so click Next>. (See Figure 7-21.)
9. The Step 5 of 5 dialog reports the template and database filenames (annoyingly, the designers neglected to account for the common case of lengthy folder structure, so the fully qualified filenames will likely

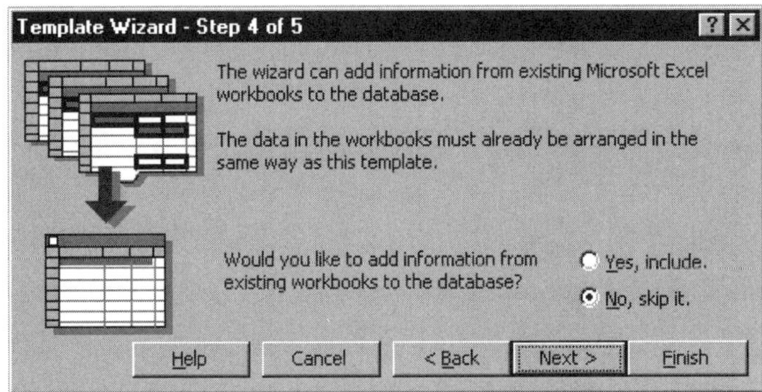

Figure 7-21: Template Wizard's Step 4 of 5 dialog box

be truncated) and allows you to specify a routing slip. Let's keep it simple for now and click Finish. (See Figure 7-22.)

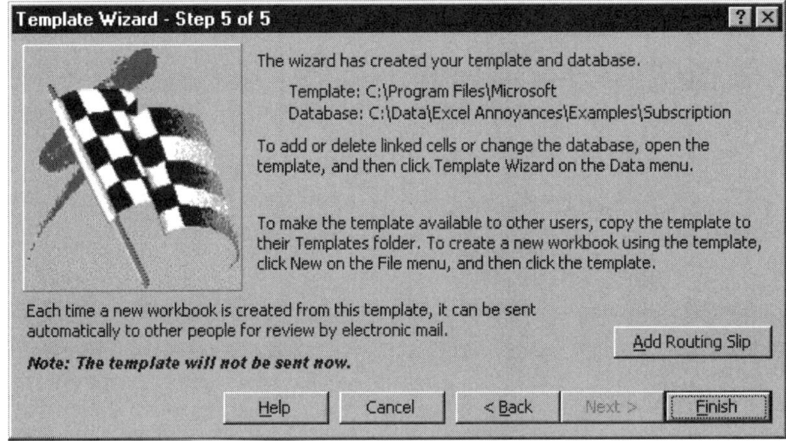

Figure 7-22: Template Wizard's Step 5 of 5 dialog box

10. After clicking Finish, the template is automatically saved and closed, and you're back in *Subscription list (form template).xls.*

Follow these steps to add a record to your subscription list using the form template you just created:

1. Create a new workbook based on *Subscription list (form template).xlt*, which should appear in the General tab of the New dialog box, and click Enable Macros when prompted. The new workbook will be captioned *Subscription list (form template)1.*
2. Fill in the field values, then save the workbook. After a few seconds you'll see the Template File—Save to Database dialog box as shown in Figure 7-23.

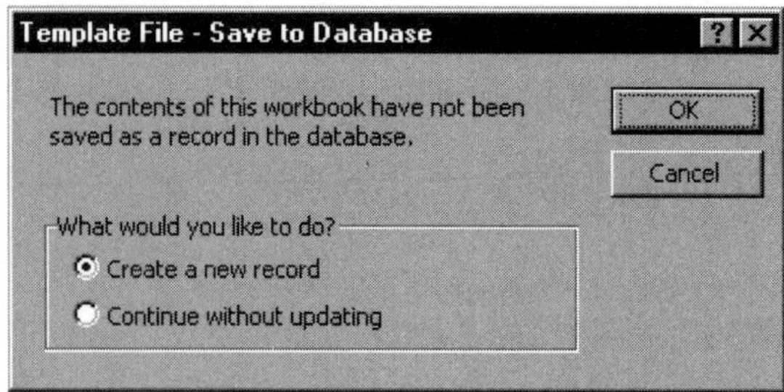

Figure 7-23: Template File—Save to Database dialog box

3. The default is to create a new record, so click OK. After a few seconds you'll be prompted to save the workbook form as *Subscription list (form template)1.xls*. Do so.

WARNING The form template will suggest this same filename for subsequent workbook forms, so you must choose to overwrite it or explicitly amend the filename to store each form separately. If you overwrite the workbook form, then you won't be able to use the wizard to update records it has added to the list. Since this update capability is a compelling feature, we find it annoying that the wizard's designers elected to reuse the same name for each workbook form.

---

4. Open up *Subscription list.xls* to see that the record has been added.

NOTE Annoyingly, if your list has the special range name Database, the form template doesn't extend the range to include the new record.

---

5. To update a record added via the wizard, open its associated workbook form, make any changes, save the workbook, and you'll be prompted to update the existing record, create a new record, or continue without updating. The wizard has no record deletion capabilities, so you must delete records from directly inside the list (you could, of course, use a data form to do this).

Access forms

You can create and use Access forms to work with a list, but a discussion of these capabilities is beyond the scope of this book. Check the relevant Excel and Access on-line Help topics.

Excel workbook forms

Semantically, things get a tad confusing here. You can use a Template Wizard form template and its workbook forms to update a list. You can also design your own form template and workbook forms (remember, Excel Help confusingly refers to these as worksheet forms) without using the Template Wizard technology; such forms are not automatically connected to a list. (For example, a department needs to produce typographically consistent medical claim forms that are then manually data-processed in paper form by someone else—yes, this still happens—so there would be no justification for a database link). If you elect to roll your own all the way (meaning, write all the code to update a database), then be prepared for a significant Excel/VBA coding effort.

Whether you roll your own or use the Template Wizard, you can always avail yourself of Excel's extensive Forms controls and ActiveX controls. Forms controls are best for Excel-centric forms; ActiveX controls are best for forms you intend to use outside Excel or in a Web context, although if you're willing to invest the time to work with ActiveX controls, you'll benefit from their wider set of features (read: methods and properties).

Whiz-bang controls notwithstanding, for simple validation needs, Excel's new data validation feature is the ideal solution. For example, in the subscription list form template, you could set data validation for the Type input cell B3 to be restricted to a list of values as shown in Figure 7-24. Here are the steps:

1. Create a new workbook. Follow along now, referring to Figure 7-24.
2. Add the data-entry labels: **`Journal`** in A1, **`Subscriber Info`** in A2, **`Type`** in A3, **`URL`** in A4.
3. Select cell B3.
4. Choose Data, Validation..., click the Settings tab, select List in the Allow drop-down list, and in the Source field enter the following text precisely as shown (including the commas and spaces): **`Advertising General, Clothing Catalog, Digital General, Fun, Health, Kids, PC General, Programming`**. Then click OK. What you've done here is enter a list of valid items right into the Source field; you could also store these values as a list on the worksheet and refer to it by name in the Source field.
5. Make sure the "Ignore blank" and "In-cell dropdown" check boxes are checked (they should be now by default), then click OK.
6. To test this, click the drop-down arrow in cell B3, and there's your list of valid entries.

B3 =

	A	B	C
1	Journal	Surfer	
2	Subscriber Info	800-999-9999	
3	Type		
4	URL		
5			
6			
7			
8			
9			
10			

Advertising General
Clothing Catalog
Digital General
Fun
Health
Kids
PC General
Programming

Figure 7-24: Data validation using a restricted list in a form template

Sorting

Filtering a list and sorting a list are two entirely different operations. When you filter a list, you might get back zero, a few, or all rows, depending on what your filter criteria are. When you sort a list, you always end up with the same number of rows as when you started, possibly in a different order.

Moral: filtering a list does not automatically sort that list, and sorting a list never filters it.

To sort a list, select any cell inside the list, select Data, and choose Sort. Excel's Sort dialog pops up as shown in Figure 7-25. If you select more than one cell, Excel sees the adjacent data and asks if you want to expand the selection or continue with the current selection.

Figure 7-25: The Sort dialog box applied to the Northwind Orders list in Lists.xls

Excel sorts by category in the following order:

- numbers
- text
- logicals
- errors
- blanks

You can read more about this in the Help topic "Default sort orders," but there are no surprises lurking there. Some tips: It is the value of a cell, not its format, that dictates how it is sorted. For example, a cell containing `=NOW()` may be formatted to display 4/25/1997 12:04:17 PM, but actually contains the value 35545.5029782407. For text, the space character comes in between the "9" character and the "!" character. For logicals, FALSE precedes TRUE. Errors appear together in their original order, that is, are all weighted equally; this means they don't get rearranged by a sort operation. Blanks are always last whether the sort is ascending or descending.

Should you anticipate the need to return your list to its original order, *before sorting the list* insert a new column that contains sequential order IDs for each row. (AutoFill is the fastest way to do this.) Hide the column until needed.

When a column contains mixed numeric and text data and you want the contents to be sorted as if all the data is text, some folks manually insert an apostrophe prefix into each numeric cell. While this works, it can be mildly tedious to downright infuriating. Since this technique alters the original data, there has to be a better way.

Instead, insert a column to the right of the source data, make sure you're in R1C1 notation, copy the formula `=TEXT(RC[-1],0)` into each cell, then base the sort on this new column. Hide or delete this interim column after the sort, at your discretion. For proper sorting, you may have to use a formatting parameter other than 0 in the function, say, `=TEXT(RC[-1],"0.##")`, depending on the maximum number of significant digits in the source data series.

NOTE The positions of hidden rows in a list don't change under any circumstances during a sort.

You can perform non-alphabetic, non-numeric sorts by using custom lists, as we discussed in Chapter 4. Excel ships with several date-based custom lists (see Tools ➤ Options ➤ Custom Lists), and it's easy to add your own, for example, a scale of Poor, Fair, Good, Excellent or simply Low, Medium, High. Tell Excel which custom list to use in the Sort dialog by clicking Options then selecting the desired custom list in the "First key sort order" drop-down control.

Distill Your Data with AutoFilter

AutoFilter is a feature that converts the header of each column in a list to a searchable drop-down control. The control, in turn, contains several predetermined choices—All, Top 10..., and Custom... (plus Blanks and NonBlanks choices, which appear at the bottom of the control list, but *only* if there's at least one blank cell in the column)—followed by a sorted list of all the unique values in the column. So with one click of your mouse, you can quickly filter the entire list based on the contents of the current column of interest.

To activate AutoFilter, select any cell inside the target list, then select Data ➤ Filter ➤ AutoFilter. Excel converts each column label cell into a drop-down control, as shown in Figure 7-26.

NOTE If you select more than a single cell but less than your entire list before AutoFiltering, Excel interprets this selection as a list within a list. Excel uses the cells in the top-most row as filter cells without prompting or warning. Most annoying.

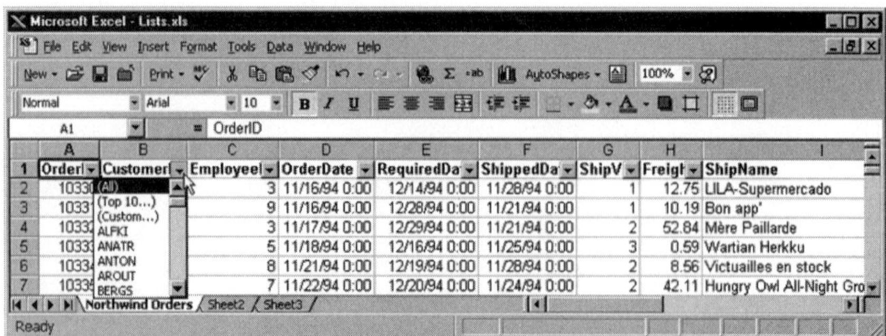

Figure 7-26: AutoFilter mode active in the Northwind Orders list

As you can see in the drop-down in Figure 7-26, you can include all records, include the top or bottom 10 records (either on a value basis or a percentage basis, as shown in Figure 7-27), perform a Custom filter, select from a sorted list of field contents, and filter all blank or all nonblank records. To turn AutoFilter off, select Data ➤ Filter ➤ AutoFilter.

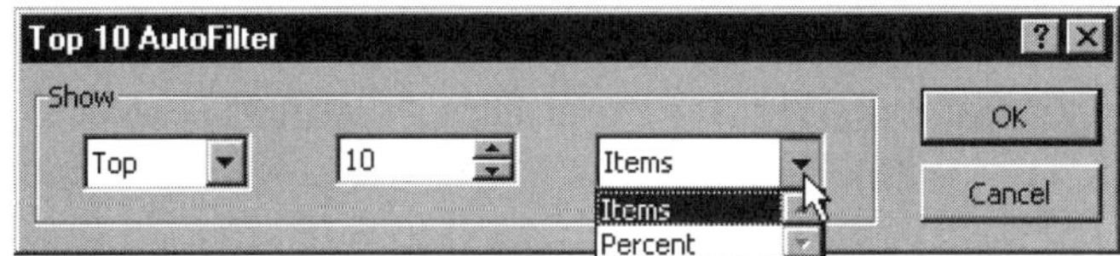

Figure 7-27: The Top 10 AutoFilter dialog box

Let's filter the list to show only the orders destined for Kirkland, WA. Open the Ship City drop-down, scroll down, select Kirkland, press `Enter` or double-click, and the list is filtered to the three matching records, as shown in Figure 7-28. Note that the status bar reveals the matching record count. To return the list to display all records (no filtering), select Data ➤ Filter ➤ Show All (alternately, click in any drop-down control and choose All at the top of the list).

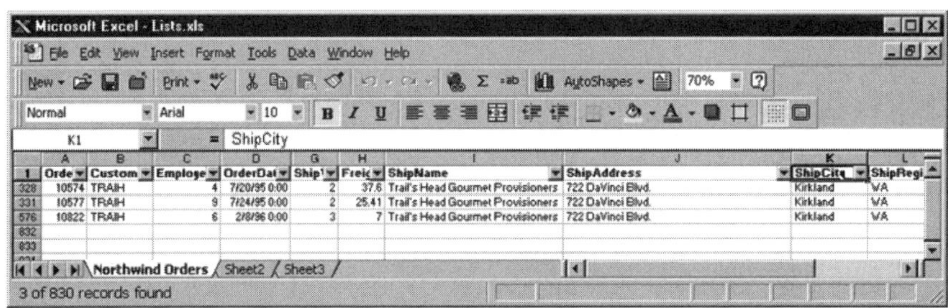

Figure 7-28: AutoFilter showing the three orders destined for Kirkland

What exactly is AutoFilter doing in the background? The Kirkland search can be logically translated as, "Show rows where ShipCity = Kirkland." When performing custom or advanced filtering, AutoFilter supports all of Excel's standard comparison operators.

The Custom item in the AutoFilter drop-down list displays a dialog box that allows you to build a more, well, complex query based on a single field (more about multi-field filtering in a moment). You can have up to two criteria operating against this one field (using either a logical AND or an OR), and each criterion provides a rich assortment of comparison operators (expressed in English as opposed to mathematical symbols) along with a complete list of current values for this field. See Figure 7-29 for an example of a filter to show all foreign orders.

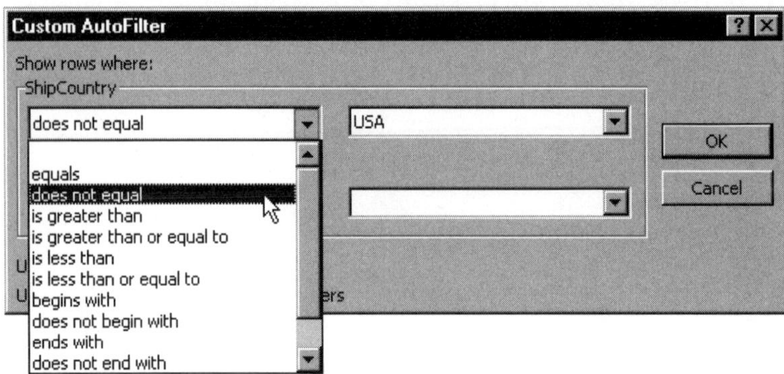

Figure 7-29: A rich set of English language comparisons are supported in the Custom AutoFilter dialog box

If you have criteria that are too complex for the basic AutoFilter dialog box or that involve more than one field, you need to use Excel's Advanced Filter feature. For example, if you want to see all foreign orders with a freight charge of $500 or more, the logical expression is:

```
Show rows where (ShipCountry <> USA) AND (Freight >= 500)
```

The key to Advanced Filter is the criteria range, an area on the sheet separate from the list that contains field names and associated criteria for those fields. Here are the steps to follow for this advanced filtering operation:

1. Insert three empty rows above your list.
2. Copy the column label `ShipCountry` to A1.
3. Copy the column label `Freight` to B1.
4. Type **`<>USA`** into A2. (Note: there should be no space between the operator and the comparison value.)
5. Type **`>=500`** into B2.
6. Click anywhere inside the list.
7. Select Data ➤ Filter ➤ Advanced Filter to display the Advanced Filter dialog box, as seen in Figure 7-30.

NOTE When performing an Advanced Filter, Excel automatically applies the built-in name Criteria to the range you specify in the dialog box (here, $A$1:$B$2). If you already have a range name of Criteria in the sheet, that range's coordinates automatically appear in the Criteria range text box.

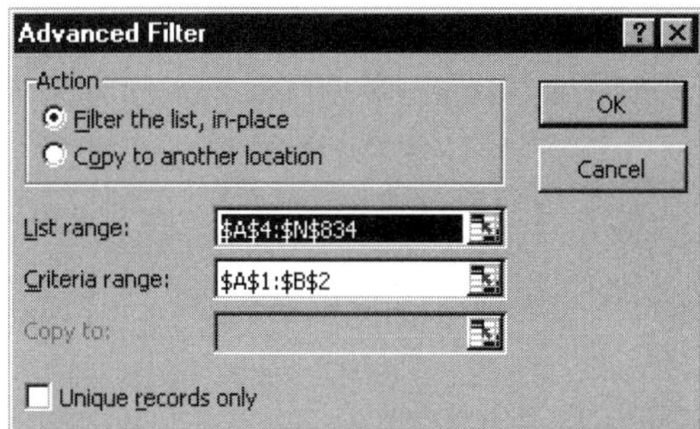

Figure 7-30: The Advanced Filter dialog box at work

8. Select A1:B2 for the criteria range, leave the Advanced Filter dialog's other settings alone for now, then click OK. Seven records should match.

The rules that apply to the criteria range are as follows (for examples, see the Help topic "Examples of advanced filter criteria"):

- Criteria on the same row are evaluated as an AND expression.
- Criteria on different rows are evaluated as an OR expression.
- Criteria can include wildcard characters. Precede a wildcard character with a tilde (~) to treat it as a normal character.
- Formulas and range references (named or unnamed) are legal inside criteria expressions.

Look back at Figure 7-30 and notice that you have the option of copying the filtered results to another location. The "Unique records only" check box, if checked, shows only the first record in a set of duplicate records; if it's not checked (the default), then Excel shows all duplicate records (if any) that match your criteria.

AutoFilter helps you quickly locate records within a list that match criteria in a specific column. This is a process of raw data filtering and does not involve any formulas. However, Excel 97 has a new feature called the Lookup Wizard that enables you to locate information in a list—if that information can be represented as the intersection between a row and column—and it does so by producing a formula. To activate the Lookup Wizard, select any cell in your list, and select Tools ➤ Wizard ➤ Lookup. The wizard then walks you through the column and row selection process (it's a modeless dialog, so you can select the desired ranges with the dialog still visible). You can choose to have the wizard build just the formula or provide your lookup parameters as stand-alone cells that are in turn referenced in the wizard-generated formula. If you have named your list, a minor annoyance with the wizard crops up if you don't start out with the active cell somewhere inside your list. In this case, you can't use Excel's powerful Paste Names feature—a feature that is available if you build the formula without the wizard—to automatically insert the list's range name into the wizard dialog. Instead, you have to manually highlight the list or remember its name.

Subtotals

Excel's automatic subtotals feature set works wonders on a list. Subtotaling is not limited to a one-dimensional summation, but includes some exceptional grouping capabilities as well. Using our orders list, let's do some automatic subtotal calculations starting with freight amount subtotals by destination country.

1. First sort the list by the column you're interested in—ShipCountry.
2. Choose Data ➤ Subtotals, then choose ShipCountry in the "At each change in" drop-down control.
3. Uncheck ShipCountry in the "Add subtotal to" list box, then check Freight in the same list box. Scan this list box to make sure only Freight is checked. The "Add subtotal to" list allows you to specify which fields you want running subtotals for. In this case, Excel will produce subtotals of freight by country.
4. Set "Use function" to Sum.
5. Select or clear any of the three check boxes that determine formatting at your discretion.
6. Now click OK.

Excel automatically outlines the list, subtotaled by country, and supplies a Grand Total row at the bottom of the list. To collapse the list one level, press the level 2 outline symbol (outline symbols appear in the area immediately to the left of Excel's standard row headers). Since there are several columns between Freight and ShipCountry, to see the figures next to the country labels, you may want to hide columns J through M. You're not limited to a Sum operation; subtotals can calculate Sum, Count, Average, Max, Min, Product, Count Nums, StdDev, StdDevp, Var, and Varp.

You can perform grouped subtotals—for example, you might want to subtotal Freight by ShipRegion by ShipCountry. All blank ShipRegion records are grouped together after non-blank records as you would expect (in the case of the UK there are three ship regions—Essex, Isle of Wight, and blanks), but the blanks don't get an explicit subtotal row. In such a case the outer group's total is calculated correctly, but you can't compress these blanks down to a single subtotal row. While some may consider this to be normal behavior of the outline feature set, we find it annoying and would prefer to have an option to turn on or off the explicit use of an outline level for blank records in a grouped subtotal operation.

To perform a nested subtotal: sort the un-subtotaled list first (by ShipCountry by ShipRegion), subtotal normally on the first group (ShipCountry), then subtotal again using the second group (ShipRegion), and make sure you clear the "Replace current subtotals" check box.

You can get Excel to jump through a wide variety of hoops when working with its outline/subtotal feature set, but as the complexity of your analysis increases, you will probably find yourself using Pivot Tables instead. For example, the annoyance mentioned earlier regarding the non-compressibility of a group of blank records for a particular field is eliminated in a pivot table, where a constellation of blank records is clearly shown with the label "(blank)."

Data Analysis with Pivot Tables

If you thought Excel's list management tricks were impressive, hang on to your hat! While the first implementation of pivot tables (several versions of Excel ago) was annoying with a capital A, Microsoft has pulled out all the stops for pivot tables in Excel 97. Annoyances are at a minimum, and the 'Softies have ratcheted up ease of use several notches.

Think of a pivot table as an interactive summary of your data (read: list). You can quickly change the functions you use for this summarization (from counts to sums to averages, and so on), change the fields across which the data is tabulated, flip through groupings and subgroupings (pages), chart these groupings, refresh the source data, drill down or up to see more or less detail, change formatting, and more. There's no substitute for the real thing, so let's begin our exploration of pivot tables using the Northwind Orders list (introduced earlier) by conducting an analysis of freight amount by destination country by employee.

1. If your list is still subtotaled from the previous section, choose Data ➤ Subtotals, and click Remove All; otherwise go to step 2.
2. Click any cell in your list, then choose Data ➤ PivotTable Report to start the wizard (see Figure 7-31).
3. Select the default source button—"Microsoft Excel list or database"—then click Next>.

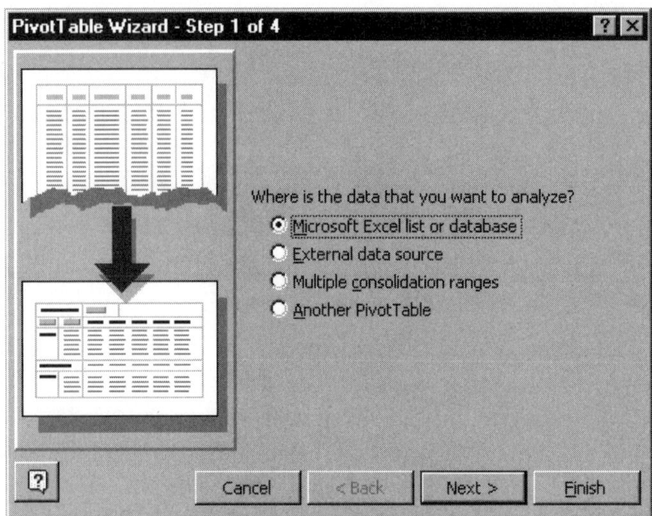

Figure 7-31: PivotTable Wizard—Step 1 of 4

4. The PivotTable Wizard—Step 2 of 4 dialog box will already have selected your list, so click Next>. The wizard's Step 3 of 4 dialog appears next, as shown in Figure 7-32.

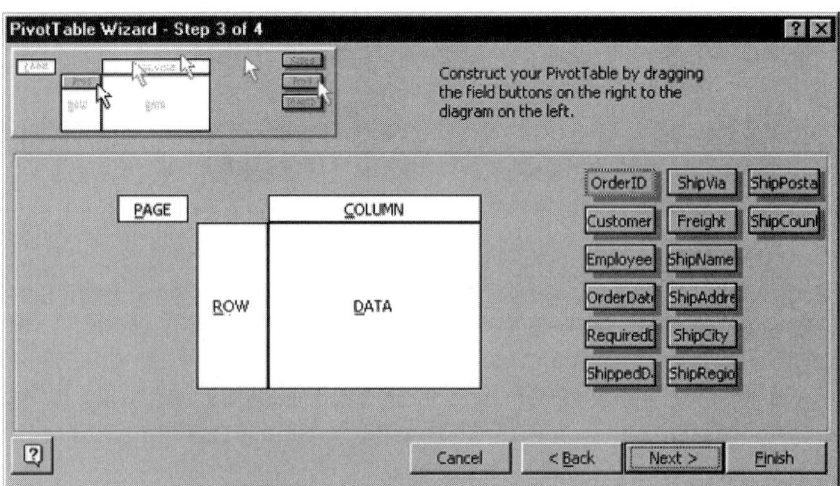

Figure 7-32: PivotTable Wizard—Step 3 of 4

5. Drag the ShipCountry field's button into the Row area.
6. Drag the Employee field's button into the Column area.
7. Drag the Freight field's button into the Data area. Excel defaults to a Sum function (more on how to change this in a moment).

8. Click the Next> button, and then click Finish to accept all of Step 4 of 4's defaults. Excel inserts a new sheet with the pivot table on it.

Once you've created a pivot table, you manipulate it with the PivotTable toolbar. To quickly update the format of the calculated field (here, Sum of Freight), click any detail cell inside the table, click the PivotTable Field button, click the Number button, select the Currency format from the Category list, set Decimal places to 2, choose the bottom-most Negative numbers format, and click on OK twice.

To see just how flexible a pivot table is, let's count the mouse strokes required to change the analysis from Sum to Average: (1) click any detail cell inside the table, (2) click the PivotTable Field button, (3) click Average, (4) click OK. An astonishing four mouse strokes (three, if the active cell is already inside the table).

To compress the pivot table's display such that you see employee orders in a single column instead of across multiple columns (as is the current format) that's selectable by employee, you need to use the Page feature: click the PivotTable menu item, then choose Wizard. Now you're in the Step 3 of 4 dialog, so drag Employee from the Column area to the Page area, double-click on the Average of Freight button to change the calculation back to Sum of Freight, then click Finish. Column B is now an AutoFilter-like column with a drop-down control in B1 showing "(All)," which can be changed to show any one of the nine employee IDs or to tabulate data for each country for all employees. Try it, and compare your results with ours in Figure 7-33. Cool, isn't it?

But wait, there's more. Say you want to see the total freight, minimum freight, maximum freight, and order count values for each country by employee: click the PivotTable menu item then choose Wizard, drag Freight to the Data area (the button label reads "Sum of Freight2"), drag Freight again to the Data area (the button label reads "Sum of Freight3"), drag OrderID to the Data area, double-click on the Sum of Freight2 button to change the calculation to Min, double-click on the Sum of Freight3 button to change the calculation to Max, double-click on the Sum of OrderID button to change the calculation to Count, then click Finish. (See Figure 7-34.)

See Figure 7-35 for a display of how pivot tables solve the noncompressible blank records annoyance that affects subtotals.

In these examples, you've seen how a pivot table can help you quickly and readily determine freight revenues by salesperson, with other slice and dice 'em analyses just a mouse click away. Take the concept behind

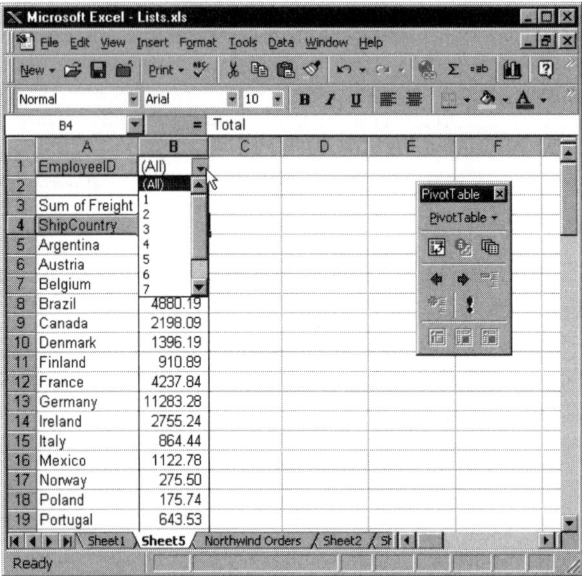

Figure 7-33: This pivot table shows total freight by country by employee in a format that's "paged" by employee

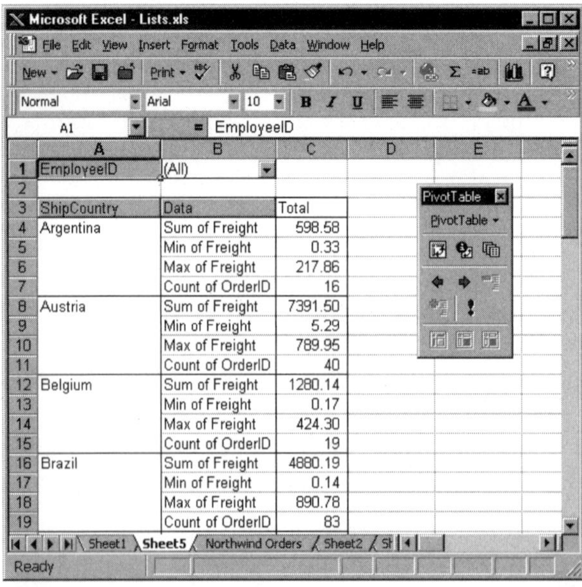

Figure 7-34: This pivot table shows total, minimum, and maximum freight plus order count by country by employee

these intentionally simple examples, and you can see how easy it is to wring the last drop of information out of any list you have, no matter the

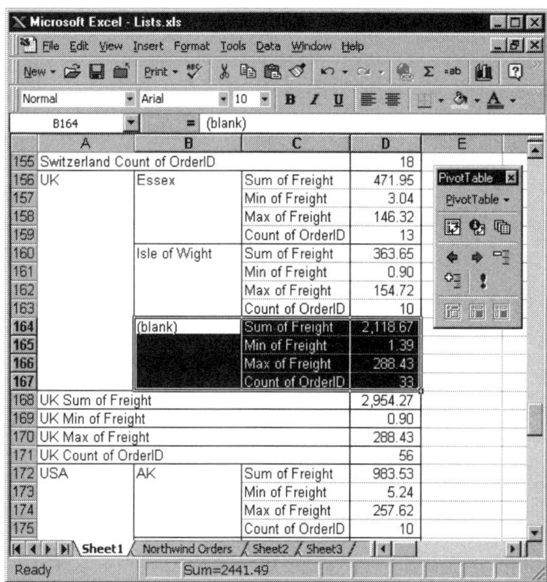

Figure 7-35: In a pivot table, grouped blank records get an explicit label of "(blank)"

list's density or complexity. A most amazing feature with the barest minimum of annoyances.

8

In this chapter:
- *The Horse's Mouth*
- *Magazines*
- *Newsletters*
- *WOW*
- *Other Places of Interest*

Where and How to Get Help

Excel has been around for a long, long time, and there are a number of rich resources for information on this great product. Of course, some sources are better than others.

The Horse's Mouth

You might try Microsoft's Product Support people. In the U.S. the number is 425-635-7145. Be prepared with your registration number (click Help ➤ About), and if at all possible be sitting in front of your PC when you call. Keep in mind that, like all the major software companies, Microsoft has started outsourcing its support services, and you might be talking with someone that knows less about Excel than you do. We've heard a lot of horror stories about PSS over the years: they're good at the basic stuff, but getting answers to complex questions can take forever. Assuming you get an answer at all.

Microsoft maintains several Excel-related newsgroups on the Net. The names of the groups change from time to time, but as we went to press, the important ones started at *microsoft.public.excel.*

Microsoft puts a lot of effort into its web site, and as long as you don't mind looking for your own answers, they can be very helpful.

NOTE Microsoft doesn't support these newsgroups. They're "peer to peer," which means the people who provide answers are acting out of the goodness of their hearts. Many of them are quite knowledgeable and have developed large-scale, industrial-strength applications used by Fortune 500 companies. Others come across as well-meaning but not terribly well-informed. Keep that in mind as you struggle through your problems.

- *www.microsoft.com/excel* contains the latest information on Excel, although sometimes it's scooped by *www.microsoft.com/office.*
- *www.microsoft.com/msexcel/* is as assemblage of current news headlines regarding Excel.
- *www.microsoft.com/officedev* is the place to start for VBA FAQs.
- *www.microsoft.com/kb*, the Microsoft Knowledge Base (MSKB), remains the indispensable source of information, albeit occasionally with a pro-Microsoft spin. The MSKB contains a veritable plethora of articles (each one has a "Q" number for identification purposes), covering all manner of Microsoft product quirks, known bugs, neat tricks, explanations, ruminations, and the like. For example, enter a search of "excel bug" (no quotation marks) and you'll get back a hit list of 100 articles with titles ranging from *BUG:XL97 Errors Using OLE Automation (Q165273)* to *Excel 5.0 for Windows: Summary List of Known Issues (Q112180)*. Fun reading!
- *www.microsoft.com/OfficeFreeStuff/excel/* for the latest for latest Wizards, templates, workbooks, tools, and Microsoft offered add-ons for Excel.
- *www.microsoft.com/support/tshoot/excelworkbook.htm* is a Microsoft-sponsored troubleshooter that gives boilerplate responses on a small number of common Excel problems.

Every serious Excel user should have those on their browser's Favorites list.

Magazines

All three of us write for both *PC Computing* and its sister publication, *Office Computing*. We naturally recommend both of those publications highly for their in-depth coverage of Windows, Office, and Excel. In particular, if you're interested in creating custom solutions for Excel with VBA, templates, forms, or just about any other advanced technique, *Office*

Computing (*www.officecomputing.com*) can't be beat. Much of what you read in *Office Computing* had its start here in the three *Annoyances* books by the authors—*Word 97 Annoyances*, *Excel 97 Annoyances*, and *Office 97 Annoyances*, published by O'Reilly & Associates.

Newsletters

For companies knee-deep in virus concerns, we strongly recommend *Virus Bulletin, www.virusbtn.com*, a pricey but key source of virus-related news.

WOW

We strongly urge all *Annoyances* readers to subscribe to WOW, *Woody's Office Watch*, our free weekly electronic bulletin with up-to-the-nano-second news about Office. From the latest rumors, to warnings about viruses, bugs, and patches, to contrarian opinions by Word's most devoted (and knowledgeable!) detractors, to the famous ask.woody column, WOW keeps you abreast of the good, the bad, and the ugly of Microsoft Office. And the price sure is right.

To subscribe, send email to *wow@wopr.com*.

Other Places of Interest

The World Wide Web has a number of excellent sites dedicated to all things spreadsheet. This list is by no means exhaustive, just a few of the spots we like and where you'll find stuff of interest.

- *www.j-walk.com/ss* is where you'll find *The Spreadsheet Page*, by John Walkenbach. Lots of top-notch material on Excel, including FAQs, sample files, utilities, and the like. Highly recommended.
- *sunsite.univie.ac.at/Spreadsite/spreaded.html* has information targeted at users with math, science, and statistical applications.
- *www.vex.net/~negandhi/excel/* calls itself *The Unofficial Microsoft Excel Page*, and while it's a bit outdated (most of the material is based on Excel 95), there's still a lot of relevant content.
- *www.primeconsulting.com/faq13.shtml* is worh checking out for a general listing of numerous Microsoft resources and white papers on Microsoft Office 97.

Index

Symbols, Numbers

A

B

C

K

L

M

P

Q

R

S

T

U

V

X

Y

Z

About the Authors

Woody Leonhard's books include *Windows 3.1 Programming for Mere Mortals, The Underground Guide to Word for Windows, The Hacker's Guide to Word for Windows, The Mother of All PC Books, The Mother of All Windows 95 Books*, and several others. He was series editor for Addison-Wesley's *Underground Guides* (11 books) and A-W's *Hacker's Guides* (4 books). Along with T.J. Lee and Lee Hudspeth, he's editor-in-chief of PC Computing's *Undocumented Office*, a monthly hardcopy newsletter. He's a contributing editor at *PC Computing* (circulation 1,000,000+), and productivity editor for *Office Computing* (circulation 400,000), a new monthly magazine from the editors of *PC Computing*. He also publishes a free weekly electronic news bulletin on Microsoft Office called WOW ("Woody's Office Watch"), available by sending email to *wow@wopr.com*. Woody's software company makes WOPR, Woody's Office POWER Pack, the Number-One Enhancement to Microsoft Office. A self-described "grizzled computer hack, frustrated novelist, and Office victim," by day he's a Tibetan human rights activist and co-founder of the Tibetan Children's Fund. Woody lives on top of a mountain in Coal Creek Canyon, Colorado.

Lee Hudspeth is a co-founder of PRIME Consulting Group, Inc. in Hermosa Beach, CA, a Microsoft Solution Provider. His background is in operations research, financial analysis, and marketing analysis (formerly with Unocal Corp.). He has co-authored several books on Office, including *The Underground Guide to Microsoft Office, OLE, and VBA*, and *The Underground Guide to Excel 5.0 for Windows*. He is co-editor-in-chief of *Undocumented Office*, he's a Microsoft MVP (Most Valued Professional), co-author of the Microsoft course on application development using WordBasic, and a certified Microsoft trainer in Visual Basic and WordBasic. Along with other PRIME Consulting staff, Lee has developed innumerable lines of VB, VBA, and WordBasic code for the firm's numerous Office add-ins (PRIME for Excel and PRIME for Word), going way back to Word 2.0. Lee also writes and delivers Office usage and development custom courses to hordes of interested parties the world over.

T.J. Lee, also a co-founder of PRIME Consulting Group, has a background as a certified public accountant and has done computer and management consulting for years. He has co-authored several books on Office, including *The Underground Guide to Microsoft Excel 5* and *The Underground Guide to Microsoft Office, OLE, and VBA*. T.J. is co-editor-in-chief of *Undocumented Office* and a certified Microsoft trainer. He has written countless courseware packages and manuals, co-authored the Microsoft Education Services course on Developing Applications in Word, and taught and lectured for thousands of developers and end users.

Colophon

Our look is the result of reader comments, our own experimentation, and feedback from distribution channels. Distinctive covers complement our distinctive approach to technical topics, breathing personality and life into potentially dry subjects.

The animal on the cover of *Excel 97 Annoyances* is a wild boar. The wild boar, a member of the family *Suidae,* is know for its sharp teeth, quick speed, intelligence, and keen sense of smell. The wild boar was first bred as a domestic animal about 9000 years ago. It is a very useful domesticated animal, as it provides humans with meat, leather, lard, and bristles for brushes, in addition to serving as a draft and riding animal.

The wild boar is the most widely distributed of all pigs, having been introduced to many regions of the Western hemisphere for sport hunting. While the natural inclination of the wild boar is to sleep at night, approximately 11 hours at a time, and search for food during the day, in heavily hunted areas boars will reverse this pattern. Like most species of pig, the wild boar eats a varied diet of grass, herbs, insects, small animals, and carrion. Wild boar are a nuisance to farming communities because their rooting damages the soil.

Edie Freedman designed the cover of this book, using a 19th-century engraving from the Dover Pictorial Archive. The cover layout was produced with Quark XPress 3.3 using the ITC Garamond font.

The inside layout was designed by Edie Freedman and Nancy Priest and implemented in FrameMaker 5.0 by Mike Sierra. The text and heading fonts are ITC Garamond Light and Garamond Book. The illustrations that appear in the book were created in Macromedia Freehand 7.0 by Robert Romano. This colophon was written by Clairemarie Fisher O'Leary, with assistance from Kevin O'Leary.

More Titles from O'Reilly

Annoyances

Windows Annoyances

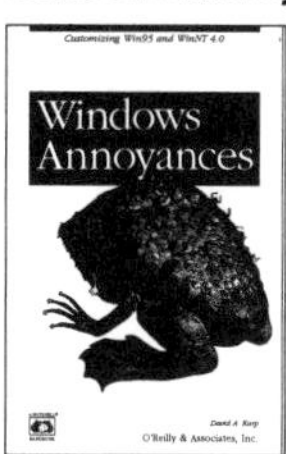

By David A. Karp
1st Edition June 1997
300 pages
ISBN: 1-56592-266-2

Windows Annoyances, a comprehensive resource for intermediate to advanced users of Windows 95 and NT 4.0, details step-by-step how to customize your Win95/NT operating system through an extensive collection of tips, tricks, and workarounds. You'll learn how to customize every aspect of these systems, far beyond the intentions of Microsoft. This book shows you how to customize your PC through methods of backing up, repairing, compressing, and transferring portions of the Registry. Win95 users will discover how Plug and Play, the technology that makes Win95 so compatible, can save time and improve the way you interact with your computer. You'll also learn how to benefit from the new 32-bit software and hardware drivers that support such features as improved multitasking and long filenames.

Word 97 Annoyances

By Woody Leonhard, Lee Hudspeth & T.J. Lee
1st Edition August 1997 (est.)
352 pages (est.)
ISBN: 1-56592-308-1

Word 97 contains hundreds of annoying idiosyncrasies that can be either eliminated or worked around. Whether it's the Find Fast feature that takes over your machine every once in awhile, or the way Word automatically selects an entire word as you struggle to highlight only a portion of it, *Word 97 Annoyances* will show you how to solve the problem.

It's filled with tips and customizations, and takes an in-depth look at what makes Word 97 tick—mainly character and paragraph formatting, styles, and templates.

This informative, yet humorous, book shows you how to use and modify Word 97 to meet your needs, transforming the software into a powerful tool customized to the way *you* use Word.

Excel 97 Annoyances

By Woody Leonhard, Lee Hudspeth & T.J. Lee
1st Edition September 1997 (est.)
224 pages (est.)
ISBN: 1-56592-309-X

Learn how to shape Excel 97 in a way that will not only make it most effective, but will give you a sense of enjoyment as you analyze data with ease. Excel 97, which ships with Office 97, has many new features that may be overwhelming. All of the various toolbars, packed with what seems to be an unending array of buttons, might seem a bit intimidating, not to mention annoying, to the average user. *Excel 97 Annoyances* is a guide that will help create some order to the plethora of available options by providing many customizations that require only a few simple clicks of the mouse button.

Office 97 Annoyances

By Woody Leonhard, Lee Hudspeth & T.J. Lee
1st Edition October 1997 (est.)
200 pages (est.)
ISBN: 1-56592-310-3

There is an enormous group of users who are either running Office 97 or will be installing it in the near future. Immediately after installation, the user will notice two dozen shortcuts scattered on the Start menu in no apparent beneficial order. In the same fashion, the Shortcut Bar is filled with an overwhelming number of applications. There are even many hidden gems tucked away in various places on the Office 97 CD that are worth hundreds of dollars if the user knows where to look for them and how to set them up. *Office 97 Annoyances* illustrates step-by-step how to get control over the chaotic settings of Office 97 and shows the user how to implement and utilize this new Office suite in the most efficient way.

How to stay in touch with O'Reilly

1. Visit Our Award-Winning Site

http://www.oreilly.com/

★"Top 100 Sites on the Web" —*PC Magazine*
★"Top 5% Web sites" —*Point Communications*
★"3-Star site" —*The McKinley Group*

Our web site contains a library of comprehensive product information (including book excerpts and tables of contents), downloadable software, background articles, interviews with technology leaders, links to relevant sites, book cover art, and more. File us in your Bookmarks or Hotlist!

2. Join Our Email Mailing Lists

New Product Releases

To receive automatic email with brief descriptions of all new O'Reilly products as they are released, send email to:
listproc@online.oreilly.com
Put the following information in the first line of your message (*not* in the Subject field):
subscribe oreilly-news "Your Name" of "Your Organization" (for example: subscribe oreilly-news Kris Webber of Fine Enterprises)

O'Reilly Events

If you'd also like us to send information about trade show events, special promotions, and other O'Reilly events, send email to:
listproc@online.oreilly.com
Put the following information in the first line of your message (*not* in the Subject field):
subscribe oreilly-events "Your Name" of "Your Organization"

3. Get Examples from Our Books via FTP

There are two ways to access an archive of example files from our books:

Regular FTP

- ftp to:
  ftp.oreilly.com
  (login: anonymous
  password: your email address)
- Point your web browser to:
  ftp://ftp.oreilly.com/

FTPMAIL

- Send an email message to:
  ftpmail@online.oreilly.com
  (Write "help" in the message body)

4. Visit Our Gopher Site

- Connect your gopher to:
  gopher.oreilly.com
- Point your web browser to:
  gopher://gopher.oreilly.com/
- Telnet to:
  gopher.oreilly.com
  login: gopher

5. Contact Us via Email

order@oreilly.com
To place a book or software order online. Good for North American and international customers.

subscriptions@oreilly.com
To place an order for any of our newsletters or periodicals.

books@oreilly.com
General questions about any of our books.

software@oreilly.com
For general questions and product information about our software. Check out O'Reilly Software Online at **http://software.oreilly.com/** for software and technical support information. Registered O'Reilly software users send your questions to:
website-support@oreilly.com

cs@oreilly.com
For answers to problems regarding your order or our products.

booktech@oreilly.com
For book content technical questions or corrections.

proposals@oreilly.com
To submit new book or software proposals to our editors and product managers.

international@oreilly.com
For information about our international distributors or translation queries. For a list of our distributors outside of North America check out:
http://www.oreilly.com/www/order/country.html

O'Reilly & Associates, Inc.
101 Morris Street, Sebastopol, CA 95472 USA
TEL 707-829-0515 or 800-998-9938
(6am to 5pm PST)
FAX 707-829-0104

International Distributors

UK, Europe, Middle East and Northern Africa *(except France, Germany, Switzerland, & Austria)*

INQUIRIES
International Thomson Publishing Europe
Berkshire House
168-173 High Holborn
London WC1V 7AA, UK
Tel: 44-171-497-1422
Fax: 44-171-497-1426
Email: itpint@itps.co.uk

ORDERS
International Thomson Publishing Services, Ltd.
Cheriton House, North Way
Andover, Hampshire SP10 5BE,
United Kingdom
Tel: 44-264-342-832 (UK)
Tel: 44-264-342-806
(outside UK)
Fax: 44-264-364418 (UK)
Fax: 44-264-342761 (outside UK)
UK & Eire orders:
itpuk@itps.co.uk
International orders:
itpint@itps.co.uk

France

Editions Eyrolles
61 bd Saint-Germain
75240 Paris Cedex 05
France
Fax: 33-01-44-41-11-44

FRENCH LANGUAGE BOOKS
All countries except Canada
Tel: 33-01-44-41-46-16
Email: geodif@eyrolles.com

ENGLISH LANGUAGE BOOKS
Tel: 33-01-44-41-11-87
Email: distribution@eyrolles.com

Australia

WoodsLane Pty. Ltd.
7/5 Vuko Place, Warriewood NSW 2102
P.O. Box 935,
Mona Vale NSW 2103
Australia
Tel: 61-2-9970-5111
Fax: 61-2-9970-5002
Email: info@woodslane.com.au

Germany, Switzerland, and Austria

INQUIRIES
O'Reilly Verlag
Balthasarstr. 81
D-50670 Köln
Germany
Tel: 49-221-97-31-60-0
Fax: 49-221-97-31-60-8
Email: anfragen@oreilly.de

ORDERS
International Thomson Publishing
Königswinterer Straße 418
53227 Bonn, Germany
Tel: 49-228-97024 0
Fax: 49-228-441342
Email: order@oreilly.de

Asia *(except Japan & India)*

INQUIRIES
International Thomson Publishing Asia
60 Albert Street #15-01
Albert Complex
Singapore 189969
Tel: 65-336-6411
Fax: 65-336-7411

ORDERS
Telephone: 65-336-6411
Fax: 65-334-1617
thomson@signet.com.sg

New Zealand

WoodsLane New Zealand Ltd.
21 Cooks Street (P.O. Box 575)
Wanganui, New Zealand
Tel: 64-6-347-6543
Fax: 64-6-345-4840
Email: info@woodslane.com.au

Japan

O'Reilly Japan, Inc.
Kiyoshige Building 2F
12-Banchi, Sanei-cho
Shinjuku-ku
Tokyo 160 Japan
Tel: 81-3-3356-5227
Fax: 81-3-3356-5261
Email: kenji@oreilly.com

India

Computer Bookshop (India) PVT. LTD.
190 Dr. D.N. Road, Fort
Bombay 400 001 India
Tel: 91-22-207-0989
Fax: 91-22-262-3551
Email:
cbsbom@giasbm01.vsnl.net.in

The Americas

O'Reilly & Associates, Inc.
101 Morris Street
Sebastopol, CA 95472 U.S.A.
Tel: 707-829-0515
Tel: 800-998-9938 (U.S. & Canada)
Fax: 707-829-0104
Email: order@oreilly.com

Southern Africa

International Thomson Publishing Southern Africa
Building 18, Constantia Park
138 Sixteenth Road
P.O. Box 2459
Halfway House, 1685 South Africa
Tel: 27-11-805-4819
Fax: 27-11-805-3648

O'REILLY WOULD LIKE TO HEAR FROM YOU

Which book did this card come from?

____

Where did you buy this book?

- ❑ Bookstore
- ❑ Computer Store
- ❑ Direct from O'Reilly
- ❑ Class/seminar
- ❑ Bundled with hardware/software
- ❑ Other ________________________

What operating system do you use?

- ❑ UNIX
- ❑ Macintosh
- ❑ Windows NT
- ❑ PC(Windows/DOS)
- ❑ Other ________________________

What is your job description?

- ❑ System Administrator
- ❑ Programmer
- ❑ Network Administrator
- ❑ Educator/Teacher
- ❑ Web Developer
- ❑ Other ________________________

❑ Please send me O'Reilly's catalog, containing a complete listing of O'Reilly books and software.

Name ____________ Company/Organization ____________

Address ____________

City ______ State ______ Zip/Postal Code ______ Country ______

Telephone ____________ Internet or other email address (specify network) ____________

Nineteenth century wood engraving of a bear from the O'Reilly & Associates Nutshell Handbook®
Using & Managing UUCP.

PLACE
STAMP
HERE

BUSINESS REPLY MAIL

FIRST CLASS MAIL PERMIT NO. 80 SEBASTOPOL, CA

Postage will be paid by addressee

O'Reilly & Associates, Inc.
101 Morris Street
Sebastopol, CA 95472-9902